Quotable

"... Verily, God does not change the condition of a people until they first change that which is in their hearts; ..."
— Qur'an 13:11

"In religion and politics people's beliefs and convictions are in almost every case gotten at second-hand, and without examination, from authorities who have not themselves examined the questions at issue but have taken them at second-hand from other non-examiners, ..."
— Mark Twain. American Author & Humorist (d. 1910)

"Rarely do we find men who willingly engage in hard, solid thinking. There is an almost universal quest for easy answers and half-baked solutions."
— Martin Luther King, Jr. American Clergyman, Activist (d. 1968)

"...God is with those who are mindful of Him and who do good."
— Qur'an 16:128

[2nd Edition With A New Supplemental Essay]

QUEST FOR ISLAM

The Qur'anic phrase *"I take refuge in God"* written in *tughra* form by the Turkish calligrapher Mustafa Rakim (d. 1767).

Also by Jamal Khwaja

* Living The Qur'an In Our Times

* Authenticity and Islamic Liberalism

* Five Approaches to Philosophy

* The Call Of Modernity And Islam

* Essays On Cultural Pluralism

* The Vision Of An Unknown Indian Muslim

* Numerous articles and scholarly essays

To learn more about the author, visit

www.JamalKhwaja.com
Download free Digital Books, Lectures, Essays and more ...

Cover illustration
The process of revelation of the Qur'an by God to His messenger, Muhammad ﷺ began in the cave of Hira (610 A.D), when the archangel Gabriel, forcefully commanded him to say; "Iqra!" (Qur'an 96:1).

The Arabic word "iqra" shown on the cover in traditional calligraphic style has been variously translated as: "Read", "Recite", and "Proclaim".
Once started, the process of intermittent revelation continued for the next twenty-three years. Read the following Qur'anic verses to get a better idea of the phenomena: 2:1–5, 2:97, 7:204, 7:157, 17:106–108, 20:2–4, 25:32–33, 33:40, 43:3–5, and 75:17–19, etc.

[2nd Edition With A New Supplemental Essay]

QUEST FOR ISLAM

A Philosopher's Approach To Religion In The Age Of Science And Cultural Pluralism

Jamal Khwaja
Professor of Philosophy

Aligarh Muslim University

ALHAMD PUBLISHERS, LLC

Los Angeles

Second Edition With A New Supplemental Essay
Copyright © by Jamal Khwaja 1977, 2015

All rights reserved. Copyright under Berne Copyright Convention, Universal Copyright Convention, and Pan American Copyright Convention. No part of this book may be reproduced, stored in a retrieval system, or transmitted in any form or by any means, electronic or mechanical or otherwise, including photocopying and recording, without prior written permission of the publisher, except for the inclusion of brief quotations in a review.

For permission to reproduce selections from this book contact the Publisher.

Published and distributed worldwide by ALHAMD Publishers, LLC.
3131 Roberts Ave, Culver City, CA 90232, USA.
www.AlhamdPublishers.com

Printed and bound in the United States of America
Book and Jacket Design by Sandeep Sandhu and Raisa Shafiyyullah.
Author Photo by Kenny Zepeda

More information about the Author and his works can be found at
www.JamalKhwaja.com
Look for FREE Downloads of Essays & Articles written by the Author.

ISBN: 978-1-935293-75-0 (Hard cover)
ISBN: 978-1-935293-69-9 (Soft cover)
ISBN: 978-1-935293-73-6 (Epub)
Publisher's SAN #: 857-0132
BISAC Subject Headings: Religion/Islam/Koran & Sacred Writings (REL041000), and Religion/Philosophy (REL051000)

In the name of God, the Beneficent, the Merciful.

For the Emerging Generation To Which Belong
Mansoor Hasan, Jawahar Kabir, Gita Anjum, and Satish Aggarwal

Quotable

"... We raise to degrees (of wisdom) whom We please: but over all who have knowledge is the All-Knowing."
– Qur'an 12:76

"Not every poem's good because it's ancient,
Nor mayest thou blame it just because it's new,
Fair critics test, and prove, and so pass judgment;
Fools praise or blame as they hear others do."
– Buddhist Saying

"Anyone who conducts an argument by appealing to authority is not using his intelligence; he is just using his memory."
– Leonardo Da Vinci. Italian Polymath (d. 1519)

"We are either progressing or retrograding all the while. There is no such thing as remaining stationary in this life."
– James Freeman Clarke. American Author & Preacher (d. 1888)

"Lo! Religion with God is Islam (submission to His will and guidance)."
– Qur'an 3:19

Contents

Author's Preface to the Second Edition xi

Acknowledgments xiii

Author's Preface to the First Edition xv

Chapter 1:
Introduction: The Problem & Its Historical Background 1

Chapter 2:
The Dominant Traditional Conception Of Islam 69

Chapter 3:
A Restatement Of The Islamic Thought System 89

Chapter 4:
A Restatement Of The Islamic Thought System (Contd.) 139

Chapter 5:
A Fresh Look At The Islamic Value System 171

Chapter 6:
A Fresh Look At The Islamic Precept System 185

Chapter 7:
A Secular Approach To The Islamic Institutional System 195

Chapter 8:
Concluding Reflections 225

Afterword 245

(Continued)

Contents

Notes And References 251

Supplemental Essay:
Modernism And Traditionalism In Islam 273

Appendix 1:
Introducing Jamal Khwaja And His Works 293

Appendix 2:
Select Bibliography 321

Index 333

Author's Preface to the Second Edition

Quest for Islam first appeared in 1977. Since then much water has flown down in the rivers of the world and some might even have dried up. I, therefore, would have loved to re-write several portions of the text and notes of the work to improve the quality and utility of a work done a quarter of a century ago. However, my basic response to the human situation and the position I adopted in the *Quest* remain unchanged, though I have kept an open mind on all matters. I have, however, added as an appendix, a paper, *Modernity and Traditionalism in Islam*, I presented at the *Institute of Advanced Study*, Shimla.

Meanwhile the cumulative fund of knowledge and wisdom has grown considerably, thanks to the work done by several outstanding thinkers and scholars in the field of Islamic Studies. Yet the crux of the issues with which I am concerned remains constant. The fact of the matter is that the human family cherishes not one but several religions and every religion, in turn, has several versions and levels. Moreover, there is no agreed method of justifying or validating the different beliefs and values of the different religious traditions. In the final analysis, religious faith, at its best and highest level, is an authentic and free commitment to a spiritualistic perspective on life and the Universe, and at its popular or folk level, a matter of cultural 'conditioning'. However, different believers occupy different points on the continuum of 'transcendental' beliefs that cannot be confirmed through deductive reasoning or scientific investigation and inquiry. I shall, therefore, leave the matter here, though I must mention one point where my approach has considerably changed from what it was a quarter of a century ago.

Thirty years ago the directive or volitional power of human reason appeared to me to be far more efficacious or effective than what I now think. Indeed, elemental passions and unconscious vested interests almost strangulate, at every step, the soft sweet voice of reason and conscience. The result is that the pace of conceptual and spiritual growth of the individual and society is miserably slow because of natural human resistance to new

Author's Preface to the Second Edition

ideas as also because their truth or validity cannot be objectively proven in the scientific sense.

I, therefore, submit that the ideal of searching for and propagating '*the*' truth should be substituted by the search for authenticity or authentic being on the part of all believers, no matter what their religious affiliation or tradition. Every believer should be content if he or she at all does touch the ever-slippery shore of genuine inner conviction. As is well-known, real conviction brings inner peace and joy. But we all learn the hard way how fleeting are such moments of blessedness. They appear to vanish the moment we think we have finally arrived. Moreover, every individual being unique, the graph of the journey and the final port of destination for every soul is also unique.

To conclude, loving tolerance and genuine respect for the existential choice every individual pilgrim makes to reach the shore of truth is the essence of true religious faith and piety, irrespective of how one conceptualizes the mystery of existence. However, I have come to the firm conclusion that seekers of truth attain the highest level of peace and felicity when they do not throw away the cultural roots and fruits of their tradition but rather lovingly cherish and creatively nourish them as a mother nourishes the child.

Jamal Khwaja
Aligarh, June 2015

Acknowledgments

I express my sincere gratitude for all that I have learned from the writings of H.A.R. Gibb, Professor Montgomery Watt, Professor Von Grunebaum, Professor Cantwell Smith, and Erich Fromm. The balanced writings of Professor Aziz Ahmad gave me a wealth of reliable background information for which I am thankful to him.

My long talks on Islam, spread over the past twenty years, with my former teacher, Professor Z.A. Siddiqui, have stimulated me deeply. The personality and views of the sage of Allahabad, Pandit Sundarlal, have been a formative influence on my life. The romantic religious idealism of Raja Mahendra Pratap—the Indian lone star in the saga of contemporary Asian history, if I may so refer to him—has also moved me deeply. I have also profited from the vast erudition of Professor S.A. Akbarabadi and intellectual chats with the late Professor Hamied Uddin Khan. My colleague Mr. Irfan Ahmad Khan has always been very helpful to me. The comments of Dr. Abdul Haq and Dr. N.U. Siddiqui on an earlier draft were also useful.

Late Ali Yavar Jung, who was Vice-Chancellor of the Aligarh Muslim University when I began this project, was deeply interested in this work. I am very grateful to him for his encouragement and also appreciation of my efforts. My mother always gave a sympathetic ear to my remarks on Islam or religion in the course of numerous family chats. My wife took down the dictation of a good deal of this work. Despite her onerous duties as an Indian housewife, she never hesitated to help me in my project. Her intuitive intelligence and common sense no less than her unfailing love have silently contributed to my work. My thanks are due to Mr. Naushad Husain in the Department of Philosophy, for his help and courtesy in taking down the dictation of many sections of this book, and to Mr. Farrukh Jalali of the Azad Library for his documentation help. I also thank Mufti Raza Ansari for kindly helping me with Qur'anic references.

It is also my pleasant duty to express my profound gratitude to Mr. Fazlur Rahman, former Pro-Vice-Chancellor, Aligarh Muslim University, and my sincere thanks to Professor K.A. Nizami and Dr. Bruce Lawrence for their valuable suggestions which have helped me immensely.

Acknowledgments

The English translation of and references to Qur'anic verses are from Pickthall's well-known *The Meaning of the Glorious Koran*. Certain portions from my paper *'Religion and Conceptual Evolution'* (read at a seminar at Chandigarh) and my papers *'Modernity and Traditionalism in Islam'* and *'Science and Religion'* (both read at seminars conducted at *The Indian Institute Of Advanced Study*, Shimla, and already in print) have been incorporated with and without amendments in the *Introduction* to this work.

Jamal Khwaja
Professor of Philosophy
Aligarh Muslim University
January 1977

Author's Preface to the First Edition

I had long cherished the idea of writing a book on my understanding of Islam. But I was in no hurry to do so. When, however, I realized that my eldest son, Jawahar, had entered the university with no religious education, apart from a basic moral training, I advised him to read some suitable literature on Islam. I wished that he should study books giving a systematic and sympathetic exposition of the main Islamic tradition. But over and above this, I felt it was my duty to share with him the fruits of my own quest for truth, not as an exercise in indoctrination, but rather to help and encourage him in undertaking his own independent spiritual journey. It was then that I felt the need for a systematic exposition of Islam in the light of the contemporary conceptual framework.

My interpretation of basic Islamic concepts and values does not question the authenticity of Prophet Muhammad ﷺ *, but seeks to remove the intellectual difficulties in the traditional Islamic thought system. Since, however, the leitmotif of the work is a quest for truth rather than apologetics, it should appeal not only to Muslims, but to others as well. The plan of the work is as follows: the *Introduction* discusses the theoretical and methodological aspects of the question: 'What is Islam?' and gives a brief but critical survey of the approaches of some recent Muslim thinkers in the Indo-Pakistan subcontinent. Chapter 2 briefly describes the dominant traditional version of Islam. Chapters 3–7 contain my restatement of the tradition. The last chapter is, in a sense, a continuation of the *Introduction*, as it rounds off methodological issues and deals with the attitude to other religions.

Every religion begins as a cultural organism comprising a thought-cum-value system, a symbolic precept system, and an institutional system. With the exception of the symbolic precepts, all the systems must grow, if the religion is to survive as a living cultural organism. All religions, which have endured, have reinterpreted themselves from within in response to the ever-changing human situation. Perhaps the most striking reinterpretation of religion occurred during and after the 18th century in Western Europe

---

* "Peace be upon him" in Arabic

due to the secular revolution. This in turn was due to the impact of science and technology and their socioeconomic consequences in Western Europe. Hindu and Buddhist religious thought in the 19th century readily assimilated the Western concept of secularism, implying the institutional system should not be deemed to be an integral part of a religion. But Muslims have shown the greatest reluctance to secularism, even though Islam is closest to many basic features of the modern outlook.

Muslims the world over have been adjusting traditional patterns of political, social, and economic behavior to present needs. But there is very little effort to relate these changes to the basic concepts and values of Islam. This state of affairs has resulted in a deep spiritual unrest and inner conflict between the pressures of modernity and the pulls of a romanticized and glorified past. The logic of traditional Islam pulls the Muslim in the direction of monolithic theocracy, while the logic of his historical situation pushes him in the direction of secular democracy. He can have no inner peace unless he resolves this conflict. Monolithic theocracy, which finds the most logical formulation in the works of Maududi, presupposes that religion is a complete code of life without any separation between the religious and the secular. Thus, Islam, as understood by the average educated Indian Muslim, is neither a mere schedule of prayer and fasting, nor a mere personal relationship between man and his Creator, nor mere 'morality tinged with emotion', but a monolithic map of the good life intended by the Creator for the true believer, who surrenders his own essentially fallible judgment before the infallible Divine will revealed to the Prophet ﷺ.

Secularism, as understood in the Indian Constitution, presupposes that religion is a personal relationship between the believer and God, and leaves the individual and society free to determine democratically the ordering of human society in all other spheres—social, economic, political, and cultural, etc.. Secularism includes religious tolerance in its essential connotation, but it signifies something more than this, namely, the judgment that the proper role of religion in the total economy of life is essentially inspirational and spiritual rather than legal or institutional. Thus, secularism, as understood in the Indian Constitution, demands a conception of religion which does not harmonize with Islam, as understood by the average educated Indian

Author's Preface to the First Edition

Muslim, even when the person concerned might honestly praise the virtues of secularism. This constitutes the basic spiritual predicament of the Indian Muslim.

Most Muslims the world over lack an Islamic perspective in which secular democracy and humanist internationalism have been organically integrated into their religious thought-cum-value system. The basic task of the Indian Muslim, rather Muslims the world over, is precisely the acquisition of an unified Islamic perspective which could resolve the conflict between the traditional conception of Islam as a complete code of life and the Western secular revolution. Mere piecemeal pragmatic adjustments to the new situation without any reinterpretation of the basic concepts and values of the Islamic tradition will not prove satisfactory. Nor is the program of Islamic modernism advocated by Turkish, Iranian, and Arab liberals the adequate response, since these Islamic modernists accept the secular revolution and propose to modernize institutional Islam, but do not appear to give much importance to the theoretical task of reconstructing the basic concepts and values of Islam. Unless this is done, the average Turkish or Iranian Muslim, who knows that the Qur'anic punishment for adultery or theft differs from the actual legal punishment in his own state, is most likely to feel that there is something wrong either with his rulers (who claim to follow the Word of God, but defy it in practice), or alternatively, that the Word of God, though suitable in the past, is not so in the present. Such a Muslim will not be free from inner perplexity and will be unable to function as an integrated and authentic person committed to his faith, as were the early Muslims. In like manner the average Indian Muslim just cannot conceive how it is possible for a sincere Muslim to be free to shape human society on the basis of the decisions of the majority, instead of implicitly following the will of God as revealed in the Qur'an and the *sunnah*. Consequently, the average Indian Muslim just cannot help suspecting that those Muslims who actively associate themselves with secular political parties and claim to be committed democrats, nationalists, or socialists, are either atheists or communists at heart, or are opportunistic self-seekers and careerists out to please the Hindu majority. These perplexed Muslims honestly feel that the primary loyalty and concern of the true Muslim could only be for the Muslim brotherhood, irrespective of region or race, rather than for a particular territorial state or a secular cause like socialism. In contrast, a Muslim who has freely assimilated secularism into his authentic Islamic perspective would be likely to function as an integrated person, though he might become alienated from the common Muslim who does not accept the secular revolution.

The Muslim's reservations about secularism and the modern conception of religion, as a personal relationship between man and God, are perfectly natural and understandable. These reservations should be viewed with sympathy rather than anger or negative despair, and at the same time all efforts should be made by Muslim intellectuals to educate the Muslim mind in its basic task of cultural self-evolution. Muslims as a body must be helped to liberate themselves from a rigid fixation upon the medieval *gestalt* of Islam as distinct from its essence as such. They must be helped to realize that while the essence of Islam is eternally valid, no particular interpretation of the basic essence should be regarded as immutable, such that the slightest departure from it amounted to disbelief, disrespect, or disloyalty to God and the Prophet ﷺ.

Western orientalists may well deem it both polite and expedient not to deal with, what Professor Kruse calls '*the ultimate data of Islam*', namely the conception of God and revelation, etc. But it would be fatal no less for the spiritual integrity and maturity of Muslims, than for their worldly progress, if their own intellectuals were to abdicate their duty to subject their cherished tradition to an honest self-criticism.

Obviously any alteration in one's religious perspective due to fear, political pressure, expediency, or opportunism will be repugnant to all sensible persons. But a genuine reconstruction of basic concepts and values as a result of deeper insight into the human situation signifies spiritual growth rather than an opportunistic adjustment in one's beliefs as a concession to situational demands or pressures. This spiritual growth, which is a slow and painful process, requires intellectual honesty and clarity, which are certainly not easy to attain. Consequently, the more or less inevitable conceptual lag or cultural resistance of the traditional Muslim should not be construed as obtuseness or obstinacy and generate anger or despair among those liberal Muslims or non-Muslims who have already inwardly accepted the secular revolution without compromising their spiritual integrity.

Author's Preface to the First Edition

Turkey was the first Muslim country to accept the secular revolution. However, this momentous breakthrough was not the result of an inner transformation of the Islamic perspective of the people, but was thrust upon a bewildered nation smarting under the shock of defeat. Even today a sizable section of the people is reported to be feeling nostalgic about the good old and only true style of Islamic piety, which has been corrupted by the spurious Islam of the modernists. The traditionalists hope the true Islam would once again be restored in Turkey and elsewhere, in accordance with a Divine plan no human mind could presume to fathom. But instead of the Turkish secularists recanting their earlier errors or being ousted from power by the traditionalists, other countries have started following the Turkish example. Indonesia, which today has the largest Muslim population in the world, has adopted a secular constitution, and Bangla Desh has just joined the secular club. Thus, about 250 million Muslims constituting more than half the total world Muslim population are already citizens of independent states, which have opted for secularism by choice and not by compulsion. The Arab countries too are groping for an integrated Islamic vision, which would enable them to reconcile the ideal of Arab nationalism with Islam, and many secular and socialist intellectuals are trying to separate the grain of the ideals of Islam from the chaff of the illusions of Muslims. This desired spiritual and political maturity presupposes an honest self-reinterpretation of the great Islamic tradition.

This work is precisely such an attempt to satisfy the above need and to project a systematic conceptual framework built around contemporary knowledge enabling the Muslim to combine authentic commitment to Islam with secular democracy and a humanistic internationalism. The work is meant for intellectuals, and to begin with, it can only have a rather limited appeal. But the basic approach to Islam, as projected in this work, is most likely to appeal in the long run to a growing cross-section of the professional and educated Muslims who are being progressively exposed to the secularization process under the impact of contemporary industrialized society. These professional classes can be counted upon to play an important role in reshaping the religious sensibility of the urban lower middle class Muslims whose acute spiritual perplexity is most resistant to the secular stimuli of the contemporary environment.

Author's Preface to the First Edition

At present there is a great dearth of literature on Islamic liberalism, while the market is literally flooded with books and tracts with the traditional approach. This state of affairs reinforces the religious sensibility of the medieval period, and perpetuates the cultural isolation of the Muslims, thereby obstructing their full participation as Indian citizens in the democratic shaping of our national destiny. Indeed, the concept of two cultures, as applied by Sir C.P. Snow to the humanities and the sciences, seems to apply with equal force to the cultural isolation between the lower middle class urban Muslims and the advanced modernized Muslims, who are ideologically nearer the modernized Hindus rather than their own traditional co-religionists. This intragroup cultural isolation of the modernized Muslims inevitably tends to escalate into their spiritual alienation. This leads to mutual suspicion, dislike and intra-Muslim polarity, which at times becomes more intense than even the Hindu-Muslim polarity in recent times.

The education of the common Indian Muslim will succeed only if there is abundant literature of Islamic liberalism suitable for the average reader. Philosophical works, like the present one, will cut no ice with him. But the propagation of any new perspective requires a solid intellectual base, just as the mass production of consumer goods presupposes an adequate base of heavy industry. The present project is precisely an attempt to fill this urgent need.

Ignorance of the Arabic language is a great handicap for anyone writing on Islam. Indeed I would never have undertaken the project if my primary objective were Qur'anic exegesis or a contribution to Islamic theology or classical Islamic philosophy. My aim is merely to reinterpret the basic concepts and values of Islam (which I could presume to understand as a born and educated Muslim) in the light of the contemporary conceptual framework. I dare say, in this context, the ignorance of the Arabic language may not vitiate the methodological propriety of my attempt, while the ignorance of the language of contemporary thought would have been just unpardonable. Indeed there would have been no point to the present undertaking.

I feel a sense of belonging to the *'Aligarh Movement'* initiated by Syed Ahmad Khan and nourished by his distinguished colleagues. It seems to me that in my own humble way I am trying to carry on the great task, which it initiated just one hundred years ago. It is a pity that the solid work done by Syed Ahmad and his associates was not followed up by the Aligarians of the succeeding generations. None of the writers on Islamic hermeneutics after Syed Ahmad, like Iqbal, Azad, Mohammad Ali (of Lahore) belongs to Aligarh. Not only this, the post-Syed Ahmad generation of educated Muslims went back upon the rationalism and secularism of Syed Ahmad, under the growing influence of Pan-Islamism which culminated in the *Khilafat* Movement of 1921.

The *Khilafat* Movement, which was supported by the Indian National Congress, was no doubt wedded to the ideal of liberal nationalism and Hindu-Muslim unity. But a deeper analysis shows that Syed Ahmad's approach was more rational, secular, and nationalist than that of most of his successors, who could not resist the appeal of Pan-Islamism. Syed Ahmad's politics of conciliation with the British was rooted in his genuine Victorian vision, while his successor's politics of militant nationalism was a shaky synthesis between nationalism and Islamic communitarianism, rather than a clear and consistent vision. Realizing this lacuna, Iqbal undertook to reconstruct Islamic thought. But he could not accommodate either secularism or nationalism, both of which were integral parts of Syed Ahmad's dynamic vision. It was Azad who stressed these concepts, although he ever-remained critical of Syed Ahmad's loyalist stance. Unfortunately, Azad's secular nationalism was misconstrued by many Muslims as politically motivated, even as Syed Ahmad's friendliness to the British was misconstrued as an exercise in prudence.

It would be an unrealistic expectation that my general approach to religion and its detailed application to the Islamic tradition would find ready acceptance by most Muslims. But a debate could be set in motion, so that the flame of ceaseless inquiry does not get dimmed or choked due to the lack of fresh air in the portals of the Muslim mind. The Islamic vision of the Muslim should never become closed, but must possess the resilience to appreciate and assimilate the ceaseless growth in the knowledge and wisdom of the human family as a whole. No vision can be final. My own Islamic vision cannot claim to be more than one existential perspective which appeals to a particular individual, attempting to spell out the meaning of Islam (or what being a Muslim ought to mean) in the contemporary human situation.

Author's Preface to the First Edition

The dates given in the work are all in the Christian era, and all Arabic and Persian terms and names have been spelt according to their correct original pronunciation in the Indian environment. In view of this, diacritical marks were not needed.

Jamal Khwaja

Note: Suggested reading pattern for the book

The explanatory notes (pp. 251–271) are meant to develop the theme and the line of the argument in the text. Each note contains some important information or insight. Reading each note along with the text should considerably add to the pleasure and the profit of reading the book.

Using two bookmarks, one in each section, would make the process effortless. This arrangement aims to serve the requirements of readers who are hard pressed for time as well as readers who can devote more time for pondering highly complex issues.

CHAPTER 1

INTRODUCTION: THE PROBLEM AND ITS HISTORICAL BACKGROUND

I

THE QUEST FOR THE MEANING OF ISLAM

It is quite common for learned scholars and laymen alike to raise the question 'What is Islam?' and answer it with a sense of assurance and certainty, as if their answer is the only conceivable one. Such persons hardly suspect that this simplicity is superficial. The reason is that Islam is neither a logico-mathematical or scientific concept that could be unambiguously defined, nor a physical object like a chair or table, or a biological organism like, a horse or cow whose properties could be catalogued or described without any room for controversy. The question 'What is Islam?' is very close to the questions 'What is justice?' and 'What is beauty?' and answers to these questions can never be simple, since the nature of justice or beauty is not out there for our perceptual or intuitive inspection, but is chosen by us out of several competing meanings of the words 'beauty' and 'justice'. The individual assimilates the concrete meaning of such abstract words from his milieu, just as he assimilates the language, gestures, or morals of the group. But the individual remains unaware of the fact that his conception of beauty or justice or, for that matter, of Islam is only one particular model among other actual or possible models.

According to the orthodox view, Islam is a set of basic beliefs, values, and practices, which are the defining coordinates of Islam. The core of these beliefs was formulated by the divinely inspired Prophet Muhammad ﷺ *. One who accepts these beliefs accepts Islam, while one who denies or doubts their validity repudiates Islam. The basic beliefs or pillars of faith are:

---
* "Peace be upon him" in Arabic

(**1**) unity of God (*tawhid*), (**2**) revelation (*wahy*), (**3**) life after death (*akhirat*), (**4**) angels (*malaika*); while the five pillars of action are the formula of faith (*kalima*) 'There is no God but Allah, and Muhammad is His messenger', prayers (*salat*), fasting (*soum*), wealth tax (*zakat*), and pilgrimage to Mecca (*Hajj*). But this simplicity is deceptive, for the moment we try to determine what exactly is meant by such words as 'God', 'prophecy', and 'angels', etc., we find ourselves immersed in a sea of difficulties.

The difficulty is due to the fact that one's concrete understanding or interpretation of religious concepts is an integral part of one's basic worldview, which, to begin with, is a product of cultural conditioning. The individual assimilates the interpretation current in his own milieu and accepts it as true. This was as true for the period of the Prophet ﷺ as for any other. Even granting that the Prophet ﷺ was the recipient of Divine revelation, his basic conceptual framework was as much derived from his Semitic milieu as that of his contemporaries. It seems to me that just as the Prophet ﷺ spoke the Meccan style of Arabic, used Arabic syntax and grammar, wore Arab dress, lived in a pre-industrial desert economy, the Prophet ﷺ also shared the generally accepted historical, geographical, cosmological, and medical ideas or beliefs of his times. Most probably the Prophet ﷺ believed that the sun went round the earth which was flat, that mountains and rivers were instantly created by the Creator, that different species of animals were separately created, that plants had no sex, that epidemics and natural calamities were Divine punishment for human wickedness, that women were mentally and morally inferior to men, etc. It seems the Prophet ﷺ must have interpreted the Qur'anic verses about God saying 'Be', and of the Universe coming into being,[1] in the sense of instant creation rather than in the evolutionary sense. Again, if asked to explain the Qur'anic verse which refers to the motion of the earth, the Prophet ﷺ probably would not have interpreted it to mean that the earth moves round the sun, but in some other sense, which is difficult for us to pinpoint. The implication is that the 'cognitive concretion', that is, the concrete understanding and clarification of generalized concepts such as creation, revelation, and God, etc., is always done within the conceptual framework current in the individual's milieu.

Concrete interpretations need not always be explicitly formulated, but are implicitly present in the general conceptual framework or background of a given period. An implicit interpretation will be formulated or expressed only when there is some stimulus or need to do so. In this process the implicit beliefs become explicit. This is exactly what happened as a result of the impact of Darwin's theory of organic evolution upon Christian beliefs, and the subsequent heated dispute between Christian theology and science. Before Darwin every Muslim and Christian believed that the original ancestors of the various species of plants and animals were first separately created by God, and subsequently they perpetuated themselves through sexual reproduction. This concrete interpretation may or may not have been formulated by any individual. But this was the actual view of almost all Christians and Muslims before Darwin. Similarly, some idea of the total time span was certainly implicit in the awareness of men living before Darwin. We may say that Christians usually believed the world to be about four or five thousand years old. But the geological assessment, as we know, was quite different.

Religion as an Existential Interpretation of the Universe

Historically every religion has been an organic whole of **(a)** a thought-cum-value system, **(b)** a symbolic precept system, and **(c)** an institutional system. The thought-cum-value system interprets man's cosmic situation and projects intrinsic values and also instrumental rules for realizing them. The precept system comprises the symbolic practices dealing with the transcendental sphere, while the institutional system comprises the approved patterns of behavior in the social sphere.

Thought systems arise because man is never satisfied with bare perceptual experience, but wants to interpret or understand it as part of a wider contextual whole. All human experience stands in need of interpretation in order to become functionally significant for man, since isolated bits of information cannot be used for satisfying human needs. Science is not merely systematic description, but also systematic interpretation of empirical data. The interpretation consists of empirically verifiable and quantitative causal laws connecting different phenomena. Such laws are essential for controlling and manipulating the physical environment. This mode of interpreting physical data is called scientific explanation whose chief feature is its direct or indirect verifiability in terms of human sense-experience. Scientific explanation always has some empirical evidence on the strength of which one explanation is preferred to another.

The above type of explanation, however, does not exhaust the full range of human interpretation, which includes man's ethical, aesthetic, religious, and metaphysical responses, which are not less significant for man's life than scientific explanation. Without the latter man cannot use the environment for satisfying his needs, but without ethical evaluation he loses his sense of direction. Similarly, without the aesthetic response man cannot create or appreciate beauty, and life without beauty lacks a dimension of value. As we know, beauty evokes aesthetic joy, which brings about the spiritual revitalization of man.

The metaphysical or existential response is rooted in man's yearning to decipher the total meaning or significance of the Universe as a whole, and to relate himself to it accordingly. Man yearns to grasp the depth-significance of the Universe as a complex state of affairs, whose empirical structure is disclosed by science. Biology, for example, tells us about the nature of life and death, but not how to relate oneself, or what attitude to adopt toward life and death. Man could respond to the Universe at the empirical, ethical, or other levels without its existential interpretation. But this would amount to ad hoc responses to ad hoc environmental stimuli, and man would not be able to give any inner justification for his different responses. Let us examine this point in some detail.

The Universe has some basic features which maybe said to be its warp and woof, and which remain the same throughout history, e.g., the features of law and order, harmony and beauty of nature, man's moral sense, as distinct from concrete moral codes, the struggle for survival of the species and of individuals, pain and suffering, hope and joy, birth, growth, decay, and death. Natural science does not concern itself with the significance or meaning of these features of the Universe, that is, whether they are just accidental features and could, therefore, disappear from the cosmic scene, as accidentally as they appeared, or whether they stand rooted in the constitution of the Universe and thus have an *ontic* status or permanent reality. Now the way in which one interprets these features simultaneously influences the personality orientation of the individual, and is, in turn, influenced by the original bent of the personality itself. In other words, there is a dialectical relationship between the existential interpretation and the personality orientation. The interpretation becomes important, since it influences man's inner responses to the Universe in a most subtle manner, though the interpretation has no prima facie bearing upon man's empirical, ethical, or aesthetic response. But the fact is that different existential

Introduction: The Problem And Its Historical Background

interpretations constitute different ways of treating the Universe or relating oneself to it, and this inevitably influences the individual's lifestyle and also raises the question as to which particular style is right, and why so.[2] To give an analogy, the practicing scientist does not concern himself with the question whether or why nature behaves uniformly, but takes it for granted, as if it were self-evident or necessarily true, or because it works. But the denial of causal uniformity does not involve any logical contradiction; nor can it be logically proved. We accept it for two reasons: first, our actual experience suggests as if it were true; and, second, if it were not true, no point would be left in our scientific inquiries, which we deem as valuable and worth pursuing. Likewise, there would be no point left or, to be more accurate, the urge to pursue values would be far less intense, if values were chance and ephemeral products of the blind dance of atoms, without the conservation and growth of values being ontologically guaranteed, despite all seeming obstacles. The concept of God is precisely one particular form of this faith. Belief in God implies that values like truth, goodness, and beauty are neither chance products, nor ultimate and un-derived features of the Universe, but have their source in the ultimate and Supreme Being with whom man could establish an '*I-Thou*' dialogue. The existential interpretation is neither a hypothesis, nor a partly justifiable postulate; it is a motivational re-enforcer that integrates the individual's thoughts and feelings into a stable inner way of life or mode of treating the Universe, as distinct from ad hoc and ever-variable responses or attitudes.

An existential interpretation maybe compared with dream interpretation or with a poetic metaphor without being reducible to them. The significance of the dream is not a matter of verifiable knowledge but of insight, intuition, or personality projection upon the canvas of the dream. Likewise, the poetic metaphor is not a matter of verifiable description or theory, but of expression of the feelings, emotions, and imagery evoked by some object, situation, or experience. The object of dream interpretation is self-understanding, that of a poetic metaphor self-expression, while that of an existential interpretation, the person's stable attitudinal adjustment or orientation to the Universe as a whole, or to some significant aspect of it, e.g., death, conscience, and sexual love, etc. One may, for instance, interpret death as the final release from the tyranny or tragedy of life, or as the blind axe that destroys the tree of life, or as a change of abode or of bodily apparel, or as the destination of life, or as a welcome union with the Infinite. These interpretations have a poetic flavor, no doubt. Their primary aim, however, is not to give pleasure, but to give meaning and direction to life. Likewise, the interpretation that life is a hard and rocky battleground differs from the interpretation that life is a blooming garden, not merely in terms of the imagery, but also in terms of its directive function. The first interpretation suggests the ethic of power and of action; the second the ethic of beauty and of contemplation. Similarly, different interpretations of Eros will imply different codes of sexual conduct, even when there maybe agreement on all the relevant facts of life. Similarly, to interpret conscience as the voice of God within man or as the Divine spark makes for a different quality of man's inner life as well as his relationship with society than to interpret conscience as the 'internalized censor'. These existential interpretations enable man to conduct his life in a consistently meaningful manner. In one word, their primary function is orientative rather than aesthetic, although when the proffered orientation really grips the individual, his entire being is suffused with a sense of profound joy, perhaps, more intense than aesthetic pleasure itself.

The existential interpretation is not a substitute for, and hence not a competitor with, scientific explanation, just as a poetic metaphor is not a substitute for a scientific description or theory. But an existential interpretation, by virtue of its essential directive function, may well promote or impede scientific inquiry, or in some cases, even of a particular scientific hypothesis. For example, the interpretation that man is the vicegerent of God, Who has granted man power and dominion over the rest of creation, including the sun and the moon, the wind and the ocean, tends to promote scientific inquiry, while the interpretation that man is only an accidental self-glorifying worm, born out of a cosmic accident, tends to inhibit the arduous and sustained labor which science demands. Indeed, as Whitehead points out, the theistic interpretation of the Universe facilitated the belief in the ultimate rationality and orderliness of nature as the creation of a perfect Creator.[3] Likewise, the idealistic interpretation of Reality being ultimately mental or ideal might have facilitated the empirical discovery that conation is present in plants and minerals. It also seems to me that Spinoza's concept of *Substance and Psycho-physical Parallelism* was congenial to the growth of an integrated and inter-disciplinary approach to the physical and the biological sciences. Whether or not this likely interaction factually occurred is a matter of research in the field of history of ideas. The crux of the matter is that while an existential interpretation always has an ethical function, in some cases it could also stimulate scientific theories.

Introduction: The Problem And Its Historical Background

An existential interpretation of the Universe is by definition not verifiable. However, it must take into account the full range of the different features of the Universe without suppressing any feature, which may not harmonize with the favored interpretation. This task presupposes a base of reliable factual knowledge as the data of the interpretation. Thus, one must be aware of the evolutionary feature of life, though knowledge of factual details is not called for. Likewise, one must be aware of the extent of struggle, suffering, and tragedy in the Universe (and not merely of its beauty and harmony) to avoid the existential interpretation from being weighted in favor of some selected features of the Universe. The interpretation must thus harmonize with the data and reliable conclusions of science. For example, the interpretation that every event serves a cosmic purpose does not appear to harmonize with geo-biological blind alleys and waste. Or the interpretation that God loves and cherishes His meanest creation does not appear to harmonize with the biological struggle for survival. Likewise, the interpretation that the Universe was instantly created out of absolute nothingness does not appear to harmonize with the scientific concept of evolution.

If, and when, the interpretation does not harmonize with the scientific conceptual scheme, a revision of its concrete sense may remove the prima facie discord. We may say, for instance, that God's love for His creation is not the same as a mother's love for her child, or that what appears as evil works as an instrumental good in a larger context. This task involves redefining, analyzing, explaining, making distinctions or comparisons either in the spirit of a free exploration of the given data or in the spirit of a defensive reconciliation between theology and science. In the former case, the role of reason is primary, while in the latter it is secondary. The theologian explores new meanings of traditional concepts in a spirit of defensive reverence to the tradition, while the philosopher freely reflects upon the validity of the religious interpretation. He checks whether the actual data of human experience harmonize with the religious interpretation. This activity, however, does not involve deductive or inductive reasoning but existential elucidation, that is, the illumination of one's hidden depth attitudes, choices, interpretative responses, or images. An existential interpretation which is chosen by the philosopher is thus functionally similar to, but genetically or methodologically different from, religious faith.

An existential interpretation of some kind or other is unavoidable. We can only opt for this or that interpretation, but we cannot opt to do away with all interpretation as such. We may claim to avoid all contact with metaphysics or religion, which we may view as the hallmarks of a pre-scientific mentality. Yet the fact is that we cannot live as integrated human beings without some kind of world view or total perspective on the cosmos. [4] And this total perspective, be it religious or philosophical, is at bottom always an existential interpretation of the basic features of human experience cosmic law and order, the mysteries of birth, growth and death, the beauty as well as the fury of nature, good and evil, joy and tragedy. [5] Religious faith is the pre-logical acceptance of an interpretation because of its existential grip over the believer.

Religious faith should not be confused with credulity or trust. A person, for example, may come to have 'faith' in any belief in the sense that he maybe subjectively certain of its truth, and feel no need for testing his belief. Thus, a mother may have such strong faith in the integrity of her daughter or the intelligence of her son, that she may not be bothered by the adverse opinion of neighbors and teachers about her children. Since, however, these beliefs are of a type that can be tested and proved, the refusal to test them cannot be accepted as reasonable. Unshakable faith in beliefs, which could be verified, is not justifiable. But faith in God or life after death is a different matter, since no argument or observation could clinch the issue. It is here that genuine faith touches its proper sphere, and can realize its full possibilities of growth and maturity.

As already mentioned, man passes judgments of fact as well as judgments of value. Those states of affairs which are judged to be good in their own right and, hence, worthy of being established, preserved, or fostered, as the case maybe, are intrinsic values, while the means or conditions required for realizing them are instrumental values. For example, punctuality, moderation, courage, industry, endurance, cooperativeness, etc., are all necessary for establishing such states of affairs as universal love, justice, the equality and dignity of man, and his integrated growth. Instrumental values are thus dependent variables, while intrinsic values are independent coordinates of any value system.

The distinction between intrinsic and instrumental values is, however, not rigid. Indeed some values maybe both intrinsic and instrumental, while some others maybe regarded as intrinsic in one context and instrumental in another. Thus, good health is both an intrinsic and an instrumental value. Similarly, the good will, in Kant's sense, namely man's general desire to do

Introduction: The Problem And Its Historical Background

his duty rather than seek pleasure, is both an intrinsic and an instrumental value. Similarly, a clearly instrumental value such as physical cleanliness tends to become an intrinsic good when its cultivation produces aesthetic delight in the individual. Again, an intrinsic value such as social justice or respect for human beings operates as an instrumental value for promoting the self-realization of the members of a group. Nevertheless, the distinction between intrinsic and instrumental values becomes crucial in those cases where adherence to an instrumental value may ultimately obstruct intrinsic values as such.

This tension or clash is not merely a theoretical possibility or a hypothetical situation, but repeatedly occurs in man's history. For example, the early Jewish and Islamic injunction to grow and multiply in order to glorify God was obviously necessary (hence, an instrumental value) for the survival of a nascent group. But under entirely changed demographic conditions, the adherence to this rule obstructs universal self-realization or the integrated growth of human beings. Similarly, many age-old and respected rules, regulations, and social customs such as the position of women and children, rules of marriage, etc., may turn out to be misconceived in the light of factual knowledge, which was not available when the rules were framed. Fidelity to the end is thus more important than obedience to the rules that might stultify the end. This, however, does not imply that means are unimportant and maybe ignored without peril. Indeed, the usual formulation of the problem of ends versus means is very misleading, since a complete separation of the means from the actual concrete end is not possible. Nevertheless, intrinsic values or ends desirable for their own sake must be accorded primacy over values that are mere means to their realization.

The emphasis upon intrinsic values encourages the individual to strive for the more important goals of life and not to feel satisfied with mechanical compliance with instrumental rules without bothering to assess their relevance in a changing world. A lopsided concern with intrinsic values occupying a relatively lower rank in the hierarchy of values must also be avoided. Without the concept of rank of value the individual fails to develop a sense of proportion, which is essential for the good life. [6]

All value systems acquire concrete meaning for a group in its concrete situational context. Without situational concretion abstract values such as justice, charity, chastity, and honesty function as variables whose validity cannot be ascertained. However, no situational concretion can be final.

Every age inherits the values of the past but gives them a fresh interpretation. The failure to distinguish between an abstract value system and its situational concretion inclines one to think that any change in the latter destroys the basic value system as such. This makes one cling to the past and stops all ethical growth.

II

FIELD TENSIONS AND FIELD INTEGRATION

There is a continuous interaction between the life experience of a religious group and the growth of its religious concepts and values. All cultural systems including the religious are situationally evoked. Many of us are apt to hold that while the beliefs of other religions have been so evoked, our own religion did not grow within an historical situation but was born ready made. But this amounts to the adoption of double standards and is invalid. Even the same individual does not stick to the same meaning at different stages of his life, since experience and reflection continually modify his concrete understanding of general concepts. In the formal sense the nuclear core may remain identical, but, in the concrete functional sense, even the core may change. The concept of God, for example, may evolve over a long period of time, so that the concrete meaning of the word 'God' becomes quite different from its earlier concrete meaning. Yet, the word 'God' may remain intact. Sometimes a new expression, say, 'Being', 'Reality', 'First Cause', may come into use. The choice of words depends upon whether or not one wants to break away from the tradition.

The illusion of changeless fundamental concepts arises through the tendency of words and names to persist in our living vocabulary, in spite of changes in their concrete connotation. Even a radical shift in ideas may take place without a corresponding change in our linguistic habits or vocabulary. This is quite natural though highly misleading, since it tends to conceal the fact of change.

The history of culture shows that all fields of human culture, such as religion, art, philosophy, science, etc., interact and influence each other, so that the total culture of a group is an organic whole. A change in one-sphere spills over into all others. There is regional resistance to begin with.

Introduction: The Problem And Its Historical Background

But in the course of time significant changes in any one sphere of human culture penetrate the total cultural *gestalt*. To give some illustrations, the invention of photography had its repercussions for painting, the scientific formulation of the theory of evolution profoundly altered philosophy and Christian theology, the industrial revolution led to social, moral, and economic revolutions, and the advent of contraception is gradually influencing the norms of sexual morality. Religion, as a segment of the cultural *gestalt*, cannot escape transformation in this evolving Universe.

Not only the fields of art, literature, and science, but also those of economics, politics, religion, and morality all interact. Religion may claim the right to legislate for all the fields, as if it were the sovereign. Even so, the religious authority is influenced by the inevitable interaction between the different fields of human life. There is a dialectical interaction between a religion or an ideology and the socioeconomic field rather than a one-sided dependence of ideology upon the economic structure. In practice this produces field tensions or conflicts between the pull of two or more fields of human experience. Thus the thought-cum-value system of a particular religion may pull us toward a male dominated society, while its techno-centric economy may pull us toward a more or less complete equality between the sexes. Similarly, tensions may develop between the fields of art and science, or art, religion, and morality, etc.

Field tensions may also arise due to conflict between the value system of the religion and the authentic values of the individual, for example, if his religion prescribes human sacrifice, while his conscience rebels against the idea, despite all his sincere efforts to accept it. Likewise, if the Qur'an were to prescribe stoning as a punishment for adultery (as a matter of fact, this is not the case), and the Muslim's conscience were to revolt against the idea, a field tension would arise and raise the problem of authenticity. [7] The believer could either suppress this tension, or rationalize the command, or, without concealing his disagreement surrender his judgment to the wisdom of the Qur'an. But if he is not prepared to do so, and wishes to live as an authentic integrated person, he must either attempt the task of field integration or repudiate his religious tradition altogether. In the West, Whitehead and Tillich have followed the first course, while Freud and Russell the latter. [8] It seems the latter course is fraught with the danger of throwing away the baby with the bath. Let us consider in greater detail the various types of response to field tension. They maybe called repression/suppression, isolation, rationalization, and, finally, integration.

Field repression/suppression implies that some field or dimension of experience is repressed/suppressed by the individual in order to escape the pain of conflict. One individual may repress the dimension of reason, while another that of spirituality. But neither the intellectual yearning for clear concepts and a unified world view, nor the spiritual yearning to transcend one's private interests and reach out for some higher impersonal values can be destroyed, no matter how much these yearnings maybe repressed or suppressed. Even as the sex instinct finds other outlets in the case of repression/suppression, so do the above needs. It appears that class hatred, bigotry, racial prejudice, and chauvinism, etc., are all partly the products of suppression of either the dimension of spirituality or reason or both. Field repression, therefore, does not produce a lasting inner peace.

Field isolation means that the different fields of human culture are deliberately kept isolated from each other. This approach again proves highly unsatisfactory, since it denies the organic unity of culture. Field isolation cannot withstand the natural impact of the different fields of human culture. The attempt at field isolation leads to a painful sense of fragmentation and the fear of facing life as a whole. Field isolation breeds an inner sense of uneasiness, though it may outwardly help to keep one's faith.

Rationalization is the attempt to overcome tensions by explaining them away with the help of far-fetched alterations in the meaning of words, false generalizations, selective sampling of data, seductive but weak analogies, confusion of meanings, or types of discourse, and, last but not the least, a defensive or justificatory use of reason as distinct from the analytical and exploratory. Field rationalization is a more or less conscious attempt to justify a traditional thought system as a partisan rather than as an autonomous person.

Field integration means a systematic dialogue between the different fields of human experience with a view to overcoming actual or possible tensions between them. The process of integration involves the pruning or revising of definitions or uses of the basic words in question such as God, creation, and justice, etc. A striking need for field integration arose due to the impact of the theory of evolution upon the concrete interpretation of the Bible and the Qur'an. Intelligent believers felt uneasy at the conflict between the religious concept of Divine creation and the scientific concept of evolution. The concept of 'evolutionary creation', as distinguished from 'instantaneous creation out of nothing' removes the conflict partly, but not completely, between the fields of religion and science. The notion of gradual

Introduction: The Problem And Its Historical Background

emergence still conflicts with Divine omnipotence, and the existence of pain and evil conflicts with either God's omnipotence or goodness. These difficulties prompt one to make still further alterations in the concept of God and Divine creation or goodness, etc. The need for field integration cannot be dismissed as the intellectual luxury of philosophical minds. It is rooted in a concern for one's intellectual integrity and disinterested search for truth instead of fragmented loyalties. In the final analysis, field integration is more a search for authenticity than for intellectual curiosity.

The search for authenticity prima facie clashes with an existential surrender to God or Scripture, and appears to be rooted in pride, or a reliance on one's own judgment, and hence the negation of genuine religion, which is supposed to be rooted in surrender to God. But many highly intelligent and deeply religious minds hold self-authentication as an essentially religious surrender to the God within man rather than as a species of pride. This is the existential approach to religion and it enables the individual to retain his spiritual autonomy without the danger of the autarchy of his surface self, or the Freudian '*id*'.[9] This approach, however, does contradict the traditional conception of religion, as surrender to an external authority.

The existentialist approach to religion, as I understand it, affirms a three-fold autonomy of science, of individual conscience and of society. This means affirming the autonomy of science in the sphere of empirical truth; the autonomy of individual conscience in the sphere of values; and finally the autonomy of the human community in the sphere of institutional matters. According to my approach, religion belongs primarily to the second category and only marginally to the third. Religion thus becomes an authentic concern with the meaning of the Universe rather than an institutional way of life. The meaning is not a propositional truthclaim, but an existential interpretation, which quenches the restless longing of man for a stable total perspective or worldview. Spiritual satisfaction can, however, occur only when the perspective is existential and authentic, that is, it wells up from the depths of the person.

A religious response degenerates into a pseudo-religious one, if it fails to grip the individual. A religion should rise from the heart rather than the head, even as maternal love is a demand of her innermost being without the aid of Kant's categorical imperative, or Bentham's (d. 1832) hedonistic calculus. Neither the laws of logic, nor the rules of verification, nor the lure of utility, whether temporal or eschatological, but only the soft whisper of the spirit wields the final authority in the sphere of religion.[10] It may happen that while the basic world view of a particular religion appeals to the believer, he is unable to agree with a particular point or norm of the tradition. Should he then reject the religious tradition, which nurtured him and in which his spiritual roots are embedded? It seems, in such a case self-authentication rather than rejection of the tradition is the proper response. This response presupposes religion in its mature form, that is, religion as surrender to an internal authority rather than to an external.

The inner authority is man's creative conscience or God within man. Submission to an external authority obviously negates freedom, while submission to an internal authority is quite compatible with freedom. Spiritual autonomy is the inner spontaneous demand of man, and submission to an external authority goes against the grain of man, so to speak, even though he maybe quite happy and productive, if there be no conflict between the prescriptions of the authority and his own inner demands.

There is another significance of the distinction between an external and an internal authority. If man could submit to an external God without any reservation and with complete authenticity, he would certainly have the inner satisfaction that he would never err to the extent that he obeyed the commands of the infallible God. But the difficulty is that man never encounters God in a direct manner in the same way as he encounters his conscience, or a book, or a person. Submission to God means, in the functional sense at least, submission to God through some mediator or channel. Man's submission to God is thus always indirect and mediated rather than direct and immediate. For example, to a Christian, submission to God amounts to submission to Jesus, the Christ; and to a Muslim, submission to God amounts to submission to the Qur'an as the revealed Will of God, or, in most cases, to the Qur'an plus *hadith*. To certain persons, such an indirect submission may not raise any difficulty, and their commitment or faith maybe perfect. Indeed, they maybe blissfully unaware of the distinction between an immediate submission and a mediated submission to God, just as most non-philosophers are blissfully unaware of the various problems connected with the perception of physical objects, or the mechanism of the perceptual process. They perceive things and are not bothered by the problems or theories of perception. Similarly, many deeply pious believers just believe without being bothered by the intellectual difficulties involved in those beliefs. They honestly feel and believe that the Qur'an is the Word of God, or Jesus the Son of God, and readily submit themselves before them, as if they had submitted before an unmediated God. But once the reflective impulse or process is set in motion, no matter how or why, man loses the original innocence of faith or commitment. His joy in surrender is corroded by doubts and felt intellectual difficulties. Once the reflective process starts, it cannot arbitrarily be stopped at the portals of sacrosanct beliefs. The reflective process is like an all-consuming fire, which spares nothing. The goal of this process is complete field integration. Should the movement of thought be checked or suspended, man becomes inwardly restless and fragmented. The reflective attitude conflicts with submission to external but not to an internal authority. This makes the distinction between the two crucial.

The difficulties of submission to an external authority have been pointed out. But submission to an internal authority is not free from difficulties of its own. The principal difficulty lies in the fact that man can easily deceive himself into believing that he is submitting himself to the internal authority of his conscience, when, in fact, he maybe guilty of rationalization or inauthenticity. Thus, man's spiritual autonomy or freedom is ever-perilously near the dark leap into license. *'The fear of freedom'*, as Erich Fromm calls it, is thus quite natural and understandable. [11] Rationalists are often inclined to dismiss this fear as born of immaturity or distrust in the essential goodness of human nature. But their confidence in human capacities is as one-sided and dangerous as is the fear of freedom, or the evasion of self-responsibility and the resultant surrender to an external authority, whether religious or secular. Consequently, the inwardly free man needs to be extremely cautious that his freedom does not degenerate into license under one garb or the other. [12]

FIELD INTEGRATION, SCIENCE AND RELIGION

Man cannot function in an interpretative vacuum, in the belief that pure morality and science would jointly suffice. To ignore this truth was the crucial mistake committed by many Western science-oriented thinkers in the late 19th and early 20th centuries. The concept of the supposed selfsufficiency of pure morality without some metaphysical foundation or other was generated by the erosion of the traditional Christian theistic interpretation. The case of morality without metaphysics or religion appeared to grow all the stronger with the gradual realization that no metaphysical or religious belief could be proved to be true either deductively or inductively.

The Western intellectual's despair pushed him into a positivistic humanism or pure 'ethicism', according to which morality is sufficient for man, and that religion is either a pre-scientific illusion or, at best, a consolation for William Jame's tender folk. [13] This implied that the progress of science and technology and the eventual eradication of social evils such as poverty and exploitation would ultimately deprive religion of its function as well as its present appeal in the presence of widespread insecurity and injustice. But this belief in the all-sufficiency of science and morality is only a product of man's incurable romanticism.

The history of Western Europe after the First World War shows the inadequacy or falsity of the belief in pure scientific morality without any interpretative support or base. The mono-dimensional fixation upon the peculiar methodology of the natural sciences, or, in other words, viewing scientific explanations as the only model of valid interpretation, generated a new variety of skepticism alter the First World War. This variety embraces not merely particular religious beliefs, but all values as such. This total and all-embracing skepticism or nihilism saps the springs of all human endeavors, generating in man a total despair and a sense of futility or absurdity of life. The logical terminus of this attitude is the quest of death, which is judged as the only means of release from the tyranny of being aware of absurdity, but helpless to overcome it. In some cases this basic despair seeks to disguise itself in a total hedonism. The quest of pleasure and the quest of destruction are desperate attempts to overcome the growing and creeping crisis of the spirit through killing or benumbing the body. The phenomena of drug addiction, alcoholism, 'sexualism', and even such apparently disconnected 'isms' such as extreme nationalism, religionism, scientism, and 'artism', etc., are symptoms of an inner spiritual imbalance or 'ontological deficiency'. They all betray an inauthentic human existence clinging to either escape mechanisms or fragmented loyalties instead of loyalty to an integrated value system. This inauthentic existence turns man into an insecure and anxious being. This breeds suspicion, aggression, and intolerance, etc., and also an inner resistance to the promptings of man's creative conscience. This condition may aptly be termed as a hardening of man's spiritual arteries. Neither the reiteration of traditional creeds nor their intellectual defense cures this malady. Only a dispassionate self-confrontation and more refined methods of philosophical analysis can liberate Western man from his unfortunate nihilism.

Introduction: The Problem And Its Historical Background

The Eastern man, whether Muslim or Hindu, has not yet fallen a victim to this nihilism. He is, however, inwardly uneasy and in need of firm support. Outwardly he maybe serene and self-assured, but various field tensions do inwardly disturb him in proportion to his awareness of the contemporary conceptual framework. He is not fully aware of the need of field integration, but inner conceptual fermentation is unmistakably present.

The Muslim having a traditional or conservative approach to Islam would not concede this point. He would assert that the different sciences, both natural and social, do not have any bearing upon or relevance to the proper understanding of Islam. This contention is true in the sense that the detailed theories and hypotheses of science are not relevant to the truth or falsity of fundamental religious beliefs and moral values, which remain unaffected and untouched by the modifications in our scientific theories or advances in factual knowledge. But the scientific perspective or world view comprising such basic concepts as universal causation, uniformity of nature, evolution, relativity, etc., do profoundly affect our concrete understanding of such essentially religious concepts as creation, revelation, miracles, etc. It is true that religious faith is essentially a matter of an existential commitment rather than of a logical or scientific proof; it is also true that the scientific worldview cannot be established through deductive or inductive reasoning alone, but also needs an extra-rational ontological commitment. Nevertheless, the concrete interpretation of every worldview is inevitably molded by the thought system of the person. Since all social and natural sciences are nothing but critically organized thought systems, they are directly relevant to such concrete interpretations. To the extent that an individual refuses to enter into a dialogue with science, he is like a person who refuses to observe or perform a certain experiment, lest this may go against his established beliefs or attitudes.

The reason for this field isolation is perhaps due to a totally false conception about a complete discontinuity between the field of religion and of science. This belief is fairly widespread. It is, however, only due to an oversimplified conception of both science and religion. Science is viewed as purely factual, while religion as purely valuational or spiritual. It is then held that there is no connection whatsoever between facts and values, or between science and religion. Consequently, it is thought, there is no need for a mutual dialogue between these two fields of human experience.

This approach completely ignores the complexity of both religion and science. It is highly misleading to say that religion has nothing to do with facts, which come under the domain of science, or that science has nothing to do with values, which come under the domain of religion. On the one hand, every religion has its distinctive thought system or worldview, apart from a distinctive value system. Every religion thus has a connection with the realm of facts. On the other hand, science generates its own distinctive values, even though it is admittedly not concerned with values, but with the explanation of facts. In other words, science has a 'valuational temper' of its own. For example, the scientific methods of observation and experiment and formulation of verifiable hypotheses lead to a distaste for speculative metaphysics or a hair-splitting theology, both of which fail to possess any operational definitions or concepts. Similarly, a techno-centric society generates the new value of equality of the sexes, or the value of speed, or the ethics of planning, etc. Moreover, science is not only relevant, but also crucial for realizing basic values, and it also has a positive bearing on the concrete interpretation of these basic intrinsic values. The inevitable conclusion, therefore, is that the slogan of a neat demarcation between the domains of science and religion breaks down.

Scientific developments, however, do not prove or disprove religious beliefs such as the existence of God, or life after death. In fact, if religious beliefs could be proved or disproved on the basis of evidence, religious faith would forfeit its distinctive flavor and become just like other beliefs. Religious faith is 'existentially certain', not 'inductively certain' like the factual truths of science, or 'deductively certain' like the truths of mathematics or logic. The developments of science do not, and cannot, prove or disprove our religious beliefs, qua existential interpretations of man-in-the-Universe, as distinct from pseudo-scientific or pre-scientific truthclaims, involving the subject matter of science itself. But the concrete interpretation of religious beliefs cannot help being influenced by the impact of scientific developments. Science and religion thus interact, and yet they do not interact, in the sense in which interaction takes place between two elements within the same field. The interaction between religion and science is complex, like the relationship between facts and values. Though distinct, facts and values cannot be totally segregated. Concrete value judgments can neither be justified nor realized without adequate factual information supplied by science.

The most significant feature of man's present situation is science or technology. Perhaps the two most vital consequences of this are man's experience of power over nature and progressive inter-cultural communication. The exercise of power over nature tends to corrode those conceptions of religion

Introduction: The Problem And Its Historical Background

that discourage man's self-reliance and encourage the ethics of surrender to an all-powerful Divine will.

The ever-growing communication between different cultures progressively transforms more or less stagnant mono-cultural societies into more or less dynamic multicultural ones. This renders the traditional commitment to the 'faith of one's forefathers' more difficult. The diversity of thought-cum-value systems generates a healthy doubt as inevitably as prosperity generates parking difficulties in the big cities. The individual is conceptually uprooted from his traditional conceptual soil and pushed into a multicultural universe where he has to choose his own conceptual latitude and longitude. Tensions arise between his religious beliefs or thought system and the thought systems of other fields of culture. Tensions may also arise between his expected course of events and the actual course of events or between his aspirations and their fulfillment. This experience of tension, frustration, surprise, and doubt is as essential for man's conceptual growth as is the experience of wonder, uniformity of sequence, success in prediction, and manipulative control over his environment. Tension and frustration induce him to reexamine his beliefs and to remove their inadequacies or mutual contradictions. The leisure generated in affluent societies also tends to promote a growing concern with fundamental human problems, even though this concern is likely to be preceded by a period of an immature hedonism. Affluent societies would eventually be drawn toward a reflective multicultural interpretation of religious experience, or a faith that inquires rather than shuns inquiry.

The concrete re-interpretation of basic Islamic concepts thus becomes inevitable due to the growth in our factual knowledge and improved conceptual tools. This reinterpretation involves an ever-growing convergence or integration of the basic concepts of all the different natural, social, and humanistic sciences. This integration does not imply the creation of a super-science or super-philosophy sitting in judgment on the conclusions of the different sciences. All it means is that the basic well-established concepts of the various fields of human knowledge cannot be viewed as irrelevant for the concrete interpretation of the faith. For example, the geological concept of time, that is, an enormous time span with many distinct long periods; or concepts of biology, such as the gradual emergence of life, ceaseless variations, mutations, evolutionary blind alleys; or the conceptions of sociology, such as the impact of patterns of production and distribution on moral and religious ideas; or the concepts of psychoanalysis, such as man's fear of freedom, defense mechanisms; or the concepts of semantics, such as the different functions of language-all these basic concepts are crucially relevant for a more mature understanding of one's religious tradition.

Let us now examine in some detail how some of the above concepts of the natural and social sciences have demanded the reconstruction of basic religious concepts in the case of Christianity.

Darwin's Theory of Evolution

The conflict between Newtonian physics and Christian theism was very mild indeed in relation to the conflict between Darwin's theory of organic evolution and theism. Newton's theory had only turned the Creator into a super-mathematician but had not abolished the concept as such. Darwin's theory, on the other hand, abolished the Divine office, since the concept of evolution was supposed to explain and account for all the marvels and complexities of living beings and the Universe as a whole.

The entire Christian world was shocked and baffled by this challenge. Initially the Church totally rejected Darwin's theory of organic evolution. But the evidence marshaled by Darwin was too systematic to be ignored. Soon scientists all over the world accepted Darwin's approach. Later on the majority of the Protestant and even Catholic intellectuals assimilated the concept of evolution into their religious framework in varying degrees. This assimilation was done through the belief that evolution was the mode of Divine creation.

This assimilation or integration of biological evolution into the Christian framework satisfied the religiously oriented scientist on the one hand, and the scientifically oriented theologian on the other. But very soon fresh intellectual difficulties were generated. For example, why should an omnipotent God choose such a wasteful and tortuously long road of creation through evolution? The facts of dysteleology and of pain and evil also continued to oppress the religious consciousness. Consequently, the highly sensitive and well-informed intellects of the late 19th century such as Bergson, William James, Paulsen, and Lloyd Morgan, etc., rejected the pre-Darwinian religious conception of creation on the one hand, and Darwin's concept of mechanical natural selection on the other. These thinkers formulated their own conceptions of evolution or evolutionary creation, which are basically similar in spite of differences in terminology. [14]

Introduction: The Problem And Its Historical Background

The Islamic conceptual framework or thought system is, however, still pre-Darwinian. Consequently, a tension exists between science and religion in the deeper recesses of the educated Muslim mind. Integration of scientific concepts with religious concepts is imperative in this crucial matter. To the extent that the official Islamic thought system rejects evolution and its philosophical bearing on traditional theism, it will lack real conviction for the contemporary mind. Only when the followers of the different religions can integrate their respective religious thought systems with well-established contemporary concepts will they become integrated believers who are not pulled in different directions by science and religion.

KARL MARX'S CONCEPT OF SOCIAL EVOLUTION

The next tension between religion and science was generated by the work of Karl Marx, who may aptly be regarded as the 'Darwin' of Sociology. Marx forcefully and strikingly projected the concepts of social evolution and social causation. What natural selection was in the scheme of Darwinism, technological changes were in the scheme of Marx. Just as the basic concepts of organic evolution and ceaseless variations have been firmly accepted by biologists, the concepts of social evolution and social causation have been firmly established in the conceptual scheme of contemporary man.

A sociological cause is an organic blend of economic, political, cultural, and ideological forces acting upon the human individual or group. Social phenomena are determined by such laws and can be altered or manipulated with their help. Poverty, social inequality, and hereditary class domination, etc. are therefore, in principle, alterable. The prospect of the conquest of poverty was enough to generate a tension between this approach and the traditional view, that the division of people into the rich and the poor is God's own act, just like His creation of mountains, rivers, or deserts, and that man could only shower charity on the poor rather than seek to abolish poverty as such. The actual success of modern Western man in abolishing poverty in the developed nations has prompted creative Western thinkers to redefine the concept of God. This reconstruction has generated a religious ethic of planned action and life-affirmation, as distinguished from the medieval religious ethic of fatalism and other-worldliness.

The traditional Islamic approach, however, continues to be pre-sociological. According to it, social or political changes such as the rise and fall of nations or groups, the fluctuations in wealth, power, or rank, the states of prosperity and adversity, etc., are either due to Divine providence, or at most due to individual human merit. The traditional Muslim is apt to suppose that poverty as well as affluence is the way of God to test the faith and character of human beings, or that the number of children born to a couple is decided by the Will of God, or that poverty can never be abolished. Consequently, the sociological approach that poverty or other social evils are as much eliminable as the physical diseases such as plague, and smallpox, etc. appears to him as being a tall and arrogant claim. He believes that such irreverent interference with a Divinely established social order is inspired by the atheistic materialism of Karl Marx and his tribe.

A corollary of this 'asociological' orientation is a mistaken reading of history by the average Muslim. History shows many instances of good men or causes losing to bad men or causes supported by brute force. Even where good causes win, careful sociological analysis reveals that mere goodness is not the total cause of victory, but technological superiority always plays a crucial role in such victories. This approach appears to conflict with the traditional Islamic interpretation of history according to which the affairs of the Universe including victory or defeat in wars are regulated by Divine providence.

Logically speaking, there should be no difficulty in reconciling the operation of Divine providence with the advantages of technology or the operation of social laws on the analogy of natural laws. But the concept of social law is usually absent from the conceptual framework of the average Muslim. Consequently, he attributes the success or failure of nations in peace and war to purely ethical or moral factors, apart from the Will of God. Thus, sexual laxity, drinking, and gambling, etc., to the neglect of religious obligations and duties, is adjudged the main cause of the defeat and decline of nations. This naive pre-sociological approach is equated with a genuinely religious approach, and contrasted with the atheistic or materialistic interpretation of human history. The average educated Muslim thus misses the complexity of social causation, and mistakes the part for the whole. He misses the relevance of technology and ultimately of the crucial role of the scientific attitude in the rise and fall of nations and the march of history.

The traditionalists as well as many liberal Muslims of the 'Syed Ameer Ali School' are also not sufficiently aware of the depth and range of modi-

Introduction: The Problem And Its Historical Background

fications necessary in the traditional understanding of the basic values of Islam, such as brotherhood, equality, and tolerance, etc., for making them relevant to contemporary Muslims who are exposed to the thought of Mill, Marx, and Freud. Unless this is done, many new sociopolitical and economic patterns are liable to be rejected straight away by Islamic societies, even though those patterns might promote the basic intrinsic values of Islam itself. It is indeed a pity that reputed Muslim writers such as Abul Hasan Ali Nadvi, go on repeating that it is not Islam but the Muslims that need reformation. This is indeed true in the sense that moral and social evils such as dishonesty, selfishness, ignorance, etc., are traits of Muslims rather than of Islam or the Qur'an. But such a formulation is highly misleading as it obscures the need for the emergence of new dimensions in the Islamic thought-cum-value system.

RESEARCHES IN PSYCHOLOGY

Another tension is generated by the concepts of modern psychology and psychoanalysis. Religions affirm that God grants the petitionary prayers of His supplicating creatures. Modern psychology, on the other hand, has empirically proved the crucial role of suggestion and other positive mental attitudes in promoting or maintaining human health, happiness, and success. This approach clashes with the view that health, happiness, and success are the fruits of Divine favors. The psychological approach, on the other hand, implies that human success and happiness are governed by social-psychological factors.

Freud's psychoanalysis poses a still more powerful challenge to religion, as he provides us with a complete scheme of psychological dynamics governing all mental phenomena without exception. Freud's concept of unconscious motivation is the counterpart of social causation. His concept of sexual or libidinal determinism is the counterpart of the economic determinism of Marx. Again, Freud's concept of repression of the libido is the counterpart of Marx's concept of exploitation of labor. The concepts of '*id*', as a surging sea of irrational drives and repressed impulses, and of the death instinct have debunked man much more seriously than Darwin's theory of man's animal ancestry, or of Copernicus's heliocentric theory. While Darwin's theory had debunked man, it had not destroyed man's confidence in his future. If he had evolved from anthropoid ape to man, he could evolve still further from man to superman. Indeed, this was the actual line of thinking adopted by most of the late 19th century and early 20th century Western thinkers. Freud's debunking of man, on the other hand, left him without hope and faith.

Freud's conception of religion as an illusion is rather dogmatic and one-sided. But the awareness of the numerous elements of value in Freud's depth-approach is essential for acquiring insight into the complexities of human nature. A critical concept of man is the prerequisite of a mature and adequate conception of God. The concepts of suggestion or autosuggestion, father image, fixation, resistance, compensation, wish fulfillment, guilt or inferiority complexes, defense mechanism, neurosis, neurotic fear or anxiety, etc., are highly significant for understanding the dynamics of human behavior and for a genuine and authentic religious commitment, as distinguished from inauthentic faith. But almost no notice has been given to the above concepts by Muslim religious thinkers, apart from literary critics and poets.

The Presence of Suffering in the World

Another major tension is generated by the extent of suffering in the world. The tension arises due to the conflict between the course of events expected in a world created by an omnipotent and benevolent God and the actual course of events. For example, when a virtuous woman is raped, or a child murdered in front of his parents, or when a life full of promise is cut short by an untimely death, while insane or physically crippled patients live on to a ripe old age, or the indiscriminate suffering caused by natural calamities, accidents or infectious diseases; all these facts evoke serious doubts about God's goodness or power. It is the solemn duty of all authentic theists to resolve this tension without intellectual dishonesty.

Technological Research

In the end, here is an example of a hypothetical tension generated by an ever-advancing technology. Let us suppose man eventually acquires control over the sex of the unborn child. Then there would be a tension between the belief that the determination of sex is an act of God, Who produces the male or the female according to His own sweet will and man's actual control over the sex of the unborn. It should be obvious that if the concept of God has to be retained, it will have to be reconstructed in order to resolve this hypothetical tension and harmonize it with man's actual experience. We could then maintain that natural laws gradually unfold themselves to the inquiring human mind, and that the postulation of natural laws does not contradict the concept of God, viewed as the Primal Source of the law and order in the Universe, rather than as an invisible Old Man with a magic wand in His hands.

Tensions arising out of the different fields of human culture must first be acknowledged before they can be removed. The denial of religious difficulties, on the other hand, creates mischief precisely because this merely serves to conceal rather than heal the tensions. The function of field integration is, therefore, strikingly similar to the function of psychoanalysis. Psychoanalysis leads to the integration of the total human personality, while field integration to that of different languages and concepts of the different streams of human culture.

III

FIELD INTEGRATION IN EARLY AND MIDDLE ISLAM

Every religion in its early phase is free from interpretative complexities of dogma and doctrine and thus also free from field tensions. This state may well be called the stage of ideological innocence or non-differentiated integration. But with the passage of time field tensions arise and demand resolution.

The germs of inquiry and of field integration in Islam were present in the intellectual approach of the fourth *Caliph*, Ali (d. 661), and later on of Hasan al-Basri (d. 728) and Jafar Sadiq (d. 765). But the need for field integration came to the fore in a big way with the rise of Mutazilite dialectics (*kalam*) in the ninth century. This movement was followed by the more orthodox Asharite School, which continued to dominate the Islamic world right up to the last century. These movements were considerably influenced by Christian theology and Greek thought and, in all probability some *Sufi* doctrines and practices of a later period were influenced by Vedantic Monism and Yoga. Let us briefly review these efforts at Islamic self-understanding in the early and middle period.

THEOLOGY AND PHILOSOPHY

The first source of field tension was the conflict between the belief in free will (which seemed to be a pre-supposition of morality) and the belief that nothing happens without the will of God, and the inequity of Divine punishment if human beings were not free agents. This field tension led to the emergence of the theories of pre-destinarianism and freedom of the will, with their protagonists attempting to justify their views with the help of Qur'anic verses of their choice.[15] In general the Mutazilites stood for free will, while the Asharites for a qualified pre-destinarianism (*kasb*). This is not the place to go into the details of this controversy. Suffice it to say that it helped in the clarification of the concept of God and His attributes of justice, omnipotence, and omniscience, etc., as well as the nature of man and his capacities and limitations. In other words, the controversy led to field integration between philosophy, psychology, theology, and ethics.

The next source of field tension was the Aristotelian distinction between substance and attributes. God was one, but His attributes were many, like mercy, knowledge, love, power, and creation, etc. It was felt that a plurality of attributes eroded the unity of the Divine Being. Let us see why this difficulty arose. When, for instance, we say that God is forgiving, we do not mean that He became forgiving at a particular time when He forgave a sinner, but that He is always forgiving or that the attribute of forgiveness is part of His eternal nature or Being. But then, this makes the attribute of forgiveness coeval and co-eternal with God and thus erodes the concept of God's unity. The Mutazilites, therefore, tended to conceive God as pure Being without attributes, which were viewed as anthropomorphic projections upon God's Being, which was essentially unknowable. But this position was difficult to reconcile with the Qur'anic references to God's attributes and with the orthodox conception of God.

The Asharite theologians held that God's essence is not a bare unity devoid of all qualities. Rather, Divine qualities are the modes of the one Divine Being or Essence, though we are unable to grasp the nature of the Divine attributes, except in metaphorical language, which is only partly ap-

Introduction: The Problem And Its Historical Background

plicable to God. It seems to me that the Mutazilite theologians overplayed the distinction between substance and attributes, and rushed to the conclusion that attributes erode Divine unity, and therefore, cannot really inhere in God as Substance. The Asharite doctrines of Divine attributes based on the union of metaphor and transcendence (*tashbih wa tanzih*) was far more balanced. In any case, this particular field tension or controversy did a lot to clarify the concept of God.

The most explosive field tension was the controversy about the nature of the Qur'an. The Mutazilites held that belief in the eternity of the Qur'an eroded the Islamic doctrine of the unity of God, since; in this case, the Word of God (which is not literally identical with God Himself) becomes co-eternal in time. Moreover, being in the Arabic language, the Qur'an follows the man-made grammar and syntax of that language, and thus could not possibly be eternal or uncreated. This was not acceptable to many orthodox Muslims for whom the Qur'an was the pure locus of Divinity without any human elements. The Qur'anic reference to the preserved tablet (*lawh-e-mahfuz*) also seemed to imply the eternity of the Qur'an.[16] This position was taken up by the Asharites. They held that the Qur'an was eternal in the sense that God foreknew the contents of what He would subsequently reveal in time to His chosen Prophet ﷺ. It is true that before the creation of the world there was no language including Arabic. But God's foreknowledge included the Qur'an in the Arabic language with all its man-made vocabulary, grammar, and syntax, apart from Divine ideas, which, however, our finite minds cannot grasp. However, even if we accept the above Asharite approach, the Qur'an, in its concrete Arabic form at least, would seem to comprise some human or temporal elements, thereby ceasing to be the pure locus of Divinity. Thus the same difficulty would arise once again. The only way out would be to claim that Arabic has a supernatural origin and a higher status than the other languages of the human family. Perhaps this line of thinking (which was implicitly present) was acceptable to the Asharites, but not to the Mutazilites, who were relatively less susceptible to Arab ethnocentricity and more speculative in their theology.

The above and similar other field tensions were sought to be removed by Mutazilite theologians like Abul Hozail (d. 841), Nazzam (d. 845), and Jahiz (d. 868) and Asharite theologians such as Ashari (d. 935), and by philosophers such as Kindi (d. cir. 870), Farabi (d. 950), Ibn Sina (d. 1037), and Ibn Rushd (d. 1198) who dealt with a wider range of philosophical problems. In the course of time neo-Platonic theories of emanation and Aristotle's theory of the immanence of form in matter led to the radical redefinition of concepts such as God, creation, revelation, personal immortality, and the eternity of matter, etc. Many theories such as perpetual Divine Creation, the negation of causality in the sense of necessary connection, the growth of lower forms of being into higher, the distinction between metaphorical and literal uses of language, and the essential unity of all religions, etc., were raised and discussed with remarkable thoroughness and perspicacity.

Muslim philosophers had been profoundly influenced by Neo-Platonic thought and held Aristotle and Plato in the highest veneration. Farabi, Ibn Sina, and Ibn Rushd, among others, maintained that there was no essential difference between the basic truths of Greek philosophy and the principles of Islam, such as the unity of God, revelation, and life after death, etc., apart from the difference in the language of philosophy and of religion. The language of philosophy was abstract and logico-metaphysical, while the language of religion was concrete, anthropomorphic, or metaphorical. But their essential import or significance was the same. Thus, according to them, the Lord of the worlds, as mentioned in the Qur'an, is the same as Plato's Idea of good or Aristotle's Prime Mover. Similarly, the creation of the Universe by the God of Islam is the same as the emanation of different levels of being from the Primal Source, which is pure Spirit. Again the Divine revelation of the Qur'an to the Prophet ﷺ through the agency of Gabriel (*Jibrael*) is the same as the illumination of the finite mind by the Active Intelligence. Thus the revelatory process is of the nature of melting or fusion of the finite mind into the Infinite or of illumination rather than of the transmission of sounds or signals from an external communicator. It seems this conception of revelation is free from the difficulties in anthropomorphic ideas about God's attributes or acts. But the trouble with Muslim philosophers was that, like all speculative thinkers of the past, they did not bother about agreed criteria of validity of their truthclaims.

SUFISM

The other movement, which led to field integration, is *Sufism*, which partly overlaps, but primarily succeeds, the movements of Dialectics and Greek Rationalism. *Sufism* lays primary emphasis upon direct spiritual illumination rather than on reason for removing field tensions and achieving inner peace and serenity (*nafs-e-mutmaiinah*). The seeds of *Sufism* were

Introduction: The Problem And Its Historical Background

present in the Qur'an and the life of the Prophet ﷺ. Instead of giving arguments for God, the Qur'an repeatedly asks man to reflect on the marvels and mysteries of the outer world and his own self. Many verses of the Qur'an have a mystical flavor, and the Prophet ﷺ used to meditate throughout his life. Ali was especially interested in esoteric knowledge (*ilm-e-batin*), as distinguished from external knowledge (*ilm-e-zahir*). In the early phase of Islamic political and religious expansion, the influence of Greek thought and Christian theology stimulated the growth of external knowledge, both religious and secular. The spate of philosophical and theological controversies, the barrenness of external morality and legalism as well as later sociopolitical changes led to the growth of Islamic mysticism.

Islamic mysticism or *Sufism* is, however, far from being a way of pure gnosis without any rational or speculative elements, just as Ibn Sina's or Farabi's rationalism is far from being a pure intellectualism without mystical elements. Islamic rationalism is inextricably mixed with mysticism, though in varying proportions in different personalities.

The earlier *Sufi's* were simple pietists who emphasized the inwardness of morality and love of God without neglecting the Islamic religious law and without any metaphysical speculation on the nature of God, soul, and prophecy, etc. But mystics emphasizing the Gnostic dimension gradually emerged and acquired a position of pre-eminence. This in turn was followed by the systematic conceptualization of mystical experience, since no individual can avoid the task of field integration. Even the mystic who stresses direct mystical experience as the true source of knowledge has to live and act at the non-mystical plane for the greater part of his life. Consequently, even he cannot abjure the need of a coherent interpretation of the basic features of the Universe, including his mystical experience itself. He cannot avoid reflecting upon the nature and meaning of his mystical experience and its reconciliation with his own normal experiences such as perception, causality, a sense of space and time, a sense of *ego hood*, a sense of freedom, and a measure of control over the environment. The *Sufi*, no less than the philosopher, is thus drawn into the vortex of interpretative activity, whose range and depth, however, depend upon his intellectual powers over and above his spiritual talents. Some *Sufi's* (like philosophers and theologians) have, therefore, reinterpreted the basic concepts and values of Islam. But the philosophers were confined to external knowledge alone, while *Sufi* thinkers claimed access to both external and esoteric knowledge. They thus went back to the tradition of Jaffar Sadiq and ultimately of Ali, who was the intellectual and mystic par excellence, while the theologians and philosophers remained at the level of Aristotle and Plato. Perhaps the two most outstanding *Sufi* thinkers are Ghazali (d. 1111) and Ibn Arabi (d. 1240).

Ghazali is the greatest mediator between the three main streams of Islamic thought and culture; the legalistic-cum-theological, the rationalistic and the mystical. Up to his time these three streams had developed more or less in relative isolation from each other. The mystical and the metaphysical approaches coalesced in such remarkably gifted figures as Farabi, and Ibn Sina, etc. But the mysticism of such philosophers was speculative rather than pietistic and hence did not attract the notice of the common man who cared for myths and miracles rather than metaphysics and mathematics. Many pietist mystics, on the other hand, were not sufficiently well-equipped with philosophy to remove various field tensions. The jurists and theologians, on the other hand, were sharp dialecticians and experts in casuistry, but failed to distinguish religious feeling from religious conformism, and to progress from the realm of law into the realm of the spirit. Thus there was a clear lack of authentic communication between the philosophers, mystics, and jurists of Islam. The genius of Ghazali led to an integrated multidimensional approach which repudiated neither reason, nor intuition, nor law. Unfortunately the cultural stagnation and decay in the Islamic East due to the Mongol violence in the 12th and 13th centuries did not permit further growth or refinement of Ghazali's irenic approach.

Many Western Orientalists are of the view that the decline of the rationalist temper and of science in the Islamic world was mainly due to the anti-rationalism or mysticism profusely injected by Ghazali into the arteries of Islamic culture. Ghazali's masterpiece *'Destruction of the Philosophers'* is regarded as Ghazali's arrow that pierced into the heart of the philosophical or rationalist movement in Islam and literally destroyed philosophy. This is not the whole truth. What Ghazali had attacked with great skill and power was not reason or philosophy as such, but rather Greek speculative metaphysics. Indeed Ghazali's approach in the *'Destruction of the Philosophers'* bears some striking points of similarity with the analytical-cum-positivistic approach of Kant and also of the present. His approach to proofs of God and faith is in tune with contemporary religious existentialism. But Ghazali, who was so systematic and methodical in his treatment of Greek philosophy, lacked a critical approach in the field of *hadith* literature. Moreover, he could not emancipate himself fully from the pre-scientific thought patterns, prejudices,

Introduction: The Problem And Its Historical Background

and limitations of his age, as is indicated by his disapproval of friendly and intimate relations between Muslims and non-Muslims. [17]

Ibn Arabi is, by far, the most daring speculative *Sufi* who has left a permanent mark on the Islamic thought system. He reinterpreted the Islamic formula of faith *'There is no god but Allah'* as *'There is no being but the Being of Allah'*. The monistic interpretation of Divine unity, as the Unity of Existence (*wahdat ul wajud*), in contrast with the traditional interpretation that God had created the Universe out of nothing, was a redefinition of the concept of God. Ibn Arabi also redefined other concepts to fit them into his peculiar conceptual framework. His influence upon *Sufi's* with an intellectual bent of mind has been very great, though in his own day the establishment rejected him.

It seems to me that the crucial flaw in Ibn Arabi's approach is the lack of a critical epistemology or methodology, since there is no criterion to test the validity of his mystical-speculative ontology. The traditional Islamic criterion lay in conformity to the Qur'an, as interpreted by the Prophet ﷺ and his trusted companions. If, however, the mystic feels free to give his own interpretation to Qur'anic verses in the light of his own mystical experiences, but fails to give any criteria of validity, his interpretation becomes an exercise in uncontrolled speculation. The stand that others could test the truth of the mystic's claims through their direct experience is misleading, since it does not distinguish the conceptual interpretation of the mystical experience with the experience as such. It is quite possible for two mystics to have a similar experience, but they may differ in its conceptual interpretation. Now Ibn Arabi can give us no criterion for the validity of his interpretation of his mystical experience. In this crucial respect Ghazali scores over Ibn Arabi, since the former is much more cautious in making Gnostic claims. But at times even he floats in the thin air of speculative interpretation of his mystical experience without bothering about the question of validity. The mere fact that the truthclaim does not clash with the Qur'an cannot suffice to make it valid.

After Ghazali and Ibn Arabi, *Sufism* loses its intellectual vigor and becomes institutionalized. This was perhaps the social consequence of the sociopolitical upheavals caused by the Mongol invasions of the Eastern Islamic world in the late 12th and 13th centuries. *Sufism* in this period ceased to do the job of field integration. But it did promote the personality integration of individual Muslims in troubled times, and also helped in propagating Islam in India and elsewhere through its exalted morality and spirituality. However, spiritual culture without the cultivation of reason is as lame as the latter is blind without the cultivation of spirituality.

The consolidation of Muslim rule in India by the 12th century led to the emergence of a plural society. The vast Hindu population with a rich cultural tradition had accepted the political presence of Islam, but they were in no mood for Islamisation, which had occurred in Iran and Egypt after the Arab conquest. The orthodox theologians stood for the cultural and social isolation of the Muslims, as far as possible, from non-Muslims. But the *Sufis* of the Chishtia order were quick to grasp the social and psychological aspects of the historical situation and stood for a liberal spiritual humanism in place of a theological legalism. This attracted many Hindus to the faith and practice of Islam. [18]

Muslim rulers and administrators in general tended to be guided by reasons of state and preferred the policy of tolerance and non-interference in the religious matters of their subjects. But the orthodox theologians ever-demanded the subordination of the state to the Islamic religious law. It appears that but for the pressure of public opinion, under the influence of the orthodox theologians, many more Muslim kings and administrators would have leaned far more to the liberal approach symbolized by Emperor Akbar (d. 1605).

The strongest opposition to the spiritual humanism and liberalism which was gaining ground in the highly sophisticated urban elite during the time of Akbar and his successors in the latter half of the 16th century came from Shaikh Ahmad of Sarhind (d. 1624). The Shaikh, who belonged to the *Nakhshbandia Sufi* order, made it his life mission to rectify the wrongs perpetrated by Akbar and his host, and to restore Islamic *Shariah* to its rightful place in India. He was also deeply opposed to the monistic philosophy of Ibn Arabi, which according to him, had corrupted the true Islamic notion of Divine unity. The Shaikh was on strong ground when he said that Ibn Arabi's conception of God was quite different from the orthodox view of God as the Supreme Creator and Lord of the worlds, the Beneficent and the Merciful, the Hearer of prayers and the Fulfiller of needs, etc. Ibn Arabi, on his part, could justifiably say that no finite mind could claim to understand God's attributes. The only way to understand the nature of God is to suggest a comparison and immediately to transcend it (*tasbih wa*

Introduction: The Problem And Its Historical Background

tanzih). So far Ibn Arabi would be in accord with the orthodox position. But when he claims direct knowledge of hidden realities through mystical experience (*kashf*) without giving any criteria of validity of his interpretations his position becomes shaky.

Shaikh Ahmad's critique of Ibn Arabi's position was thus quite powerful and made a considerable impact on *Sufi* circles. But the unfortunate thing was the Shaikh's rejection of the spiritual humanism and liberalism of the Persian mystical tradition represented by the classical Persian poetry of Attar (d. 1229), Rumi (d. 1273), Sadi (d. 1291), and Jami (d. 1492), which was flourishing at court circles ever since Akbar. The Shaikh on the other hand stood for a rigid adherence to the *Shariah* as a complete and closed code of conduct rather than for a creative fidelity to the Qur'an. The Shaikh had no understanding of the requirements of a plural society and the point of view of his non-Muslim Indian brethren whose ideals and interests pulled them toward a secular polity rather than the rule of Islamic law. He was also not sympathetic to the *Shia* Muslims. He, thus, put back the clock of the Indian secular movement, as it were. [19]

In the 18th century Shah Waliullah (d. 1763), the greatest Muslim philosophical theologian of the age, brought some fresh air and light into the portals of the Muslim mind through his concept of a common '*deen*' underlying the revealed Semitic religions, his permissive approach to denominational conformism within the four orthodox *Sunni* sects, his rationalistic approach to Qur'anic hermeneutics, and his irenic approach to the controversy between Ibn Arabi and Shaikh Ahmad. But he accepted the Islamic *Shariah* as an organic totality, and his approach to the putative sayings of the Prophet ﷺ was not sufficiently critical. Moreover, his approach to sociopolitical issues was rooted in concepts and values common to both medieval Islam and Christianity. These ideas, which had started changing in Western Europe during the Renaissance, underwent a perceptible difference by the middle of the 18th century. This is the century, which witnessed the American and French revolutions, and also the industrial, the secular, and the sociological revolutions, which were rooted, in the earlier scientific revolution of the previous two centuries. The 18th century enlightenment blossomed into the knowledge explosion of the 19th and 20th centuries. This has now compelled the Islamic thought-cum-value system to come to terms with modernity.

IV

FIELD INTEGRATION IN RECENT ISLAM

The 19th century is of crucial significance for not only Islam but all other religions, since it was in this period that Darwin's theory of evolution brought the conflict between modern science and religion to its sharpest point. For Islam it is significant for the additional reason that the process of slow cultural and political decay going on in the entire Islamic world for several centuries reached its point of culmination. The entire Islamic world became a virtual dependency of some European power or other, and all hopes of success in the future appeared illusory. This total political and economic defeat of the bearers of the Qur'an and of God's best community (*Khairul Umam*) inevitably evoked fresh questionings in the minds of the thinking Muslims the world over from Egypt to Indonesia. Thus the nadir of defeat and despair proved to be a stimulus for a constructive probe into fundamental problems of religion and human destiny.

Of all those who reflected on these problems in the 19th century three persons stand out as outstanding; Jamaluddin Afghani (d. 1897), Muhammad Abduh of Egypt (d. 1905), and Syed Ahmad of India (d. 1898).

JAMALUDDIN AFGHANI

He vigorously pleaded for a united pan-Islamic state as a precondition of the political and cultural re-emergence of Islam in the modern world. Gifted and dynamic as he was, Afghani had a merely pan-Islamic rather than an international perspective. He was certainly right in criticizing the evils of theological hair-splitting and a static religious piety totally divorced from a living concern with sociopolitical problems and concerns. But he was unable to register the full meaning and implications of the scientific attitude, which is the differentia of the modern age. Grievances against the excessive conservatism of the Mullas does not constitute the full meaning of a truly liberal and rationalist approach to religion and life. Afghani was thus more of a dashing publicist for a pan-Islamic Renaissance rather than a creative scholar who could integrate contemporary concepts and values into the traditional Islamic thought-cum-value system. [20]

Introduction: The Problem And Its Historical Background

MUHAMMAD ABDUH

He took inspiration from Afghani but did not entangle himself in politics. He devoted himself to reforming both the administration and the teaching of al-Azhar, the oldest living university in the world. Abduh played a crucial role in weakening the hold of a static tradition upon the Arabic-speaking Muslims. He never abandoned the traditional interpretation of fundamental Islamic concepts and values, but only stood for a limited adaptation of the institutional system of Islam to contemporary needs and the aspirations of a liberal mind. His reconstruction of basic Islamic concepts and values was marginal. Perhaps this cautious and moderate approach, together with the great prestige of al-Azhar, as a symbol of traditional Islamic learning, greatly facilitated the propagation of his ideas in the Egyptian milieu. His ideas were different from those of the conservative and stagnant minds of his associates, but not too different to isolate him from the broad thought patterns of his associates. He was a modernist in relation to the outlook of his milieu. But in comparison with Syed Ahmad or Iqbal he was rather conservative.

SIR SYED AHMED KHAN

He was the principal architect of the Aligarh Movement, the father of Islamic Modernism, and the first to be aware of the need of field integration between religion and modern science. His sharp mind pierced through the armor of the medieval pre-scientific understanding of basic Islamic concepts. He realized that Islamic thought had not even caught up with the Copernican revolution, to say nothing of the Darwinian. One cannot help admiring his efforts, even though one maybe unable to agree with some features of his approach.

Syed Ahmad was a great admirer of Shah Waliullah, but knew that the latter's basic conceptual framework was essentially medieval. Waliullah, for instance, retained the medieval polarity between the Islamic religio-political community and the non-Islamic world. Syed Ahmad, on the other hand, had outgrown this Islamic communitarianism.[21] He had genuinely accepted secular democracy and liberal nationalism with the implication that religion was a personal relationship between man and God rather than a total way of life in the medieval sense. In other words, the cast of mind of Syed Ahmad was almost (though not completely) modern. He went further than any previous

Islamic thinker in viewing Islam as a simple Qur'anic theism without an all-embracing institutional system. He separated the proper spheres of religion and the state within the organic unity of a spiritual perspective, which was rooted in religious tolerance. This approach led to a pluralist fellowship of faiths in the place of the traditional concept of a religious brotherhood or community, be it Islamic, Christian, or Hindu.

Syed Ahmad was, however, primarily a philosophical theologian and apologist for Islam who used all the resources of his fertile mind to reconcile science with the Qur'an, accepted as the infallible and literally revealed word of God. His basic thesis was that science accurately and objectively describes the physical world, which is the Work of God. Now there cannot be any contradiction between 'the Word of God' and 'the Work of God'. The seeming contradiction was due to the mistaken interpretation of Qur'anic texts on the basis of pre-scientific ideas. In the light of this basic assumption Syed Ahmad proceeded to reinterpret those Qur'anic passages which seemingly violated the postulate of the causal uniformity of nature and also other well-established scientific theories of the time. This led Syed Ahmad to deny the actual occurrence of miracles, though he conceded their logical possibility, or God's power to perform them. Since, however, God had Himself willed the laws of nature and expressly said in the Qur'an that there is no change in Divine ways, nature always behaved uniformly.

The other basic thesis of Syed Ahmad was the essential harmony between reason and revelation, both of which were Divine gifts for man's guidance. Reason was given to all, but revelation was confined to the prophets alone. Their source was one and the same, though their spheres of operation might be different. Syed Ahmad thus stood for a scientific empiricism and speculative rationalism without, however, having a clear and critical methodology of science and philosophy. He accepted the findings of science as well as the findings of reason no less than the Qur'an, which is infallible, and then, proceeded to reconcile any apparent discrepancy between them with the help of a speculative hermeneutic. The attempted reconciliation involves rejecting the ordinary meanings of Arabic words or expressions. Syed Ahmad thus rejects the separate existence of Satan (*Shaitan*), of angels, of heaven and hell as locales, and of the literal truth of verses about the creation and fall of Adam, the ascension of the Prophet ﷺ, and the virgin birth of Jesus, etc.,

Syed Ahmad's metaphorical or philosophical reinterpretation of the Qur'anic texts in question was bound to disturb, nay alarm, the religious

Introduction: The Problem And Its Historical Background

establishment. The orthodox and conservative sections naturally dubbed him as a naturalist or as a champion of reason rather than of revelation. But the truth of the matter is that Syed Ahmad was not a pure rationalist philosopher, but a scholastic with a pre-rational faith in the Qur'an, as the revealed word of God, as well as a pre-critical faith in the harmony between revelation and reason. This concept of a pre-established harmony between revelation and reason was his heritage from classical Islamic philosophers: Farabi, Kindi, Ibn Sina, and Ibn Rushd, etc.

Let us now briefly examine the validity of Syed Ahmad's position. It seems to me that Syed Ahmad commits what maybe called the *rationalistic fallacy*; a fallacy which is committed by all those philosophers or theologians who claim to prove the truth or validity of their faith, which (according to them) was initially accepted because of the accident of their birth, but which is retained by them because of its coercive rationality or objective truth. This approach was the common feature of medieval Islamic and Christian thought, and continued right up to the time of Kant. Descartes, Leibniz, Locke, Paley and many others always stressed the reasonableness of the Christian faith, and advanced putative conclusive proofs of God. It was Kant who denied the coercive power of such proofs and examined the proper scope and limits of reason. Barring a brief interlude of Hegelian rationalism, almost all post-Kantian philosophers and theologians such as Schleiermacher, Kierkegaard, William James, Bergson, Otto, and many others have abandoned the rationalistic approach to religion in favor of a broad voluntaristic or existentialist approach. According to this viewpoint, religious faith is qualitatively different from logical or objective certainty, and is essentially incapable of any coercive proof. Thus there can be no proof of the existence of God, Divine incarnation, prophecy, and life after death, or of the truth of a particular religion. Indeed, if a coercive proof were possible, either in the logico-mathematical or scientific sense, no occasion or need for faith will be left at all, just as there is no need for faith in the spheres of logic and mathematics, etc. Religious faith presupposes that the beliefs in question are not logically provable. In other words, faith is not like objective knowledge, but like the subjective truth of ethics and aesthetics. It is this essential non-provability, which gives religious faith its inwardness, tension, depth, and poignancy as distinct from the external or objective tension-free certainty of science or logic. Syed Ahmad's rationalistic approach to Islam thus can be said to be valid only in the sense that it does not shun rational or scientific inquiry but affirms its need. But his approach is invalid when it claims that the truth of religion in general and Islam in particular could be rationally proved.

Syed Ahmad's approach to Qur'anic miracles and his Qur'anic hermeneutics are also invalid. The Qur'an contains several references to miracles performed by God or His prophets, even though Prophet Muhammad ﷺ had no power to perform miracles (according to the Qur'an). Now Syed Ahmad explains away the prima facie Qur'anic references to miracles by interpreting them as reports of natural events, which were misconstrued as supernatural due to the general human craving for the supernatural. Perhaps the most striking instance of this type of Qur'anic hermeneutics is Syed Ahmad's interpretation of the Qur'anic verse that no man had touched Mary who was with child. [22] Syed Ahmad interprets this verse to mean that no man, other than her husband, had touched Mary who had conceived a child. Another instance is the Qur'anic verse that God punished sinners through natural calamities. Syed Ahmad says that natural phenomena are governed by natural laws, but men view them as a punishment for their sins. Similarly, he gives a naturalistic interpretation of verses describing angels, demons and the people of the cave (*ashab al kahaf*), etc., Syed Ahmad shows great linguistic skill in reinterpreting Arabic expressions, even though his command over the language may not be perfect.

Syed Ahmad had a twofold orthogenetic justification for this type of hermeneutic. The first was the clear statement of the Qur'an that the Prophet ﷺ had no miraculous powers and was an ordinary mortal like other human beings, the only difference being that he was the recipient of Divine revelations. (The logic was that if the greatest of all prophets could not perform miracles, other prophets too must have been without any supernatural powers.) The second justification was the Qur'anic statement that it contained two types of verses; the clear and categorical commands (*muhkamat*), and the metaphorical or ambiguous verses (*mutashabihat*). Armed with this twofold principle of interpretation, Syed Ahmad perhaps felt no qualms in explaining away all Qur'anic references to the supernatural. This approach is quite valid and fruitful up to a point, but Syed Ahmad did not realize its limitations and went to the extremes of semantic speculation just to prove his point.

Forced interpretations of a text involve the fallacy of projection of one's own ideas upon the revealed text. It maybe said that, by the very nature of the case, there can be no standard meaning of Scripture, and that all meanings are inevitably cases of projecting our own ideas upon the propositional

Introduction: The Problem And Its Historical Background

canvas of the Qur'an. But it seems to me that the interpretations made by the Prophet ﷺ and his trusted companions, who were directly inspired and instructed by the Prophet ﷺ himself, must be treated as normative interpretations, at least in spiritual and moral matters. Now if the Prophet ﷺ believed in miracles, but miracles do not really occur, the Prophet ﷺ was mistaken in his interpretation of the Qur'an. This would imply that though he was the messenger of God, he was not the infallible interpreter of the Word of God. Syed Ahmad did not actually draw this inference but, it seems, this approach was latent in his thinking.

Syed Ahmad's attempted field integration led to his denial of miracles, including the Prophet's ﷺ bodily ascension to the highest heaven (*Miraj*), his affirmation of revelation as the highest form of Divine illumination of the human consciousness without any intermediary role of angels, in the literal sense, his denial of the virgin birth of Jesus; in brief, a thorough 'de-mythologisation', of the Islamic thought system. This was no mean achievement, and one cannot but admire Syed Ahmad's imagination, clarity, candor, and courage.

But in his quest for integrating religion with science and philosophy, Syed Ahmad deprived Islam of its mystique or spiritually romantic elements, without, however, providing a critical and mature philosophy of religion, which could appeal to the modern Muslim mind. His approach lacked the organic unity and inner consistency of an authentic existential interpretation of man in the Universe. This is why neither his closest friends and admirers nor the orthodox could agree with his peculiar blend of faith and reason. However, as the principal architect and inspirer of the Aligarh Movement, which produced or influenced a whole galaxy of liberal Muslims such as Chiragh Ali, Mehdi Ali, Imtiaz Ali, Hali, Shibli, Amir Ali, and Ghulamus Saqlain, among several others, Syed Ahmad acted as the master trend-setter. The work initiated by him in the 19th century was carried-forward in the present century by Muhammad Iqbal (d. 1938) and Abul Kalam Azad (d. 1958), both of whom were men of genius.

Muhammad Iqbal

Through his book, '*The Reconstruction of Religious Thought in Islam*' as well as his moving philosophical poetry, Iqbal has reinterpreted Islamic concepts and values in the light of contemporary thought. Iqbal realized that one's concrete understanding of religious concepts is organically related with one's basic conceptual framework, which grows with the growth in man's factual knowledge. But he also held that scientific knowledge based on sense perception could not disclose the nature and destiny of the human ego and of ultimate reality, as distinct from its appearance to our sense organs, or its conceptual reconstruction in scientific theories. The ultimate nature and destiny of the human ego, its relationship with God; the ultimate Ego, the attributes of God, the nature of prophecy or revelation, etc., are beyond the ken of human reason and can be known only through revelation or spiritual intuition which is a Divine gift to a chosen few. Iqbal, therefore, makes no attempt to prove God's existence, and immortality, etc., but follows Kant in rejecting the putative coercive power of the classical proofs for God. He emphasizes love and intuition rather than reason as the path, which leads to God, so that his approach to religion is existentialist. At the same time Iqbal reconstructs the concrete meaning of basic religious concepts to integrate them with the conceptual framework of contemporary science. He was an erudite scholar, though not an analytical thinker of genius like Kant, Jaspers, or Wittgenstein.

Iqbal rejects the anthropomorphic concept of God's attributes and actions such as creation, guidance, and punishment, etc. Though the nature of God can never be grasped by man, He may best be viewed as the Infinite Ego Who is the Source of all finite egos or monads which are centers of energy or the will to affirm one's existence. The ultimate reality for Iqbal is thus not matter, or even matter in motion, but the Divine Ego Who creates finite egos or centers of will as a manifestation of His creative powers and glory. Man is the highest created being. But his latent powers have not yet been realized with the exception of the Prophet ﷺ who was the perfect man and exemplar for all mankind.

Man, as the vicegerent of God on earth, can subjugate and direct all creation through the application of natural laws, which have been willed by God. God does not change them to perform miracles though He may do so. Scientific laws are not logically necessary but are empirical generalizations.

In Iqbal's view, the proper way of self-realization or the growth of the ego is neither metaphysical speculation, nor mystical absorption into

Introduction: The Problem And Its Historical Background

the Infinite Ego, but the conquest of nature through science and the conquest or disciplining of the human ego through obedience to the Qur'an and the *sunnah*. The conquest of the ego does not mean the suppression of its individuality but rather its growth through the full cultivation of the Divine attributes of power, wisdom, love, mercy, etc. The developed ego can then control and discipline its lower urges, not at the behest of external commands of God, but as the inward demands of his own developed nature due to the assimilation of the Divine attributes. The developed ego, however, remains the servant (*abd*) of God and at the same time experiences itself as free or autonomous.

The commands of God are to be found in the Qur'an, which is the revealed Word of God. We cannot understand the mechanics of revelation, but the conviction of its Divine Source may arise in us if we approach the Qur'an and the Prophet ﷺ with receptivity and humility in an earnest search for truth. Iqbal rejects all anthropomorphic models for understanding the mechanics of Divine revelation, that is, the model that Gabriel first gets the message from God and then communicates it to the Prophet ﷺ, or that Gabriel appears in the human garb before the Prophet ﷺ, or the model of an angel on the sky, or of mysterious sounds reaching the Prophet ﷺ, as if from nowhere. The Qur'an does refer to these modes of revelation, but they fall in the category of metaphorical verses whose mystery cannot be deciphered. However, poetic and artistic inspiration as well as psychical phenomena such as telepathy and veridical dreams do confirm the existence of modes of human experience over and above normal perception and reasoning. Just as the gift of poetic or musical genius is not universal, the gift of prophecy is confined to a few Divinely chosen persons. Iqbal's concept of prophecy is thus basically the same as that of Syed Ahmad, who in turn followed Waliullah and the tradition of classical Muslim philosophers.

Iqbal rejects the literal interpretation of the Qur'anic verses dealing with the creation of Adam and his expulsion from the garden, universal resurrection of the human body, heaven and hell as external locales. Iqbal accepts the evolutionary hypothesis. But he qualifies the mechanistic conception of Darwin since he holds that the evolutionary force is rooted in the individual will to live and to assert its power, corresponding to its endowment (*taqdir*).[23] Evolutionary change, therefore, is not the mechanical result of the combination of chance variations and natural selection (in Darwin's sense) of the better adjusted species, but rather the result of a striving for self-perfection and a more intensive and permanent *ego hood*. The peak of evolutionary growth is man who is next only to God. Iqbal agrees with the famous lines of Rumi describing the different stages of growth; minerals, plants, animals, man, and higher still. [24] The urge to grow and develop comes from God Who is the ultimate Source of all being and value, and without Whom the evolutionary process would not have begun at all.

Iqbal's conception of evolution is very similar to Bergson's Creative evolution. But while Bergson posits an *'Elan Vital'*, which is the vital ground or immanent principle of movement.

Iqbal holds the vital ground to be not merely an impersonal immanent *Elan* but a supra Personality or Super Ego, Whose mode of existence is, however, beyond human comprehension. The Divine Ego responds to human prayer, though not in the sense of a Heavenly Father wiping the tears of His children and giving them sweets. Iqbal's concept of evolution adumbrates Aristotle's view that every member of a species strives to reach the perfection appropriate to its form. Iqbal holds that Islam is not merely a set of metaphysical beliefs and rituals but also a complete code of conduct. It thus differs from Christianity, which makes a clear distinction between the church and the state and enjoins on the Christians to render unto Caesar and Christ what respectively belongs to them. Iqbal holds that from its very inception Islam has been an organic whole demanding a total loyalty from the Muslim. Thus the Prophet ﷺ and the pious *Caliph's* were the spiritual and temporal heads of the Islamic community, and there was no distinction between the sacred and the profane or the spiritual and the secular. However, the law and polity of Islam are not intended to be static. Indeed they must ever be renewed within the framework of the Qur'an and the *sunnah* to keep pace with the ceaseless creativity of human values. The Qur'an only gives basic guidance to the Muslim and exhorts him to exercise his reason within those limits. The *sunnah* too must be given the utmost importance but it can never equal the status of the Qur'an. This is because human reports about the Prophet ﷺ maybe mistaken, unlike the complete authenticity of the Qur'an.

The principle of movement or independent reasoning, however, applies only to the institutional system (*muamilat*) and not the prescriptive system

Introduction: The Problem And Its Historical Background

(*ibadat*) as fixed by the Prophet ﷺ. Independent reasoning maybe exercised not only through the consensus of the jurists (*ijma ul ulama*) but also through the consensus of the Islamic community (*ijma ul ummah*). Iqbal, however, does not give any further constitutional details in this context.

Let us now attempt a critical estimate of Iqbal. His existentialist approach to religion, his vitalistic and voluntaristic ontology and evolutionary cosmology, his rejection of life-negating mysticism, his ethic of self-realization through the conquest of nature and a dynamic religious morality and law, his awareness of the limitations of scientific knowledge, his emphasis on creativity of values, his concern for social justice, and his rejection of narrow nationalism are all very valuable. But Iqbal's concept of Islam as an organic total code of conduct (even though possessed of an inbuilt mechanism for inner growth); as well as his theory of Islamic communitarianism, is not valid for our times. Let us examine in some detail why this is the case.

Iqbal does not seem to realize that right up to the 18th century not merely Islam but all religions had been total guides to life rather than merely a set of rituals. It is true that the church and the state were never one in Christianity, though the two were united in Islam. Thus in Christendom the Pope and Emperor symbolized the domains of Christ and of Caesar, while in Islam the Caliph (*Khalifa*) was at once the spiritual and the temporal head of the Islamic community. This difference was, however, due to the historical situation of Christianity and Islam in their early history. [25] When Christianity became the state religion of the Roman Empire in the fourth-century, the Christian Church too claimed spiritual jurisdiction over the state, and the Church held Christianity to be a complete code of conduct for the believers. When Martin Luther (d. 1546) repudiated the authority of the Pope in the 16th century, this repudiation was made in the name of true Christianity represented by his own Church, rather than in the name of secularism. The break from the Church of Rome did not imply any change in the conception of Christianity as a total conduct of life. Likewise, Calvin (d. 1564), who also founded his own church soon after Luther, claimed to provide complete guidance to his followers, including the spheres of trade, industry, education, law, and government, etc.

The effective breakthrough in the conception of Christianity however came in the 18th century as the cumulative result of the gradual scientific revolution in Western Europe between 1500 and 1700, and its impact upon the social and industrial life in the 18th century. The scientific revolution was nurtured by the works of Copernicus (d. 1543), Kepler (d. 1630), Galileo (d. 1642), Newton (d. 1727), and Descartes (d. 1650), while the revolution in social and religious ideas by the impact of Locke (d. 1704), Voltaire, (d. 1778), Rousseau (d. 1778), Adam Smith (d. 1790), and Kant (d. 1804), *et al.*

Let us now consider the exact way in which scientific developments led to the gradual transformation of traditional Christianity as a complete way of life. Traditional Christian theism implied that every event, whether social, natural, or Divine, was purposive. The category of purpose or final end was the supreme explanatory principle of the cosmic process, though finite mind could not grasp the purpose of many events, which prima facie went against reason or justice. Human reason had, therefore, to be subordinated to faith. However, the rise of Mechanics and Dynamics culminating in the grand Newtonian cosmology showed that natural events could be accurately described and predicted in terms of pure mechanical causes without any reference to any purpose or end, whether human or divine. Reason was still necessary for formulating hypotheses and developing their implications, which were empirically tested. But reason was no longer the supreme and sufficient oracle, which decided what was the case.

The steady growth of natural science inevitably led to technological innovations for the satisfaction of man's practical needs. Technological innovations in turn led to social and economic innovations, like mass production factories, banks, joint-stock companies, insurance firms, managing agencies, auditing firms, etc. In the course of time these social forms or phenomena became objects of systematic theoretical study like natural phenomena in the earlier period. In other words, social phenomena also came under the jurisdiction of the scientific method, first, the economic behavior of man, and later his social, moral, and religious behavior. All this naturally led to a shift of intellectual influence and power from the church leaders to the university intellectuals and the business and industrial community whose interests lay in adopting a secular and scientific approach to problems of social organization in place of the closed ecclesiastical approach of the medieval period. This maybe called the secular revolution of Western Europe, partly overlapping and partly succeeding the Industrial Revolution of England. The secular revolution was nurtured by Locke, Hume, and Adam Smith in England, Voltaire, Rousseau, and Montesque in France, Kant and Lessing in Germany, and Benjamin Franklin and Jefferson in America. The secular revolution did not dislodge religion but transformed Christianity as a complete code of conduct into the modern conception of religion, as

Introduction: The Problem And Its Historical Background

primarily a spiritual perspective upon the Universe. In other words, religion came to be viewed as a personal relationship between man and his Creator rather than as total guidance or a mandate for every sphere of human life. [26]

It seems Iqbal was unable to look upon the secular revolution as a factor in the evolution of a mature religion. This was because Iqbal remained under the spell of the medieval conception of religion as a complete code of conduct, or what maybe called *'religionism'*, in short. Iqbal does not realize that 'religionism', be it Islamic, Christian, or Hindu, raises quite unnecessary social, psychological, and administrative difficulties which make it unfit for plural societies, even though it may work relatively better in the case of the homogeneous. Iqbal's approach is utterly unsuitable for plural societies where it is absolutely essential to separate macro-social matters involving the entire nation, from micro-social or transcendental matters touching sub-groups or individuals. Muslims living in plural societies cannot accept Iqbal's understanding of Islam, which is rooted in medieval 'religionism' rather than in modern secularism.

The rejection of 'religionism' is not dictated by prudence or the situational compulsions of a plural society, but is the result of mature insight into the essential and non-essential functions of religion and the role of reason in human affairs. To hold that Iqbal's conception is true, but not prudent for Muslims of mixed societies would imply that such Muslims are second class Muslims who are compelled by their historical situation to acquiesce in the rupture of the organic unity of their religion. Nothing could be more misleading than this conclusion, which seems to be logically implied by Iqbal's conception of Islam. Just as Iqbal holds that a dynamic approach to the *Shariah* is intrinsically desirable and valid rather than merely prudent, similarly, many contemporary religious minds, be they Muslim, Christian, or Hindu, genuinely accept the religion of the spirit rather than medieval 'religionism'. This implies that secularism is right and valid not only for plural societies like, say, India or Nigeria, but also for predominantly Muslim countries, say, Pakistan or Turkey, or a Hindu country like Nepal. Indeed secularism becomes a principle of the good life, like democracy or socialism, rather than a matter of policy or prudence.

It maybe that Iqbal was prejudiced against the 18th century concept of secularism because it eventually led to agnosticism and atheistic materialism in the succeeding centuries, though the founding fathers of the secular revolution (like the earlier creators of the scientific revolution) were all sincere

Christian deists. But secularism as such is pre-eminently neutral toward the truth of religion or the truth of a particular religion, though it does clearly and emphatically reject religionism.

It is noteworthy that while many brilliant Western minds of the late 19th century rejected not only religionism but also the religion of the spirit, the best Western minds of the present century are much more cautious in this respect. Indeed they have become deeply aware of the dangers and limitations of a new brand of dogmatism, termed scientism; the belief that scientific knowledge exhausts the full description and meaning of the Universe. Contemporary thought has realized that reality is far more complex than the scientific picture paints it to be. [27] Many eminent thinkers now seem to be willing to concede that mere morality without an existential interpretation of the Universe fails to sustain man's quest for value and plunges him into a destructive nihilism. In other words, though morality without God or Spirit may and does flourish, the cultivation of the spiritual dimension of man reinforces morality and creativity in general, thus enhancing the inner quality of life. Iqbal's fear of secularism, as it were, is thus not justified, in view of the perfect compatibility between secularism and the religion of the spirit.

Let us now examine Iqbal's theory of Islamic communitarian ism and the implied critique of nationalism. According to this theory, the primary determinant of group identity and loyalty is the religious community rather than the nation, race, etc. He repeatedly criticizes nationalism as a narrow and restrictive focus of loyalty, as compared to a religious community rooted in shared ideas and values transcending all barriers of race, region, and language, etc. Iqbal was even critical of the League of Nations since its basis of membership was the nation-state, thus perpetuating the very evil it sought to cure.

Consistency demands that Iqbal concede that all religious communities are justified in making their religion the primary determinant of group identity and focus of loyalty. Iqbal cannot deny them this right on the ground that religions other than Islam are false. Now the moment this is done, humanity again becomes divided into rival religious groups, if not warring nation-states. Is not strife between partisan ideological groups as bad as strife between partisan nation-states? The answer is quite plain. Moreover, if relations can be friendly between different religious groups they could also be friendly between different national groups. What makes nationalism

Introduction: The Problem And Its Historical Background

harmful is thus not territorialism as such but rather chauvinism and aggressive intolerance. And these can also vitiate the virtues of communitarianism. It seems Iqbal equated nationalism with chauvinism just as some tend to equate faith with fanaticism. But one equation is as wrong as the other.

It is true that nationalism or rather nationalistic chauvinism has played havoc in modern Western history and Iqbal's fear of nationalism is, therefore, not groundless. But it is equally true that communitarianism or rather ideological fanaticism had played havoc in the medieval period producing endless strife between Catholics and Protestants or between Christians and Muslims, etc. Indeed reliable historians have claimed that casualties in the religious wars or persecutions of the medieval period far exceed the losses inflicted by nationalist wars in the modern period. Thus, in view of the smaller world population in the medieval period, religious communitarianism caused greater friction than has nationalism in the modern.

Let us now see how far communitarianism is feasible in the present world situation. We find that human societies have gradually become mixed or plural due to migrations, wars, and political integration, etc. Communitarianism with its stress on religious differences creates problems of emotional integration for the different religious groups, while territorial nationalism makes for a smooth and harmonious relationship between the different subgroups composing the nation. Again, the world is today organized on the basis of nation-states, while communitarianism demands an entirely different focus of primary loyalty. Communitarianism thus leads to emotional stress for minority groups in mixed societies, as it tends to displace the state as the primary basis of macro-social identity and the focus of loyalty.

Take for example an American Jew, who is a member of two classes; the class 'American' and the class 'Jew', and by implication, of a third class, 'American Jew'. Now no conflict would arise as long as the class 'American' is deemed to be the primary group which includes Jew, and Christian, etc., as secondary classes or, in other words, when the dominant principle of functional classification is membership of a common state rather than a common church. When, however, religion seeks to become the dominant basis of functional classification in a mixed society tension is inevitable between the two rival bases of classification, each of which seeks for the pride of place.

Even if human society becomes religiously homogeneous, it is condemned to be spatially, racially, and occupationally plural and sexually dual, and all these differences will inevitably generate special affinities over and above the bond of religion. Under these conditions the administratively most convenient basis of macro-social unity is the nation-state comprising all the different religious, racial, linguistic, regional, occupational groups as parts of an harmonious and integrated nation.

Nationalism is not opposed to internationalism or humanism since both complement each other. Nationalism is also not opposed to religion but only to religionism. Again, nationalism does not imply the rejection of local or professional loyalties and interests since there is no mutual conflict, provided we accept a scale of values. Suppose several candidates apply for a job, or several sites clamor for a steel plant, or two nations dispute over some matter. Now nationalism, properly understood, does not mean siding with my country, right or wrong. Likewise, professional or local loyalty does not mean siding with my club, my profession, my city, my team, right or wrong. We must always back the right principle and not any religion, nation, or region. However, a conflict may arise between patriotism and justice in the case of a war. But this conflict is also possible when the belligerents are divided into religious communities rather than nation-states. This problem is thus not peculiar to nationalism.

The nation-state, as it now exists cannot, however, be deemed to be an immutable and sacrosanct institution. The concept of sovereignty in the classical sense is in the process of being transformed into the concept of national autonomy within a supra-national confederation based upon cultural and economic interests. In the past smaller principalities combined, whether by force or by free will, to form the nation-state. In the future the present sovereign nation-states may evolve further into supranational confederations, like multi-national common markets and corporations within the present framework. Religious ties will facilitate economic and cultural cooperation since a common religion does constitute a powerful bond between individuals or nations. But a common religion is not the only bond, and by itself alone it can never suffice for inter-regional collaboration unless the people share common politico-economic ideals and interests. Consequently, if the emphasis on religious brotherhood does not lead to religious parochialism or communitarian discrimination in international relations, the forging of special relations between sovereign states with a common religion is quite justifiable. This is the only valid sense of the traditional notion of Islamic brotherhood.

Introduction: The Problem And Its Historical Background

The history of the pan-Islamic movement also points to the same conclusion. Jamaluddin Afghani stood for the political union of all Muslim countries and Iqbal shared this ideal. But gradually Iqbal veered to the idea of a confederation of Muslim states functioning in close harmony but retaining their separate identity. But even this would not work in the absence of shared politico-economic ideals and international cooperation on secular lines. Pan-Islamism, therefore, must be secularized and not merely regionalized in Iqbal's sense.

There is nothing wrong with Iqbal's deep concern for the welfare of the Islamic community and the touching lamentations in his poetry over the decline and fall of the political and cultural glory of Islam in the past. But what strikes me as odd in a philosophical poet of Iqbal's stature is that he never sheds tears at the decline of other great cultures. Again, he is severely critical of the evils of Western diplomacy, but is apt to overlook the core of genuine idealism in the life and work of Western savants such as Mill, Matthew Arnold, Tolstoy, Max Mueller, and Blunt, etc. Iqbal gives the impression of being a devoted partisan of the Islamic community rather than a universal savant who can look upon the fads and foibles of the human family with a sense of detachment rather than of resentment or bitterness.

To turn to another aspect of his social philosophy, Iqbal seems to waver in his evaluation of democracy and socialism. He believes in Islamic democracy and socialism but does not spell it out anywhere. He is apt to confuse the question of the structure of Islamic polity with Islamic piety. Thus he dwells on the need to avoid pomp and show, to be charitable and kind to the needy, to be prompt in paying wages to the worker, etc., but he does not spell out the ideal Islamic polity.

Iqbal's approach to the status of women is also unsatisfactory. Iqbal does not permit his ideal woman to be man's equal partner in life but regards woman as a perpetual ward and man as her natural guardian. Iqbal's ideal woman at best can only aspire to be the mother of the male super-man but not super-man herself.' [28]

In conclusion, it maybe pointed out that Iqbal omits to deal with the crucial problems of pain and evil and of authenticity. But his greatest shortcoming is his rejection of secularism and inter-religious fellowship or universalism. It is important to point out these limitations of Iqbal since his medium is poetry, which, as sheer poetry, is one of the treasures of world literature. Indeed, as a poetic genius, Iqbal has the power to cast a spell on his readers through his word-magic even when one may totally disagree with his social philosophy.

MAULANA ABUL KALAM AZAD

In his early *al-Hilal* phase, Azad stood for a romantic pan-Islamism and a more or less traditional interpretation of Islamic concepts and values. But in his second phase, represented by his monumental commentary on the Qur'an, Azad formulates his mature conception of Islam. [29] His existentialist approach to proofs of God is much more in harmony with contemporary thinking than the pre-Kantian rationalism of Syed Ahmad. Azad outgrows the Muslim scholastic or rationalistic approach to the proofs of God and confines himself to the Qur'an, which does not give any arguments for God's existence, but only invites the reader to ponder over the mystery of the various aspects of nature and of man's inner self, and then listen to the inner response of his total being. The implication is that if man looks at the order, harmony, and beauty of the macrocosm and the microcosm, in the spirit of pure receptivity without any preconceptions or theories, the inner conviction will well up from the depths of his being that the Universe is not a chance or accidental event or a brute fact, but a purposeful cosmos. [30] This cosmos cannot be the result of the blind dance of atoms without serving some end or purposes, even though the purpose may not be primarily anthropocentric, that is, centered on human welfare. This inner existential conviction can of course never be proved in the logical sense. But then logical proof is needed only when one is in doubt and not when one is existentially certain. When the lover's eyes meet those of the beloved in wordless communion, is there any need left to prove that one loves the other?

The intuitive conviction of the existence of God does not imply that we have intuitive knowledge of His attributes as well. In fact the finite mind can never grasp the Infinite. But the attributes of God, as mentioned in the Qur'an, do give us analogical or metaphorical knowledge of the Divine Being. Azad thus steers the middle way between theological gnosticism and philosophical transcendentalism or 'negationism'. He is at once aware of the limitations of the popular anthropomorphic conception of God and also of the extreme agnostic negation of Divine attributes. The view that no attribute like love, wisdom, mercy, power, and creativity, etc., could be predicted of God, and that all we can properly do is to affirm His existence but negate

Introduction: The Problem And Its Historical Background

every quality (in order to avoid inner contradictions) virtually amounts to the negation or denial of God. The qualified analogical affirmation of Divine attributes, on the other hand, leads to the spiritual growth of the believer through the partial assimilation of the Divine attributes. Azad thus believes in a personal God in the non-anthropomorphic sense.

Likewise, Azad accepts that God reveals His will to His chosen prophets through revelation (*wahy*), but Azad's conception of Divine guidance is rooted in his philosophical conception of fourfold Divine guidance through instinct, perception, reason, and revelation. Let us examine his conception in some detail.

Azad points out that the Qur'an uses the word '*wahy*' in the wide and narrow senses. In the wide sense '*wahy*' refers not only to suggesting or making signs by one man to another but also to God's guiding the bee to collect honey. [31] Azad holds that the instinctive behavior of animals is not the product of blind impulse, but of God's guidance to animals to perform those actions which are essential for their preservation and the realization of their potential excellence, in the Aristotelian sense. Thus Azad regards unlearned drives which have survival value for a species as a Divine gift to animals. In a similar vein, the capacity for sense perception through different sense organs is another form of God's guidance to His creatures. Sense perception enables the individual to perform instinctive actions more accurately and effectively. In many cases perception triggers the instinctive response and gives it concrete content and direction, as in the case of the searching for food or a mate. Thus instinct and perception fuse into each other in the economy of life.

The capacity to reason is the next mode of Divine guidance to His creatures, but this form of guidance is restricted to man alone, animals possessing it only in its rudimentary form. When the conditions of perception, whether internal or external, are not standard, that is, not in accordance with the Divinely intended structure and functioning of the sense organs, reports given by the senses are not reliable, for example, the sun appears to be a disc when it is, in fact, much bigger than the earth itself, or the stick appears to be bent in water, when it is, in fact, straight. In such cases reason corrects or amends perception. Moreover, reason also enables man to intuit logical truths or the connections between concepts and propositions through direct inner vision, as if reason were a spiritual lamp, which illumined man's consciousness. Thus reason and perception mutually complement each other at the human level, just as perception and instinct do at the animal level.

The last form of Divine guidance is revelation. But even in this case there are two levels-the lower level of the intuitive flash of the poet, artist, and scientist, etc., and the higher level of prophecy (*wahy*). We can never understand the nature and dynamics of '*wahy*', which is restricted to the prophets alone. But it is clear that revelation is the highest level of the fourfold Divine guidance, since it complements and completes God's guidance to His creatures. There is no clash between revelation and reason if their proper spheres are not confused. Revelation guides man in the sphere of spiritual and moral truths, while reason, in the sphere of logico-mathematical and perceptual truths. However, reason does help us to discover instrumental rules for realizing basic ethical truths disclosed by revelation. Man's conscience, as a form of reason, also gives ethical guidance up to a point, but such reasoning in the sphere of morality and spirituality, without the confirmation of '*wahy*', ever-remains subject to doubt and disagreement between men.

The net result of Azad's concept of Divine guidance is to demarcate the proper spheres of the operation of instinct, perception, reason, and revelation and to put forward the ideal of a balanced and integrated conception of Islamic piety and of obedience to the Qur'an and the *sunnah*. Neither the Qur'an nor the *sunnah* is treated by Azad as a textbook of law, politics, economics, physics, or astronomy, but as the fount of spiritual and moral truths. The Muslim must use his powers of perception and reason, which are as much Divine gifts as revelation, for acquiring knowledge of nature and also for the detailed ordering of society.

Azad makes a clear distinction between Islam as '*deen*' and as '*Shariah*'. '*Deen*' maybe defined as authentic faith in God and an authentic concern for right action for its own sake. *Shariah* is the law rooted in the Qur'an and the traditions of the Prophet ﷺ. Now Azad holds that all prophets have preached the same '*deen*', though legal codes have differed from prophet to prophet. But these differences do not negate the essential oneness of all religions. Doctrinal differences arose because of misunderstanding the original '*deen*'. The removal of these misunderstandings plus righteous action rather than a formal acceptance of the Islamic '*Shariah*', suffice for inter-religious understanding and salvation. Just as the biological structure of man is the same despite differences in complexion or facial features, similarly, the basic oneness of the '*deen*' is the same despite differences in the religious law. This leads Azad to the concept of a federal religious unity of mankind rather than a conception of unity, which deems conversion to Islam as the condition of brotherhood in this world and of salvation in the next.

Introduction: The Problem And Its Historical Background

Azad's stress on religious tolerance and pluralism, however, does not imply that he gives up his belief in the uniqueness of the Qur'an and of the Prophet ﷺ as the last of the long line of prophets. What Azad rejects is the view that a Muslim, as a member of Muhammad's ﷺ community (*ummat-e-Muhammadi*), has a higher spiritual status than non-Muslims without any consideration of his ethical or spiritual condition. Spiritual merit and status depend upon spiritual attainments rather than upon membership of a particular race, family, religion, etc. It is sheer conceit to hold that an immoral Muslim ranks spiritually higher than a highly moral non-Muslim simply because of the formers faith in the Qur'an and the Prophet ﷺ.

Azad rejects Iqbals conception of Islam as a total guide to the good life without any distinction between the spiritual and the secular, and also Iqbal's conception of the Islamic community (*ummah*) as the primary and supreme determinant of group identity and loyalty. In these two respects, Azad accepts the essentially secular and nationalist or rather humanist outlook of Syed Ahmad. Both Syed Ahmad and Azad stand for Islamic universalism as distinct from the Islamic communitarianism of Iqbal. They also have the same concept of '*deen*' as the basic unity behind the variety of religious laws. Their common emphasis on '*deen*' as the essence of religion enables them both to accept the special status of the Qur'an and the Prophet ﷺ, without the implication that non-Muslims will not be saved, or that a formal Muslim is *ipso facto* superior to the non-Muslim, or that human brotherhood is not possible without a world Islamic umbrella.

Azad's Islamic universalism made him full of sympathy and concern for the welfare of the human family rather than the Muslims alone. It seems to me that Azad's spiritual humanism was unfortunately misconstrued by his political opponents as an ideological concession to his political ambitions in a country where the majority consisted of non-Muslims. Many alleged that Azad had compromised his authentic faith of the *al-Hilal* period at the altar of political ambition. This most unfair interpretation of Azad's genuine spiritual evolution must have weakened the potential appeal of his line of thought to his fellow Indian Muslims.

The crucial issues not raised by Azad are the problems of pain and evil, the problem of authenticity, the problem of moral and legal growth, and the concept of social justice. Let us now briefly deal with the above matters.

The problem of pain and evil arises when we encounter unmerited suffering and evil in a Universe created by an all-loving and all-powerful God. Azad emphasizes the beauty, harmony, and goodness of the Universe and dwells at great length upon the wonderful ecological balance and teleology of nature. But Azad almost completely ignores the suffering caused by different species and members of the same species struggling for existence, and also ignores the presence of evil. Azad follows the traditional approach that evil is merely a means for promoting a greater good. But this leaves unanswered the crucial enigma why an all-powerful Creator should resort to evil for promoting good.

The problem of authenticity arises when the individual experiences an existential conflict between his conscience and some scriptural injunction. One's conscience, for example, might demand complete equality between men and women, while the Qur'an definitely gives a higher status to man. Or, one may have a conscientious objection against the penalty of severing the hands of the thief, or against whipping. Azad's distinction between '*deen*' and '*Shariah*' is very pertinent, and it maybe said that the above matters are not part of '*deen*' but of the '*Shariah*', and that Muslims are free to modify the law. But any amendment of any clear Qur'anic injunction implies that the Qur'an is not perfect.

Azad stands for secularism but he nowhere spells out the details of the politico-economic and social institutions, which he approves. One would like to know, for instance, what Azad thought about inter-religious marriages. We know that many individuals, both Hindu and Muslim, who loudly proclaim the virtues of secularism, view inter-religious marriages as an obnoxious evil, without realizing that this violates the meaning of secularism.

Similarly, Azad did not spell out his concept of social justice and socialism, which he professed. Azad did not concern himself with the crucial question as to what were the features of the ethically good society over and above the virtues of the good individual.

MAULANA ABUL ALA MAUDUDI

According to Maududi, Islam is the acceptance of unqualified and exclusive sovereignty of God in every sphere of human activity. In practice this boils down to implicit obedience to the Prophet ﷺ. Islam's ethic of

Introduction: The Problem And Its Historical Background

submission is totally opposed to the humanist ethic of inner freedom, which is the common denominator of all man-made 'isms' like Democracy, Rationalism, and Communism, etc. The individual Muslim, however, retains ample scope for exercising his freedom within the bounds of the sacred law. Similarly, the Islamic community also retains ample scope for the joint exercise of its discretion (*ijtehad*) to meet new problems in accord with the spirit of the Qur'an and the *sunnah*. This reform must conform to the spirit of the *Shariah*, and only the Islamic scholar-jurists are qualified to decide what the spirit is. Hence, for all practical purposes, Maududi makes the consensus of the scholar-jurists (*ijma til ulama*) the supreme arbiter of the destiny of the Islamic state. Perhaps his followers do not adequately realize this crucial implication of Maududi's interpretation of God's sovereignty.

Maududi, indeed, speaks of the need of a new Islamic reconstruction of the basic concepts of all the natural and social sciences. Yet he rather dogmatically rejects the evolutionary hypothesis about the origin of the human species. Although he criticizes traditional Muslims for their conservatism and mechanical conformity to the letter of the *Shariah*, in practice, Maududi himself remains as much tied down to the letter of the *Shariah* as any other theologian, except in rather minor and marginal issues. He thinks that his significant message to contemporary Muslims is that they should reconstruct the traditional Islamic institutional system. But Maududi's concrete views on social or politico-economic matters, such as the position and status of women, polygamy, socialism, and equality of opportunity, etc., reflect an essentially justificatory approach to tradition rather than its sympathetic but critical appraisal.

The burden of Maududi's thought is **(a)** the sovereignty of God, **(b)** the organic totality of Islam as a complete code of conduct, and **(c)** Islamic communitarianism. The implication of the first is the rejection of the Western concept of the autonomy of the individual and the sovereignty of the state; the implication of the second is the rejection of secularism; the implication of the third is the rejection of nationalism and secular internationalism. It will be seen that all these are already found in Iqbal, so that there is nothing new in Maududi. What is new is his political activism and dedication to the party, which he founded and still continues to lead. The secret of his appeal, in my opinion, is his simple but polished and powerful Urdu prose, the sheer volume of his writings on themes, which really touch the interests and imagination of his audience, his valuable translation and commentary on the Qur'an, together with a remarkably detailed and systematic index and, last but not least, the fact that much more than Iqbal, Maududi's understanding of Islam remains closer to the traditional thought-cum-value system. Iqbal had rejected many traditional concepts, such as, the view that the sayings of the Prophet ﷺ were implicit revelation (*wahy-e-khafi*) as distinct from explicit revelation (*wahy-e-jali*) or the Qur'an. It is Maududi's great contribution to the full understanding of Islam that he makes explicit what was implicit in the traditional concepts. Maududi thus cannot be ignored. The contemporary Muslim must either accept Maududi or the secular revolution.

GHULAM AHMED PARVEZ

The voluminous writings of Ghulam Ahmad Parvez (containing Qur'anic quotations in almost every paragraph) attempt a systematic reconstruction of the basic concepts of Islam in the light of modern ideas. He takes from Azad the concept of Divine Providence (*nizam-e-rububiyat*), but in all other matters he relies upon Iqbal without, however, being a mere imitator. [32]

Parvez' uniqueness lies in his Islamic or Qur'anic socialism. Iqbal had also criticized capitalism because of its exploitation of the poor, but he had never claimed that the Qur'an prescribed socialism. Similarly, Ubaiduallah Sindhi and Hifzur Rahman had also stood for socialist ideas on secular grounds. [33] But Parvez actually deduces a socialist polity from the Qur'anic text by giving novel interpretations to Arabic words such as '*salat*', '*zakat*', and '*akhirat*', etc. Thus Parvez holds that '*salat*' or establishing of prayer does not mean merely the ritual of prayer but the establishing of a just social order. Likewise, '*zakat*' does not mean merely a tax on savings, but the appropriation by a welfare state of all the surplus wealth of individuals for running a planned economy. Similarly, Parvez interprets the term '*akhirat*' as worldly welfare in addition to its usual eschatological sense.

To the objection that, if the Qur'an stood for socialism, why does it give such detailed attention to the laws of inheritance, Parvez replies that socialism could not come about at a stroke; detailed laws were, therefore, given for the transitional period. The advent of socialism will make these laws infructuous rather than invalid, even as improvements in hygiene eliminate the need for curative medicines. To the further objection that if this were the real intention of the Qur'an why was this not accepted by the earlier Muslims, Parvez holds that the vested interests of the establishment

Introduction: The Problem And Its Historical Background

and the essentially non-Arabic (*ajami*) ideas of the previous ages distorted the proper interpretation of the Qur'an and *hadith*.

Let us examine the above claims. Parvez commits the fallacy of projectionism by reading his own thoughts and values into the propositional canvas of the Qur'an. While it is quite permissible to interpret the Qur'anic reference to instantaneous creation as an evolutionary beginning, or the Qur'anic reference to six days as six geological periods, or the Qur'anic reference to the motions of the sun and the moon as motion in the Copernican framework, the situation becomes quite different if one interprets '*salat*' as an injunction to establish socialism. This amounts to a far-fetched stretching of the plain meaning of terms to make them conform to one's own ideas. One may well accept socialism on rational or ethical grounds and hold that, since the Qur'an does not oppose socialism, Muslim society ought to go socialist. In other words, matters of polity should not be mixed up with transcendental matters.

It seems Parvez attempts to seek Qur'anic support for a socialist polity for two reasons; firstly, because he thinks this would strengthen his case, and, secondly, because Parvez (under the influence of Iqbal) accepts Islam as a complete code of conduct meant for every walk of life. But his purpose is totally defeated, as is evident from the situation in Pakistan where the opposition to politico-economic leftism has not been softened or overcome merely by finding Qur'anic sanctions or support for socialist ideas. In fact, as sociology tells us, the roots of the opposition lie in the vested interests of the privileged classes who will quite understandably continue to support the status quo, justifying it in the name of orthodoxy. Thus Parvez' socialistic interpretation of the Qur'an will not work even in a Muslim society. But even if it did to some extent, it would not work at all in plural societies especially where Muslims are in the minority. Parvez's approach will give a religious turn to an issue which cuts across religious groupings and which, as an essentially politico-economic matter, requires a national rather than a group consensus in a democratic state. In the final analysis, therefore, secularism provides the only route to socialism for Muslims, whether in homogeneous or in plural societies.

The difficulties of Parvez arise because he is unable to accept secularism, which implies delinking the politico-economic system from the purview of religion. It is significant that out of the about 6,200 verses of the Qur'an only about 250 are prescriptive in character, and out of these only about 10 deal with politico-economic issues. [34] Thus, for all practical purposes the Qur'an does not prescribe any polity. This was worked out by the early Muslim jurists and administrators starting from Umar, and will have to be modified by each generation to suit its own situational needs. If so, there is no point left in Iqbal's theory (faithfully reiterated by both Maududi and Parvez) of the organic unity of Islam and the implied rejection of secularism.

Secularism does not erode the Muslim's freedom in the transcendental '*I-Thou*' sphere. However, every society, whether homogeneous or plural, and every state, be it secular or religious, must inevitably constrain the freedom of the individual in social relationships. Consequently, the sense of external restraint is inseparable from the individual consciousness as such. The only difference is that in a plural society, which is predominantly non-Muslim, the sense of restraint will appear to flow primarily from an out-group, while in a homogeneous Muslim society, from an in-group. But it is pertinent to note that since the in-group itself can never be absolutely homogeneous, social-psychological tensions will again tend to arise between the constituent sub-groups. This is happening in Pakistan, which was established as a pure ideological state. Consequently, mutual understanding between different religious, linguistic, regional, and occupational groups becomes equally essential in both homogeneous and plural societies. Secularism is, thus, more relevant to the human situation in general than Iqbal's communitarianism with its restricted appeal to Muslims in a homogeneous or predominantly Muslim society.

V

A New Look

Arab, Turkish, and Iranian Islamic modernists such as Ali Adbul Raziq (d. 1965), Taha Husayn (b. 1891), and Ziya Gokulp (d. 1924), *et al.* also accept secularism, but they take another stand. They want the 'essence' of Islam to be maintained, while all accretions and details to be thrown away

Introduction: The Problem And Its Historical Background

unceremoniously without any qualms of disloyalty to a long tradition. They are quite right up to a point, but unfortunately they oversimplify the issues involved and miss the essentially organic character of religious faith.

Ziya Gokalp and Raziq identify the essence of Islam with a simple monotheism minus the traditional conception of revelation, according to which the Qur'an is the infallible revealed Word of God. The conception of Islam, as entertained by Gokalp thus reduces Islam to a sort of 18th century British or French Deism, and to the view that religion is a matter of a personal relationship between the individual and God, without any bearing upon the collective life of mankind. In other words, man is left free to order the social web of human life in accordance with his collective wisdom. The assumption is that men are quite capable of regulating their affairs satisfactorily in a democratic manner without any religious authority. This is a rejection of the traditional conception, according to which Islam offers complete and perfect guidance in every walk of life.

Ali Raziq's radical conception of Islam is marked by the incongruity and inadequacy of retaining the traditional Islamic conception of God without the corresponding traditional conception of revelation. If the traditional Islamic conception of God is retained, but the traditional conception of revelation is repudiated, mere belief in a God Who creates but does not guide His creatures, either through incarnation, in the traditional Christian sense, or through revelation, in the Islamic sense, satisfies neither the heart nor the head. A lacuna is left in this approach to Islam. Turkish and Arab Islamic modernists do not seem to be aware of the intellectual and spiritual difficulties inherent in combining an unqualified secularism with traditional Islamic monotheism. What Muslims all over the world require is the reconstruction of the traditional Islamic concepts of God and revelation so that they no longer conflict with science and secular humanism. In the absence of such a reconstruction the combination of secularism with Islamic monotheism strikes a jarring note of discord between two incongruous concepts. Such a combination is an artificial or mechanical juxtaposition without inner organic harmony, and is liable to disintegrate. Such a patchwork synthesis leaves men as divided selves and split personalities, even though they may not be fully aware of their subtle spiritual predicament.

The same remarks apply to all those persons who are inclined to think that all will be well with Muslims, if their economic problems are solved, and that the reformation of Islamic concepts does more harm than good as it generates religious controversy. This line of thinking completely ignores the vital relationship between theory and practice in human life. Just as man finds it very difficult, if not impossible, to pursue morality without some sort of a theoretical basis or set of reasons for being moral (whether this base be supplied by theism, pantheism, or humanism, etc.), similarly it is very difficult, if not impossible, to pursue socioeconomic objectives without a suitable theoretical rationale. Thus, if the members of a society consciously or unconsciously believe that poverty and riches are created by God rather than the results of human actions, their motivation will never be as powerful as of those who regard poverty a man-made evil. Similarly, the ideal of human brotherhood will never inspire a group, if it believes those who are outside the group will not find a place in heaven, no matter how morally good they might happen to be. Modernism as a mere sociopolitical expression will never suffice unless it touches those depths of the human personality where religion resides and operates.

We are thus justified in concluding that reconstructing the basic concepts and values of Islam is an unavoidable responsibility of Muslim intellectuals. Mere changes in sociopolitical infrastructure or, in other words, the schemes of modernization, as advocated by some Islamic liberals in India, Pakistan, and West Asia, will never prove effective unless they are rooted in a systematic and consistent thought system. Similarly, Maududi's program of the marginal reconstruction of Islamic polity will also not prove satisfactory. Neither Maududi nor the Turkish and Arab modernists attempt to reconstruct the basic Islamic thought system in the light of the ever-expanding frontiers of human knowledge. All said and done, only Indo-Pakistan thinkers like Iqbal (d. 1938), Azad (d. 1958), Fyzee, and Fazlur Rahman (d. 1988), et al, are sufficiently aware of this vital need. [35]

FIELD INTEGRATION, CONTINUITY, AND CHANGE: THEIR PSYCHOLOGY AND ETHIC

A fresh look at Islam by Muslim intellectuals is essential for giving enlightenment and guidance to the common Muslim, who stands totally perplexed by the antagonistic pulls of theocracy and democracy, clericalism and secularism, traditionalism and modernity. The average Muslim is more or less a split personality and must be helped to integrate himself.[36] The traditional conception of a monolithic religion poses a serious problem

Introduction: The Problem And Its Historical Background

to him. As long as the inner logic of traditional Islam leads the Muslim in the direction of monolithic theocracy, and at the same time the logic of his historical situation pulls him in the direction of secular democracy, he can have no inner peace. To the extent that he refuses to come to grips with this basic conflict, he will continue to remain a split personality. The split is due to the basic conflict between the contemporary concept of secularism underlying the present Indian polity and the traditional concept of Islam, as a revealed code of conduct for every facet of human life.

The traditional conception further implies not only the Muslim's duty to submit himself to the discipline of the *Shariah*, but also to try to convert non-Islamic states into Islamic ones. This approach makes non-Muslims suspect that all Muslims perpetually attempt to convert, if not subvert, their ways of life. The Muslim resents the suspicion of his loyalty, and feels that his loyalty to the Sovereign Lord of the Universe is immensely more important than his image in the eyes of others. He believes that in trying to establish a Qur'anic world state he is really serving his fellow men better than they know how to serve themselves, rather than imposing an alien way of life.

Any alteration in one's religious convictions on grounds of political expediency or improving the community's image in the eyes of others is definitely wrong in principle. What is really needed is a genuine field integration and the realization that all cultural traditions, including Islam, need ceaseless self-authentication, if they are not merely to endure but also prevail. This approach stands in quite a different category from opportunism and signifies inner growth rather than the loss of one's soul for the sake of worldly gain. It leads to an integrated human vision rather than to an eclectic compromise or patchwork synthesis dictated by situational needs or demands.

A mere pragmatic adjustment can never convince the person at the existential level, that is, in the depths of his being, even though it may appear to possess the virtue of situational expediency. No matter how well such a position may have served in the past and may promise to serve in the future, it will lack that power of existential conviction that prompts a Socrates to drink the hemlock with a smile, or a Husayn to embrace death as his highest destiny, or a Vietnamese woman to accept destruction in a foxhole, without the consolation of heaven, just for making the socialist dream come true for posterity. Now, whether we like it or not, some of the Western secular thought-cum-value systems such as Democracy, Socialism, and Communism, etc., do possess this inner structural harmony and existential appeal to their respective followers. This fire of conviction, needless to say, had once burnt in the hearts of the early Muslims also. But the fire gradually cooled down leaving behind only the ashes of a once living conviction. Religious faith is indeed like passionate love, which cannot be produced or extinguished at will. If love be present, the lover is carried on the wings of a sacred passion which makes the sacrifice of his comforts, nay life itself, a ready giving to the beloved rather than a painful duty. But if love be absent, neither logic, nor allurement, nor force suffices to impel such sacrifice, though prudence or a sense of duty might prompt the service of others.

A basic difficulty that besets the traditional Indian Muslim is that he honestly believes in the superiority of his religion to all other religions, especially to polytheistic Hinduism, as he understands it. At the same time he finds himself in a hopeless minority as a result of the new democratic set-up in the country. Right up to 1750 A.D. the Indian Muslims had been the politically dominant minority in the country. Later the advent of British rule had deprived them of their dominant position, but they had never become dependent upon the Hindus. At present, however, the Indian Muslim is at a loss to know how to relate himself to Hinduism about which his information is very meager, in spite of the long contact between Islam and Hinduism. All that he does know about Hinduism is derived from a period in which Hinduism was decadent in many respects. The vital and creative period of Hinduism had ended with Harsha (d. 647 AD) almost four centuries before the effective political penetration into north India by the Ghorid Pathans in the late 12th century. Indian Muslims, therefore, never had any opportunity of seeing or studying Hinduism in its earlier period of creative glory. The early Arab scholars of the Abbasid period, who avidly translated Sanskrit classics into Arabic and learnt Indian numerals, astronomy, arithmetic, and chess, etc., must have entertained an image of Hinduism considerably different from that of the Ghorid soldiers and administrators who established themselves in Hindustan without much opposition. Perhaps something of the unconscious group pride still clings to the Indian Muslim mind. This was precisely the situation, which prevailed during the latter half of the 19th century after the establishment of British rule in 1857. But then the problem was posed by Christianity and the Englishman, with the result that Syed Ahmad was perpetually on the defensive against charges of appeasing the English and of watering down Islam to suit the then existing conditions.

Introduction: The Problem And Its Historical Background

It is thus necessary to correct and supplement the rather distorted and one-sided image of Hinduism in the minds of many Muslims. The grave evils that unfortunately crept into Hindu society long ago need not be glossed over by Muslims. Nor should the rather chauvinistic approach of some Hindu sections be silently accepted. At the same time the numerous elements of value in the long and rich Hindu tradition should be appreciated by the Muslim. In doing so the Muslim would find himself in a very distinguished company, indeed the company of some of the finest intellects of the world: from al-Beruni to Max Mueller. It goes without saying that the Indian Hindus too must acquire an authentic and well-informed understanding of Islam, as distinguished from the rather superficial social contacts or mere political cooperation for short-term objectives.

Man is born egocentric, bred ethnocentric, but he is potentially 'value centric', that is, inwardly free to assimilate new values or to cultivate new dimensions in the traditional values. The inwardly free man is engaged in an eternal pilgrimage with no sectarian barriers in his way. His heroes are not Muslim, Hindu, or Christian, but just beacons of light that guide his own authentic quest for value. He is neither an imitator nor an originator, but only a truth-seeker gathering the pearls of truth wherever he finds them.

The study of the history of other religions will prove useful for acquiring a deeper insight into our own. Just as it is easier to detect the psychological defense mechanisms or motives of self-interest of others than one's own, so is it with groups. The limitations of other religions are much more easily grasped than those of one's own. Consequently, a critical sociological survey of other religions helps us to understand better the stages and laws of growth of our own culture or religion, its strength and its limitations. This comparative sociology of religions tends to dissolve our natural ethnocentricity and group self-conceit. Self-conceit prompts us to treat our own religion as a class by itself, and hence exempt from sociological laws that apply only to religions other than our own. Once we put aside natural ethnocentricity or 'group snobbery', if I may call it so, we are in a much better position to appreciate the points of excellence of our own religion and its unique contribution to the human family at large.

History avers that no group or tradition can grow and prosper without intelligent self-interpretation. Modern Western culture has been particularly receptive to self-criticism and it is precisely due to this that it continues to grow and flourish. Protestant Christian thinkers such as Matthew Arnold,

Tolstoy, Schweitzer, Bultmann, Tillich, Niebuhr, Ramsey, Robinson and others have revised traditional Christian concepts and values without breaking away from the tradition. The Catholic Church has not approved of these essays in conceptual reconstruction, and remains conservative in its approach. But now it is also displaying a new dynamism. Hinduism has been reinterpreted by Rammohun Roy, Vivekananda, Tagore, Aurobindo, and Radhakrishnan, *et al*. But it appears to me that the systematic reconstruction of Islamic concepts and values has relatively trailed behind in the modern era, though Muslim thinkers were in the vanguard of field integration in the medieval age.

The spiritual and religious history of the West is deeply relevant to Muslims. The achievements of Christian thought must be sympathetically studied for the light it could throw on our own problems and prospects. The counsel of some to accept Western science and technology, but not bother about its spiritual and religious history is both superficial and barren. Conceit is as irrational as blind imitation.

It seems to me that Muslims are relatively more sensitive than non-Muslims to criticism, no matter how objective and academic, on religious issues. It is a common grouse of even highly educated Muslims that Western non-Muslim scholars knowingly or unknowingly distort the truth about Islam due to religious prejudice or political hostility, etc. This makes Western scholarship suspect in the eyes of traditional Muslims. This is indeed most unfortunate. While most Christian writers were manifestly prejudiced against Islam right till the closing years of the last century, the approach of contemporary Western scholars of non-Christian cultures has undergone a qualitative change due to a number of reasons. It would be sheer folly and misfortune for the Muslims to ignore the sympathetic yet critical and balanced evaluations and findings of a Gibb or an Arberry merely because their agreement with traditional Islamic views may not be complete. A dogmatic or defensive rejection of the fruits of free inquiry is no less undesirable than mere fashionable imitation of things Western.

No cultural system, whether religious or secular, can be completely free from spatiotemporal traces. The sincere effort to transcend the limitations of the tradition while remaining loyal to its basic values constitutes creative fidelity to the tradition. The jurists of Islam have in theory evolved a very rational procedure for bringing about orderly changes in the situational concretion of the Islamic value system. But changes based on individual reflection (*ijtihad*) have been very slow and halting, utterly failing to keep

Introduction: The Problem And Its Historical Background

pace with a rapidly changing and fast moving world. Even when changes have been accepted by some liberal Muslims, others have continued to question their bona fides. The true conservative seldom gives up the pious hope that the erring members of the group will recant one day. Consequently, he is averse to the 'legitimization' of even the *de facto* changes wrought by time into the religious tradition. However, if the changes take deep roots, showing no sign of dislodgement from the liberal sections of the group, the conservative in time becomes partly reconciled to them.

The creation of new values and the conservation of the old ones that have stood the test of time are both equally necessary. In fact they depend upon each other. The creation of new values presupposes a valuational base or support. Similarly, the effective maintenance of this base demands awareness of the subtle changes in the nuances of human experience. Eternal and intelligent vigilance is the price of keeping old values alive in the condition of dynamic interaction with the environment, rather than as showpieces in the museum of man's heritage.

Creativity ever-spurs men to go ahead in the realm of values and to yearn for the better rather than be content with the good. The function of tradition, on the other hand, is to strike a note of caution, lest the pace of change increase to the point of giving diminishing returns. The function of tradition is not the stoppage of growth but only the regulation of the speed of growth. Thus the conservative approach has its own function in the economy of human progress, provided it does not overreach itself. However, the pure conservative or modernist approaches tend to assume the two dimensional, either/or, logic of evaluation, according to which an object is either good or bad and should either be conserved or rejected. This type of blanket evaluation misses the complexity of the object judged. Evaluation must be preceded by an analysis of the elements and structure of the object in question and separate elements must be evaluated separately. All cultural traditions comprise separate elements of value and of disvalue, instead of being monolithic structures of either value or disvalue. The evolutionary approach ensures the blending of continuity and change. It criticizes and overcomes the elements of disvalue in the tradition while making the elements of value the nucleus of further growth.

Creativity and conservation should, therefore, dovetail into and supplement each other. Without creativity conservation leads to fossilization, while without conservation, creativity leads to irresponsible experimentation. While such adventures in the realm of art and literature may not be injurious, they could prove catastrophic in the realm of moral and social relationships. The new sex morality of Western Europe and America, according to which the game of sex maybe played between any two willing parties without any mutual obligation arising there from, has played havoc with the spiritual growth of the contemporary Western man. It appears to me that the West is gradually realizing its fallacy and that a more balanced interpretation of sex is in the process of crystallization. Similarly, the limitations of different movements such as nationalism, capitalism, socialism, and scientism, etc., are being acknowledged. Humanity would have been spared countless tears, had the human judgment been more balanced and well-informed. But man blunders, pays the penalty in the course of time, and forges ahead.

The revision of concepts is a continuing and self-correcting process. All attempted revisions are rooted in the concepts and values of the time and place of the integrating individual, though creative individuals are never merely reflections of their environment. No particular integration, whether made by an Ibn Sina or a Ghazali, an Aquinas or a Kant, a Syed Ahmad or an Iqbal, can be accepted as final. The task of the systematic interpretation of the human situation is an unending collective task, at once the burden and the privilege of the human species rather than of any individual.

This conceptual evolution or reconstruction in the meaning of traditional symbols and images takes time. There maybe said to be a 'conceptual lag' just as there is a cultural lag. The concept of conceptual lag makes us tolerant toward the tradition-oriented person. In this context the methodological approach of some Western philosophers is illuminating. They hold that philosophical or theological disputes arise because different persons select different features for emphasis within the same set of facts. Hence, the important thing is not the verbal formulation but rather the full awareness of the complexity of the set of facts. Provided this complexity is grasped, any formulation maybe retained. This principle maybe called the 'principle of formulational tolerance'. This together with the concept of conceptual lag should help our modernists in carrying out an authentic and fruitful dialogue with the traditionalists, as recommended above.

The principle of formulational tolerance is not an innovation in the cultural tradition of Islam, as is attested by the well-known story of *Moses and the Shepherd* in the *Masnawi* of Maulana Rumi. [37] Earlier still, both

Introduction: The Problem And Its Historical Background

Ghazali and Ibn Rushd had said that truth must be communicated to suit the mental level of the hearer. This approach releases us from the monopolistic grip of traditional formulations and also the jargon of our own pet interpretative system. [38]

The concrete life situation of every person being unique, the concrete problems or tensions arising out of the different fields of human experience vary from case to case. The need, urgency, and range of field integration can, therefore, never be uniform for all persons. Where field tensions are not pronounced and an individual is happy and satisfied with his religious beliefs field integration is unnecessary. To make him aware of field tensions that have been registered by philosophers or other sophisticated intellects, but not by an average person, and then to help him overcome those tensions through field integration would be partly similar to raising the blood pressure of a healthy individual to a high degree, and then again bringing it down to normal through some therapy. Nevertheless, the generation of doubt in a satisfied individual is not pointless, since this encourages the conceptual or spiritual growth of individuals by increasing the area and depth of their awareness. This is the legacy of Socrates. The average believer, however, no matter what his religion, does not realize the need for the continuous search for new meanings of old concepts in the light of advancing human knowledge.

The cumulative growth in man's factual knowledge in the modern era has profoundly modified the basic conceptual framework of those who are aware of these developments. Now many such people just find it impossible to accept traditional interpretations. At the same time they do not see any point in repudiating or rejecting their cherished tradition with which they continue to feel a sense of emotional involvement and identification. They still draw inspiration from the tradition, but are not prepared to abdicate their own spiritual autonomy. It is these people who yearn for a new interpretation of basic religious concepts in the idiom of contemporary thought. This is not tantamount to making concessions or 'adjustments' for the sake of expediency or material gain, but reflects an awareness of the intellectual difficulties in the traditional thought or value system.

The quest for growth, must not, however, blind us to the power of the symbols and images of a tradition. These symbols must be retained and at the same time they must be reconstructed. If the symbols are discarded, the creative person isolates himself from the tradition and his new insights have no prestigious vessels to be poured into. If on the other hand the symbols are retained, it becomes very difficult to make them first absorb or assimilate and then convey the new ideas and values in question. The symbols cast their shadows and tend to obscure and distort the fresh stirrings of the human soul. Moreover, even if this difficulty be overcome there is another dilemma. If the symbols are retained in their traditional sense the reformer is heard and understood by the group, but the group does not move forward toward the vision of the leader. If the symbols are formally retained but their meaning or significance radically altered, he tends to suffer from a sense of intellectual dishonesty, and is also liable to be charged with hypocrisy by those who do not feel dissatisfied with the traditional meanings of the symbols in question. Every creative individual, therefore, has to solve this predicament. The fear of the charge of hypocrisy should not deprive him of the advantages of his membership of a living church or tradition. Provided he feels an emotional involvement with the tradition and genuinely finds many elements of value in the historical personalities and events of that tradition, he should go ahead with the task of reconstructing the tradition. The charge of hypocrisy cannot after all be treated as more discouraging or demoralizing than the charge of apostasy that was the order of the day in medieval times, nay, right up to our own.

The charge of hypocrisy will be valid only if the individual distorts his authentic meanings in order to get an audience. If the recommended changes in the meanings of the traditional symbols are fully and frankly acknowledged, employing those symbols for facilitating the genuine creative growth of the community can never be regarded as hypocrisy. Indeed this is the only way to further the cause of cultural evolution. The modifications in the traditional concepts and values should be viewed as fruits growing upon the tree of a living tradition rather than as alterations in an inherited inert brick and mortar structure for the sake of a better *'adjustment'* to life. This concept of growth, as distinguished from alteration, should dispel any lingering sense of disloyalty to the tradition.

Chapter 2

The Dominant Traditional Conception of Islam

Introductory Remarks

Every developed religious tradition has historically been an organic whole of a thought-cum-value system, a prescriptive or symbolic system and an institutional or legal system. The traditional version of these four aspects or dimensions of Islam are so well known and so much has been written about them by competent scholars, whether Muslims or Islamists, that there is no need for my describing the traditional conception in detail. [39] Since, however, my purpose is a critical examination of the tradition and its actual reconstruction, to the best of my limited abilities, it is essential to state the traditional version in its basic outline. I will, however, restrict myself to the thought system (making only brief reference to the institutional system, and entirely omitting the symbolic and value systems), since it is primarily the thought system that needs restatement in the light of the contemporary conceptual framework. Islamic symbolic practices do not come into the picture at all, since their modification would amount to instituting a new religion rather than a restatement of the old in a new idiom of thought. However, any serious and consistent attempt at conceptual reconstruction is bound to lead to a fresh interpretation of basic values or the emergence of new dimensions therein, and also to some shifts in emphasis. This will be very obvious to the reader as he proceeds.

GOD, PROPHECY, AND LIFE AFTER DEATH:
Unity of God

The unity of God is the foundation of the Islamic thought system. God is the only Primal and Self-Existent Being and the Creator of all phenomenal existence. God created the world out of nothing, directs the affairs of the world, and everything is under His absolute control. If asked to explain the exact nature of God's attributes and activity, the common Muslim would take the stand that neither the mode of God's activities nor His purposes can be fully grasped by man's limited reason. Thus, if we were to say that the purpose of God in creating the Universe was to be acknowledged and glorified as God, this would imply some desire or aspiration in God. This in turn would imply some dissatisfaction on the part of God, vitiating the concept of a Perfect Being. Thus, the traditional position leans to the view that the nature and attributes of God are ineffable, even though belief in the existence of God is rationally justifiable.

Man yearns to understand the nature of God just as he tries to understand things in general. This quest for understanding is natural and there is nothing wrong about it. But man's capacities of understanding and reason are limited. He cannot help projecting his own ideas and experiences into his concept of God. Thus when the Qur'an says that God creates, sees, listens, punishes, etc., man is inclined to understand the attributes and the activities of God in his own image. This inevitably creates difficulties and contradictions. It does not, however, prove the non-existence of God. It only proves that the projected conception of God is not valid or applicable to God as He is in Himself; it merely reflects God as He appears to our imperfect reason.

Another reason for the difficulties arising in connection with the conception of God is that we are inclined to think that our conception of God is the same as God Himself, and that anyone who rejects our conception of God, therefore, rejects the existence of God as such. This makes us unnecessarily dogmatic. The attempt to establish a detailed conception of God is basically ill-conceived. We must accept that God is ineffable, and be content with a sense of mystery and awe in the heart of the Universe. We must accept God as the Supreme Power before Whom we surrender ourselves and should not venture to say anything more (*iman bila kaif*). The moment we say anything further we involve ourselves in the fruitless task of trying to comprehend, through finite concepts, the Supreme and Infinite Source of all existence. If the ray can never comprehend the sun, or the drop contain the ocean, we too cannot comprehend God. Even if we could prove the existence of God, His attributes, no matter what they are taken to be, are not a matter of logical proof. It is in the last analysis a question of faith (*iman*). This, however, does not mean that one's faith is necessarily irrational but only that it is 'supra-rational'.

The Dominant Traditional Conception of Islam

The contention of some philosophers and sociologists that the idea of God has evolved through a long process is not correct, according to the traditional or orthodox Islamic view. Monotheism is not the product of a slow and gradual evolutionary advance of ideas through interaction between man and his environment; it is rather the first or primitive religion. These ideas constituting the content of the '*deen-e-Islam*' have been revealed by God to prophets from Adam onwards. The ideas and concepts of philosophy, on the other hand, are the product of man's own attempt to interpret the human situation. Revealed religion is superior to philosophy, whose proper function is not to compete with religion or rather the '*deen*' but to act as a handmaid for serving the basic values taught by the eternal and universal '*deen*', that is, Islam from Adam onwards.

The so-called laws of nature, which appear to regulate natural events, are in reality descriptions of the uniform behavior of nature at the behest of Divine commands. Thus, far from rendering the concept of God superfluous, these laws proclaim the majesty, wisdom, and beneficence of God. It is through these laws that God enables man to control nature for his own benefit.

These laws do not in any way limit the power of God Who can suspend or change them at will. A miracle is nothing but just an instance of God's power. However, since God is just, He usually does not interfere in the working of these laws. Consequently, regular and uniform laws govern the events of the world. In this way God combines His omnipotence with uniformity of nature.

Every event, apart from human actions resulting from the operation of man's free will, has a place in the Divine management of the Universe. The finite human mind, however, is unable to grasp this Divine scheme. Hence it is baffled by many apparent contradictions that seem to belie any coherent purpose of the Universe. Yet these contradictions dissolve in the fuller Divine perspective, which also includes the events of life after death. Death is not the final destruction but only a change of state.

God knows the future beforehand. But this foreknowledge does not in any way deprive man of his freedom of will. Consequently, no blame can be attributed to God for the various man-made evils in the world. Physical evils such as natural calamities, diseases, accidents, etc., prima facie contradict the benevolence of God. But according to the traditional conception, what appears to be evil to man may not really be evil at all. Human reason being finite, it should not surprise us if we are unable to comprehend the wisdom of God.

Prophecy

God has created all living and non-living things to carry out His Divine commands. But God, in His wisdom, has bestowed the gift of freedom upon man who can either surrender himself to the commands of God or violate them. God was not content with the eternal praise offered to Him by angelic beings, who were not capable of any evil. In this respect they were like the inanimate objects referred to above. God decided to make man free by creating temptations for him, on the one hand, and by giving him Divine guidance and help, on the other. The instrument of temptation is Satan who has deliberately been given the ability and power to make evil attractive to man. The instrument of guidance is the human conscience or the moral sense of man as guided by Divine revelation. The revelation is communicated to God's chosen prophets and messengers by God's angels. Man is potentially stronger than Satan. With God's help he can conquer temptation and achieve salvation as well as success in this life through following God's commands delivered through His messengers. But those who reject the revelations of God will be punished and will come to an evil end.

The messengers of God have been continually appearing everywhere to warn and guide people to the straight path. But Satan has also been busy tempting human beings to go astray. The conflict between good and evil is the unending theme of the cosmic drama. The Divine laws promulgated from time to time by His messengers were meant for their respective communities. But the Qur'an revealed to the Prophet ﷺ in the seventh century A.D. was meant for all men and for all time. The Qur'an, as the final and infallible version of God's will, cancels all previous revelations and is the sole criterion of truth in all matters. In case of conflict between human reason and any Qur'anic statement the former must be in error.

The Qur'an indicates the various ways or modes in which God communicates His will to His prophets, namely, through angels or through a vision or from behind a veil or through sounds or other signals or through dreams, etc. But obviously these descriptions do not give the reader any concrete understanding of the exact mechanics of revelation, which remain as unknown or mysterious as ever before. It would not be wrong to say that the concept of Revelation is the ultimate mystery of Islam, just as the Divine Sonship of Christ is the ultimate mystery of Christianity. Just as it would be futile to expect a Christian to be able to give an exact and clear conception of the phrase *'the only begotten Son of God'*, so it would be futile to expect a Muslim to be able to have a clear and agreed conception of the expression *'the revealed Word of God'*. The meaning of the expression *'the Word of God'* is not any easier to understand than the meaning of the expression *'the son of God'*, provided, of course, these words are used in their ordinary literal sense. Since the spirit of critical inquiry or questioning is judged to be contrary to the spirit of faith in the unseen, a Christian attempting to analyze the various meanings of the expression *'the only begotten son of God'* maybe deemed as a good philosopher, but this activity will not make him a good Christian. Similarly, a good Muslim (on the traditional view) is one who does not worry about the exact mode and mechanics of revelation but who acts upon the Word of God. Not clarity but rather faith is crucial for salvation. The passion for clarity is the fad of the philosopher rather than the crown of the believer. If, however, the average Muslim be pressed to clarify the expression *'the Word of God'*, he would give the following account:

By God's command the angel Gabriel, either **(a)** appeared before the Prophet ﷺ in a human form and made him recite the words composing the Qur'an after hearing them from Gabriel; or **(b)** appeared before the Prophet ﷺ in his (Gabriel's) original angelic form and performed the same function; or **(c)** without making himself (Gabriel) visible to the Prophet ﷺ he performed the same function. The Prophet ﷺ memorized the verses and later dictated them to his scribes. The Prophet ﷺ himself indicated the textual sequence of the verses, as distinguished from the chronological sequence of their revelation. This process of intermittent revelation continued for twenty-three years.

To the question whether the textual sequence was the result of the Prophet's ﷺ own decision, or was itself communicated by Gabriel, the average Muslim will probably be unable to give an answer. [40] But this question does not touch the essential concept of revelation as such. The Prophet ﷺ played no part in either the subject matter or the moment of revelation. God Who acted through Gabriel and determined all the matter, manner, and moment of revelation. This does not imply a higher rank for Gabriel than the Prophet. As an angel, Gabriel's capacity for glorifying God maybe much greater than that of any human being. But it is man who is the peak of God's creation, and the Prophet ﷺ is the peak of humanity or the perfect man. He is the perfect model for all men for all times.

While the revelations of the other prophet's were provisional the revelation given to Prophet Muhammad ﷺ is final. Moreover, while the previous revelations were corrupted by the ravages of time the Qur'anic text will ever-remain free from any possible interpolation. This is God's own guarantee contained in the Qur'an itself. Consequently, the Islamic community, as the bearers and human guardians of the Qur'an, is unique. While nations and communities may come and disappear from the stage of history the Islamic community will eventually triumph in the final scene of the final act of the cosmic drama. This is not because the Muslims as individuals will be given special treatment by God, but because the Qur'an has a special status among God's revelations.

The Qur'an, as the Word of God, is final and infallible. But the Word of God needs to be interpreted and amplified in order to be applied to concrete human situations. This interpretation is the task of the Prophet ﷺ. The Prophet ﷺ is not merely the recipient of the Qur'an but also the interpreter and commentator of the Qur'an. Hence, the words or actions of the Prophet ﷺ, though not Divine like the Qur'an, are almost as binding and authoritative as the Qur'an itself. A saying of the Prophet ﷺ, provided it is authentic, is for all practical purposes infallible, since the Prophet ﷺ, as the recipient of the Word of God, enjoyed a unique access to the will of God. To hold that the Prophet ﷺ was fallible is to reduce his status to that of a mere messenger in the literal sense, while he was a messenger in the spiritual sense, with full authority and competence to interpret and apply the Qur'anic commands to the concrete human situation. Barring the authority to contradict the Qur'an, the Prophet's ﷺ authority, moral and legal, is absolute, unconditional, and unlimited. Anyone who denies this absolute authority of the Prophet ﷺ is guilty of rejecting the Qur'an and God Himself, since the Qur'an, without the *hadith*, remains incomplete and inapplicable to the concrete human situation. Moreover, the Qur'an itself repeatedly commands obedience to the Prophet ﷺ. The example and the judgments of the Prophet ﷺ are thus binding on all Muslims.

According to the earliest view, the Qur'an alone is the 'begotten' Word of God. This belief accounts for the significant fact that no attempt was made to collect and classify the Prophet's ﷺ sayings for almost two hundred years after his death. But later on the view developed that some sayings of the Prophet ﷺ, namely, the *Hadith-e-Qudsi*, were the product of Divine inspiration, though admittedly not a part of the Qur'an. Theologians started to make the subtle distinction between manifest revelation (*wahy-e-jali*) and hidden revelation (*wahy-e-Khafi*). It was held that while the Qur'an was a product of manifest revelation, the amplification and interpretation of the non-specific or general injunctions of the Qur'an were the product of hidden revelation. Thus the prescribed mode, timings, and other details connected with prayers, and fasting, etc., were not the result of the Prophet's ﷺ thinking, as a human being, but were inspired by God. Other men may excel the Prophet ﷺ in worldly wisdom or knowledge, but no man can excel him in the spheres of morality and spirituality, that is, ethical insight and the knowledge of the nature of God, angels, revelation, and life after death, etc. Consequently, the Prophet ﷺ will ever-remain the infallible guide and preceptor of men. His vision of human society cannot be improved upon. All schemes of reform and improvement that seek to go beyond the sociopolitical or economic vision of the Prophet ﷺ are, therefore, *ipso facto* unsound and uncalled for. They imply the tampering by human reasoning with the infallible Word of God, as interpreted by the Prophet ﷺ. Hence, they are bound to lead to mischief. This may escape human detection but it inevitably harms man. The duty of man in the post Qur'anic phase of human history is nothing but a corporate attempt to apply the principles of the Qur'an and the *sunnah* to the concrete human situation. All possible progress in the future is progress toward the ideal already enshrined in the Qur'an and the *sunnah*. The idea of progress in the ideal itself or the idea of the reconstruction and reformation of Islamic concepts and values implies an imperfection or inadequacy in the Prophet's ﷺ ideal or vision. This would amount to a virtual rejection of the finality and perfection of the Word of God, as interpreted by the Prophet ﷺ.

Once we commit ourselves to the Qur'an, as the infallible Word of God, we cannot at the same time claim to follow our own independent reason or go wherever the argument leads us, in the language of Socrates. An existential commitment or submission, by the very nature of the case, can only be to a single object or person. An individual may get along pretty well with two centers of commitment, so long as their demands do not conflict with each other. But the moment a conflict arises the individual must opt either for one or the other as the focus of his existential commitment.

Islam is nothing if it is not the total surrender or submission to God. But man cannot directly know the Divine will, which is revealed only to

His chosen prophets. From the functional point of view, therefore, surrender to God is surrender to the Qur'an, or to the Qur'an as interpreted and supplemented by the Prophet ﷺ. Man cannot, however, surrender himself both to the will of God and to the voice of his own individual reason or conscience. In this sense there is a conflict between commitment to revelation and commitment to reason, or between faith and autonomy.

If one commits oneself to the Qur'an he will have to subordinate his own judgment to the Divine judgment in case of conflict between them. A conflict only shows that human reason is in error and is unable, for some reason or other, to comprehend the truth of the Qur'anic judgment. In all such cases the individual is very likely to realize his error, provided he sincerely and patiently tries to grasp the truth of the Divine judgment in question. The Qur'an is the literal revelation of God's will to the Prophet ﷺ, while the faculty of reason is the gift of God to all men. If properly used, reason also gradually brings us to the truths revealed in the Qur'an. In this sense there is no conflict between revelation and reason. Reason supports revelation.

The *Shariah* of the Prophet ﷺ is not only last but also perfect. Obviously new situations may always arise for which there maybe no specific provision in the *Shariah*, but in all such cases the Islamic jurists are competent to frame rules of guidance through analogical reasoning (*qiyas*) from the clear and specific provisions of the Qur'an and *sunnah*. In case no analogy be available, the jurists are competent to exercise their independent reasoning (*ijtihad*) without violating basic Qur'anic principles.

Fresh legislation may also be made to solve new problems with the help of the consensus (*ijma*) of Muslim jurists. It appears that this method is not in addition to the above two but is only a collective exercise of the procedures of analogical reasoning and independent reflection, and should presumably command greater authority than reasoning by individual jurists. This consensus of jurists, however, should not be confused with the democratic consensus of the Islamic community at large.

LIFE AFTER DEATH

The affairs of the Universe are under the full control of God Who allows men to exercise their free will up to a predetermined point of time. When the Hour comes, God would wind up the affairs of the cosmos. Henceforth God will not permit any defiance of His will. The freedom of will enjoyed by man will be withdrawn and the dispensation of Divine justice will commence. The contradictions of this life, which apparently belie or negate the rationality of the Universe and the supremacy of the moral law, will be removed through the unhindered operation of the omnipotence and justice of God.

The operation of Divine justice will lead men into either heaven or hell, according to their earthly record of good and evil. The Qur'an describes these two states, as if they were locales. Heaven is described in terms of shady gardens full of fruits, luxurious couches, and flowing rivers and inhabited by beautiful men and women. Hell is described as a furnace of raging fire, which consumes human logs. The occupants of hell are given fresh bodies to be burnt again and again by the flames. The drinking of blood and pus, etc., as a punishment is also mentioned. Muslims will ultimately get a place in heaven after suffering the penalty for their sins in this life. But atheists and polytheists will be placed in hell, though they will suitably be rewarded for their good deeds in this world. Those who believe in one God, but not in the Qur'an as the final revelation, and Muhammad ﷺ as the last prophet, will not enjoy the highest bliss of heaven, even though they maybe spared the worst regions of hell. In other words, their salvation will not be complete.

FAITH, MORAL CONDUCT, AND SPIRITUALITY

The highest virtue is Islam or '*iman*'. Consequently, even if a Muslim is ethically inferior to a non-Muslim he has a higher spiritual status and is nearer God than the non-Muslim. No matter how intellectually or ethically superior a nonbeliever (*kafir*) might be, his denial of God and the Prophet ﷺ cancels all his claims for a place in heaven. Even the most spiritually developed non-Muslim monotheist who does not believe in the prophecy of Muhammad ﷺ cannot attain the spiritual status of a Muslim. Whether such persons will be saved is controversial. According to some, they will ultimately be consigned to hell, though they will suitably be rewarded for their good deeds in this life. According to others, they will ultimately find a place in heaven after undergoing just punishment for their refusal to accept Islam. However, their position in heaven will be lower than that of the Muslims. According to some others, no human being can know the fate of such people.

Faith is incomplete without action in conformity with the sacred law (*Shariah*). The tradition places the greatest emphasis on regular prayers and fasting. The emphasis does not entail neglecting the value of good conduct in everyday matters (*muamilat*), though in practice Muslims usually do so.

Adherence to the *Shariah* is only the first stage of spiritual growth. To begin with, evil is avoided because of the fear of God. Fear of God may mean two things: fear of being punished by God, and fear of losing nearness to God. The first kind of fear is essentially fear of the loss of things or goods, be they of this world or of the next. The second kind of fear is the fear of loss of one's soul or of appreciation by God, without any consideration of the consequent loss of the first type. The first type of fear of God is ego-centered, while the second is value-centered. The first kind of fear is the fear of losing one's possessions, while the second is the fear of losing one's spiritual qualities. These fears may coexist in different degrees or proportions in the concrete motives of men. In Islam, as in all developed religions, fear of God, in the second sense, indicates a higher level of spiritual development, spiritual merit depending upon the relative preponderance of the higher kind of fear. In *Sufi* thought fear, in the second sense, merges into or becomes the love of God. The love of God gives rise to abiding concern for carrying out the commands of God, just as a lover is ever-eager to fulfill the slightest wish or even the whim of his beloved.

The next stage comes when the Muslim becomes interested in the education of his emotions and inner attitudes rather than in mere conformity to the *Shariah* or the external law. As long as he experiences a tension between his natural inclinations and the *Shariah* he realizes that he is not a true Muslim or *Momin* in the highest sense. This education of the emotions cannot, however, be enforced by any laws and external sanctions, just as true love cannot be produced in a person by any legislation or punishment. This growth can only be brought about through a regular and systematic training or education of the spirit under the guidance of a spiritual master (*pir o murshid*). This disciplined life is known as '*tariqat*'. We may say that while the first is the legal stage the second is the ethical stage. However, the full growth of the individual is completed only when he passes on to the third stage, which maybe called the spiritual stage (*haqiqat*).

At the spiritual stage the individual acquires true knowledge of God (*marifat*) which leads to the deep love of God. Such an individual has a mystical experience of God as the eternal Source and Preserver of value in the Universe. Other mystical experiences may also accrue. These experiences bring about a spiritual rebirth of the individual who is purified of all the dross of base passions, vices, or diseases of the soul. In *Sufi* language, this is the death of the ego (*fana*) and the permanent establishment of the Divine attributes (*baqa*). This does not mean the absorption of the individual ego into God but only his complete purification, leading to the removal of all tensions between his lower passional self (*nafs-e-ammara*) and the higher judging self (*nafs-e-lavvama*) and the establishment of the beatific self (*nafs-e-mutmainnah*). Such a person rejoices in his free surrender to God (*abdiyat*) and becomes the friend of God (*wali Allah*).

The *Sufi* path has several stages or stations (*manazil*) of growth through which the individual passes under the guidance of his spiritual director (*pir*). The *Sufi* discipline consists of austerity, litanies, and prolonged meditation apart from the usual obligatory discipline prescribed by the *Shariah*. Different *Sufi* orders differ in minor details only.

The stage of friendship with God (*wilayat*) is the highest stage, which a *Sufi* may reach by God's grace (*tawfiq*), after the advent of the Prophet ﷺ, who was the last and the greatest in the line of prophets starting from Adam. The status of the Prophet ﷺ, other prophets and saints, and matters dealing with angels, Satan, life after death, etc., are matters of esoteric knowledge (*ilm-e-batin*) as distinct from external knowledge (*ilm-e-zahir*). The Prophet ﷺ was the perfect teacher and guide who passed on esoteric knowledge to Abu Bakr and Ali, especially the latter. And *Sufi* orders, with the sole exception of the Nakshbandi, regard Ali as their founder. [41]

SOCIAL PHILOSOPHY

According to the traditional view, God created Adam and placed him in heaven to enjoy the blessings of celestial life. Later on, in response to Adam's desire for company, God created Eve. The two lived happily in paradise until Adam violated God's command by eating prohibited food. Adam and Eve were thereupon expelled from heaven to earth. But God promised to guide Adam and Eve and their progeny back to their previous state of celestial bliss. Those who followed the revealed Word of God would be properly guided in this world and achieve salvation in the next, while those who rejected the revelations of God would be doomed. Satan (*Iblis*) was, however, permitted to tempt Adam and Eve and their progeny, since without such temptation there could be no test of the inner moral and spiritual growth of the individual. Moreover, struggle and resistance against temptation are necessary for spiritual development. *Iblis*, therefore, is unconsciously and unwillingly collaborating with God in the un-foldment of His Divine plan.

The progeny of Adam and Eve gradually increased on this earth. In the beginning there was love and understanding in the small human family. But with the growth of numbers rivalries, jealousies, and conflicts emerged. The murder of Abel by Cain is a landmark in the story of man. The love of individual possession and the will to power led to mutual frictions and later on to the division of society into the rich and the poor. The existence of wealth or poverty is, however, not without the will or the permission of God, Who, had He so desired, could have made every one rich or poor. God ordains different individuals to be born in different strata of society in order to test the rich through their wealth and the poor through their poverty. Those wealthy persons who help the poor and needy for the sake of God rather than their own egotistic satisfaction find favor in the eyes of God. Those who are proud of their possessions and waste wealth through ostentatious expenditure incur the wrath of God, and will suffer in the hereafter. Wealth is a trust given by God to the wealthy to be used for the good of all rather than as a luxury for the few. Similarly, poverty is a Divine means for developing the character and testing the patience and faith of the poor. In life after death God will rectify any injustice that any individual may have suffered in this life.

Every individual who is born is actually sent by God as a part of His inscrutable plan in which every living individual (*nafs*) has been allocated his own share of provisions (*rizq*). God is the great Sustainer or Feeder (*Razzaq*) and provides sustenance to some in abundance while he straightens the means for others. Consequently, one should cultivate the virtue of contentment (*raza*) at his state, though he should not sit idle or abandon his trust in God (*tawakkul*).

Since God is not only the Creator (*Khaliq*) of the Universe but its wise, loving and all-powerful Sustainer (*Rabb*), man need not worry about such problems as overpopulation, crowding, unemployment, undernourishment, and poverty, etc. The concept of the voluntary control of population is not only unnecessary, in view of God being the Great Feeder (*Razzaq*), but is also useless. It is useless because man has no control over the number of souls sent into the world in accordance with the command of God (*Amr*). Try as we may, we can never interfere with God's plans and commands. Consequently, the number of mouths to be fed in each family and hence in the world at large is an issue in the hands of God rather than of man. Modern man is unwilling to have a large family because this involves sacrifice of his own comfort and share of wealth. His outlook is materialistic and he wants to enjoy his stay in the world as much as possible, since he is not certain of life after death. But those who are certain of life after death attach more importance to the afterlife, and do not mind the discomforts of this life. Hence, the problem of controlling the growth of human population does not trouble the believers at all.

God is not only the Creator of the Universe but is its Governor and Controller. Nothing happens without His will and His awareness. The course of natural events and the march of history are both under His firm grip. He, however, does not give immediate reward or punishment to His creatures, but allows the march of events to continue. Man does not know either the future or the purpose of God in delaying the administration of justice. This, however, does not mean that there is no purpose, law, or order prevailing in history. The Qur'an itself repeatedly draws our attention to the fate of nations who invited the punishment of God upon themselves on account of their blatant misdeeds and rejection of the messengers of God. But the general conception or view held by the Muslims is that the affairs of history are decided by the inscrutable will of God, Who gives victory or defeat according to His will. He does not necessarily grant victory to the Muslim. Instead of losing their faith in God the Muslims should ponder over their own weaknesses and shortcomings.

THE TRADITIONAL INSTITUTIONAL SYSTEM

According to the traditional view, the institutional system of Islam is perfect and satisfies every human need. The Qur'anic teachings, as interpreted and developed by the *sunnah*, provide the Muslim with an ideal code of life for all its facets. Consequently, there is no need of any change or reform in the Islamic institutional system. The evils that may exist in Muslim societies are due, not to any inadequacy or shortcomings of Islam, but to the defects and shortcomings of the Muslims who do not live up to the ideal of Islam.

To give a few examples, Islam has done full justice to the rights and status of women. Men are superior to women not only in physical strength but also in intelligence, wisdom, and courage, etc. [42] Moreover, women are economically dependent upon men, since temperament makes them fit only for maternal and household tasks rather than those requiring physical strength, intelligence, wisdom, or courage. Consequently, God has made a few distinctions between the civic rights and privileges of men and women. For example, daughters have been given half of the share of sons, and the evidence of two women is equivalent to that of one man. This, however, does not involve any injustice or discrimination against women since this difference is not arbitrary, but is a function of the genuine difference between the capacities and aptitudes of men and women.

The penal code of Islam is again perfect and, therefore, must be applied in all Islamic societies. For example, if the Qur'anic punishment of severing the hand of the thief were actually put into practice theft will become extremely rare, if not totally extinct. Similarly, the Qur'anic punishment for adultery is also the ideal punishment. Its implementation would eliminate this evil and bring about a true moral reformation of society. No other type of punishment could have the same powerful deterrent effect as public whipping for the foul sin of adultery. To suppose that men and women could ever-succeed in controlling their sexual behavior in the absence of such a drastic punishment is unrealistic.

The socioeconomic system of Islam is also perfect. Consequently, there is absolutely no need to turn toward either socialism or capitalism or any other man-made 'ism' to solve the common problems of mankind. Islam prescribes a balanced approach, which combines the virtues of all the different man-made ideologies without their vices. For example, the Qur'anic law of inheritance promotes social and economic equality through the wide dispersal of inherited wealth. Similarly, the wealth-tax (*zakat*) is a tax on wealth rather than merely on income, and has more far-reaching consequences than mere income tax. Furthermore, the functions of the '*bait-ul-mal*' were the prototype of the functions of a welfare state. Again the Islamic emphasis on social and political equality of all persons irrespective of their race, religion, or wealth is the greatest example of democracy and fraternity. Hence Islam has no need to learn any lessons from other religions or cultures. Indeed all others should learn from Islam.

The Qur'an prohibits interest. The practice of charging interest is the root of all economic evils and exploitation of the needy. The prohibition of interest cuts at the root of all socioeconomic evils. The socialistic or Communistic projects of nationalization of the means of production or the abolition of class privileges or unearned wealth, etc., are all quite unnecessary. And these man-made schemes create more evils than they remove.

It is true that Islam did not legally abolish slavery. But short of abolishing this institution, every effort was made to humanize it, and also to encourage Muslims to free their slaves. This institution was so deeply entrenched in the society of the period that a sudden abolition of the institution was not feasible. But the spirit of the Qur'an is categorically against the enslavement of man by man. Islam clearly and forcefully affirms that God is the only Master, and that the worth or value of an individual depends on nothing except his nearness to God. Hence the abolition of slavery in the 19th century by the Western world was in perfect accord with the spirit of Islam and the unsurpassable humanitarianism of the Prophet ﷺ, who had not only preached but practiced equality, providing the same food and clothes to his slaves as used by himself or his family.

Reasoning from analogy (*qiyas*) or the principles of equity (*istehsan*) and consensus (*ijma*) of the *ulema* on the basis of independent reflection (*ijtihad*) will jointly suffice to solve (within the basic framework of the *Shariah*) new problems or difficulties posed by novel situations in the onward course of human history.

THE MUSLIM'S SELF-IMAGE

The concept of self-image is applicable as much to groups as to individuals. Unless the members of a group learn to make the vital distinction between 'self-image' and 'observer-image', that is, how other observers view the group, the self-image is bound to remain pre-critical and rather lopsided. Attaching significance to the observer-image, however, does not imply its uncritical acceptance. The ideal is a balanced self-appraisal or self-interpretation in the light of reliable data.

The following self-image of Islam has been drawn from my own inside knowledge as a member of the group as well as from the actual writings of the established leaders of the group. The delineation of this image is illustrative rather than exhaustive.

1. Islam is one of the very few, if not the only religion, which is not named after an individual. The reason is that Prophet Muhammad ﷺ or any other prophet did not found Islam. Islam is merely the submission of man to God, and all prophets of God have preached this from the very beginning of time. Islam is the only religion that recognizes all other prophets and the truth of all other religions and scriptures. Islam is not a new religion, but an authoritative and final confirmation and completion of all previous religions. The message of the Qur'an is the same as that of all previous scriptures. It is unique only in the sense of being completely authentic, and hence it alone is fully reliable.

2. Islam is the only religion whose scripture, namely, the Qur'an, is fully preserved in the memory of numerous individuals. The Qur'an is the only scripture, which exists, in its original form at least ever since the first *Caliph*, Abu Bakr, who died only two and a half years after the death of the Prophet ﷺ himself. A scripture like the Bible is known to us only in the form of a translation from the original Hebrew into Greek. Similarly, the different *Vedas* or other scriptures of Hinduism came to be written down much after their original composition. Consequently, no scriptures can equal the Qur'an in the matter of authenticity. The Prophet ﷺ was very particular in committing to writing the verses of the Qur'an as soon as they were revealed to him.

3. Islam is the only religion whose Prophet's ﷺ life is known to us in such great detail. In other words, the life of the Prophet ﷺ possesses the greatest degree of historicity. The Bible contains numerous details about the life of Judaic prophets including Jesus. But it is very difficult to regard the Bible as a historical work. Similarly, the lives of the ancient heroes and spiritual leaders of India, such as Ram or Krishna, are not described in any historical works. The great epics of *Mahabharata* and *Ramayana* cannot be regarded as books of history. Gautam Buddha, however, undoubtedly possesses historicity. But the details of his life have not been as well-preserved or historically established as those of the Prophet ﷺ.

4. There are no superstitions or myths in Islam. Other religions contain stories concerning mythical heroes and their exploits. These heroes may or may not be historical figures. Even when they are historical, history and myth are so deeply blended that it is impossible to sift one from the other. Islam, however, is purely rational in its teaching. The Qur'anic stories about the very early prophets like Adam, and Noah (*Nuh*), etc., and even the details of the creation and fall of Adam and Eve are factually and literally true.

5. Islam is a universal religion meant for all people at all times. Consequently, the Qur'an consists of different levels of thought, which are suitable for people of different levels of intelligence. This is a great blessing and achievement of the Qur'an. Thus, for example, heaven and hell are described in physical terms for the person of ordinary intelligence and limited vision. For the philosopher or mystic the Qur'an promises the pleasure of the vision of God. The different levels of the Qur'an, however, do not imply any diversity in the basic principles or beliefs of Islam.

6. Islam has no official priesthood as some religions such as Christianity or Hinduism have. Consequently, it does not recognize the need of any intermediaries or professional priests to conduct religious ceremonies or fulfill religious functions at crucial life situations such as birth, marriage, prayer, death, etc. Any Muslim can perform the religious ceremonies associated with such moments. There are no ordained priests in Islam.

7. Islam is a very tolerant religion. The Qur'an specifically declares that there is no compulsion in religion. It repeatedly points out that the duty of the Prophet ﷺ was merely to deliver the message of Islam. The Prophet ﷺ was not sent as a guardian over men.

Members of different religious communities lived peacefully and honorably in Islamic states throughout the centuries. Their customs, religious institutions, and places of worship, etc., were as much sacrosanct as those of the Muslims. Non-Muslims occupied high posts and positions in the states and participated in trade and industry. They were called "*dhimmis*", that is, those whose security was the responsibility of the Muslims. The word "*dhimmi*" was not a word of abuse.

The "*dhimmis*" were obliged to pay a separate poll tax (*jiziya*). But this was only a substitute tax for those "*dhimmis*" who wanted to be exempted from military service, which was compulsory for the Muslims. It is significant that women and children among the "*dhimmis*" were exempted from "*jiziya*". This clearly shows the real nature of this much-misunderstood tax. The Muslims had borrowed this idea from Persia.

8. Islam has not only preached but practiced the ideal of the brotherhood of man. The Qur'an declares that most respectable among men is he who possesses religious piety. This approach destroys the myth of racial superiority, of distinctions based on caste, color, or religion. The only criterion of superiority or status is the degree of one's spiritual merit.

Christianity has also preached the fatherhood of God and the brotherhood of man. It is also true that Christians are found among all races of mankind. But the Christian Church has not been able to create the same degree of fraternity and sense of kinship among the Christians belonging to different races as has been done in Islam.

Hinduism not only believes in the fatherhood of God, but in the essential Divinity and unity of all living beings, including animal life. It should, therefore have resulted in an even greater sense of solidarity and oneness among not only its own followers but of the human family in general. But the actual practice of Hinduism has been surprisingly very different from its theory, as maybe gathered from the extremely strong and deep hold of the caste system on the Hindu mind. Thus no religion has promoted the ideal of human brotherhood to the same degree as Islam has.

9. Muslims have been very liberal in admitting their debt to other cultural traditions such as the Chinese, Indian, Greek, or Christian. When the Arabs adopted the Indian numerals they called them *"Hindsa"* after the country of their origin Similarly, they continued to call their own system of medicine as Greek or *"Unani"*, even though the original Greek system had been enormously improved upon due to the efforts of the Arab scientists. Muslim philosophers also paid the highest tributes to Greek philosophers especially Plato and Aristotle.

10. Islam does not preach asceticism. It has a very balanced approach to the various dimensions of the human personality or the needs of man. It is the only religion, which is fully practicable for all men. It does not degrade the physical needs of man like food or sex. The pursuit of the means of livelihood, marriage, and the procreation of children, are not only permitted as concessions to the flesh, but are regarded as the duties of a good Muslim, equally important as other religious duties. In fact, there is no distinction between the spiritual or the profane in Islam. Everything depends upon the motive (*niyat*) of the individual. All actions from prayer to entertainment can be performed in the spirit of devotion to and service of God. In such a case every moment of one's life maybe said to be spent in the worship of God (*ibadat*).

11. Islam has attached the greatest importance to social justice and to the promotion of a healthy and balanced collective life, in addition to the individual salvation of its members. Consequently, the Qur'an repeatedly exhorts the Muslims to pay the wealth tax (*zakat*), which was meant, for the poor and the needy sections of the people. The regular payment of *"zakat"* is one of the five pillars of Islam. The first *Caliph* attached such great importance to *"zakat"* that he actually waged war against those Muslim tribes who had refused to pay it. The institution of *"zakat"* was quite distinct from that of private charity. This shows that Islam has always been wedded to the concept of a welfare state from its very inception.

12. Muslims are the chosen people of God, just as the prophets are chosen individuals. God, in His Wisdom, chose Arabic to be the instrument of the propagation of "the Word of God" in every nook and corner of the world. This is the Divine mission with which every individual Muslim is charged. It is in this sense, rather than in the sense of enjoying special privileges or being immune from the laws of God, that Muslims are the chosen people. The Muslim will not be shown any favored treatment at the expense of other communities. It is precisely the task or the "burden" of the Muslim that constitutes his only claim to a special status in the family of nations. Should the Muslim neglect his duty God will not help him. The duty to propagate the Word of God, however, does not imply any forceful imposition of belief upon others.

13. Islam is perfect. Muslims, however, are not and it is Muslims rather than Islam that stand in need of reform. The concept of the reconstruction of Islam is totally invalid and is the product of aping Christian modernism. Christianity or Christian thought might have needed such reconstruction because of the alterations and corruptions that had crept into its Scriptures. But the Qur'an being incorruptible and infallible, Islam does not require any reform. Nor is there any conflict between Islam and science clamoring for reconciliation. The spheres of religion and science are entirely different. Religion deals with moral and spiritual truth, while science with material or physical facts. The conflict arises only when religion attempts to encroach upon the field of science, or science upon that of religion. But if science is used, as it should be used, for giving man technical knowledge or the means for attaining his basic values, as given by religion, then no conflict arises. Both religion and science are essential for the complete good life. Islam has always encouraged the cultivation and growth of every branch of knowledge. The Qur'an repeatedly exhorts man to ponder and reflect and also to observe the phenomena of nature. It also extols wisdom as a blessing of God. Similarly, the Prophet ﷺ exhorted the Muslim to treat knowledge like his lost property and to acquire it wherever he encounters it.

The social system of Islam is also perfect. Certain marginal changes maybe needed due to changes in the external environment and the posing of fresh problems. Such changes are desirable. Islam never stands in the way of such change as is amply shown by the example of Umar and others. The concept of independent reflection (*ijtihad*) is a recognized and integral part of the Islamic tradition. This *ijtihad* must, however, be subject to the authority of the consensus of the religious scholars (*ijma*).

14. Islam is a complete code of life in all its varied aspects. There is no distinction between the religious and profane or secular spheres of life. Consequently, there is also no distinction between civil and religious laws in an Islamic community. Islam, in all its completeness and fullness, can exist only when the Islamic code of life acquires the force of law. Otherwise only the "*deen*" or the basic principles of Islam could be followed on an individual basis. The full flowering of Islam presupposes the enforcement of the *Shariah* in all its ramifications. Consequently, it is a religious duty of the Muslim to see that the state is run according to the *Shariah*. In other words, if the state be an Islamic state (*dar-ul-Islam*), the Muslim must work for the enforcement of the *Shariah*. Where the state is non-Islamic, but where Muslims are permitted to live peacefully and allowed to believe in and practice their religion (*dar-ul-aman*), they should try peacefully to convert the majority of the people to Islam. Thus, in either case, the Muslim is deeply concerned with the establishment of the *Shariah* or the peaceful creation of conditions for its eventual establishment.

15. Secularism, in the sense of a clear distinction between the sphere of religion and other spheres of human life such as politico-economic, legal, scientific, etc., represents an entirely different approach from that of traditional Islam. But the denial of secularism must not be misconstrued as the denial of tolerance. Tolerance can coexist within an Islamic theocracy. In fact, the long history of various Islamic states is notable for good will and tolerance toward non-Muslims.

CHAPTER 3

A RESTATEMENT OF THE ISLAMIC THOUGHT SYSTEM

I

INTRODUCTORY REMARKS

The concrete interpretation of the basic concepts and values of Islam or any other religion should remain a matter of continuous reflection. The search for truth can never be completed. Religious faith or commitment should not preclude attempts at fresh interpretations of its thought-cum-value system. The Qur'anic verse *'This day have I perfected for you your religion'*, by no means implies a closed and static approach on the part of the Muslim as regards the concrete understanding of basic Islamic concepts and values.

According to the traditional conception, God is the Creator, Sustainer and Beneficent Lord of the Worlds, ever-concerned with the welfare of His creation and responding to the supplications by His creatures. Several features of the Universe suggest and support this conception. The earth is a part of the solar system, which is characterized by mathematical proportions between the orbits of the various planets. The movements of the sun, moon, and planets, etc., have been predictably regular for millions of years, the cycles of the seasons and of night and day have been going on for millennia. Similarly, the structure of the atoms and molecules of different elements, the cells composing different organisms, the intricate ecological balance between the different spheres of nature, the amazing complexity, adaptiveness, and creativity of the human organism, etc., are extremely difficult to account for as products of mere chance. The contemplation of the above and similar other phenomena strongly suggests that the Universe is the product of a grand design or purpose, which in turn presupposes a Being with purpose as one of its attributes or qualities. Even if a purpose of the Universe is not accepted, it is undeniable that the sequence of events is not at random, but in accordance with ascertainable laws.

THE CONCEPT OF GOD

The traditional concept of God is a very understandable and reputable interpretation of the law and order and prima facie design in the Universe. At the same time, there are a number of other features of the Universe that pose serious difficulties in the way of the traditional theistic interpretation as, for example, the fact and extent of pain and evil in the Universe, the data of biology and geology, etc. We shall now examine these difficulties. In the end we shall deal with some crucial semantic problems posed by the language of religion.

DIFFICULTIES RAISED BY PAIN AND EVIL IN THE UNIVERSE

According to the traditional conception, God is the all-powerful Creator Who ever-showers infinite love and mercy upon all His creatures. But the question arises: Why do His creatures experience prima facie unmerited suffering and why is there so much evil in a Universe created by an all-powerful and loving God? Some examples of prima facie unmerited suffering are: **(a)** ghastly accidents killing or mutilating innocent individuals, infant mortality and premature deaths; **(b)** diseases, epidemics or natural calamities which cause untold suffering to human beings; **(c)** psychological traumas which impair the normal human personality; **(d)** insanity and other severe mental diseases that deprive the individual of his rational faculties and render him a lifelong burden upon society; **(e)** congenital diseases and monstrosities such as Siamese twins, dwarfs, and giants, etc.; **(f)** the suffering of the underprivileged and suppressed sections of society due to social evils or moral vices like exploitation, corruption, and prejudice, etc.; **(g)** the suffering of innocent persons due to chance errors and miscarriages of justice, etc.

Now either God permits all the above instances of suffering or these instances occur against Divine will. The first supposition contradicts the love and mercy of God, while the second supposition contradicts the power and wisdom of God. It appears that, unlike Christian theology, Muslim theology has not come to grips with this serious problem. Buddhism and Hinduism do not face this problem in the same sense, because they accept the working of an impersonal moral law (*karma*) instead of the theistic creation and governance of the Universe. If suffering be the effect of causes, even as the cosmic process is subject to inherent laws, the presence of pain and evil ceases to be a riddle. The only question, which arises, is how to conquer suffering rather than how to explain or interpret evil. Prima facie the concept of *karma* eliminates the riddle of pain and evil, but the concept is not entirely free from some difficulties of its own. I shall, however, not pursue this matter in this work.

Let us now briefly examine how traditional theism solves or attempts to solve the problem.

One of the earliest Christian attempts to explain the presence of evil is Saint Augustine's thesis that evil is only the absence of good and has no independent or objective existence, just as darkness is the absence of light, or death is the absence of life. [43] A little reflection, however, makes it clear that this argument is invalid for the simple reason that the analogy does not hold in the case of pain and evil. Pain is not merely the absence of pleasure but a concrete experience with innumerably different specific features. The absence of pleasure is not necessarily pain, since an organism might remain in a neutral state. The same remarks apply to good and evil. Evil has its own varieties and specific features in different cases, and the sheer absence of good is not evil, unless some of the specific elements of disvalue be present.

Another very common explanation is that suffering and pain constitute Divine punishment meted out to man for his own misdeeds. But there are numerous cases of the suffering of innocent people, for example, inherited diseases, and epidemics, etc. To say that the people who suffer are not really innocent but only appear to be so (due to limitations of human understanding) does not solve the difficulty. Who, for example, could honestly and seriously doubt the innocence of the newly born baby unless, of course, one subscribes to the theory of rebirth?

Another attempted justification of prima facie unmerited suffering is that God tests the faith of the individual. But when God is all-knowing He has no need to test individuals who are transparent to their Creator. Moreover, testing in the absence of proper training and education is not just. Now it can hardly be said that all those who suffer have been given proper training in the graceful and serene endurance of suffering. Sometimes children have to endure hardships and pain which, instead of being a fair test of their endurance or faith, actually destroy their basic capacity for happiness and fill them with abnormal inhibitions, fears, or complexes which are difficult to remove for the rest of their lives.

Some theologians hold that God educates and develops the individual through suffering. But this attempted justification also breaks down. Firstly, God, being omnipotent, could have brought about human development without pain and suffering. Even if it is conceded that some frustration or suffering is logically necessary for human growth, the actual quality and quantity of suffering might have been less destructive. For example, many loathsome diseases and excruciating pains may conceivably have been absent from the Universe. Moreover, in many cases, instead of having an educational value, suffering leads to the degeneration of character, insanity, and suicide. Furthermore, in some cases of extreme suffering any improvement of the individual is *ipso facto* ruled out by the very nature of the case as, for example, congenital idiocy, lunacy, and total paralysis, etc. The view that such suffering is meant to promote the moral growth of others is obviously untenable, since this would imply that God uses some individuals only as a means for the good of others.

Some religious thinkers differentiate between different sources of human suffering, for example, natural causation, logical necessity, and human free will, etc. They say that analysis of the sources of suffering puts the problem in its right perspective.

Let us first consider natural causation as the source of suffering. Suppose a relief party is sailing upstream to rescue a trapped group of children. Assuming that speed is the essence of the rescue, the relief party would suffer from the compulsion of having to move upstream, and suffer still more if the wind be unfavorable. But would they be justified if they took this compulsion of moving upstream as an argument against God's supreme power or love? After all the river must flow in one direction or the other, and greater effort must be expended for moving upstream than downstream. The wind may or may not be against the rescue party since the direction of wind is never fixed. But the very moment the wind might be hindering the rescuers it maybe helping a doctor rushing in the other direction to reach a patient in a critical condition. The wind cannot blow in two different directions at the same time, just as a surface cannot be red and blue at the same time. This case of suffering is rooted in the logical and causal nexus of the cosmos. We are free to wish that causality and logic had been absent and that the cosmos had been a chaos of atoms dancing without any pattern. But this would have meant still greater rather than less suffering. Like the rule of the road, the causal nexus enlarges our freedom and our satisfactions.

Similarly, the suffering whose source lies in free interpersonal relationships cannot be said to contradict the love and power of God. For example, a person whose love is not returned or who is betrayed by a good friend cannot infer that either God is not all loving or not all-powerful. Love, and loyalty, etc., presupposes freedom of individual response, and it is absurd to demand that the all-powerful Creator should force a person to be loyal or return the passionate love of a sincere lover. In the same vein, suffering whose source lies in undesirable macro social patterns; poverty, cruelty, racial or religious hatred, distributive injustice, and corruption, etc., does not prove that God is either indifferent to human suffering or unable to remove it. These social evils flow not from Divine dispensation, but from man's freedom of response to his fellow men.

The question arises, why should man have been granted freedom, to begin with, since God must have foreknown the consequences. This is the crux of the problem of suffering arising from the operation of man's free will.

If freedom of the will be logically necessary for realizing an intrinsic value, the evils introduced by human freedom will not erode either the goodness or the power of the Creator. If, however, free will were not logically necessary, yet a perfect Being (who was all-good and all-powerful) used it as an instrument for realizing the intrinsic value concerned, this would imply an inner contradiction in the behavior of the Perfect Being, or imply that the Being was either not all-powerful or not all-knowing. Moreover, even if free will be logically necessary, why should a perfect Being endow his creatures with evil propensities of such variety and intensity as to facilitate the abuse of freedom and the generation of unmerited suffering in the Universe?

It seems to me that the following position is internally consistent: The goodwill in the Kantian sense is the highest value after the Holy Will or the Self-Existent God. The evolution and existence of the good will logically, and not merely factually, presupposes free will just as mathematical reasoning logically presupposes the cognitive dimension of consciousness, and aesthetic enjoyment logically presupposes the emotional dimension. It is, therefore, logically impossible for God to foster the growth of the good will without first granting free will to man. Now man as a finite creature abuses his free will and inflicts suffering on his fellow men. God has the power to stop this suffering through canceling man's free will, but not the power of granting free will to finite man and simultaneously canceling the logical implications of the operation of free will in finite and fallible creatures. In other words, tolerance of error and evil, for some time at least, is also a logical implication of granting free will to man. That, which is logically necessary for realizing the highest intrinsic value, after God Himself, does not erode either the love or the power of the Supreme Being.

Omnipotence does not mean the power of violating logical necessity; it only means freedom from the constraint of the causal nexus or factual necessity. Man cannot alter facts and their interrelations without first submitting to natural laws, which are not of his own making but are given to him. But an omnipotent being has no need to submit to factual laws, which He can change at will. It is this power rather than the power to violate logical necessities, which is the valid meaning of omnipotence.

Similarly, Divine love for His creatures does not mean spoon-feeding and wiping tears but rather providing the conditions for the promotion of intrinsic values and their qualitative and quantitative growth in the Universe.

The above line of thought appears to be quite valid at the level of abstract speculative thinking. The moment, however, we examine the concrete human situation, two insuperable difficulties arise which seem to erode the traditional theistic interpretation that God loves and cherishes every single creature, and that it is not God but man himself who creates moral evil through the abuse of his free will.

The first difficulty is that there are countless cases in which the conditions, both internal and external, for the growth of the human personality are miserably lacking. The internal conditions refer to the psychological endowment of the individual or his inborn personality structure, and the external conditions refer to his environment, both physical and social. There can hardly be any doubt that if Divine love means the provision of the conditions for the growth of the human personality, countless individuals, from Adam downwards, have been tragically deprived of Divine love due to the poverty or peculiarities of their psycho-physical endowment. On the other hand, many who had been favored in this respect were mysteriously denied suitable time or environmental conditions for realizing their rich potentialities.

The second difficulty is that even if man be free in his essence, men in the concrete sense are not actually free, but are in the grip of their irrational impulses or their environmental pressures. Man maybe potentially free, but men are not born free, and have to earn their freedom through an arduous and sustained apprenticeship. But then how many get this opportunity in life?

Let us briefly clarify the concept of human freedom just as we earlier clarified the concepts of Divine omnipotence and love. Human freedom is not caprice or license but self-determination of his responses. Since, however, his self is not merely the rational self but also the irrational libidinal self, his actions are partly rational and partly irrational. Sometimes the individual succeeds in subordinating his irrational drives to the control of his reason. At other times the irrational drives get the upper hand and the gentle voice of reason is drowned in the surging waves of his powerful drives. Man is only partly in command of his impulses, and no two men are alike on this scale of rational self-control. Man is potentially free in the sense that he could increase the relative dominance of his rational self over his irrational drives without, however, completely eliminating them, since their complete elimination would make man superhuman, even as the complete elimination of reason makes him sub-human. In other words, man is potentially free, but this does not mean that men in the concrete are actually free.

Thus the suffering whose prima facie source lies in human free will, ultimately flows from the irrational drives, which are an integral part of man's self as much as his rational, moral, and artistic endowment. The traditional view that social evils flow from man's abuse of his free will, points the accusing finger at his freedom (which is only potential and which is actualized only to a very limited degree) and ignores the irrational drives which are clearly not of his own choosing or making. If, and when, the irrational forces completely dominate man's rational self, we judge him to be insane, to be treated as a patient rather than condemned and punished as a criminal. But are not all of us sometimes, to some extent at least, the victims of irrational drives whose demoniac force overwhelms our free will and reason?

Take the case of a man who has an abnormal appetite, or anger or sex drive, or jealousy, or an abnormally strong need to dominate, or be loved. His sufferings will be due not to the free will of others or natural causation or logical necessity, but to the actuality of his psycho-physical endowment, which he neither asked for nor deserved as a penalty for his actions. The sufferings of a person consumed with jealousy, hate, or vengeance are far more pathetic than sufferings whose source lies in external factors. Such a person is hardly aware that the source of his suffering and the source of his hostility to others (resulting in their suffering) lie in his own self, which could have been differently structured without violating any logical necessity. That his self is what it is, and not different, is his existential pathos or the tragic contingency of his concrete being.

It is significant that Christian theologians, who have gone the farthest in attempting to solve the problem of pain and evil, eventually confess their inability to solve the riddle. They accept that it is impossible to solve the riddle of evil and also of prima facie unmerited suffering unless we have full knowledge of all facts, including eschatological facts and since this is impossible in this life, the rationale of evil and of suffering can never be understood by us in this life; even if we could know all the facts, including eschatological ones, our finite minds will never be able to comprehend the wisdom of God in creating or tolerating pain and evil.

This reaffirmation of the sense of mystery, in the face of pain, evil, and tragedy, may be called the existentialist response to the problem of evil, as distinguished from the rationalistic justification of the ways of God. In the final analysis, the riddle of pain and evil in the Universe remains unanswered by Christian and Muslim thinkers alike. Whether or not Muslim theologians turn out to be wiser than their Christian counterparts for not even initially attempting to solve the riddle, I leave to the judgment of the reader.

The upshot of the above analysis is that when, by the very nature of the case, no interpretation of the presence of pain and evil can be confirmed by us, either deductively or inductively, the grounds of assent must shift from provability to something else. As is well-known, William James opted for pragmatic utility as a valid ground of assent or criterion of validity, but somehow his approach has not worked and has left us rather cold toward it. [44] The only acceptable ground for assent to an existential interpretation of the basic features of the Universe can be the authenticity of the individual's response to the mystery of the cosmos.

Now many highly sensitive and noble souls are so profoundly impressed by the tragic dimension of life that the talk of Divine solicitude for every single creature appears to them as a case of wish fulfillment and pious sentimentality, rather than a realistic and courageous acceptance of the plain fact that the welfare of individual organisms (human, animal, and vegetative) is ever at the mercy of situational factors.

Let us, in conclusion, consider the case of a young girl who is brutally assaulted by a psychopath who soon afterward dies in an accident. It is reasonable to hold that if the girl had not come across the psychopath at the time she did (this being a sheer coincidence), probably the girl would have been spared the ordeal, which turned her into an emotional cripple for life. This and similar facts do not clinch the issue whether God loves and cherishes each individual. Nevertheless, this and similar facts do not suggest or evoke the traditional view of God as the all-powerful and all-loving Father. If the girl comes to reject this view and her rejection is not rooted in anger, bitterness, self-pity, or despair, but rather flows from the depths of her serene authentic being, her existential response to the mystery of the Universe cannot be treated as a perverse generalization from her own experience, or as satanic defiance of God or as spiritual blindness. Like the traditional view, it too is an existential interpretation of the amorphous significance or mystery of the plain observed facts of life; birth, growth, decay, death, tragedy, and joy, etc. And the measure of its truth (which can only be truth for a particular person, that is, subjective truth) lies in the degree of the authenticity of the individual's response to mystery rather than its pragmatic utility or verifiability.

THE DIFFICULTY RAISED BY THE CONCEPT OF EVOLUTION

According to the theory of evolution, the entire solar system and all the different species of organic beings have gradually evolved over the centuries from the same primordial stuff. This view contradicts the traditional religious conception that the entire furniture of the Universe and the different species were instantaneously created by God's command. According to the traditional view, God said let there be light and lo! There was light.

When the theory of organic evolution was seriously mooted by Darwin in the second half of the 19th century, Christian theologians just rejected the idea as preposterous or absurd. But as the concept gained ever-wider acceptance and respectability among scientific circles Christian theology had to come to terms with the concept. Gradually the concept was incorporated into or reconciled with Christian theology through the mediating idea that evolution is the Divine method of creation. It was said that creation by God has been evolutionary rather than instantaneous. Now apparently, this reconciliation is quite satisfactory. But a little further reflection leads to difficulties. The question arises why should an all-powerful Creator adopt the evolutionary method of creation. It may be said that there is no essential contradiction between omnipotence and gradualistic or evolutionary creation, just as an airplane, capable of a maximum speed of 1,000 miles per hour, may deliberately be flown by the pilot at 200 miles per hour due to some reason or other. According to this line of thought, God is quite capable of instantaneous creation. But He, in His wisdom, has preferred the evolutionary pattern of creation. The finite human mind can never question the wisdom of the Infinite Mind or understand God's purposes.

The above explanation is; however, very unsatisfactory since gradualness is only one of the features of the evolutionary process. There are several other features such as blind alleys, mutations, enormous waste, biological strife, and built-in ecological destruction, etc., and these features do not suggest or prima facie support the view that the Universe is the product of a supreme and all-loving Creator who loves and cherishes the welfare of the meanest of His creatures. [45]

Biology shows that the world of nature is not like a garden where species engage in cooperation and friendly competition under the tender care of guardian angels all glorifying their common Creator. Biology tells us that the world of nature is more like a battle-ground where all manner of species are engaged in a fierce and ceaseless struggle to get enough food for keeping them alive and reproducing themselves. Not only this, one species literally consumes the other as its normal diet. The tiger cannot survive without destroying the ox, the wolf without destroying the lamb, the larger fish without destroying the smaller. Finally, man cannot survive without destroying living organisms of one type or the other. The intra-species rivalry between different individuals is no less intense, so that nature is literally 'red in tooth and claw'. The cry of the dove for succor and help against the attacking hawk is literally a cry in the wilderness and vastness of nature. This built-in predatory feature of life does not harmonize with or evoke the worldview or picture of different species having been created by a loving Creator. It rather suggests the natural evolution of the species without any Divine solicitude for any particular species or individual.

But the biological features mentioned above do not disprove the creationistic view. Just as the theist claimed to reconcile gradualistic creation with his belief in an omnipotent God, similarly the theist could claim that biological strife is also a part of the inscrutable Divine plan. The sordidness and callousness man finds in nature is only due to man's fragmentary perspective on the Universe. If man could know all the facts, including those that could come to his knowledge only in life after death, the rationality and goodness of the Divine plan would become clear to man.

As remarked earlier in connection with the problem of pain and evil, no one interpretation can claim to be logically coercive or compelling. There is no denying the fact that our factual knowledge, for all its probity into the secrets of nature, is like knowledge acquired through a pinhole. It remains logically possible that pain and evil in the Universe are transient features, which have a function in the total economy of Divine Creation, which, in the language of Leibniz, is the best of all possible worlds.

It is also possible that there is no moral order in the Universe apart from natural law, which also might be a passing phase, for all we know. It is also possible that there is an impersonal moral law or power working for the promotion of truth, goodness and beauty, apart from man's own weak and halting striving for values, but that the objectives of the supreme impersonal power are different (though not totally disparate) from our own. All these different interpretations or attitudinal perspectives are available to us. What is crucially important is not which interpretation we profess or verbalize, but which interpretation really evokes our authentic commitment. Whenever the issue cannot be clinched either due to the data being insufficient or due to the inherent non-verifiability of the truthclaim (as in the case of an ultimate value judgment or an existential interpretation), the grounds for assent must shift from provability to authenticity. Now many highly intelligent, moral, and sensitive souls cannot authentically accept as a liberating truth the traditional religious interpretation of a personal Creator, who works for the individual welfare of all sentient beings with a love infinitely exceeding the fondest mother's love for her infant. The above interpretation appears to them to be a source of personal assurance and ego fortification in the task of facing the stresses and storms, trials and tribulations, frustrations and disillusionments of life. Be this as it may, this much is certain that belief in a personal God is immensely facilitated by the semi-obscure antecedent conviction that a personal God is a postulate or presupposition of optimistic life affirmation and striving by the individual.

The powerful and universal impulse of life affirmation on the one hand, and the above conviction on the other, jointly facilitate the choice of the interpretation of a personal God, since it is deeply felt to be most conducive to optimistic life affirmation. If, however, we transcend the natural human concern with one's own life affirmation and develop an active and authentic concern for collective welfare (which, however, includes one's own), we need not have an emotional investment in believing in God's special solicitude for one's personal welfare. We then cease to adopt a defensive or justificatory approach to the strife and suffering, callousness, and calamity in the world of nature, and are able to choose an authentic existential interpretation of the diverse observed features of the Universe. Let me give an analogy which appears irrelevant at first sight but which, I think, is singularly illuminating. Suppose a married woman is pondering whether to tolerate or leave her husband with whom she has been unhappy. If she is economically dependent and dreads the prospect of being thrown upon her own resources it would be more difficult for her to understand and accept her innermost inclinations than if she were free to decide without any financial compulsions. In like fashion, it is only when the individual becomes aware of his emotional dependence on, or investment, as it were, in the traditional notion of God and outgrows his half-defensive thinking into a spontaneous receptivity to the joys and sorrows, beauty and sordidness, harmony and strife, pattern and chaos in the Universe, that he can afford to plumb the depths of his authentic attitudes and choose an authentic existential interpretation, whatever it may happen to be.

THE DIFFICULTY RAISED BY SEMANTIC CONSIDERATIONS

All statements referring to God contain words and expressions of ordinary language used in the normal human context. Without being aware of what we are doing we apply the same words or expressions in a non-human context of which we have no experience whatsoever. For example, theists assert that God creates, rewards, disapproves, punishes, and guides, etc. Now all these verbs are obviously meaningful in normal human contexts. A child observes his parents or teachers when they are pleased and reward him, or are angry and punish him. Similarly, the child knows what it is to be guided by teachers or parents. The child also experiences the making of things out of raw material. But the child has no experience whatsoever of these different activities in any other context. When, however, he comes across religious statements containing the same expressions, he inevitably and quite understandably attaches more or less the same empirical meaning to them. Very often this generates problems and confusions, which the child readily brings to the notice of adults. The elders laugh away the logical blues of the child. The adults say that either the child is too small to grasp the truth or that the child is confused. But the truth of the matter is that adults are no less confused, and if they do not pose ridiculous questions concerning God, it is not because their ideas are clearer than the child's, but rather because they have lost the natural curiosity of the child, having become accustomed to ambiguity, opaqueness, and self-contradiction without feeling any logical pangs.

The traditional conception of God as Creator, Governor, and Judge, and the traditional conception of God's acts such as loving, guiding, punishing, testing, creating, commanding, revealing, raise numerous difficulties when these words are used in their plain ordinary sense.

For example, we say God has made the Universe. Now we all know that making an object presupposes the material out of which the object is made. Naturally, therefore, the further question arises; who made the raw material of the Universe? Now if we say that God made the primal matter out of nothing we retain the verb 'made', but cease to use it according to the agreed rules of ordinary language. But if we are asked as to what are the new rules for using the verb 'make' or 'create' in the context of God-statements, we are unable to specify them, for the simple reason that we have no experience either of making something out of nothing or of watching a magician literally doing so. Thus the expression 'creation out of nothing' remains an empty phrase even though it is neither logically absurd like the expression 'round square', nor meaningless like the expressions 'blue intelligence', 'quadratic equations are brittle', or 'creation flaw ice'.

Let us examine another instance of using the words 'nothing' and 'combine' in a new sense in the metaphysical context. We know what it means for water to 'combine' with tea leaves to produce tea; or for hydrogen and oxygen to 'combine' to produce water; or for two armies to 'combine' to defeat a common foe; or for self-interest to 'combine' with genuine ideals to produce the complex motivation of human beings. But do we really know or even presume to know what it means for the Platonic 'Idea' to 'combine' with 'Non-Being' to produce material objects such as tables and chairs or horses and cows?

The proper use of language requires a body of definite rules prescribing when, or under what conditions, it is proper to use a particular word or expression; in other words, when a particular statement is true or false. Unless such rules operate, our use of words will never be free from confusion and controversy, and the language game will not be played smoothly as it should. Let us consider some concrete examples. We say 'the teacher rewarded John for his good conduct', or 'the teacher punished Jane for her being naughty in class', or 'Mrs. Sinha loves her husband', or 'Mrs. Sinha is loyal to her husband but loves Mr. Sharma'. Now in all the above cases it is clear how to find out, whether or not the above statements are true, and even if we don't know whether they are true or not, we know what would be the case if they were true, and what would be the case if they were not. In other words, there are definite rules for using the above expressions just as there are definite rules for card games, chess, or cricket. But when we use ordinary expressions or words in the context of God-statements such as 'God loves all His creatures', 'God punishes sinners', 'God made the world', 'God guides the honest seeker of truth', 'God feeds and sustains His creatures', there seem to be no such rules in operation. If, for example, a father permitted the stronger among his children to mercilessly beat or even to mutilate their weaker brothers and sisters, or if a father gave all his assets to a favorite son who was a rotter, leaving his other children to starve and die from curable diseases, the rules of our ordinary language would prohibit us from applying the expression, 'the father loves all his children' to this particular gentleman, say Mr. Sultan. Now it is God Who wills that the tiger kill the ox, and the wolf kill the lamb for his food, it is God Who wills that animals devour plants. Yet the rules of the language of God-statements do not prohibit us from saying 'God loves, feeds, and sustains every single creature as no mother could love and care for her child'. Similarly, even when Mrs. Ahmad meets with a tragic accident or is raped (and we know that she was an excellent woman and, for the life of us, cannot accept that she has been punished for some secret vices or sins), we go on saying that God loves and protects every single creature. Again, when we find that an honest and intelligent person is unable to believe in his traditional religion in spite of his arduous search for the truth and prayers to God for guidance, we still use the expression 'God guides the honest seeker of truth to Islam/Christianity', as the case may be. If we were dealing with human actions and using expressions in their ordinary sense we would not be permitted to use the above expressions in the face of such contradictory states of affairs. Whenever we assert a factual statement or make a value judgment, we entertain a set of expectations. If we say 'Mr. Sinha is honest' or 'Mrs. Sinha is loyal', we expect a determinate pattern of responses or events in the universe of discourse. But if we were to assert the statement 'Mr. Sinha knows Sanskrit pretty well' but did not know whether or not to expect that Mr. Sinha would understand a simple poem by Kalidasa, then we would be using words without understanding them or without any clear rules of use. This is precisely the case with the God-statements so frequently used by traditional theists. It appears that traditional theists, unknowingly, commit what may best be called the 'fallacy of contextual transference', whenever they refer to God's qualities, attributes or acts, apart from the bare notion of some supreme Being or Reality. It is an illusion to think we understand ordinary expressions used in a trans-empirical Divine context. The illusion is partly due to the grammatical correctness of the expressions and the bewitchment of our intelligence by language analogies, as pointed out by Wittgenstein. This, however, does not imply that God-statements are meaningless or nonsense.

It has been claimed that the 'transferred' use of ordinary expressions, originally used in the human context, involves the analogical or metaphorical uses of language. But this theory of religious language, though prima facie plausible, does not bear scrutiny. Metaphors are indeed the standard type of discourse in poetry. The metaphor enables the poet to convey his feelings in a striking and economical manner and also gives keen aesthetic pleasure to the reader by stimulating his imagination. This is why the pleasures of poetry far exceed those of prose, which usually employs plain and straightforward description. But trouble will immediately arise if the metaphorical description is intended to be an objective factual one. This is the precise difference between the traditional theist and the poet. When, for example, the poet says that leaves are flying in the autumn wind as if 'from some magician fleeing', or that 'stars are diamonds studded on the robe of night', or when we say that 'technology has conquered space and time', we are aware of using figures of speech. We concede there may be a thousand and one other and even more apt metaphors than our own. The theist, on the other hand, claims his description to be 'the' true description of Reality, and also claims that its denial amounts to the rejection of truth. Thus, he views his statement 'God created the world out of nothing' not as the projection of one among many possible metaphors but as the awareness of an objective metaphysical fact. According to the theist, the cognition of this basic fact is more like cognizing a logico-mathematical or factual truth than appreciating the aptness of a poetic metaphor or the beauty of a work of art.

Religious knowledge is ostensibly factual. But if it be really so, there must be definite rules for using the expressions involved. But as pointed out above, these rules are not to be found. The semantic difficulty with the traditional conception of God may be summed up as follows: If God-statements are adjudged as metaphorical, we distort the intention of the genuine theist; if God-statements are adjudged as factual, we distort the rules of ordinary language without specifying new rules for using ordinary expressions in religious contexts.

The analogical theory of religious language also does not remove the difficulties of traditional theism. An effective analogy gives the hearer illuminating insight into a situation in a manner beyond the reach of ordinary descriptive language. But this can only happen if the analogy is strong, if not perfect or almost so. Now the analogies between human actions such as creating, loving, rewarding, and punishing, etc., and corresponding Divine acts are so imperfect that they are only analogies in name rather than in substance. The moment we take the analogy seriously by trying to discover the parallelism or isomorphism between the two sides of the analogy, it breaks down; and to resurrect the analogy we have to qualify it. This has been termed by a British philosopher as *'the death of the analogy by a thousand qualifications'*. [46]

The traditional talk about God, His attributes and acts is thus shot through with ambiguity and is not governed by agreed semantic rules. Neither the rules of factual discourse nor of metaphorical discourse are fully applicable to God-statements. This, however, does not imply that religious talk should be rejected as either nonsense or useless. But it does imply that we will be gravely misleading both ourselves and others if we go on talking about God and His acts without first caring to understand the functional logic or rules of valid use of religious discourse involving God-statements. But having done this, we can use statements such as 'God has made the Universe', 'God is beneficent and merciful', etc., without any danger of entertaining expectations that are belied by our actual experience.

The above semantic critique of traditional theism also implies that our conception of God should not be equated with God as He is in Himself or with Ultimate Reality. This is precisely the mistake made by most if not all-traditional theists whose conception of God is, patently or latently, anthropomorphic. This leads to difficulties the moment we juxtapose the actual observable states of affairs, both in nature and in history, with the expectations flowing from believing God to be all-powerful, all-loving, etc. Perhaps the best approach to God is the wordless receptivity to the mystery of the macrocosm and the microcosm. But, if conceptualize man must, it seems to me that the concept of God as a *Value Elan*, immanent in the heart of the Universe and also transcendent, relative to all finite persons or things, is free from the above fallacies and also accords with our actual experience and well-established concepts of science.

THE ELAN CONCEPTION OF GOD

Darwin claimed to have explained the emergence of developed organisms from simple ones without importing the concepts of purpose, design, creation or God. It may appear as if Darwin's conceptual scheme does not require any other assumption apart from that of ceaseless variation and natural selection. True, there is no logical impossibility in this explanation, provided we assume an already considerably differentiated cosmos, consisting on the one hand of organisms that displayed this trait of ceaseless variation, and on the other of the natural environment that performed (mechanically and non-purposively) the function of selection or preservation. As a biologist purporting to explain the phenomena of an immense variety of living organisms, Darwin was completely within his rights to assume this stage or setting for the operation of the law of natural selection. But how did the cosmos evolve up to the point at which Darwin's theory becomes plausible? In other words, what were the mechanics or dynamics of the origin of unicellular organisms themselves or, going still further back, the origin of organized matter or of the various elements and their ultimate constituents, according to the latest scientific theory? When we attempt to employ Darwin's theory as a universal and absolute explanatory formula or principle its limitations emerge. As a limited theory or hypothesis of organic evolution, it does its job satisfactorily, but as a general theory of cosmic evolution, it breaks down. It breaks down because it fails to account for the enormously differentiated cosmos prior to the emergence of the first unicellular organisms. It fails to 'interpret' the 'law' of ceaseless variation. Why is there, after all, this ceaseless variation rather than ceaseless stagnation or fixation? Assuming that the 'hitherto ultimate' of science is the electron or proton, why did not this 'state of ultimacy' continue, instead of the electrons and protons combining to form atoms or molecules of the various elements? Similarly, how was the function of natural selection performed at the very remote undifferentiated phase of cosmic evolution when the electrons and protons evolved into atoms and molecules, and non-living matter into the living organism? Was there no driving force or rationale, as it were, behind this gigantic evolutionary process?

According to the *Elan* Conception of God, this fact of ceaseless change is not a brute datum or just a contingent or accidental ultimate, but is rooted in or springs forth from a *Value-Elan* or *Nisus*, which is eternally and universally operative. Without this *Elan* the cosmos would have been a static and ossified X, no matter what the primal nature of X may have been. This *Elan* is the Divine discontent, or the aspiration or quest for the perfect, and it supplies the fuel for the motor of cosmic evolution. In man this *Elan* is more or less consciously felt and registered. But at pre-human and non-human levels of existence it operates without being registered. It is this *Value Elan* that is called God in the language of religion, which, however, attributes to this *Elan* many other features, which may or may not be acceptable to the critical and mature believer.

This eternal *Elan* toward goodness or value is embedded in the heart of all things from the elemental or primal nebula, star dust (or whatever science may establish as the primal stuff of the cosmos) to man, as the highest known product of cosmic evolution. Whether this *Value Elan* is ontologically separable or inseparable from matter is both insoluble and a fruitless query. The significant point is that the aspiration toward value or rather perfection is inseparable from the concretely real at all stages or points of its spatiotemporal history.

This *Elan* gently guides the individual toward goodness or makes him seek value and avoid disvalue. To begin with, this *Elan* is intertwined with the 'conditioned conscience' of the individual human being and reflects the value system of the group. But the 'conditioned conscience' has the potential of developing into the creative conscience of a unique bearer of this *Value Elan*. Unfortunately, the vast majority of individuals fail to actualize this potentiality and remain more or less fixated at the level of the conditioned conscience, which is the same as Freud's 'internalized censor'. Many philosophers, under the influence of contemporary anthropology, social psychology, or psychoanalysis, hold that conscience is nothing but a dignified version of the pleasure principle rather than the Divine spark in man, as religious or mystical minds are apt to believe. It is held that conscience or the moral sense is a social product or the fruit of the socialization of the individual. But this approach misses the crucial point that the concept of value as such, as distinguished from the concrete value system of an individual, is not the product but rather the condition of 'cultural conditioning'. The concrete content of a value system is certainly the product of such acculturation or socialization, but the concept of value, however undifferentiated and undeveloped it may be, is included in the original 'psycho-physical endowment system' of every individual. Even an one hour old baby functions, as if it had a system of values, albeit very simple ones; warmth, nourishment, and security, etc. But the point is that the phenomenon of preference is present even here; indeed it is co-extensive with all life.

As we move from higher forms of life to the lower, the dimensions of value correspondingly shrink until they are reduced to the pursuit of physical pleasure and the avoidance of physical pain and ultimately nothing more than the mere instinct of self-preservation. If we go still further down the evolutionary scale even this instinct tends to disappear and all that remains is the tendency of a body to remain in motion or at rest unless acted upon by some external cause. We cannot apply the words 'instinct' or 'urge' to this tendency, unless of course we enlarge the ordinary meaning or use of the words 'instinct' or 'urge'. But equally obviously the tendency of a natural material system to retain a given equilibrium or its structural-functional constancy does have a parallelism or isomorphism with the instinct of self-preservation or the organic integrity of a living system. If so, we may well say that the generic non-specific concept *Value Elan* applies not only to the operations of 'instinct' or 'purpose' of living beings but also to the 'tendencies' of the so-called inanimate bodies or systems. The conception of Divine immanence may then be regarded as a religious formulation of the primacy and universal presence of this *Value Nisus* from the electron to the solar system, and from amoeba to man himself.

According to the '*Elan*' conception, the Universe is not the creation of a transcendental Creator God out of nothing. Nor is the Universe reducible without remainder merely to a configuration of eternal matter in motion, which is explained by the laws of physics and chemistry. The Universe is a multi-layered or multidimensional emergent due to the creative activity of the primal and eternal *Value Elan* embedded in the heart of things, that is, operative in all the natural structural-functional systems in the Universe. This *Elan* conception of the cosmos is neither theistic, nor deistic, nor naturalistic, nor materialistic. It is *sui generis*, though it may have points of contact with all the above approaches. This conception cannot be called even energism or vitalism like the philosophy of Bergson or Shaw, since the *Elan* is viewed not merely as a perennial source of energy or growth, but also as the highest good in the sense that it is the basic *ontic* condition of the emergence of all subsequent concrete values. [47] So viewed this *Elan* evokes in man a sense of mystery and awe, since its status is not merely that of *ontic* primacy but also that of the Supreme Evocator of values in nature and history. In other words, the First Cause also becomes the Source of all value, and in this sense, the Highest Good. The contemplation of the *Value Elan*, as the source of all values in the cosmic process fills us with wonder and the sense of obligation to listen to its authentic promptings.

The *Elan* conception of God removes the various difficulties generated by the traditional view, for example, the problem of suffering, instantaneous creation, and anthropomorphism, etc. The *Elan* is not the Divine counterpart of a human creator. Nor is the emergence of value-bearing objects (such as stable natural elements, living organisms, etc.) the analogical counterpart of human productivity. The *Elan* conception refuses to project any concrete attributes such as omnipotence, knowledge, volition, love, and mercy, etc., on the bare notion or concept of the *Elan* as such. Hence the problems of suffering in a Universe created by an omnipotent and loving God, or the problem of reconciling the theological conception of instantaneous Divine creation with the scientific conception of evolution does not arise. The concept of *Value Elan* resembles Rumi's and Iqbal's concept of an immanent urge for self-expression and growth as a Divine gift which brings about the evolution of the cosmos from lower to higher forms of existence.

GOD AS THE PERSONIFICATION OF THE VALUE ELAN

As pointed out earlier, the conditioned conscience of an individual is the product of his socialization. With the emergence of the creative conscience the person touches a new dimension of morality. When he relates his creative conscience with the *Primal Value Elan* (with which he attunes himself through meditation) he touches the dimension of spirituality. Now numerous sages who are widely separated in space and time and profess different faiths testify that this attunement becomes far more fruitful when the *Value Elan* is personified as a *'Holy Thou'*. This personification generates an interpersonal *I-Thou* attitude toward the immanent Elan, and molds the character and conduct of the individual. The personification is thus an existential response, as distinguished from the aesthetic response of a merely poetic personification. Existential personification is a symbolic procedure for deepening the communion between the individual and the Value Elan, and not an interpretative concept like *'Value Elan'*, which refers to man's actual self-awareness or inner experience.

The validity of an existential personification cannot be judged in the same way as the truthclaim of a cognitive statement or the aptness of a poetic metaphor or the validity of an existential interpretation. An existential personification is a spiritual act whose justification should be sought in the quality of the inner life of the individual rather than in any procedure of verification or justification. If the personification maximizes the individual's receptivity to the *Value Elan* and reinforces man's fidelity to the *Elan* in the face of external threat, temptation, and tragedy, this justifies the personification. Reinforcement could also result from auto-suggestion, hypnosis, and drugs, etc. But none of these can equal the beneficent effects of spiritual communion with the Value Elan, personified as the *Holy Thou*. This *I-Thou* communion is a loving submission and spiritual prayer for guidance and grace, rather than for specific boons or favors. Its beneficial integrative effect is thus much deeper and more permanent than could ever be brought about by other means.

Personification should, however, be permissive rather than obligatory. Should the individual feel no authentic urge to establish an *I-Thou* relationship, no intellectual or moral objection could be raised, provided the individual be receptive to his creative conscience. The crucial requirement of spiritual well-being is active receptivity to the *Elan* and not its personification, even though the *I-Thou* relationship is most conducive to spiritual growth. The permissive rather than the obligatory approach to the personification of the *Value Elan* reconciles the impersonal conception of God with the personal without claiming that this or that conception is the only true one. [47] If it is realized that the function of belief in a Personal God is primarily onto-genetic, that is, the evolution or enrichment of spiritual being rather than onto-*Noetic*, that is, knowledge of ultimate being, it ceases to matter whether the individual believes in a personal God or in an impersonal Source of values. However, it seems to me that the concept of a personal God performs the ontogenetic function more effectively, since men are at times liable to be overwhelmed by the surging waves of irrational and self-destructive impulses. In such moments man's yearning for truth, goodness, and beauty is consumed in the fire of an agonizing alienation from the depths of his inner being. The interpretation that God is the immanent and impersonal Source of all values seems to break down leaving the individual at the brink of a shattering disillusionment at the impotence of an impersonal God to deliver him from the raging fire or the surging waves of his irrational impulses. Belief in a personal God comes as a soothing balm to such a person as an inner necessity when he is hemmed in by suffering, despair, and inner collapse.

The desirability or admissibility of personifying the PVE (*Primal Value Elan*) does not imply that a person who is unable or unwilling to personify the *Elan* is on a lower moral or spiritual plane than the person who does so. Spirituality does not depend upon one's conception of God but rather upon the authenticity of being. To say that God is a super-Person is quite different from living in His presence as a super-Person. It seems to me that those who do not personify the *Elan* but are receptive to its promptings stand on a higher spiritual plane than those who believe in a personal God but are alienated from Him in practice. Similarly, those who do not accept the concept of the *Primal Value Elan* but act as if this were the case are on a higher spiritual plane than those who affirm the *Elan* without proper action. [48]

It seems to me that many persons who formally deny God nevertheless do have an unarticulated faith or optimism in the conservation of values in the long run. Now to the extent that this optimism is not merely *de facto*, but somehow or other derived from some inherent features of the Universe, such persons unknowingly imply that the Universe is something more than a mere blind dance of atoms. If so, even a dialectical materialist who accepts that higher levels of being will continue to emerge should have no methodological difficulty in affirming the *Primal Value Elan*, which, as an avowed existential interpretation, is not a substitute for any scientific explanation. The concept of the *Primal Value Elan* reinforces man's unarticulated conviction or faith in the conservation of values and thus intensifies his search for perfection. It does this job not by appealing to any external authority, blind faith, philosophical or scientific reasoning, mystical experience, but by reflection upon the cosmos and man's quest for value.

It is, however, not claimed that the concept of *Primal Value Elan* or its personification suffices to resolve the mystery of being. Every effort to reduce its mystery to a conceptual scheme, rooted in either science or philosophy or mystical experience, founders at the unfathomable depths and complexity of being. Man may experience the *Value Elan* but he cannot claim to understand the nature and working of the PVE. However, the quest for value does strike me as the most illuminating and apt interpretation of the Universe, even as the image of effulgent light strikes man as the most apt physical symbol of God. In the final analysis, mystical silence is the only proper response to the mystery of being. This silence is, however, not the same as intellectual agnosticism or philosophical doubt, but an existential surrender to the mystery of being.

The concept of mystical silence is partly similar to Ibn Hazm's concept of 'faith without knowledge' (*iman bila kaif*) and the Asharite doctrine of metaphor and transcendence (*tashbih wa tanzih*). The Asharite theologians steer a middle way between the anthropomorphic conception of God and pure transcendentalism, according to which human conceptions are totally inapplicable to God. Complete silence concerning the Divine attributes makes the conception of God totally vacuous, and the word 'God' not only loses its cognitive but also its emotional significance and directive function. The middle way means affirming the attributes of God without affirming their mode of inhering in God, for example, saying that God creates, loves, and guides, etc., but in a way we can never know. The Asharite theologians called this approach '*tafwiz*', which literally means delegation, and in this context implies the delegation of right knowledge about God to God Himself.

It may be thought that the difference between Asharite '*tafwiz*' or mystical silence and agnosticism is merely verbal. But this is not the case. Agnosticism has the same practical result as the denial of God's attributes or even His existence. But the middle way leads to analogical knowledge or a *Noetic* base, if not knowledge proper. This in turn leads to the practice of meditation on the Divine qualities or beautiful names of God (*asma ul husna*) mentioned in the Qur'an. This in turn makes the believer partly assimilate those qualities. The analogical knowledge of God thus has an ontogenetic function rather than the *onto-noetic*. [49]

The ontogenetic function of belief in God is not to be confused with the psychological utility function; providing solace and a sense of security to the individual. The ontogenetic function refers to the growth of ethical and spiritual values such as love, compassion, and veracity, etc., and the removal of negative elements from the psyche such as fear, hatred, and malice, etc. Obviously spiritual catharsis leads to improved psychological health as its by-product. Likewise, the ontogenetic function cannot be equated with the ethical, understood in the sense of an external morality.

Sufism also affirms the principle of '*tafwiz*' and most *Sufi's* emphasize the sense of mystery and the inadequacy of their knowledge of God despite their mystical experience (*kashf*) of the hidden realities, though some speculative *Sufi's* do make sweeping claims of spiritual status and of esoteric knowledge of celestial beings and events. This implies that these *Sufi's* are familiar with the ways and purposes of God. This appears to be highly improper, and many sober *Sufi's* too disapprove of such practices.

Speculative *Sufi's* also claim absolute truth for their metaphysical or cosmological theories, for example, the theory of the five stages of the differentiation of the Absolute Unity of Being, according to Ibn Arabi, or the stages of descent or emanation from the Supreme Being, according to Farabi and Ibn Sina, etc. [50] In the light of contemporary meta-philosophy, all such theories are plural conceptual schemes or language games which serve to reduce the multiplicity of the world to a systematic unity, and not 'the' objectively true description of Reality, as was held by the speculative mystics or philosophers of Islam. The bewitchment of philosophers due to linguistic reasons is understandable as pointed out by contemporary linguistic philosophers. But why should the mystics have been bewitched, since they claimed to grasp reality through direct experience (*kashf*)? In the final analysis, all claims of gnosis to know God and of reason to prove God commit the 'naturalistic fallacy' of reducing faith in the unseen to objective or logical certainty. It does not matter whether the validation of faith is sought through mystical experience or through reasoning. Both approaches confuse the dimension of faith with the dimension of knowledge. According to the existentialist approach, both the metaphysical and the mystical approaches to God reflect man's craving for objective truth or verifiable knowledge as distinct from the truth of authentic subjectivity. This approach thus agrees with Abu Bakr's who stresses faith rather than knowledge or gnosis, acknowledging mystical silence and surrender as the proper response to the mystery of God. [51]

The above approach, however, may over reach itself by completely abandoning the role of reason or of direct experience available to man. Man thus seems to face two dangers; the danger of reducing faith to knowledge and the danger of field isolation and fragmented thinking without any connecting windows. Ibn Arabi and others like him must be given due credit for attempting to overcome field isolation, while Shaikh Ahmad and others like him for warning us against assimilating faith to knowledge.

THE INTERPRETATION OF THE SURAH FATIHA

The *surah Fatiha* is said to be the mother of the Qur'an (*ummul Qur'an*). It is indeed the essence of the Qur'an, which may be said to be the *Fatiha* writ large. Azad devoted the entire first volume of his great *'Commentary on the Qur'an'* to the simple seven verses comprising this foundational *surah*, which is the essential part of all Islamic piety and (properly understood) has a universal appeal. The *Fatiha* deals with ontology, eschatology, and ethics and is a marvel of utter simplicity and deep spirituality. In what follows I attempt to interpret the seven verses in the light of the *Elan* conception of God. I trust this interpretation will help clarify and develop the conception of God as the Primal Value Elan, which is immanent in the Universe and transcends every finite existent.

The *surah Fatiha* runs as follows:
In the name of Allah, the Beneficient, the Merciful.
Praise be to Allah, Lord of the Worlds,
The Beneficient, the Merciful.
Owner of the Day of Judgment,
Thee (alone) we worship; Thee (alone) we ask for help.
Show us the straight path,
The path of those whom Thou hast favored;
Not (the path) of those who earn Thine anger
Nor of those who go astray.

Verse 1: We rightly praise persons or things for their good qualities. But to the extent that they owe these qualities to external factors such as heredity, environment, chance, etc., the person or thing cannot claim absolute praise. Absolute praise is irresistible wonderment and wordless surrender to the ultimate Source of all the concrete values in the Universe. This absolute praise is due only to the *Value Elan* immanent in every particle or cell composing the Universe, and is rightly called the Lord of the worlds, in the language of religion.

The Lord of the worlds is not a patriarchal father who rules over his children according to his inscrutable wisdom, a tribal overlord who rewards the believers and punishes the unbelievers, an impartial constitutional king who may, however, grant mercy petitions at his discretion, a supermathematical architect who leaves the governance of the created world to impersonal mathematical equations, or a super magician who creates out of nothing. The Lord of the worlds is also not electro-mechanical energy that moves the cosmic machine, or vital energy that animates and moves the cosmic organism, but rather the mysterious Spiritual Pulsation, which fosters, sustains, and develops the elements of value in the Universe.

As physical bodies attract each other, as the moth is impelled toward the flame, as the sexes are impelled toward each other, as the human spirit is impelled to seek truth, goodness, and beauty, so does every particle and cell of the Universe reverberate with the passion for the conservation and growth of value. This holy passion for value is, however, not a separable transient and accidental process that emerged in the cosmic scene at some point of time, and may (for all we can tell) wither away in the future. The passion or quest for value is rather the inherent and inseparable dimension of the eternal cosmic process as time is inseparable from space. The atoms and molecules of stable elements that have evolved out of the elementary particles or cosmic dust (or whatever the primal stuff, according to science), living organisms, consciousness, self-consciousness and all other individual values together with their concrete spatio-temporal instances may come and go, but the primal *ontic* quest for value, as the eternal Ground and Source of all individual values, goes on forever.

The *Value Elan* is not concerned with the preservation of any concrete instance of the different values but only with their maximum promotion, irrespective of the concrete bearers of values on the cosmic scene. The traditional belief that God loves and cherishes every single individual creature infinitely more than the fondest mother could ever-love her infant dignifies as well as fortifies the ego, but ignores those features of the Universe which suggest a different existential interpretation.

Verse 2: The conservation and promotion of value constitutes the mercy and beneficence of the Elan. But the greatest mercy and beneficence of the

Lord is to enable man to create values—physical, moral, aesthetic, logical, and scientific, etc., which no other species can do. This requires providing the eternal conditions for man's creation of value that is, the presence of law and order in the Universe through universal causality. Causality thus becomes the key instrumental value.

Verse 3: The operation of universal causality, however, does not mean any limitation on the supreme power of the *Value Elan* to generate and promote individual values and their concrete instances to an infinite degree. Man can achieve his aims only by submitting to causal laws, which are given to and not created by him. The *Value Elan*, on the other hand, remains supreme, since causation, as an instrumental value, is itself the emergent product of the operation of the *Elan*. The supremacy of the *Value Elan* does not mean or require the negation of causality but only the ultimate and irresistible transformation of disvalue into value.

The crucial question arises as to why disvalues exist or survive despite the supremacy of the *Value Elan*. This is the well-known problem of pain and evil. All religious answers fall into two broad types; monistic and dualistic. The monistic thesis is that evil is God's instrument for the realization of value. Hence what appears to be evil, or is evil in the short run, works for the maximization of value in a way, which does not become transparent to the finite reason of man. The dualistic thesis asserts that good and evil are both primeval and in mutual conflict. Good will, however, eventually destroy evil. Thus evil is transient while good is eternal. The *Elan* conception of the God is neutral with respect to the above theses, since, no matter which interpretation be accepted, it is the ultimate victory of good over evil or the conservation and accretion of value that constitutes the essence of the supremacy and beneficence of God.

Verse 4: We rightly respect men who have power, goodness, and knowledge, etc. But we cannot worship them or surrender our own free judgment to them since no human being can be infallible. Only the Supreme Perfect Being can be worshipped. Worshipping is, as it were, the melting of one's ego and the willing abdication of one's self-affirmation, the 'dying of one's self to God'.

Worship is not merely a transient emotional state or condition but rather an ever-present disposition to act as an integrated person upon the promptings and pulsations from the depth of one's authentic being, unmindful of one's surface inclinations and desires.

Reliance upon natural laws governing the course of nature or reliance upon mutual cooperation and help of fellow human beings are essential for human life. But this reliance is qualitatively different from the help, which one may seek from the Supreme Being whom one worships. This is spiritual or existential help, which differs from the different forms of natural help; physical, technical, and financial, etc. Neither form is a substitute for the other. The primary function of existential help is not the achievement of any particular desire but the attainment or preservation of the spiritual quality of life; equanimity, integrity, and faith in the face of frustration, temptation, tragedy, and despair. This state of mind is called 'grace' in traditional religious discourse.

Moral help and exhortation also aim at the same result but they prove fruitful only if the individual's conscience is spiritually responsive. Moral stimuli are like seeds that need a fertile soil for their growth, and only Divine grace promotes this spiritual fertility. Grace is not like food or water administered from outside but an inner quickening of the spirit that leads to the stillness and peace that passeth understanding. Like the fragrance of the flower or the light of the sun, grace emanates from the deeps of the individual whose ultimate unfathomable depth is God; the immanent Value Elan.

Verses 5-7: The socialization of the child takes place in the family and the child naturally acquires the ideas and norms of the group. Later on his wider environment and experience foster his own individuality. He strives to do what is good and to avoid what is wrong. But though his intention be good his judgment is often confused, so that he errs without knowing he is wrong. In other cases his judgment of values is valid, but he is tempted into evil. Man ever-remains weak, and though his will may become good, it can never become holy, that is, above temptation, and his thinking can never become free from error. Perfect self-knowledge and self-control are only ideal limits rather than realized states, and not even the greatest of the great can claim never to have slipped from the straight path due to temptation or error or both.

To know and follow the straight path is the greatest achievement by man and also the greatest reward by God, since without Divine help man cannot accomplish this difficult task. Worldly rewards may or may not fall to the lot of the rightly guided person, since they depend upon situational factors and are by no means the test of the quality of the inner life of the individual.

Man must ever-seek Divine grace through reaching out for the ultimate depth of his authentic being rather than seek boons and favors from God. Man must seek Divine help for following the right path and avoiding the wrong; the path of those who have gone astray and evoked the wrath of God. Divine wrath does not refer to anger rooted in frustration of desire, since God is above frustration and also retribution in the human sense. Divine wrath refers to the temporary alienation of the wrongdoer from the depths of his Divine core, that is, his loss of Divine grace. A person who is alienated from this Divine core is like a fish in a waterless sealed container surrounded by water. Alienation from his Divine core or the loss of his inner integrity is the supreme penalty for going astray, and man must ever-seek to remain a whole and integrated being.

II

THE CONCEPT OF REVELATION:

DIFFICULTIES IN THE TRADITIONAL CONCEPTION OF REVELATION

The traditional conception of revelation has already been described. Let us now point out the intellectual difficulties inherent in this conception.

(i) The Arabic word for revelation, '*wahy*', as used in the Qur'an is a general word meaning 'suggestion' or 'hint' and has been used in a variety of contexts. The Qur'an uses the word '*wahy*' to refer to God's guidance to animals or birds, presumably in the form of animal instinct. The Qur'an also applies '*wahy*' to the slightly veiled remarks or gestures employed by the hypocrites in their dealings with the Muslims. The Qur'an contains some other uses of the word as well. Now, the exact sense of '*wahy*' as applicable to the Qur'an is obviously different from the above senses of the word. But we cannot understand this exact sense in the absence of any personal experience of '*wahy*'. Under these conditions, any theory or conception of '*wahy*' is bound to commit the fallacy of contextual transference—the fallacy of transferring words, understood in one context, to another context in which no clear meaning could be given to the words in question. It may be said that the Qur'an does indicate the mode of revelation. For example, the Qur'an refers to the various ways in which God has spoken to or guided man. Some possibly authentic reports or sayings of the Prophet ﷺ also purport to describe the mode and nature of revelation. But all these descriptions suffer from the same fallacy. The traditional conception of revelation is thus not at all clear.

(ii) The traditional conception of revelation is a corollary of the traditional Islamic conception of God, and both are anthropomorphic. Just as a king prefers to communicate with his subjects indirectly through a messenger rather than directly in person, similarly, it is held God communicated through Gabriel. This implies that God so completely transcends man that there is no possibility of any direct communion or communication without the mediacy of a third person who is neither man nor God. Since God is omnipotent, He could have communicated with prophets directly. Why then did He not do so? If it be said that God's majesty and glory do not permit Him to communicate directly with His human creatures, then the angels are also the creatures of God, and according to the Qur'an itself, their status is lower than that of man.

(iii) Authentic biographical records of the Prophet ﷺ show that he was completely mystified and bewildered by his early mystical experience or moment of revelation in the cave of Hira some miles away from Mecca. He returned home in a shaken condition and asked his spouse to wrap a blanket round his body, which was trembling. His dear wife, Khadijah, consoled him and said that he should not feel afraid of his experience in the cave, since his peculiar condition was not due to any disease or the work of any demon but was a sign that he was a prophet of God. It is also reported that she subsequently took the Prophet ﷺ to her cousin, Waraqa, who was a reputed Christian sage. On hearing the full report and also in the light of his intimate knowledge of the unimpeachable integrity and nobility of Muhammad ﷺ, Waraqa also concluded that Muhammad ﷺ was a genuine messenger or prophet with whom God had communicated through Gabriel. Waraqa's ready confirmation of Khadijah's interpretation greatly assured the Prophet ﷺ about the genuineness of his mission as a messenger of God.

Reports further say that soon afterward there was a complete cessation of the Prophet's ﷺ mystical experience and that he received no revelations for a period lasting from about six months to two years. During this period the Prophet ﷺ was rather unhappy and depressed at the withdrawal of God's favor in the form of revelation. However, the process of revelation started once again after this temporary break and continued right up to the end of the Prophet's ﷺ life. ⁵²

The above traditional account and conception of revelation is full of intellectual difficulties. It implies, firstly, that the original idea that Muhammad ﷺ was a genuine prophet emanated from the Prophet's ﷺ wife and was subsequently confirmed by Waraqa. But if God be accepted as omnipotent and Gabriel as a reliable and intelligent intermediary of God, it was Gabriel who should have adequately prepared the Prophet ﷺ for this tremendous responsibility or task. Moreover, in view of the great love and nearness between God and the Prophet ﷺ, as mentioned in the Qur'an itself, why was the Prophet ﷺ put to considerable suspense and suffering during the two year's stoppage of revelation. A similar difficulty is met with when, much later on, there was no revelation forthcoming for almost a month or more, during which time the Prophet ﷺ was profoundly disturbed and anxious about the truth or otherwise of a charge levelled against his wife, Ayesha. Perhaps the suffering of Ayesha was greater still. Since, however, Ayesha was very dear to the Prophet ﷺ, and equally dear to her father, Abu Bakr, who was himself the dearest companion of the Prophet ﷺ, the question arises why was there so much delay in God's revealing the truth about the integrity of Ayesha, when the withholding of the truth was the source of such profound suffering to the Prophet ﷺ and his near and dear ones?

The delay in the revelation of the verses exonerating the Prophet's wife from the malicious charge in question certainly goes to support the utter and unqualified integrity of the Prophet ﷺ in claiming that he was not the author of the Qur'an. But the delay certainly does raise the problem of justifying the unnecessary suffering of the Prophet ﷺ and others concerned.

The difficulty caused by delay in revelation to the Prophet ﷺ is matched by the difficulty caused by the onset of the revelatory process all of a sudden in a somewhat odd or inconvenient situation for the Prophet ﷺ, for example, when he was in company or in the middle of some work or even relaxing. On the traditional theory of revelation, it is difficult to account why God or His intermediary, Gabriel, chose such an inconvenient moment for communicating with the Prophet ﷺ, since God, as the omnipotent Being, must have known all about the situation of the Prophet ﷺ. **(iv)** Another difficulty, which arises on the traditional conception of revelation, is that there was no uniformity in the mode of Divine revelation to the Prophet ﷺ. For example, according to the traditional view, sometimes Gabriel appeared before the Prophet ﷺ in human form, sometimes in his original angelic form, while at other times the Prophet ﷺ only heard Gabriel reciting the Qur'anic verses without seeing him. At other times the Prophet ﷺ had yet another type of auditory experience resembling the sound of the ringing of bells. This variety in the modes of God's communication with the Prophet ﷺ raises the problem whether or not these different modes of revelation had the same epistemic status. *Prima facie* those revelatory episodes in which Gabriel was both seen and heard acquire higher epistemic validity or status.

(v) Why did God allow previous revelations or Words of God to get corrupted? Either God did not prevent the corruption, or could not prevent the corruption. In either case it is impossible to defend His omnipotence and benevolence. If it is said that He allowed the corruption to take place because the revelations were after all either temporary or provisional, unlike His last revelation to Prophet Muhammad ﷺ, then why was this distinction made between the prophets? It may be said that God's early revelations were adapted to the needs of immature men, and were not meant to be universally applicable, and since the Qur'an was revealed much later and was intended to be universally applicable, God has and ever-will protect the Qur'an from all corruption; this is God's own promise in the Qur'an.

This argument is, however, invalid, since the general maturity of humanity at the advent of the Prophet ﷺ was basically the same as at the time of Moses, Abraham, Jesus, Buddha, or Socrates.

(vi) Many foundational issues concerning the form of economy, the theory and practice of government, and rules and regulations for corporate living are either not mentioned in the Qur'an, or their treatment is very incomplete, when other matters, of much less or merely local importance are given much fuller treatment, such as the procedure of imprecatory oaths, etc. Consequently the social and political ideas of the Qur'an do not seem to provide comprehensive guidance to man.

(vii) According to the traditional conception, Gabriel is the intermediary between God and the Prophet ﷺ. The Qur'an, therefore, must have been first communicated to Gabriel for onward transmission to the Prophet ﷺ. Now did God communicate with Gabriel with words or without words?

In case God did not employ words, the Word of God is really the word of Gabriel. In case God employed words or language, the language must have been guided by rules of grammar, syntax, etc. What was the language in which God communicated to Gabriel in the first instance? If it was Arabic, then the Arabic language becomes unique and acquires a supernatural status, while others remain only natural languages whose vocabulary, grammar, and syntax have gradually evolved. But this singling out of Arabic from the family of human languages is clearly contradicted by philology. Philology clearly shows that all languages including Arabic have evolved as a result of man's interaction with his environment and the mutual impact of different languages upon each other. Consequently, the Arabic of the Qur'an, namely, the Arabic in vogue in Mecca and Medina in sixth-seventh century A.D., was as much a natural cultural growth as, say, Persian, Greek, or Chinese, etc. Now if God communicated with Gabriel in Qur'anic Arabic, then God used the rules of grammar and conventions of man-made Arabic.

Now there is no intellectual difficulty in the view that God employed human conventions of language while communicating with His human creatures. If the Prophet ﷺ had been born in China, we can safely assume that the Qur'an would have been revealed in Chinese. Again if the Prophet ﷺ had been born in South Arabia, the language of the Qur'an would have been slightly different from the actual Arabic employed, namely, the Meccan style of Arabic. These implications, however, go against the traditional conception, probably first formulated by Asharite theologians, that the Qur'an is eternal, and uncreated. How can an eternal and uncreated Qur'an use Arabic vocabulary and syntax, which are evolutionary products, according to philology? No wonder the keen speculative minds of the Mutazilite theologians were led to make the explosively controversial distinction between the eternal spirit of the Qur'an and its temporal Arabic form or expression.

(viii) The traditional conception of revelation implies an authoritarian ethic and character structure for the pious Muslim. To the extent that the injunctions or the commands of the Qur'an do not conflict with one's own authentic attitudes or moral judgments, no difficulty or conflict is generated. But, if there be any disparity between the two, then the traditional conception of revelation clearly implies that the Muslim must abdicate his inner freedom at the altar of an absolute and unqualified submission to the Word of God. For example, the Qur'an says that Muslims should not befriend Christians or Jews. Now should literal obedience to this command be judged as unreasonable by the contemporary Muslim believer, what should he do if he is not satisfied with mere lip faith, but wishes to mold his life after the Qur'an? The traditional conception of revelation makes a rational solution of this difficulty almost impossible, even though great efforts have been made in this regard by Muslim theologians.

During the lifetime of the Prophet ﷺ revelation was a continuing process and a particular command or set of commands revealed in a particular situational context (*shan-e-nuzul*) could be qualified, modified, or superseded by a new command in the face of situational changes. Such qualifying or modificatory commands were actually revealed a number of times. For example, the later verses concerning alcoholic drinks modified the earlier verses. Again, the later verses concerning the relation between the Muslims, Jews, and Christians, or the permissibility of intermarriages modified the earlier verses.

After the total cessation of revelation modifications or changes in the Qur'anic injunctions are *ipso facto* ruled out. But situational changes will obviously occur, since change is the law of nature. It cannot be rational to suggest that all the changes that possibly could have occurred actually did occur during the twenty-three years of the Prophetic mission, and that God has already provided for all these changes. Now if any further changes are called forth by the situation, an obvious deadlock is reached, if we accept the traditional view of Divine revelation.

The traditional solution of the above difficulty is first to make a distinction between those commandments of the Qur'an which are absolutely binding, irrespective of time and place, and those commandments whose validity is dependent upon contingent facts; next, to ascertain the situational contexts in which the latter type of Qur'anic commandments were revealed. Shah Waliullah has actually followed this procedure in his approach to Qur'anic exegesis. This approach is prima facie reasonable and helps to keep open the Islamic legal or institutional system. But this procedure involves intellectual difficulties, if we consistently adhere to the traditional conception of revelation.

The main difficulty, which arises is that, the Qur'an itself does not make any distinction between the universally or eternally binding commands on the one hand, and the temporarily binding commands on the other. To put it simply, the Qur'an does not distinguish between eternal and temporary bindingness. The Qur'an does distinguish between verses, which are clear imperatives, and those, which have a metaphorical significance. The Qur'an also mentions or implies the distinction between historical or factual verses and verses used as parables for exhorting mankind. But the distinction between verses, which contain permanent injunctions, and those that contain temporary injunctions is nowhere mentioned in the Qur'an. God must have known about the situational changes that would occur in the future and the modifications or changes that would be called forth by them. Then why did not God expressly provide a regulative principle to guide Muslims in this crucial matter for all times to come? To mention a rather small but very significant difficulty experienced by sincere and genuine believers, the Qur'an expressly declares that the polytheists are unclean and should not be permitted to enter the mosque at Jerusalem or the *Kabah*. Presumably, this prohibition would apply to an atheist or agnostic. But it is very difficult, if not impossible, for a modern mind to hold that a polytheist or atheist should be prohibited from entering any place of worship on the ground of his being 'unclean'. The modern attitude or approach in all such matters is extremely liberal and permissive. Now if the above-mentioned verse of the Qur'an had been expressly declared as temporarily binding no difficulty would have arisen. Since, however, the verse is in the form of an absolute imperative, and since the Qur'an, as the infallible Word of God, is binding upon all Muslims, the resolution of the conflict is rendered impossible by following the traditional procedures.

The same remarks also apply to the Qur'anic verse, which declares that the evidence of two women should be treated as equal to the evidence of one man. On the traditional conception of revelation, the Muslim simply must follow this command, provided he is not satisfied by lip loyalty to the Word of God. The intellectually honest Muslim must thus expressly and unequivocally repudiate all talk of equality of the sexes in the eyes of the law. Similarly, the honest Muslim must not feel apologetic about the propriety of flogging as a form of punishment, since the Qur'an expressly prescribed this form of punishment, although there is no reference to stoning as a punishment against adultery.

To cite yet another difficulty, consider the clear and categorical Qur'anic command to sever the hands of the thief. Without going into the problem of tightness or wrongness of this particular form of punishment, let us consider the phenomenon of kleptomania or a compulsive and uncontrollable urge to commit theft. Now should such a kleptomaniac thief be punished in the same way as an ordinary thief? Equity and common sense suggest that a clear distinction should be made in such cases.

But the Qur'anic injunction is categorical and unqualified and, prima facie, it does not allow any relaxation in the punishment prescribed for the crime in question. It is very significant that the Qur'an does provide for a flexible approach in respect of punishment for murder through giving to the survivors of the deceased the option between capital punishment and acceptance of blood money. Thus, the Qur'an could also have prescribed a measure of flexibility in respect of the punishment against theft. In the absence of any such prescription it is quite logical and natural to hold that the Qur'anic sanction against theft is deliberately intended to be both severe and rigid. Now if rigidity in this regard goes against the grain of an individual Muslim (no matter how hard and honestly he may try to surrender his own authentic judgment to the command of God), an inner existential conflict is bound to be generated, if the traditional conception of revelation is adhered to.

Some scholars are of the view that the punishment of severing the hands of the thief is the maximum punishment rather than the standard or normal. But this distinction between minimum, moderate, or maximum punishment, though certainly in conformity with equity, is not mentioned in the Qur'an. The Qur'anic command of cutting off of the hands is clear and categorical, although the qualifying clause clearly excludes or rules out this form of punishment for the first offense. Since the Qur'an does mention many details concerning other matters, the absence of qualifying clauses suggests that the Qur'anic punishment for theft is meant to be stern and deterrent.

It is interesting to note that the second *Caliph*, Umar, is reported to have refused to apply the Qur'anic sanction against theft in one or more instances on the ground of some situational or extenuating grounds. Assuming that the decisions of Umar were correct and rationally justified, the crucial question is whether Umar's deviation from the Qur'anic command could be justified, not on the grounds of equity or reason, but on some grounds contained in the Qur'an itself. If the second type of justification not be forthcoming, then the action of Umar must be judged as a violation of both the letter and the spirit of the Qur'an. In other words, the actual conduct of even such an orthodox and distinguished Muslim, as Umar does not solve the deadlock due to an existential conflict sometimes arising between reason and revelation. The traditional approach is thus far from satisfactory.

To sum up, the traditional view of revelation does not create any difficulties so long as the letter and the spirit of the Qur'an accord with the ideals and aspirations of the believer, even though he may be unable to live up to them in actual practice. But the moment his authentic evaluations differ from some Qur'anic command or prescription, the logical implication of the traditional conception of revelation is that he should surrender his personal and private judgment to the Divine command. This is the only straightforward and intellectually honest option, provided he accepts the traditional conception of revelation. But if he is unable to surrender his authentic judgment even after the most careful, honest, and prayerful search for authentic existence, then the surrender of his individual judgment would not heal the tragic split in the depths of his being. Even if he were to surrender his spiritual autonomy on the ground that the finite human mind can never fully grasp the infinite wisdom of God, he will still suffer from the pangs of a deep existential conflict. The faith of such a person would be haunted by ghosts of the reasons, which he has buried for the sake of an unqualified commitment to revelation. Such a person can never feel satisfied either by the surrender of his spiritual autonomy or by the traditional Islamic hermeneutics. For such persons the *Elan* conception of God and of revelation does not generate any existential conflict or tension in the depths of their beings.

THE CONCEPTUAL BACKGROUND OF THE ELAN CONCEPTION OF REVELATION

At the popular level the term 'revelation' is used loosely and refers to both the process and the content of revelation. Moreover, no distinction is made between a fact and its explanation. Consequently, any questioning of the traditional explanation of a fact is misconstrued as a rejection of the fact itself and also of the veracity of the Prophet ﷺ. A clarification of some basic concepts is, therefore, essential. These concepts are 'fact', 'paranormal fact', 'revelatory process', 'revelatory content', 'interpretation of revelation', and finally 'theory of revelation.'

A fact is any thing, process, or state of affairs that is 'given' in experience, as distinguished from what is inferred, imagined, or construed in order to explain, interpret, or evaluate the given content. Thus, the alternation between periods of light and darkness or days and nights is a fact, while the view or judgment that this alternation is due to the rotation of the earth on its axis is an explanation of the above fact. A fact that is repeated frequently and fits into or can be placed in a general frame of reference, habitually accepted by an observer, is a normal fact relative to the observer. Facts, which are normal in this sense, do not disturb our pattern of beliefs and expectations, even though we may not be able to explain them fully or to understand the laws of their occurrence. But if we actually and unmistakably experience something that is not generally experienced and which we are unable to fit into our customary conceptual framework, then we are forced to question the validity of the framework itself, rather than the veracity of our experience, assuming of course that all possible precautions were taken to exclude self-deception or fraud. A fact of the type described above may be called a 'paranormal fact' as distinguished from normal facts. Thus, if a month old baby in the cradle starts speaking or walking or running, and if we are sure about the age of the child and also sure that we are not imagining or dreaming when we hear the baby speak or see him run, but hear or see him with our ears and eyes working normally, then the above-mentioned fact is a paranormal fact.

A paranormal fact is thus as perceptible as any other fact, but strikingly deviates from normal facts in the relevant sphere and thus resists normal explanation, that is, location in the general conceptual framework. A paranormal fact may be explained in different ways. The rejection of any particular explanation is not tantamount to the rejection of the fact itself. Similarly, the rejection of any one interpretation of the revelatory process is not tantamount to the rejection of the revelatory process as such.

The revelatory process is the total psychophysical state of the 'revelatee', that is, the recipient of revelation at the moment of revelation. The revelatory content is the set of images, words, symbols of any kind that are the ostensible result or product of the revelatory process. The interpretation of the revelatory content (even by the revelatee himself) is a distinct activity that should never be confused either with the revelatory process or with the revelatory content as such. This revelatory content is given, while its interpretation is the cognitive act of the individual person, be he the revelatee himself or any other individual. The theory of revelation is a 'second order' or 'meta-theory' about the nature and dynamics of the revelatory process, while the interpretation of revelation is the 'first order' understanding of the revelatory content of the Qur'an.

Both the textual understanding of the revealed content and the epistemic theory of revelation involve the projection of the system of meanings and values of every individual. But the epistemic theory of revelation inevitably involves the projection of the conceptual framework of the age to a much greater degree. Even the revelatee himself is heavily dependent upon the conceptual framework of his age for this task. Thus the theory of revelation is at the farthest remove from the revelatory process as such, and the most liable to reflect the conceptual framework of the age, even when the revelatory content may represent a definite creative advance upon the inherited thought-cum-value system of the revelatee. The validity of the theory of revelation is thus quite distinct from the validity or the truth of the revealed text.

The theory of revelation adopted by the Prophet ﷺ to interpret his extraordinary or paranormal experience was in line with the Judaic theory of God communicating with chosen messengers through His angels. The Prophet's ﷺ contemporaries also naturally accepted it, once they accepted the integrity of the Prophet ﷺ without any mental reservations. This was a logical sequence. If, however, the Prophet ﷺ had been born in India, which had a long tradition of an entirely different conceptual framework, probably, he would have been viewed as an incarnation. It is very difficult, if not impossible, to speculate how he himself would have interpreted or explained his extraordinary experience. But even if it be assumed that he might have adopted the traditional Aryan conceptual scheme, and further, even if we were to reject this scheme, this would not at all have affected the spiritual or moral excellence of the Prophet ﷺ or of the Qur'an. Thus, there is no necessary correlation between the truth or validity of the Qur'anic thought-cum-value system and the traditional Islamic theory of revelation, or between the 'moral truthfulness' or integrity of the Prophet ﷺ, on the one hand, and the epistemic truth or validity of his own theory of revelation, on the other. His theory of revelation was not itself a revealed theory, but the traditional Semitic theory about revelation in general and also about his own extra-ordinary experiences.

These experiences were not unique to the Prophet ﷺ. As the Qur'an itself testifies, revelation has been vouchsafed to numerous messengers of God in every age and region. There is no reason to suppose that the essential features of the mystical experience of the Greek people differed from the Semitic or Aryan people. But the Greek conceptual interpretation was obviously different. Under the influence of St. Paul, Augustine and his spiritual heirs, this Greek conceptual scheme overshadowed the original Semitic conceptual scheme inherited by the earliest Christians from Judaism. The developed Christian conceptual scheme is certainly a product of the fusion of Semitic and Greek ideas.

The traditional Islamic theory of revelation was likewise inevitably generated by the conceptual framework of the age. The paranormal fact of the Qur'anic verses 'coming' unsought and involuntarily to the Prophet ﷺ was naturally and inevitably explained with the help of the prevalent Semitic concepts of the Prophet's ﷺ environment such as personal God, angels, and the 'Word of God', etc. Later on under the impact of Greek philosophy, particularly the conceptual framework of Plotinus, Muslim philosophers interpreted revelation with the help of concepts such as Logos, Active Intelligence, and emanation, etc. The philosophers and philosophical mystics of Islam are, on the whole, inclined toward the Greek conceptual framework, while the orthodox theologians and the average Muslim believer toward the Semitic. On the whole, the original Semitic scheme has maintained its identity and hold fairly successfully and persistently. Whenever neo-Platonism acquired a position of preponderance, as in the case of mystics such as Al-Bistami (d. 875 AD) or Ibn Arabi, or philosophers such as Farabi and Ibn Sina, there arose a Ghazali or Ibn Taymiyyah (d. 1328 AD) to reassert the verity of the original Semitic conceptual scheme. Perhaps this phenomenon has been a mixed blessing.

No conceptual scheme or framework need be accepted as infallible or perfect. Our framework must critically evolve rather than be a static legacy of antiquity or the middle ages or an imitation of the 'conceptual fashions' of our own day. Only a few years ago Western scientists were prone to reject alleged spiritual phenomena as fraud or delusion, while today they are keen to explain 'paranormal facts'. This should suffice to warn us against the danger of 'conceptual fashions'.

The significance of paranormal phenomena for a balanced, comprehensive, and scientific cosmology or worldview is now clearly accepted by leading contemporary thinkers. Psychical research has become an important field of investigation, and there is now an ever-growing consensus of informed belief in the occurrence of paranormal facts such as telepathy, clairvoyance, foreknowledge, and various types of hypnotic phenomena, etc., even though there may be no consensus on the explanation of such phenomena.

Morton Prince, a reputed American psychologist, personally investigated the case of an American lady who was barely literate. She was normal in all respects. Suddenly she started writing for long stretches of time. She did not know what she was writing, and had no ambition or plan to become a writer. She just felt an irresistible urge to write, and she wrote as long as the urge remained without knowing what she was writing about and why. Morton Prince obtained the manuscript. It was a historical novel about ancient Egypt. Qualified literary persons judged its English to have a fairly high literary standard and Egyptologists said that the description of social conditions and other details agreed with their findings. Morton Prince was completely satisfied that there was no fraud about the lady and that it was a genuine case of automatic writing.

Tyrell refers to a number of famous writers, poets, composers, painters, mathematicians, etc. who have claimed in all honesty and sobriety that certain works or portions of them were not produced by any conscious effort, but came to them or were 'revealed" to them in a flash. Milton, Beethoven, Mozart, Blake are some of this group.

A mathematician said that he had been working on a problem for many days without any success. One fine morning, as he arose from bed, he saw a full and satisfactory solution of the problem written on the blackboard of his bedroom in his own handwriting. He was dazed, as he had no memory of having written anything on the black board during the night.

There are numerous recorded cases of automatic speech, sudden ability to talk and lecture in foreign languages not known to the speaker, automatic calculation or computation of arithmetical sums involving many digits, and the calendar days or dates of many decades past. The phenomenon known as 'psychometry' is also recorded. In such cases an individual reads the entire past and future of an unknown person by simply touching an object belonging to the person. [53]

Many religious thinkers or persons are inclined to think that the phenomenon of divine revelation is entirely different from paranormal phenomena referred to above. But as William James pointed out long ago, it is difficult to deny that there are striking similarities between the two phenomena. [54] Moreover, no point is served by such a denial, since the occurrence of paranormal phenomena tends to strengthen rather than weaken the probability of Divine revelation. Just as the operation of intelligence or instinct in animal species in no way reduces the status of human beings as bearers of instincts and intelligence, similarly, the admission that paranormal phenomena of different types are the lower prototypes of Divine revelation, or, in other words, that Divine revelation is the highest form or version of paranormal phenomena such as clairvoyance or telepathy, etc., does not in any way destroy the value or sanctity of genuine revelation in the religious sense. From this point of view, the mystical experience of the Prophet ﷺ is the highest form of direct non-inferential awareness whose relatively lower forms are manifested in the inspiration of artists, poets, and mathematicians, etc. To admit the continuity between the *'event of the Qur'an'* and psychic phenomena should not, however, lead to the reductive assimilation of the spiritual to the psychic or, in religious language, of the Divine to the human paranormal. The similarity between revelation in the religious sphere and paranormal phenomena is only partial. [55]

THE ELAN CONCEPTION OF REVELATION

The well-established facts of the Prophet's ﷺ life make it reasonably certain that he was an exceptionally versatile, truthful, and honest person. Consequently, his unequivocal declaration that he was not the author of the Qur'an cannot be brushed aside as either a deliberate falsehood or the delusion of a disorganized mind. At the same time the traditional concept of Divine revelation also cannot be accepted due to the difficulties mentioned above. The proper approach, therefore, is to accept the Prophet's ﷺ declaration that the Qur'an was revealed to him, and to reconstruct the traditional meaning or significance of this claim. In other words, the proper approach is to accept the fact of the revelatory process, without necessarily accepting the traditional theory of revelation. Similarly, we could accept a text as revealed, without holding that its interpretation was also revealed. [56] Thus the acceptance of the Qur'an as revealed does not entail the acceptance of the traditional theory of revelation. Conversely, the rejection of the traditional theory of revelation does not entail the rejection of the belief in revelation.

According to the *Elan* conception of revelation, the *Primal Value Elan* ever-pulsates in and informs every spatiotemporal system or *gestalt*. But it is clearly and distinctively registered in man alone. He has the potentiality to identify his will, or to 'melt', as it were, into the Value Elan. Different people realize this capacity in different degrees. Revelation is the maximum possible integration with the Elan. If, and when, an individual attains this limit, his subjective and conscious *Value Nisus* is extinguished and merged into the overwhelming and shattering onrush or flow of the *Primal Value Elan* itself. He becomes like a blade of straw carried away by an extraordinarily powerful ocean current. This analogy, however, is not meant for literal consumption but only intended to point out the obliteration, as it were, of the normal conscious, self-deliberative and self-regulative human personality and its total dependence and existential surrender to some 'numinous field of presence'. ⁵⁷ This state, however, cannot be brought about at will. The revelatory content may synchronize with the revelatory process or crystallize soon after the process. In any case, no effort or labor is required by the revelatee who is 'given' the content and does not produce it. The conceptual understanding of the revelatory content may, however, involve his own labor unless, of course, the conceptualization itself is deemed to be an integral part of the total revelatory process as such. The theory of revelation, however, which seeks to interpret the event of revelation, is based on the interpretative categories current in the milieu of the revelatee.

According to the *Elan* conception, the revelatory content is not the passive reception of a readymade external communication from a totally external transcendental source or center of communication, as if the revealed content were quanta or drops of revelation falling into a passive receptacle. ⁵⁸ According to the *Elan* theory, the revelatory process is one of the maximum attunement and inner receptivity to the pulsations of the *Primal Value Elan* which is pan-immanent, yet seldom comes in the range of attunement to finite beings. Although the *sin qua non* of genuine revelation is the total surrender of the subjective desires, aims, and attitudes of the finite individual in the face of the shattering inflow of the Primal Value Elan, the particularity of the individual can never be totally obliterated. If so, the revelatory content has to be viewed as a complex deposit or crystallization of the *Primal Value Elan* in a particular individual placed in concrete social space-time. In other words, the revelatory process is a complex and bipolar rather than a simple and unipolar activity and the human pole is bound to leave its traces in the crystallized revelatory content. These traces imply the possibility of spatiotemporal limitations in the revelatory content. The *Elan* conception thus fully registers the complexity of the issue and preserves the sanctity of the revelatory content as well as its growth. The *Elan* conception certainly implies that the phenomenon of revelation is, in principle, repeatable but not that it must be or that it has been repeated after the Qur'anic revelation. As regards infallibility, the *Elan* conception holds that no revelatory content, either in the process of its conceptual crystallization or in its subsequent application to the human situation, can totally transcend the 'gravitational pull' of the conceptual framework of the revelatee. If so, the revelatory content as well as the interpretation of that content is bound to bear traces of social space-time. No revelatory content can claim to reflect the final and perfect integration with the PVE. In this sense, no revelation can claim to have exhausted all future possibilities of growth of man's thought and value systems. The reduction of the Value Elan to a particular revelatory content is a denial of the infinitude and inexhaustible transcendence of the Elan. Such a denial inevitably leads to a closed and static thought-cum-value system. A revelatory content may, however, be infallible in the sense that its basic value system is valid beyond the least shadow of doubt and reflects the integration of the individual will with the PVE. This may be termed 'nuclear infallibility' as distinguished from the traditional 'molecular infallibility'. Nuclear infallibility does not preclude the emergence of new dimensions or molecular levels in the basic nuclear values or concepts of the revelatory text. The emergence of new levels constitutes growth in the realm of thought and value. Such growth is not merely permitted, but is encouraged and promoted by a genuine acceptance of the *Elan* conception of revelation.

The *Elan* conception of revelation does not involve the abdication or dilution of man's spiritual autonomy and responsibility for growth; it makes ceaseless growth the prime duty of man. This growth can only take place if it actualizes the potentiality for freedom. Freedom, in the highest sense, is not the gift of nature or nurture but rather the fruit of a long process of growth. This process consists of continual attempts at authentic self-insight or self-awareness. Freedom implies the courage to act or grow in accordance with one's deepest choice. But before one can choose, one must know or be aware of the possibilities of the self. Thus freedom presupposes self-knowledge. This self-knowledge itself requires a measure of courage; the courage of self-acceptance. The *Elan* theory nourishes the courage to be and to choose, and also affirms man's essential kinship with the *Value Elan* or the God within man. The traditional theory of revelation, on the other hand, strengthens man's fear of his own freedom, his distrust of his own self, and his need to surrender himself before an external authority.

In the ultimate analysis, it is futile to try to explain or interpret an experience, which one avowedly has not had. Even if one does have the experience its adequate explanation or interpretation is extremely difficult, if not impossible. Consequently, all attempted theories of revelation, including the *Elan* theory, are bound to be inadequate in some respect or other. One cannot, however, totally avoid the issue, since Muhammad's ﷺ claim that he was not the author of the Qur'an is a part of history and must be reckoned with by all men, be they Muslims or not. If one rejects the veracity of the Prophet ﷺ then obviously the problem of a valid interpretation does not arise at all. But if one cannot reject the veracity of the Prophet ﷺ, since he finds no evidence that could possibly compromise the truthfulness of the Prophet ﷺ, then one cannot totally avoid the task of interpreting the Prophet's ﷺ claim that the Qur'an was revealed to him.

The *Elan* conception is an attempt to conceptualize an experience, which is the most complex and the rarest form of awareness. Whether the *Elan* conception is adequate or inadequate is not crucial. The crucial matter, in the last analysis, is the veracity or otherwise of the Prophet ﷺ. As long as one authentically accepts the Prophet's ﷺ veracity one may be said to believe in Allah and His Prophet ﷺ, no matter what theory of revelation may be most acceptable to him. In the final analysis, the crux of faith in the Qur'anic revelation lies in faith in the veracity of the Prophet ﷺ, and in experiencing in the depths of one's being a sense of profound mystery and wonder while hearing or reciting the verses of the Qur'an.

LIFE AFTER DEATH

Belief in life after death is not a scientific hypothesis that could be verified or falsified. It is an existential interpretation of man in the cosmos and a corollary of belief in God just like the corollary beliefs of revelation or incarnation. Belief in life after death implies that worldly time is only a slice or portion of an infinite duration.

The traditional Islamic faith in life after death consists of two correlated beliefs; the resurrection of the individual and his everlasting survival either in heaven or in hell, and the Divine reckoning of man's earthly actions and final dispensation of justice. If God's existence be accepted, the above beliefs do not raise any theoretical difficulties of the type raised by the antecedent belief in Divine existence or revelation in history. An omnipotent God Who creates individual organisms in the first instance could surely resurrect them after any length of time.

Similarly, what could be more desirable and logically consistent than the just reward and punishment of man as the eschatological finale of his temporal sojourn? As a matter of fact, belief in life after death helps to solve the difficulties raised by the presence of pain and evil in a Universe which has been created by an all-good and all-powerful God. Theologians, therefore, do not attempt to prove a belief, which is the logical corollary of the antecedent belief in God, which they claim to demonstrate.

Even if it be conceded that theism could be demonstrated, an individual's living belief in God and life after death is not the product of deliberation, but a pre-logical faith or conviction which is obviously culturally conditioned. This conviction or faith is, however, nourished and reinforced by three factors. Firstly, man's inalienable passionate longing for establishing truth, goodness, and beauty here and now, and his utter helplessness to do so (except to a marginal extent) which impels him to look up to God for establishing these values in eschatological history, if not in the temporal. Secondly, the very common belief that men would have no reason or motive for practicing morality, if they did not believe in God and eschatological reward or punishment. It is held that men may be forced into discipline due to the fear of the policemen, but they can never be persuaded to embrace genuine morality unless they first believe in God and life after death.

The third factor that reinforces our pre-logical faith in life after death is man's lust for life itself; the elementary will to live. If man cannot live forever in this world he is prompted to seek immortality in life after death. These three factors; the lust or passion for life, the passion or quest for value, and the belief that personal immortality is the postulate of morality; existentially push man toward belief in life after death.

The functional significance of belief in life after death is both to enhance the value of the individual in the cosmic scheme of things and also to enhance the significance of man's actions, both good and bad. Belief in life after death is thus one of the greatest means of reinforcing man's quest for value and helping him face the tragic and evil dimensions of life with equanimity and an unshakable faith in the ultimate triumph of good over evil. In the ultimate analysis, this belief is the only antidote to the nihilistic and self-destructive impulses, which, according to depth psychology, coexist in the depths of the human psyche with the positive quest for value.

Non-belief in the immortality of the soul prompts the individual to view himself as a transient bubble or fleeting cloud rather than a permanent ego with solemn duties and responsibilities to his Creator, his co-creatures, and finally his own self. In the words of William James, belief in life after death raises man's stakes in the enterprise of living the good life in this world, not merely as a member of a perishable society, but as a member of an imperishable kingdom based on Divine justice. [59]

A Restatement of the Islamic Thought System

The undeniable advantages of this belief, however, do not necessarily make it logically coercive or inductively true. The only coercive proof can be the actual experience of life after death and this proof is ruled out in this life. It may be held that when by the very nature of the case a belief cannot be confirmed or falsified, the fact that it is an inalienable demand of our passional nature suffices for its truth. But it is precisely here that the inner experience of many highly intelligent, morally developed, and spiritually sensitive persons makes it doubtful whether belief in life after death is in fact an inalienable demand of our passional nature. When these persons come to realize that belief in a personal God and personal immortality, though immensely useful, is not logically necessary for morality, the existential concern for personal immortality withers away. The prospect of nothingness, that is, total loss of individual consciousness, does not frighten or depress them and the prospect of everlasting personal happiness in heaven does not attract them. They seem to realize the vanity of all finite individuation, be it joyful or tragic, temporal or eschatological, and this realization fosters in them the longing to lose rather than preserve their selfhood. This satiety with *ego hood* is not rooted in frustration, bitterness, or despair but in the authentic longing to transcend the limitations of finite *ego hood* or individuation. This longing leads to the voluntary abdication of self-affirmation by the finite ego. This state of mind does not promote passivity, indifference, or life negation, but rather generates a deep and dedicated concern for the universal good, irrespective of personal loss or gain. Consequently, the individual does not neglect the duties and obligations of his station in life, nor does he forego the authentic joy of life through the pursuit of values. But perhaps the intensity of the instinctive lust for life is reduced along with a concomitant reduction in the intensity of the sexual drive, which propagates *ego hood* and is also the most intense form of self-affirmation.

Satiety with *ego hood* or individuation is a fitting preparation for welcoming death interpreted as the glorious release from the shackles of finite egohood; the return of the drop into the ocean or of the part into the wholeness of some tremendous mystery, or maybe even a reversion into the primal elements from which life first emerged. In other words, whether death be an evolution of the ego into a higher level of life or awareness, or its devolution into the lower, the dread of losing one's hold on life (as a drowning man dreads losing his hold, howsoever slight, on something solid) is gone for the individual who outgrows the instinctive lust for life or passion for individuation. Such an emancipated person is joyfully prepared for his eschatological destination, whatever it might be, without any anxiety and dread or a defensive and self-assuring ratiocination. Only such an individual can know what is his authentic response to the mystery of being.

As long as a man holds personal immortality to be necessary or useful for morality, a utilitarian interest or concern for individuation lurks in the depths of his being. Now utilitarian considerations make it difficult to assess how far the faith in life after death is an authentic response to the mystery of being rather than an option of convenience for preserving or promoting morality. After all man is strongly prompted to choose what is more useful to him rather than what authentically grips him.

Now the crucial question is this: If one finds that one has neither the desire nor the faith left in personal immortality, whether in the purely spiritual or in the psycho-physical form, does this mean that one is denying life after death, which is obviously an integral part of the Islamic thought system? It seems the answer is in the negative due to the following two reasons.

Although the Qur'an refers to resurrection, the final reckoning and the rewards of heaven and the punishments of hell in language which prima facie suggests eschatological personality, it is impossible to claim any clear-understanding of the Qur'anic verses on this subject. [60] To claim that fire, heat, fuel, boiling water, fountains of water, trees, fruits, and the human body, etc., as mentioned in the Qur'an, refer to these objects as they exist in this world is to commit the anthropomorphic fallacy. In the same vein, to claim the knowledge of the mode of survival in life after death is also to commit the same fallacy.

Secondly, it seems to me that the spiritual and functional core of the belief in life after death is not individual survival but rather the ultimate vindication of the truth and the majesty of the moral law whose violation on earth often goes unpunished. And for this vindication personal survival is not necessary, even though it maybe an eschatological fact. Whether the individual bearers of value or disvalue in temporal history survive as persons in eschatological history does not matter. What really matters is the triumph of the moral law, whether in temporal or eschatological history, as the case maybe. It is this belief rather than belief in a personal God or belief in the reward and punishment in after life that is the minimum psychological necessity for sustaining man in his moral striving.

Consequently, all that is necessary for belief in life after death as an essential and integral part of the Islamic thought system is the belief in the ultimate continuity of life and the triumph of value over disvalue. Provided a man is committed to these beliefs, he may well remain non-committed to any particular concrete conception of life after death found in the Semitic milieu of Judaism, Christianity, and Islam. Just as we must make a distinction between God, as He is in Himself, and our finite human conception of God, similarly we must make a distinction between life after death, as an objective though as yet undisclosed feature of man's total history, and the concrete human conceptions of life after death, as envisaged by this or that religion. The doubt or even denial of a particular mode of afterlife should not be misconstrued as a denial of the concept of life after death as such.

The essence of the doctrine of *karma* is also that man must reap what he sows in virtue of an inviolable metaphysical law. The only difference between the suggested Islamic reinterpretation and the Hindu doctrine lies in their respective theories of time. The Islamic view presupposes the serial conception of time while the Indian view is cyclical.

The views of the classical Muslim philosophers, Ibn Sina and Ibn Rushd, on the subject of immortality of the soul or life after death are significant. Both Ibn Sina and Ibn Rushd believed in the impersonal conception of immortality, that is, the ultimate absorption of the finite soul into the Universal Soul, which is one of the emanations of God. This conception obviously differs from the dominant traditional anthropomorphic conception of immortality, that is, bodily resurrection and immortality of human beings qua separate personalities.

The classical Muslim philosophers stood for interpreting concepts like God, life after death, etc., in accordance with the intellectual level and personality needs of different individuals. The conception of life after death, as reconstructed in this work, is based on the methodological principle of avoiding all unverifiable speculative concretion of concepts like God, creation, revelation, and life after death, etc., and holds the wordless surrender to the sense of mystery as the essence of a mature faith. Even if knowledge of the above concepts were possible, doing right or being good will remain infinitely more precious than knowing the geography of heaven and hell, and the physiognomy of man in life after death.

CHAPTER 4

A RESTATEMENT OF THE ISLAMIC THOUGHT SYSTEM (CONTD.)

AN ANALYTICAL AND EXISTENTIALIST APPROACH TO THE QUR'AN

I

THE LANGUAGE OF THE QUR'AN

The Qur'an is the concrete mode in which the Muslim believes to come in contact with God. As the Word of God, the Qur'an is the concrete locus of Divinity for the Muslim, just as Jesus, the Christ, is for the Christian. In the presence of the Qur'an the Muslim is face to face with the Source of Divine mercy and guidance. Indeed it is impossible to say for a Muslim, from within the Islamic frame of reference, which is the greater blessing or mercy of God: the Qur'an, or the Prophet ﷺ himself. If the Qur'an had not been revealed to the Prophet ﷺ his status would not have been extraordinary. On the other hand, the Qur'an itself declares the Prophet ﷺ to be a 'mercy for the worlds' (*rahmatul lil alamin*), while God is the 'Lord of the worlds' (*rabbul alamin*).

The Qur'an has been the primary focus of Islamic religious thought, and perhaps no other scripture can claim to have inspired a greater volume of exegetical literature than the Qur'an. This very concern for the Qur'an has tended to put a human gloss upon the Divine word thereby blocking the Muslim's creative response to the Qur'an. A measure of human cognitive projection upon the propositional canvas of the Qur'an is inevitable, and no interpretation could ever-claim to be free from the concepts and values of a particular time and place. But our understanding of the Qur'an will be considerably helped if our interpretation of the text is preceded by a careful analysis of the language of the Qur'an in the functional sense.

The Qur'an may not be a book in the ordinary sense of the term, but it must be accepted as a body of statements, which are as amenable to the basic principles of semantics as any other meaningful communication. We must determine the type of discourse to which a Qur'anic statement belongs before we can claim to understand it properly. This approach is implied by a Qur'anic Verse itself, according to which the Qur'an consists of two types of verses; one clear, definite instructions known as the *'Muhkamat'*, while the other similes or metaphors, known as *'Mutashabehat'*. The verses of the Qur'an go on to say that those in whose hearts is a disease, try to confuse these two verses. [61] The implication is that the first type of verses have a clear meaning and it is these verses which constitute the main truthclaims and the fundamental principles of the Qur'an, while the other type of verses are perhaps not so essential and are to be understood not literally, but in some other way. The point is that the Qur'an itself refers to this distinction between two types of verses. Therefore, a fuller analysis of the verses of the Qur'an on the same lines is certainly not a philosophical luxury. Indeed, such a type of analysis is absolutely essential for identifying the exact purpose or function, which lies behind a particular Qur'anic statement. Only when its true function or purpose has been grasped can it properly guide the believers.

Language serves several functions. Confusing one function with the other leads to problems, which would not arise at all if we knew the actual functions prior to our using the statement. Language serves the functions of description, exhortation, evaluation, interpretation, interrogation, prescription, instruction, and amusement, etc. But people are inclined to stress the representational or descriptive function of language to the exclusion of the other functions. Even these broad heads have many sub-varieties subsumed under them and it is essential to be aware of these distinctions. [62]

The language of the Qur'an, from the functional point of view, comprises factual, evaluative, exhortative, prescriptive, parabolical, metaphorical, interpretative, invocative, and mythical types of discourse. After dealing briefly with the earlier types I shall deal at some length with the mythical type, since it raises intellectual difficulties for the critical mind. [63]

Factual statements purport to describe facts and thus inform us about what is the case in the objective world open for public inspection and verification. Factual statements grow out of the primitive use of language to give names to observable objects. This is followed by combining names into expressions which describe how individual objects are interrelated to

A Restatement of the Islamic Thought System (Contd.)

constitute simple or complex facts, for example, the Qur'anic statement that Abraham had a dream or that the Meccans attacked the Muslims, or that every soul tastes of death.

Evaluative statements are judgments of value indicating what ought to be the case, for example, the Qur'anic statement that fulfilling one's contracts is right, or that murder is wrong. Exhortative statements presuppose evaluative judgments, and exhort man to strive for values, for example, the Qur'anic statements exhorting Muslims to establish righteousness, or to do their duty. Prescriptive statements are commands to promote values, whether intrinsic or instrumental, such as, the Qur'anic statements commanding Muslims to pray at stated times, or pay the wealth tax, or stop infanticide, etc.

Parabolical statements are functionally exhortative but their form is of very short narratives invented for a didactic purpose, for example, the Qur'anic parable about two gardeners. [64]

Metaphorical statements are either descriptions or evaluations in non-literal analogical language. Metaphors are used to describe, evaluate, or exhort with the utmost brevity, beauty, and force at the command of the communicator, for example, the Qur'anic statement that God seals the eyes and the ears of the hypocrites, so that seeing they see not, and hearing they hear not, or that God created the world in six days, or that God is the light of the heavens and the earth, etc. [65]

Interpretative statements are existential interpretations of the Universe, their function being to provide a stable attitudinal orientation toward the Universe. Interpretative statements are partly similar to explanatory statements in the sense that both go beyond the immediate data supplied by perceptual knowledge. But while scientific explanations are verifiable, existential interpretations are accepted or rejected primarily on the basis of authenticity, such as, the first three verses of the *surah Fatiha*, and numerous other verses describing the glory and majesty of God, or the harmony and purposiveness of the Universe. Interpretative statements are the most characteristic type of discourse (next only to the invocative) to be found in religious literature in general.

Invocative statements are appeals, prayers, and petitions for obtaining the love, forgiveness, blessings, or wrath of God. The most notable Qur'anic invocation is the last four verses of *surah Fatiha*.

Out of about 6,200 verses of the Qur'an, probably the vast majority belongs to the evaluative-exhortative type of discourse, perhaps followed by the descriptive-narrative type, describing in very general terms the events in the life of the different prophets. The prescriptive statements number only about 250, the vast majority of which deal with symbolic rites and personal law. [66] Confusing one type of statement with the other leads to contradictions and intellectual difficulties. Let us now see in some detail how this comes about.

The Qur'an says that God seals the heart of the unbelievers and throws veils over their eyes and ears, and such persons will never listen to the Prophet ﷺ. But when God Himself seals the heart of man how can He later on punish him for his disbelief? Similarly, God's sitting on the throne of glory or God's placing some men on His right hand, while others on His left, cannot be literally understood, for the simple reason that God cannot be regarded as a physical object occupying a definite spatio-temporal position. [67] Again, God's creation of the Universe out of nothing cannot be understood in any one of the plain descriptive meanings of the word 'creation', for example, the sense in which Shakespeare created Hamlet, or Shahjahan created the Taj Mahal, or the carpenter makes a chair, or an organism begets its offspring. But then can we claim that the word 'Divine Creation' has any meaning at all? There are numerous other cases where a plain literal interpretation of the text generates obvious difficulties. The point is that all these difficulties arise only when we accept such statements in the literal sense and as belonging to the descriptive type of discourse such as the statements 'the office clerk sealed the envelope before handing it over to the peon", and 'the railway station is to the left of the post office', etc. But if it be the case that the Qur'anic expression *'God has sealed the eyes and ears of the hypocrites'* is an elliptical way of referring to the inevitable psychological effects on the disbelievers due to their repeated arrogant refusal to give a patient and honest hearing to the Prophet ﷺ, then the difficulty disappears. Indeed the actual function of a statement maybe quite different from that of its formal type of discourse. The actual function of the interrogative expression 'Do you think I am a fool', for instance, is not interrogative. Similarly, what appears to be a descriptive statement in the future tense may really be an existential interpretation, for example, the Qur'anic statement that God will seat some on His right and some on His left on the day of judgment. Again, the Qur'anic statement about God's creation of the Universe is not a super scientific hypothesis, but an existential interpretation. The expression

'Divine Creation' does not have any factual meaning, but only provides man with a stable attitudinal orientation and mode of treating the Universe. [68]

A person who is not aware of the plurality of language functions is apt to commit at least three types of mistakes: **(i)** to accept all the statements of the Qur'an as being literally representational and then project anthropomorphic elements into his conception of the nature and behavior of God, without being bothered by the intellectual difficulties that must inevitably arise when ordinary words, primarily meant for describing human experience, are used for describing God or other supernormal beings, **(ii)** to reject all statements describing God on the charge of anthropomorphism, and **(iii)** to adopt a polemical approach to different religious or philosophical views and demand their proof. The first two mistakes would be avoided, if it were realized that statements about God should be understood not in the literal but in the metaphorical sense, and metaphors are neither true nor false, but simultaneously illuminating and misleading. The third mistake would be avoided if greater importance were given to the function of religious statements than to their grammatical form. For instance, the form of such Qur'anic statements as God is the light of the heavens, or God is the first and the last, the manifest and the hidden and knower of all things, or to God belongs all that is between the heavens and the earth, is factual or descriptive, but their function is to evoke a sense of mystery, awe, trust, and security in the believer, and to reinforce his quest for value, rather than to describe the features of the Universe in the scientific sense. [69] Hence, the demand for their verification in the empirical sense is pointless.

The analysis of disagreement between rival philosophical or theological beliefs is also instructive. One person may assert that every event in the Universe is controlled by an omnipotent God, and not even a leaf moves without His Will or permission, while another person may assert that all events are determined by causal laws. Now, these formulations are widely divergent, but they agree in the sense (which is apt to be ignored) that both deny haphazard or lawless sequences in the Universe. One formulation regards will or purpose, while the other empirical uniformity as the inherent '*ontic*' feature of these events. These two interpretations thus partly agree and partly disagree. But if a person holding that not a leaf moves without Divine Will, actually uses medicines for curing illness or a person who says that empirical laws are 'Divine commands' functions in the same way as the empirical scientist, then perhaps their divergent formulations conceal a partial agreement at a different level of belief. It is true that a person who asserts that natural laws are merely empirical generalizations would never pray to God for the temporary suspension of these laws for a particular purpose, while the person who asserts that natural laws are 'imposed' by a Creator could see a point in such a prayer. But to the extent that a theist excludes the occurrence of miracles violating the established laws, the directive function of believing in causal uniformity or believing in Divine regulation of events is basically similar.

Let us analyze another very vital religious belief; the belief in Divine justice. The Semitic interpretation of God's justice implies a linear view of life in a single backward-forward direction, while the Aryan interpretation of justice or *karma* implies a cyclical theory of birth and rebirth. The two formulations partly differ and partly agree. But in so far as the directive functioning of both is the same, namely, restraining the individual from wrongdoing, their operational significance maybe said to be the same. Formulational pluralism may thus conceal functional similarity of statements.

The practical implication is that many controversies and confusions could be avoided, if **(a)** the different functions of language are not confused with each other, **(b)** the function or use of an expression is not confused with its prima facie grammatical form, **(c)** the demand for validation or verification of the different types of statements takes into account their functional peculiarities without trying to assimilate them to a rigid empirical scientific model. These steps would enable us to do full justice to the wide variety of human discourse rather than reduce one to the other, or needlessly restrict man's range of discourse to select types.

MYTHS IN THE QUR'AN

Let us now turn to the mythical type of discourse. In many circles the word 'myth' is equated with illusion, unreality, and falsehood, etc. This is indeed one of the meanings that this word has acquired in the English language. But in the original usage 'myth' is an imaginative tale of primitive pre-philosophical times dealing with the basic themes and values of life. Myths were thus the source of both entertainment and edification. In the absence of a written language, these myths were orally transmitted from generation to generation and represented the accumulated wit and wisdom of the ages. Myths, therefore, should not be brushed aside as mere concoctions of barbarous times. The myths of different societies should rather be treated as the pre-philosophical literary output of a society. Credit must be given to the insight of the great 19th century French thinker Comte, according to whom there are three stages of human thought, namely, religious or the mythical, the metaphysical, and finally the positivistic or scientific. [70] But Comte was inclined to underestimate the significance of the first stage, since mythical thinking does not help us to build bridges or fly in the air. Nevertheless, myths can convey profound moral and even metaphysical insights in a most concrete and dramatic manner just like parables. The only difference between a myth and a parable is that the latter does not include any supernatural concepts, themes, or persons, while a myth is precisely a supernatural parable possessing a deep and timeless significance for man. The educative or existential value of myths is, however, destroyed if the myths are accepted in the literal sense. The rejection of the literal truth of the myth is not the negation of the value of the myth as such. Indeed, the making of this distinction between literal truth and mythical truth is the only way to preserve the myth from extinction. What applies to myths also applies to poetry and art in general. Poetic and artistic excellence are *sui generis* and should not be assimilated to scientific or logical truth. [71]

The mythical mode of thinking is universal but the mythology of some societies is much more developed than that of others. For example, Hindu mythology is much richer than the mythology of, say, the Arabs or the Chinese. This is not the place to try to discover the basic reasons for such differences in the mythological aptitude and output of different societies. What matters is that there are several stories in the Qur'an that significantly resemble the stories current elsewhere and whose tone and texture is plainly that of myths.

The traditional Muslim does not look at these stories in this way but regards them as literally and historically true. Thus, for example, the traditional Muslim accepts in the literal sense the creation of Adam as the first man or the dialogue between God and angels and God and Satan, the expulsion of Adam and Eve from heaven, etc. But it is not all necessary to accept the literal truth of such statements just as it is not necessary to accept the Biblical or Qur'anic parables or Aesop's fables as literally true, in order to profit from their profound wisdom or be inspired to live the good life. While the person straightway rejecting the myths as fairy tales, which need not be taken seriously, misses their profound ethical or spiritual significance, the person who insists on the literal truth of the myths confuses the different types of discourse and the different functions of language. Wisdom lies in profiting from myths, whether of this religion or that, without being caught in the web of uncritical dogmatism. It must, however, be pointed out that by the very nature of the cause no finality can be claimed for any particular interpretation of a myth. The interpretation of myths is like the interpretation of dreams. Though this activity is not entirely arbitrary and not every interpretation of a dream could claim to carry conviction, either with the dreamer himself or the listener, there can be no clear-cut proof that a particular interpretation or a particular line of interpretation is valid. Some methodological principle underlying different interpretations may, however, appeal to us. If so, we could adopt it as a general principle of interpretation. But the final test of its validity would be its consistency and its ability to illumine our understanding of the complexities of man's nature or the cosmos and to deepen our self-insight.

I shall now attempt a very brief interpretation of the myth of the creation of Adam and the expulsion of Satan from heaven. The literal Qur'anic version is to the effect that God had originally created the angels and the heavens. Later on He decided to create Adam from common clay but breathed His spirit into the material configuration. He then commanded all the angels to prostrate themselves before Adam. On refusal the chief angel, *Iblis* or Satan, was banished from God's grace, but was given the power to tempt man. However, those who have faith cannot be ensnared by Satan. [72]

The above statements are perhaps a mythical representation of some such truth as follows. Man is a very late arrival on the stage of cosmic history. The raw material of his psychophysical constitution is the same as that of the most insignificant organism or living form, but there is a *'Divine spark'* in man that makes him superior to all creation. This Divine spark is the creative conscience or the Value Elan, which, though present in all creation, to some extent or other, is most conspicuous in man. Man is, however, not entirely good, and left to his own resources, is always in danger of falling a prey to his own vanity and negative impulses such as hatred, malice, fear, pride, etc. The power of these negative emotions or passions is very great indeed, and the highest among us is liable to be carried away by their inner fury as well as man's inner blindness or self-deception. This loss of authentic being is the greatest tragedy that can befall man, since this throws him into the darkness and wilderness of a constant flight from truth. But surrender before God saves man from such dangers. God is, however, not some Being external to man. Rather God is the ultimate depth of Man's authentic existence without being reducible to any particular depth or the depth of any particular being. God's command to Satan to prostrate himself before Adam was the declaration of the Divine immanence in man. Satan who was proud of his intelligence and knowledge, claimed to be constituted from 'fire', while Adam was made out of 'clay'. Probably 'fire' in this context symbolizes dynamic intelligence or reason, while clay stands for surrender and humility. Satan's logic stood in the way of the growth of spiritual insight. In other words, rationalism without spirituality is superficial and one-sided. Just as *Iblis* suffered due to his rationalist pretensions, similarly, all those who reject the spiritual dimension of human experience in the name of a lopsided scientism or positivism cut themselves away from the depths of their own being, or the God within man. These people maybe totally unaware of their loss, and maybe highly successful from the worldly point of view, but their loss is indeed tremendous.

Again Satan's refusal to honor Adam or to concede that Adam could act rightly, even though he had received God's own breath, implies Satan's doubt in the ultimate supremacy of good over evil. Satan's cardinal sin, thus, could be said to lie in doubting God's power to ensure the triumph of good over evil in the long run. Had he not doubted this, he would not have refused to obey God's command to honor Adam. It was his doubt that led to his disobedience, his subsequent disgrace, and his self-chosen career as a constant tempter of man. The existential as distinguished from the literal truth of this myth, therefore, is precisely that though evil is inseparably interwoven in the fabric of the cosmos, yet good will triumph over evil in the long run, no matter how difficult or tortuous the path to victory. This is the functional meaning of faith in God.

This bipolar conception of man and the Universe as a whole is amply supported by the findings of psychoanalysts and also the well-established conclusions of science. Scientists maintain that there is no absolute exclusivity between, say, the male and female, the organic and the inorganic, the positive and the negative charges of electricity, but only a relative or proportional dominance of one type or factor over the other. It is this dominance that gives a typological identity to a person, thing, or attribute. Similarly, psychoanalysts have been led to the view that absolute sanity or insanity are only 'limit concepts' rather than actual facts. Individuals occupy infinitely varying positions on the scale of normality-abnormality. It is only when abnormal syndromes outnumber or preponderate beyond a certain point over the other syndromes that an individual may rightly be deemed as abnormal or psychotic. Furthermore, psychoanalysts have concluded that irrational drives and destructive urges are as much built-in traits of the human personality as the aspiration for truth, goodness, beauty, etc. According to them, man is neither wholly good nor wholly evil, but partly good and partly evil, with the good elements preponderating. Thus it maybe said that the concept of *'Iblis'* is the mythical counterpart of the concept of irrational drives embedded in the human psyche or man's total personality structure. [73]

MIRACLES AND THE QUR'AN

The Qur'anic reference to extraordinary events or miracles in the past also raises intellectual difficulties for the critical mind. A miracle is any event that violates the established laws of nature. The Qur'anic approach to the subject of miracles is very puzzling to the critical mind, in that while the Qur'an refers to the miracles performed by prophets in the past, it categorically denies that Prophet Muhammad ﷺ had the power of performing any miracles. When he was asked to show miracles in support of his claim to be a prophet, the Qur'an itself dismissed this demand as wrong in principle. The Qur'an repeatedly declared the Prophet ﷺ to be an ordinary human mortal who could not change the laws of nature. His only distinction was that he was the recipient of Divine revelation, over which, again, he had no control. [74] It is well-known that the Prophet ﷺ sometimes yearned for enlightenment through revelation, but that he had to wait for unpredictable and indefinite periods before the revelation came. [75]

The Islamic tradition, however, contains numerous stories and anecdotes to the effect that the Prophet ﷺ performed a number of miracles. Since these stories categorically contradict the Qur'anic approach, they are interpolations reflecting the universal tendency toward the glorification of one's heroes and attributing a supernatural status to them. [76] We find this tendency in the followers of every religion without any exception. Gautam Buddha probably had the most rational and philosophical mind among the spiritual geniuses of the world. But he too was credited with possessing supernatural powers, which he vigorously denied.

The Qur'anic references to the miracles performed by the Semitic prophets, however, pose an intellectual difficulty. It may significantly be asked as to why God's gift of miracles was withheld in the case of the Prophet

A Restatement of the Islamic Thought System (Contd.)

Muhammad ﷺ. It maybe said that the Qur'an was the greatest miracle, and that there was no need for any lesser ones after the revelation of the Qur'an. But according to the Qur'an itself, all other prophets had been the recipients of Divine revelation from the very beginning. Therefore, this argument seems to break down.

Again, it maybe said that miracles were necessary means for convincing mankind in its infancy about the existence of God. Since mankind had become mature and rational at the time of the advent of the Prophet ﷺ, such modes of persuasion were no longer necessary. But ancient Egyptians, Iranians, Jews, Greeks, Chinese, Aryans, and Dravidians were not any less mature than the Arabs of the sixth century. In fact, their intellectual and cultural level was much higher than that of the pre-Islamic Arabs who were the original audience of the Prophet ﷺ.

The above difficulties have led Syed Ahmad and some others to the denial of miracles. In defense of this view they have given the most far-fetched interpretations of plain and simple Qur'anic texts, which prima facie affirm miracles. For example, the Qur'anic reference to the drying up of the sea to help the flight of Moses from Egypt is interpreted as the natural phenomenon of the ebb and flow of tides, rather than as a miracle. Similarly, the reference to water gushing forth from the soil at the touch of Mose's rod is also interpreted as his exploring the soil for water and being very lucky in the first few attempts.

Some elliptical interpretations of Qur'anic verses are quite convincing. But some Qur'anic references to the supernatural cannot be explained away in this fashion. It is true that in most cases the Qur'anic reference to the supernatural does not give any details as found in the Bible. These details may have become an integral part of the Islamic folklore, but, since they are extra-Qur'anic, they can be rejected without disrespect to the Qur'an. But some reference to the supernatural will still remain, and it would be patently invalid to twist the meanings of plain Arabic words to prove one's contention that the Qur'an does not refer to miracles. [77]

Another solution is to hold that the laws of nature are nothing but nature's regular obedience to God's commands, while miracles are nothing but obedience to God's extraordinary commands. This view is certainly logically possible. But two major difficulties arise, if one asserts it. Firstly, as pointed out by Syed Ahmad, the Qur'an clearly states that God does not change His ways, which seems to rule out the suspension of Divine commands, even though God may have the power to do so. Secondly, since no miracles occurred during the Prophet's ﷺ time, they could not have occurred earlier also, as God does not change His ways. On the other hand, if God did perform miracles before the Prophet's ﷺ time, their stoppage after the Prophet's ﷺ birth in 570 A.D. implies a change in the ways of God. Nay, it sounds paradoxical that God should have performed or granted several miracles to help His prophets such as Moses and Jesus, but none to help Muhammad ﷺ, the greatest among the prophets.

It seems to me that no clear-cut interpretation of the Qur'anic reference to miracles can claim to be the true one. It maybe the case that miracles did occur before the Prophet's ﷺ time, and he too was blessed with the greatest of all miracles; the Qur'an itself. After this no other miracle was called for. It may also be the case that some unusual events governed by natural laws were interpreted as miracles in the remote past and this memory became deeply entrenched in the collective memory of the Semitic people, who were the immediate audience of the Qur'an. Now in order to preserve the continuity of the Biblical tradition and to facilitate the acceptance of the mature Qur'anic conception of the uniformity of nature or the reign of law, the Qur'an did not specifically repudiate the false but otherwise innocent belief in miracles. [78]

It seems to me that Syed Ahmad's emphatic denial of miracles was as uncalled for as is the traditional affirmation of miracles as a part of the Islamic creed or thought system. What is important is the question whether or not the Qur'an is held as a miracle, that is, whether one holds the Qur'an to be the speech of Muhammad ﷺ, who in good faith interpreted it as the speech of God, or whether one holds that the Qur'an is God's revelation to Muhammad ﷺ, even though one maybe unable to understand the ontology and dynamics of Divine revelation.

In the final analysis, there can be no proof that the Qur'an is a miracle; there can be only an intensely personal testimony to its 'numinous' quality or flavor. I, for one, am profoundly stirred by numerous verses of the Qur'an, which appear to me as the most powerful propositional confirmation of my own authentic and deep conviction—that the heavens and the earth and all that lies between them are not mere brute facts, but immersed in a mystery I can never fathom, except that it is good and the Source of all the goodness, order, and beauty I encounter around me. The Qur'an assures me that my faith in God (which is neither self-evidently true, nor logically deducible from self-evidently true premises, nor inductively confirmable) is not an illusion or a mere culturally conditioned '*blik*', but rather a true insight. This insight liberates me from all fear and suffuses me with peace and a joyful surrender to the Lord to do with me as He pleases. Some passages of the Qur'an affect me like a symphony, which reduces one to a wave in the encompassing ocean of spiritual harmony and joy. If this be the effect of the Qur'an, then it may rightly be said that it is a miracle which terminates the need of miracles and inaugurates the age of reason.

To say that the Qur'an is a miracle does not, however, imply accepting any theological meta-theory of revelation, over and above the authenticity of the Prophet ﷺ and the sense of mystery in the face of the Qur'an. It is true that many paranormal psychical phenomena such as telepathy, clairvoyance, automatic writing, etc., also baffle our attempts to fit them into the conceptual frame, which we accept. But they do not have the 'numinous' quality of the Qur'an with its message to man, and its power to quicken man's conscience and receptivity to the Primal Value Elan. With the opening up of new frontiers of knowledge and dimensions of human experience man's contemporary conceptual framework may have to be revised, and this revised framework may easily render the presently paranormal phenomena as normal. But even if we accept (for the sake of argument) that the revised framework would also suffice to explain 'the event of the Qur'an', this will not touch the question of the spiritual impact or effect of the Qur'an, which may well remain unique, mysterious, and incomparably 'numinous'.

It maybe thought that my own or, for that matter, the typical response of Muslims in general to the Qur'an is a product of cultural conditioning, and no outsider will or can respond in the same manner. This may well be true. But even if true, it does not imply that my response is necessarily a mere conditioned response and nothing more. It is possible that this is the case, and it is equally possible that this is not the case. In the final analysis, there can be no proof as to what is the case. Nor does the lack of proof one way or the other make any difference to my response, to the extent that it is not merely culturally conditioned but also authentic, and is not concerned with vindicating itself to others as 'the' truth, capable of objective proof. Indeed, even the claim of authenticity cannot be established or proved by the individual. But there is one crucial point which goes to suggest, though not prove the authenticity of the individual; whether he, as a free individual, experiences any tension between any of his value judgments and those of the Qur'an, and if so, whether he has the moral courage to admit this and to live with this tension, rather than embrace inauthentic existence, or surrender himself into the arms of an external authority, albeit Divine. The presence of tension implies that the person is not a mass man or a mere product of cultural conditioning, but a free and authentic person who has the courage of his convictions, and whose subjectivity has not been totally merged in the objectivity of his milieu or even of the Qur'an.

II

AN ANALYTICAL AND SOCIOLOGICAL APPROACH TO HADITH

The Sociology of Hadith

The traditional concept of the sacred Islamic law (*Shariah*) applicable to all spheres of human activity has already been described. The traditional conception implies that the real task of the Muslim is to implement the sacred law as faithfully as humanly possible rather than to refine or improve the law itself. Indeed, the authority and sanctity of the authentic sayings of the Prophet ﷺ and the Word of God is thought to be almost indivisible. [79]

This was, however, not the earliest position. It is significant that almost for the first two hundred years of Islamic history relatively much less attention was paid to the collection and arrangement of *hadith* than to the study of Islamic jurisprudence (*fiqh*), which was the principal discipline that supplemented the Qur'an. [80] It has been suggested that the collection of *hadith* was not necessary as a large number of Muslims were already well-conversant with the doings and sayings of the Prophet ﷺ. According to this view, the lack of attention to the collection of *hadith* in the early period had no ideological significance. But this appears to be an oversimplification of the issue.

It is significant that Umar was very cautious in attributing sayings to the Prophet ﷺ. It is said that he only related seventy sayings of the Prophet ﷺ. The same also applies to Abu Bakr who is reported to have prepared a report of five hundred sayings of the Prophet ﷺ, but subsequently burnt

A Restatement of the Islamic Thought System (Contd.)

them lest they contain any errors. Umar also discouraged officers and others from diverting the attention of the people from the Qur'an to the *hadith*. This has been acknowledged by Zahbi, one of the greatest scholars of *hadith* literature. [81]

Umar's cautious approach to the sayings of the Prophet ﷺ, however, does not imply any indifference or disrespect to the Prophet ﷺ. Umar fully accepted that the basic precepts of Islam such as prayers, fasting, etc., could not be carried out fully without following the Prophet's ﷺ interpretation of the bare Qur'anic injunctions. But in matters of personal taste as well as in numerous institutional or policy matters Umar felt himself free to make independent decisions. In his monumental life of Umar, Shibli has devoted one detailed chapter to the changes or developments in the institutional system of Islam made by Umar during his caliphate. These changes are known as the 'firsts' (*awwalyat*) of Umar. Some of these changes or innovations were objected to by his contemporaries, and later on Shafai strongly criticized Umar for deviating from the practice of the Prophet ﷺ. He recommended that some of the 'firsts' of Umar be repealed.

Umar's approach to the Islamic institutional system remains a striking example of creative fidelity. He seems to have made, explicitly or implicitly, a distinction between directive principles and instrumental rules, and also between the precept system and the institutional system. While remaining loyal to the directive principles and the precept system as enunciated by the Prophet ﷺ, Umar felt free, rather deemed it his duty, to scrutinize all instrumental rules of the institutional system, including the ones followed by the Prophet ﷺ. Indeed, a critical scrutiny of instrumental laws or bylaws is always necessary, since a rigid and mechanical fixation upon the letter of the law often obstructs the attainment of the basic objectives of the lawgiver. What was pre-eminently useful in the past may become less useful and, at times, even positively harmful as a result of the altered conditions.

The *hadith* movement was, in fact, the response of a later age to the cumulative social and institutional variations in different segments of the vast Islamic society. Firstly, the 'reasoned opinions' of the *Hanafi* school, founded by Abu Hanifa (d. 767 AD), must have led to differences of opinion. Secondly, Islam having spread among people with different socio-cultural backgrounds, further differences of opinion were inevitable. The emergence of the other three schools of Islamic law and jurisprudence represented by Malik (d. 795 AD), Shafai (d. 820 AD), and Hambal (d. 855 AD) reflected these growing disagreements. Fissiparous and centrifugal forces were continually on the increase. The creative minds of the period must have felt that a greater stress and reliance upon the sayings of the Prophet ﷺ would effectively check the onslaughts of innovation (*bid'at*). Theologians came to interpret the sayings of the Prophet ﷺ as implicitly revealed by God (*wahy-e-khafi*), while the Qur'an was manifestly revealed (*wahy-e-jali*). This interpretation raised the *hadith* almost to the status of the Word of God. The situational logic of this striking departure from the approach of Umar is clear. *Hadith* was used to narrow down and prevent further differences within the Islamic community, which was now scattered far and wide in the world.

The sayings of the Prophet ﷺ, to the extent that they are authentic, are certainly of the greatest interest to all Muslims, for the obvious reason that they reveal the Prophet's ﷺ understanding and interpretation of the spirit as well as letter of the Qur'an. Who could be more competent than the Prophet ﷺ himself to interpret God's Word? Nevertheless, if the Prophet ﷺ was not Divine but a mortal, albeit the recipient of revelation (which is exactly what the Qur'an itself expressly and repeatedly declares), then his interpretation of the revelation must be distinguished from the actual content of the revelation.

The first and the greatest scholar-jurist who collected the authentic (from his point of view) sayings and reports about the Prophet ﷺ was Imam Bukhari. He was followed by Muslim, Abu Daud, Tirmidhi and others. I shall, however, confine myself to Bukhari alone.

Bukhari took great pains to sift the authentic traditions. The number of putative sayings of the Prophet ﷺ exceeded six hundred thousand. After immense labors in the light of carefully selected principles of evidence (which are valid, though not sufficient for excluding spurious reports), Bukhari divided the reports into four classes, **(a)** absolutely authentic (*Sahi*), **(b)** probably authentic (*hasan*), **(c)** probably spurious (*zaif*), **(d)** certainly spurious (*mauzu*). He included the first types alone in his famous collection of *hadith*.

The number of authentic sayings in the collection is 7,275 arranged under sixty-three chapters, which have been subdivided where necessary into headings or sections according to subject matter. These reports number only 2,180 in the standard abridged Bukhari (*Tajrid-e-Bukhari*) compiled by Zubaidi in the 13th century. [82]

The overwhelming number of sayings in the Bukhari corpus deal with matters connected with the precept system like prayer, fasting, pilgrimage, etc., that is, with the relationship between man and his Creator rather than with social matters. Thus out of the two thousand and odd sayings in *Tajrid-e-Bukhari* only about 300 or so deal with such matters as trade and commerce, land tenancy, money transactions, contracts, taxes, distribution of wealth, slavery, position and role of women, science or medicine, etc. While adherence to the sayings of the Prophet ﷺ in such matters as the time and mode of prayer, fasting, payment of wealth-tax and finally the pilgrimage to Mecca (for those who can afford it) does not stand in the way of sociopolitical or economic changes in response to new conditions and the ever-expanding frontiers of human knowledge, strict adherence to the sayings of the Prophet ﷺ in such matters as the status and role of women, inheritance of massive unearned wealth with only minimum taxation, private control of the means of production, family planning, social hygiene and medicine, and similar other matters certainly obstructs social progress. To give some pertinent examples, the sayings of the Prophet ﷺ maintain that women are naturally inferior to men, that slavery is permissible if one feeds slaves kindly, that Muslims need not worry about overpopulation, since God suffices to feed all mouths created by him, etc.

THE STATUS OF HADITH

The issue of the status of *hadith* is not merely a theoretical one, but has a vital practical significance. The *hadith* literature covers a wide range of individual and collective life, and many of the reported sayings of the Prophet ﷺ have a very specific and detailed content. This sharply contrasts with the Qur'an, which (barring a few specific injunctions) contains mostly broad principles of conduct rather than specific rules and regulations. Herein lies the utility as well as the potential danger of *hadith*. On the one hand *hadith* gives concrete meaning and content to the non-specific and general regulations of the Qur'an, while on the other it is precisely this concreteness of the *hadith* that injects rigidity in the institutional system of Islam.

The concept of 'prescriptive specificity' refers to the degree of generality or specificity of a prescription or rule of action. For example, the prescription to eat a balanced diet is very general, while the prescription to add fruits and vegetables to meat is relatively more specific. The naming of the specific fruits, etc., or their exact quantities makes the prescription even more specific. This specificity could be increased even further, if desired. The degree of specificity is a crucial matter, since, upon it would depend the extent of autonomy or initiative of an individual or group committed to the rules in question. If the rules are highly specific, they would proportionately restrict individual freedom. This specificity is a double-edged instrument. On the one hand, it certainly helps the individual by providing him with concrete and detailed guidance, when the mere affirmation of a general principle may not have helped him to the same degree. On the other hand, such specificity tends to check the growth of the individual through the exercise of his own reason, since it presents him with a complete and ready made concrete rule. Again, while a high degree of specificity may prevent the individual from aberrations, it may also prevent him from attaining higher levels of achievement. Now, while the prescriptions of the Qur'an are mostly general and non-specific, the prescriptions found in the reported sayings of the Prophet ﷺ are frequently highly specific. Consequently, while unquestioning submission to the Qur'an does not entail the loss of one's autonomy but only a measure of restriction within a very wide range of freedom, unquestioning submission to the *hadith* entails very drastic restrictions upon one's freedom of thought and action.

Some observers maintain that *hadith* literature does not raise any problem, provided we accept the principle that all sayings, contrary to the Qur'an, are inauthentic. But this is an oversimplification of a complex problem. The Qur'an contains very few specific or concrete truthclaims, which neither confirm nor contradict the large number of truthclaims, found in the *hadith* literature. If an agreement with the Qur'an be regarded as the sole test of authenticity or validity, this criterion will cease to be useful, since the Qur'an would neither confirm nor contradict several putative sayings of the Prophet ﷺ. To accept all putative sayings, not contradicted by the Qur'an, as authoritative or binding would drastically curtail one's independent reasoning. The utility of the *hadith* thus very easily lends itself to becoming a mechanical conformity to rules, as distinguished from a creative fidelity to basic principles and values. An excessive concern with *hadith* tends to promote a 'rule centric' morality, which stresses observance of rules, as distinguished from a 'value centric' morality, which stresses devotion to values. Obviously, the observance of rules is essential for the good life. But when rules become supreme, they tend to obliterate the crucial distinction between ends and means or between intrinsic and instrumental values. Value centricity, as I understand it, presupposes a balanced concern with both ends and means.

A Restatement of the Islamic Thought System (Contd.)

Some thoughtful persons take the stand that the prescriptions of the Prophet ﷺ are binding upon Muslims only in respect of specifically 'religious matters', but that Muslims are free to act according to their own discretion in all 'worldly matters', provided they do not violate the Qur'an. A particular reported saying of the Prophet ﷺ is quoted in support of this contention. [83] This approach certainly permits a much greater degree of individual freedom and initiative to the Muslims. But there are at least two difficulties with this approach. Firstly, it is not at all clear what is the connotation of worldly matters. For example, would such social issues as the freedom and equality of women, family planning, nationalization of industries, abolition of slavery and other forms of social exploitation, etc., come in the category of' worldly matters', or would they not? Most probably Muslim theologians and jurists would not at all agree about the exact scope of worldly matters. Consequently, as long as the unquestioning submission to the *hadith* is regarded, more or less as essential as the unquestioning submission to the Qur'an, the range of freedom of thought and action of the Muslim would continue to be severely limited.

Secondly, even if this particular *hadith* be accepted as a guiding principle, it appears to conflict with the claim that Islam is a complete code of life. Numerous theologians claim that Islam does not make any distinction between the religious and the secular spheres of life. Following this principle, Muslims have consistently refused to separate politics and economics from religion. At every stage the conservative Muslims have resisted the efforts of their liberal and more rationalistic coreligionists to keep religion confined to its own proper sphere, instead of making it a final judge in all matters. Thus the difficulty, which is posed by the high degree of specificity of the prescriptions of the Prophet ﷺ, remains unsolved, as long as *hadith* is looked upon as binding upon Muslims as the Qur'an itself.

Every religion has a dominant basic vision or thought-cum-value system as its essence. Even if the essence has a permanent validity, many elements of the concrete *gestalt* may lose their relevance or their inner appeal to the sensibility of a later period. If, and when, this happens, these features of the *gestalt* tend to become cognito-emotively insignificant rather than invalid. For example, whether women will go to hell in greater numbers than men, whether or not Gabriel's wings are correctly reported as six hundred in the sayings of the Prophet ﷺ, and whether it is true that Abraham was circumcised at the age of eighty, etc., fail to grip the contemporary mind, as they are irrelevant to the living needs and problems of the present.[84] Consequently, we tend to ignore rather than settle the truth or falsity of such issues. Now a very large number of the putative authentic sayings of the Prophet ﷺ, as found in the Bukhari corpus, are of the above type. This, however, does not compromise the dignity and sanctity of the Prophet ﷺ. Nor does the refusal to bracket the *hadith* with the Qur'an negate the many exhortations in the Qur'an to follow God and the Prophet ﷺ.[85] The real import of following the example of the Prophet ﷺ lies in a creative fidelity to the basic values he taught to mankind, rather than in a mechanical and rigid fixation upon the details of his daily life and behavior.

The static approach to the sayings of the Prophet ﷺ would only serve to alienate the contemporary mind from Islam and the Prophet ﷺ. As Tillich points out, religious symbols, like any other symbolic system, have an inner vitality and span of life, and are subject to decay and death in the course of time.[86] Unless religious symbols are nourished by fresh insights and enriched by freely accepting the growth of new dimensions in old values (due to the creativity of the in-group or the out-groups as the case maybe), the symbols of religion start losing their relevance, evocative appeal, and directive power for their adherents. Thus, today when egalitarian ideals and technological skills have resulted in the actual abolition of poverty in many Western societies, the traditional religious ethic of charity (aimed at merely ameliorating the sufferings of the needy and the poor) will never be able to inspire man as profoundly as the socialist ethic of planned welfare.

The belief that Islamic polity being perfect, does not stand in any need of growth or reform, and that all the evils that plague man are due to the faults of Muslims, rather than of Islam, maybe called the finalistic fallacy. This fallacy haunts not only Muslims but the followers of other religions as well. But perhaps its grip on the Muslim mind is the strongest. The finalistic fallacy is understandable in the case of Islam, since its polity is, indeed, firmly rooted in values possessing universal validity. Nevertheless, it is a fallacy to suppose that any code of conduct could be final in the literal sense. Perfection is the ideal limit of an infinite progression rather than an actually realized human condition. In other words, perfection is the hovering and inspiring ideal, rather than the settled or the entrenched real. Perhaps the unbounded reverence of the Muslims for the Prophet ﷺ together with the Qur'anic verse, referring to God's completing the faith and completing

His blessings on the Prophet ﷺ, have led to this static orientation of the Muslims. The fear of inner freedom and creativity, as pointed out by Erich Fromm, is another factor. But completing of faith and of Divine blessings refers only to the extra-ordinary phenomenon of revelation, the only miracle which the Prophet ﷺ really claimed to possess. The completion of the faith certainly does not imply the static finality of the Islamic thought-cum-value system or the institutional system. However, it must be conceded that the Islamic precept system, as taught and practiced by the founder, will have to be accorded an ultimate sanctity, without which Islam, as a distinct religion, will not be able to preserve its identity and personality in social space-time. The sayings and example of the Prophet ﷺ must remain unequivocally normative in the sphere of precepts, if the Islamic tradition is to continue as a living *gestalt*. The Qur'anic precept system being highly general and non-specific, an unquestioning submission to the Prophet's ﷺ example is essential for maintaining a unified precept system. But there is no justification for extending this discipline to the institutional system in all its ramifications. This implies unnecessary restrictions on man's freedom of choice and his quest for fresh values. Traditionalism in the sphere of precepts is quite compatible with dynamism in the politico-economic or social spheres.

III

GOD AND HISTORY:

The Concept of Social Causation

No worldview can be complete without an interpretation of history or a theory of social phenomena. The traditional religious view is that either God ordains the rise and fall of nations and individuals, or that God has granted freedom to man and rewards him according to his deserts. Belief in the Divine regulation of history has gradually evolved from two earlier beliefs, **(a)** primitive animism, that is, belief in natural spirits or gods of fire, rain, water, etc., who could be placated by prayer, and **(b)** the cult of magic, that is, the technique of bending those spirits to man's will. Since both prayer and magic often disappointed primitive man's expectations, this led the sensitive and creative minds of the time to the concept of a tribal god who gave victory to his worshippers. Since this approach too was vulnerable, it gradually led to the conception of the Universal Lord Who treats His creatures impartially according to their deserts, or according to His own inscrutable will. [87]

To begin with, God was conceived in anthropomorphic terms, which were gradually qualified as and when the difficulties of anthropomorphism came to light. The earlier conception was that God was a powerful and arbitrary Ruler Who rewarded His obedient slaves and punished the defiant ones. Gradually, the image of God changes to a loving, rational, and just Lord Who ordains (without any external compulsion) the rule of law, as distinct from rule by Divine fiat. In other words, the idea emerges that God does not govern the Universe as a despot, but regulates it through the imposition of Divinely willed laws which He has the power to change or suspend at will. The evolution of the idea of God thus leads to the notion of metaphysical causation—the view that the causal connection is not inherent in the nature of things, but is a Divine command. In other words, every causal connection is rooted in a Divine purpose.

The growth of science and mathematics in Western Europe in the 16th and 17th centuries, however, showed that the idea of purpose or rational end was not methodologically necessary for the empirical discovery of causal connections between natural phenomena. All that was needed was accurate observation or experiment, construction of empirical hypotheses and their verification. This understandably led to the elimination of the purposive or teleological dimension from the concept of cause, as understood in science. This implied the view that nature was a system of mechanical non-purposive events determined by natural causes. Thus in the 17th century the mechanistic cosmology of Descartes displaced the teleological cosmology of Aristotle. Descartes, however, affirmed a mental or spiritual order as coexisting with the natural, the two being entirely unconnected, except in man, in whom the two intersected and mutually interacted. Animals were pure bodies without any consciousness or feelings, while angels were pure spiritual beings. The nature of God, as the absolute Uncreated Substance, First Cause and Perfect Being could not be understood (except analogically) by the finite human minds. Descartes' dualism thus conformed to the ancient and medieval concept of man as a union of mind and body or spirit and matter, but it totally displaced the concept of purpose from the sphere of nature, including animals, which were deemed to be complicated machines. Descartes' cosmology thus had no room for life, birth, growth, decay, and death as autonomous biological phenomena, rather than as pure mechanistic events completely governed by the laws of mechanics. Descartes mechanistic approach did not admit the evolution of qualitative novelty in nature over and above mere quantitative complexity. Nevertheless, if the concept of mechanistic causation was so useful in the realm of Physics and Astronomy, etc., why should it not be used in Biology for explaining the wide variety of animals and plants? This is precisely what Darwin did.

There can be no doubt that both Descartes and Darwin succeeded remarkably well as methodological pioneers and trendsetters of subsequent scientific investigation. But Descartes failed to realize that a reductive mechanistic cosmology distorts the nature of biological phenomena and ignores qualitative difference within nature. Likewise, Darwin failed to realize that to explain the emergence of higher species as an accidental result of the cumulative effect of chance variations in the offspring of lower species leaves us totally baffled and dissatisfied, even though this explanation is logically possible. However, just as Darwin had extended the concept of natural causation from Physics to Biology, Karl Marx soon afterward extended it still further to Sociology and History. The expression 'Social Darwinism' is thus pre-eminently illuminating.

Marx's conception of natural and social causation are distinct improvements upon the older mechanistic version. Marx recognized the emergence of new qualities and higher levels of matter in the course of its dialectical development, thanks to his Hegelian inspiration. [88] But it seems to me- that like Darwin before him, Marx fails to ask the ontological significance of the emergence of higher levels of matter. No matter how much our knowledge advances, there can be no verifiable scientific explanation of the actual ascent of matter into higher and still higher levels of organization. Marx seems to accept this fact as the inherent and ultimately inexplicable feature of the cosmic process, without using the concept of chance, as Darwin had done to account for ceaseless variations and occasional mutations in the offspring of species. Nor does Marx resort to any metaphysical speculation, since he had already rejected it as an ideological superstructure devoid of verifiable scientific truth. [89]

If Marx had possessed the concept of existential interpretation (which differs from both scientific explanation and a metaphysical theory, in the classical sense), he might well have reflected upon the ontological significance or existential meaning of the Universe. As it is, Marx could neither interpret the actual emergence of higher levels of matter, nor justify his essential optimism that this pattern of dialectical development would continue in the future. In this respect, therefore, Darwin's theory of natural selection and Marx's concept of dialectical development are equally sterile. The fact that the cosmic process threw up life and mind in the past and that both continue to exist so far may suffice for a *de facto* but not a *de jure* optimism flowing from an existential interpretation of the Universe. The affirmation of a Primal Value Elan, however, does provide grounds for a *de jure* optimism, since it implies that higher levels of being emerge due to an immanent and eternally operative impulse toward the creation of values. This further implies that man's own quest for value is rooted in the PVE; the Supreme Source of all values.

Marx's concept of the withering away of the state is yet another instance of unjustifiable optimism. While the removal of class conflict will remove many contradictions and tensions of present-day society, tension, tragedy, and contradiction are the inseparable shadows of finite existence, so that the basic need for the state will ever-remain.

SOCIAL CAUSATION AND THE ELAN: CONCEPTION OF GOD

Marx's conception of historical materialism and social causation have no place for Divine purpose as distinct from the undeniable role of human purpose in the historical process. But, to my mind, the sociological interpretation of history is quite compatible with the *Elan* conception of God. Let us see in some detail how this is the case.

We have seen that the working of the immanent *Primal Value Elan* leads to the emergence of higher and still higher levels of being eventually resulting in man himself. This marks the inception of a new era in the cosmic process; the start of history, as distinct from nature.

Nature may well be conceptualized and manipulated with the help of mechanistic concepts without any recourse to purpose, though at the biological level of cosmic evolution, pure mechanistic concepts need to be supplemented by vitalistic concepts such as organism, cell, growth, assimilation, and reproduction, etc. Conscious purpose is, however, not yet in evidence, though instinct could be regarded as the rudimentary prototype of purpose-something between a pure mechanistic push or force and the conscious purposive striving to reach a goal. At the human level, purpose becomes the warp and woof of life. Man's crucial differentia from the animals is his conceptual intelligence and potential inner freedom to choose his values and purposes. This implies that man not merely makes a living, but has the latent power to make his life, and even to take his own life. It is significant that man is the only living being who commits suicide, and there does not seem to be any rudimentary analogue of suicide at the pre-human level.

The reign of purpose and inner freedom at the human level distinguishes history from nature. But, as we know, the realms of nature and of history interact within the over-all unity of the cosmic process. Man, for instance, cuts trees for firewood, only to reduce rainfall. Much later on he learns of the connection between forestation and rainfall, and also develops the technique of building dams. Similarly, geography makes history, while in its turn; history alters geography as human creativity reaches a high enough level.

Man's quest for value is the fuel, which keeps going the interaction between him and the environment, both natural and social. His most basic value is the will to live. But just as pure sensation is always embedded in apperception, similarly the will to live is almost always supplemented by other conscious or unconscious impulses, the most basic being the drive for power and prominence. This leads to the individual struggle for power, since not everybody can be supreme. Every group (whether racial, religious, occupational) also strives for supremacy and for the maximum possible share in the total wealth of society. This gives rise to the class struggle, as pointed out by Marx. Thus an inter-class and an interpersonal struggle within every class goes on all the time.

Power, whether *de jure* or *de facto* implies the ability to coerce others into submission through physical strength or through control over the environment or the decision-making process. Once the better sword or the swifter horse supplied this power, while today it comes from nuclear weapons or rather the economic and industrial base to manufacture them.

The struggle to live and the struggle for power are coextensive with life, including the animal kingdom. The will to power is not suppressed in animals who fight without any sense of disapproval by others or by themselves. But among humans while the struggle for existence approved (it being even conceded that man has the inalienable right to take another's life in sheer self-defense), the struggle for power is not approved. Both society and the individual feel uneasy at the idea of striving for superiority and power. This is because, unlike animals, man is endowed not only with instincts, including the will to power, but also with a potential conscience or the Divine spark, which is the source of man's ideals. Man is motivated not merely by instincts or interests, but also by his genuine ideals — justice, compassion, love, and truth, etc. This leads to an inevitable ambivalence in man's motives and his tendency to clothe his pursuit of interests in the garb of ideals, values, and principles. These in turn lead to the formation of total worldviews or ideologies in the Marxist sense.

Belief in ideologies is not a case of fraud or self-deceit, but is a sort of bewitchment of intelligence under the hidden influence of one's interests. Ideologies really appeal to the individual and the group who sincerely fight against their opponents, as if they were fighting for impersonal ideals rather than personal or group interests. But behind all this ideological superstructure (which is genuine up to a point) there lies the basic struggle for power and superiority, within groups, whether large or small.

Each occupational class has its own interests, and corresponding to them, its own conception of the right pattern of things (which it calls objective justice), which it seeks to impose upon others. The clash of values is thus partly the reflection of the clash of interests of different groups. The historical process consists of the interplay of ideals and interests and of cooperation and conflict at different levels. Every individual is condemned to fight at some level or the other. The vast majority struggle to establish their personal identity as members of a particular group: professional, political, or religious as the case maybe.

This struggle for superiority is not adequately recognized in the traditional thought systems of different religions, which are not sufficiently aware of the range, and depth of man's struggle in social space. Traditional religious ethics speaks of justice, righteousness, duty, truth, and compassion, etc., as if they were clear-cut and absolute values, which could guide man. But they all break down in the face of man's struggle for his interests as well as ideals. How can a person survive in his profession if he is absolutely altruistic or even just, and prefers the job to go even to a slightly more competent rival? How can a person survive as a politician, if he does not choose a party and a few comrades on the basis of shared values and goals, and then stick to them, despite minor lapses and failures? How can a politician or administrator function without giving some concession to human weakness and adjusting his ideals (to some extent) to get the willing cooperation of his group? The idealist thinker or moralist does not realize the predicament of men of action who are steeped in struggle. While the pure thinker must retain his integrity and independent judgment, he must cooperate with such men of action as are relatively, though not absolutely, in the right. The fundamental axiom of the ethics of struggle is to choose the lesser evil rather than reject a qualified good.

The mature, informed, and intellectually honest person has the capacity to become aware of the hidden influence of his interests upon his values and his group ideology. Actual insight into the power and depth of the economic motive helps man partly to transcend the gravitational pull of his individual or class interests, and to attempt to judge as an impartial observer, though he can never succeed in the attempt. But the attempt as such makes him approximate to an objective approach, namely, giving equal consideration to the interests of all concerned, rather than any particular individual or group. It seems every age or society has a few impartial observers who manage to transcend their personal or group interests and eliminate all hostility or antagonism to different classes. Their call to end the exploitation of the weaker classes does not erode their humanistic love and universal compassion.

Giving primacy to the economic factor or struggle for power should not, therefore, lead us to deny the power and role of impersonal ideas and ideals in shaping history, though the vast majority of persons do tend to reason and act under the hidden influence of their interests.

Different Factors of Social Causation

Let us now analyze two types of social phenomena, first a concrete case of politico-economic confrontation, and, second, a concrete case of the growth of ethical norms. We shall see how ethical factors enter into the fight for economic interests, and, conversely, how economic interests enter into the growth of ethical ideals. This will enable us better to appreciate the complexity of social causation and the role of different factors in social phenomena.

A trade union holds some established rule or regulation of the company to be unjust, while the management holds it to be fair and reasonable. The union threatens to go on strike. Many reasonable and sympathetic officers of the management are opposed to appeasement on both ethical and administrative grounds, but the top management succumbs to the pressure tactics of the union. Encouraged by its success, the union takes up other issues and eventually a deadlock arises and the plant is shut down. Economic hardship of the workers leads to a split in the union and a change in its leadership and policies. Meanwhile the shareholders are so disgusted that they sell the plant to a big company, which is in a much stronger position to deal with the union. Finding that the union leadership is in able hands and may pose a danger to the company later on, the new management succeeds in bribing some union members, who have a personal grudge against the leader, to form a rival union on prima facie more militant lines than the moderate approach of the then leader. Though the militancy of the rival leader is not bona fide, it makes a sincere appeal to some younger workers who are personally honest and inspired by ethical ideals. We can go on giving other details. But the point of the illustration is to show the variety of determinants, ethical, political, economic, personal, which fuse with each other and jointly produce the net result. But the economic factor remains the most important single factor, since it triggers the entire process and continues to operate throughout, though at times from behind the scene, as it were.

Let us now turn to the factors that have contributed to the steady decline of *purdah* among the Indian Muslims after independence. To explain the decline of *purdah* as the result of sheer immorality and erosion of Islamic piety is to miss the operation of situational factors, such as, **(a)** the economic consequences of the political changes in India after independence, viz., the hardship of Muslims due to the sudden abolition of reservation in services and in the legislature, and the abolition of landlordism, **(b)** the social consequences of the migration of large numbers of eligible young men to Pakistan in search of better employment prospects, **(c)** the cultural trends among non-Muslims who were socially more progressive in the matter of female education and also stood to gain economically thereby, and **(d)** the lack of women's colleges with *purdah* facilities. The joint result of all the above factors was that many Muslims who stood for *purdah* as a value were faced with an acute social problem with economic implications. They started to give much greater importance to female education, which promised economic security to girls who could not be married because of the shortage of eligible marriage partners due to the 'bachelor drain' to Pakistan. Since, however, there were no *purdah* colleges, they had to send their daughters or sisters to mixed institutions where *purdah* was almost impossible.

The point to note is that Muslims were not compelled in the literal sense to do so, since they could have decided just to trust in God for getting a suitable match for their wards (indeed this is what some families actually did), or they could have agreed to the marriage of their wards beneath their own family status. Thus economic difficulties did not determine their choice in a rigid mechanistic fashion, but facilitated the adoption of a new way of life leading to a change in their value system. Situational needs evoked a fresh response, which they did not regard as immoral or sinful because of its departure from the traditional mores, though conservative Muslims who stuck to *purdah* naturally thought otherwise. The pro-changers were enabled to reflect on the meaning of democracy, social justice, the rights of women, etc., and in this process new values or new dimensions in old values emerged on their mental horizon. They did not think that they had made an opportunistic adjustment to society for the sake of material gains, but that their values had grown or matured due to their creative response to situational challenges.

Ethical factors thus enter into the causal nexus, though their degree of causal efficacy maybe generally less than that of the economic. In an election, for example, the party or person who wins is generally the one with sufficient economic resources to be able to reach and convince the electorate that their interests will be promoted. But sometimes the public will prefer an honest mediocre candidate to an efficient, energetic but unreliable person. This clearly shows the operation of the ethical factor in politics. However, the standard of ethical integrity expected of politicians is not the same as expected of saints and savants, and very often integrity of a high order makes the politician inconvenient and unacceptable to the party bosses as well as to the masses. Similarly, while there are numerous cases of administrative favoritism, many appointments and promotions take place on the basis of merit. These cases also represent the operation of the ethical factor in administration.

Moral values and ethical motivation are thus active determinants of both micro-social and macro-social phenomena. History also reflects a broad pattern of value preservation and accretion, though without any concern for particular persons or societies. The pattern is not geometrical but organic, and can be grasped only when the historian is able to look at the broad sweep of history as an impartial spectator (as far as humanly possible) rather than as a partisan.

Evil and the Historical Process

Grave moral and social evils are a fact of history. Men not only get away with, but also succeed in attaining their objectives through flattery, bribery, deceit, fraud, exploitation, manipulation, and murder, etc. The traditional religious approach to this fact is that although evil means may bring about short-term success, the evildoer suffers in the long run in this very world. But if for some reason the evildoer escapes punishment in this life he will be punished by God in the next. The traditional religious response further implies that all the sufferings of the virtuous at the hands of the evildoers are not unmerited, since the seemingly virtuous might be guilty of sins or faults, which are known to God but not to humans. To the extent that (so the religious position goes on) the sufferings of the virtuous are really undeserved, they will get suitable compensation in life after death.

There is no contradiction in the above approach or existential interpretation of social or historical evil, just as there is no contradiction involved in the view that values have emerged purely as an accidental by-product of matter in motion. But just as this latter interpretation does not grip us because of the staggering number of chance events all converging to produce the intricate order and harmony of the cosmos, similarly, the view that the sufferings of virtuous souls are really deserved, or that the tragedies and evils of this life will be compensated in another life, somehow has lost its authentic hold on many men who believe in a spiritual dimension of the Universe but not in the traditional conception of God with its corollary of personal immortality.

If one rejects the traditional theism the ontological basis or rationale for being moral, instead of pursuing his interests, is removed from under his feet, though he can go on behaving morally due to the fear of social punishment, the force of habit or one's spontaneous preference for the right. The concept of *Primal Value Elan* (PVE), however, restores the ontological base of moral striving. The concept implies that though no umpire may regulate the struggle for existence, the historical process is not a blind dance or the victory of pure might without any right, but a dialectical process which conserves values and even leads to higher levels of value without any prima facie consideration for the individual bearers of value.

This ontological faith generates a *de jure* optimism in the individual, not for personal rewards in this life or the next, but for the promotion of the values which inspire him. Such an individual refuses to treat others as mere means nor allows others to treat him merely as a means. But in relation to the PVE he regards himself as an instrument who reaches his highest peak of self-realization in the disinterested loyalty to the promptings of the PVE. He is no doubt aware of his will to live and his fear of death. But he moderates his will to survive and conquers his fear of nothingness through an authentic surrender to the mystery of the PVE. This surrender makes him indifferent to the theological or philosophical problem of personal immortality. His faith in the eventual vindication of the moral law is enough to sustain his moral striving in the face of the failures he comes across in this life.

Faith in the invariable victory of truth or righteousness in the march of history is actually negated by actual historical evidence, and must be deemed to be only a sustaining illusion. But faith in the ultimate, if not the invariable victory of good over evil, is the functional meaning of the belief in God. It seems to me that even if a man formally denies God and life after death, he maybe said to believe in them in the functional sense if he affirms the ultimate victory of good over evil.

If one views the cosmic process before the emergence of man as a giant accident, one may well hold that the emergence of purposive human beings and of the historical process, as distinct from nature, is also a temporary and passing accident in the total cosmic process. But if one holds that even prior to the emergence of man the cosmic process had been value centric, that is, directed to the realization of values, it becomes difficult to believe that its 'value centricity' wears out in the course of time and degenerates into the blind non-purposive dance of the atoms.

If we do not initially accept the PVE, it is logically possible to maintain that chaos becomes a cosmos only to degenerate into chaos again, even as clouds on the sky might produce the most intricate patterns for a while and then dissolve. But the acceptance of the PVE makes the emergence of the historical order a link in the dialectical 'valuecentricity' of the cosmic process. This implies that the historical order remains subject to the over-all working of the PVE, despite the freedom of action enjoyed by purposive human beings to defy the promptings of the Elan. In other words, the conservation and accretion of values continues within the historical process as it does in nature as a whole. If we do not accept the PVE, does it not look inexplicable that there should be such values such as justice, loyalty, altruism, disinterested pursuit of truth, goodness, and beauty rather than a sterile Universe without any such values at all? It seems to me that the presence of these values becomes more understandable and less baffling, if we accept the eternal working of an immanent PVE in the cosmic process rather than interpret these values as accidental products of the chance permutations and combinations of elementary particles or star dust or whatnot.

The concept of PVE thus enables us to reconcile the Divine regulation of the historical process with the concept of social causation. The historical process is the highly complex outcome of the interaction of objective social conditions and man's quest for value, which is rooted in the PVE. As a partly free being man can either attune himself to the promptings of the PVE and act accordingly, or alienate himself from the PVE and get lost or go adrift in the tempestuous waves of his surface self. To the extent that the historical process is shaped and guided by the authentic promptings of the immanent PVE, history is regulated by God. The Divine regulation should not be understood in the sense of interference by an external God or Divine will in the historical process. The power of the PVE works in and through the objective and concrete social conditions or facts.

The proper sociological interpretation of history thus rejects neither the role of God and values nor the role of situational factors, particularly the economic interests of the individual and the group.

CHAPTER 5

A FRESH LOOK AT THE ISLAMIC VALUE SYSTEM

INTRODUCTORY REMARKS

All religions promote basic spiritual and moral values, which are more or less the same, even though differences of emphasis and formulation are inevitable. Since, however, people imbibe values in the context of the lives and teachings of their own saints and heroes, the followers of different religions are inclined to think that they are the exclusive custodians of those values.

The world has made tremendous advances in the realm of factual knowledge. But this does not necessarily lead to a proportionate advance in wisdom, which is primarily an insight into values as distinguished from knowledge of facts. Hence ancient wisdom and moral insights still retain their relevance and constitute a source of inspiration for all. Indeed the concrete Islamic value system of Ghazali with its elaborate classifications of virtues and vices is a significant contribution to human self-understanding, transcending all theological differences.

The traditional Islamic value system marks a distinct advance upon the traditional Christian and Judaic value system in a number of respects. For example, the Islamic conception of the near equality of the sexes, and the respectability of Eros, the contractual nature of marriage, and the wide dispersal of inheritance, etc., are more valid and relevant to contemporary man than the Judaic or the Christian conceptions. However, the cardinal virtues in the Islamic value system are primarily virtues of the good individual rather than the virtues of the good society.

Like the Judaic and the Christian value systems the Islamic also lays primary emphasis upon the ideal man rather than upon the ideal society. It supposes that the good society is nothing more than the aggregate of good men, and that if we look after the virtues of the individual such as truthfulness, sincerity, chastity, generosity, humility, and patience, etc., the society will look after itself as naturally as night follows day. But while the above virtues do promote the good society up to a point, contemporary opinion does not hold them to be sufficient for the good life. We now clearly recognize that unless a society provides equality of opportunity to all people, it cannot be deemed to be a good society in the complete sense, no matter how good its individual members might be. Now the traditional Islamic interpretation of social justice fails to provide equality of opportunity in the contemporary sense. The same applies to some other basic values.

The creative assimilation of new values or the fresh interpretations of the old that have arisen in other societies is not an easy task. Nor is it easy to be aware of the emergence of new interests and aspirations. The more or less unconscious disposition to defend group interests makes the task harder still. When the official value system does not respond to fresh situational needs it loses its grip over the minds and hearts of men, even though they may continue to pay lip-homage to it. This is precisely what has happened in the West to the Christian value system. It is, therefore, imperative to nurture traditional values in the light of fresh insights and new dimensions of old values, no matter where and how they arise. The Islamic and all other value systems must ever-remain open and resilient rather than closed and rigid.

In what follows I shall first briefly describe the main Islamic values, which, in my opinion, do not stand in any need of revision or reinterpretation. I shall later mention four basic values that do need reinterpretation in the present era; faith, piety, Islamic brotherhood, and social justice.

REMEMBRANCE OF GOD (ZIKR)

This is the active and external aspect of the inner love of God. Prayer (*salat*) is only a particular form of remembering God. True remembrance which is much more pervasive than prayer at fixed periods does not imply any verbalization or overt activity like the counting of rosary beads, etc., but only an enduring sense of responsibility and fidelity to God. Remembrance of God acts like an ever-vigilant internal censor or guardian angel, as it were, helping man to resist evil. The corresponding value in Hinduism is *Ishwar-pranidhan* (attentiveness to God).

SINCERITY TO GOD (IKHLAS)

The motive of actions is as important as the rightness of the act itself. Unless the action is motivated by respect for the moral law, or by the love of God, the action cannot be regarded as a virtuous act in the highest sense. If, for example, a person tells the truth because he is afraid of being punished by God for uttering a lie, he is certainly doing right, but this motive is not the highest motive. The classic illustration of this stand is the famous woman saint of Islam, Rabia Basri (d. 801 AD), who wanted to destroy both heaven and hell, so that people would learn to act morally without the hope of reward or the fear of punishment. [90]

This virtue is functionally the same as the virtue, which is termed non-attachment in the Gita. Non-attachment means that right actions are performed for the sake of duty without any desire for the fruits of action, that is, personal gain. The ethical philosophy of the Gita does not recommend life negation or withdrawal or the abdication of spontaneous desires and inclinations, which have no moral dimension. In the final analysis, no individual can be sure that he is solely motivated by selfless duty or love of God, since nobody can claim to see through the depths of his personality, as if it were transparent. Complete self-knowledge is only an ideal. Hence the perennial need for prayerful submission to God.

RIGHTEOUS ACTION (AMAL-E-SALIH)

The value of righteous action has been stressed time and again in the Qur'an. Muslim theologians may discuss whether Muslims professing faith in God and the Prophet ﷺ, but not acting righteously, will go to heaven. But the Scripture brackets faith and good deeds, as if they were two sides of the same coin. Indeed, faith in God without good work is empty and sterile, while good deeds without faith in God are uncertain and unstable responses.

Genuine faith in God must lead to action; otherwise the faith is a surface verbalization of a creed without authentic commitment. However, man can and often does act righteously, according to his norms, without believing in God or life after death. But if man has no ontological commitment or faith whatsoever, his good deeds will not be rooted in an existential interpretation of the Universe; hence they will lack stability and ontological justification. The good deeds of such a person will merely flow from his social conditioning and his own impulses or attitudes, which are liable to change due to external or internal factors.

TRUST IN GOD (TAWAKKUL)

Trust in God means trust in the ultimate beneficence of the laws of the cosmos. Trust in God as the loving Father is the metaphorical version of the existential trust that the uniformity of nature ultimately fosters values. Trust in God does not imply the hope or expectation that life is a bed of roses or untouched by the shadows of pain and evil, but only that man can and will successfully meet the situational challenges of life, since the cosmic laws including the laws of his own psycho-physical organism are ultimately 'valuepetic', that is, promoter values. This trust in God is the *ontic* ground or basis of self-confidence and positive thinking which are the avowed ingredients of all 'formulas' of success.

Trust does not imply passivity or inaction or complacency, but positive activity rooted in a serene self-confidence and reliance on the 'valuepetic' character or potentiality of the cosmos. Trust does not preclude but only precedes or accompanies human effort or striving.

CONTENTMENT (SHUKR)

This means acceptance of reality. It implies the enjoyment of what one has unclouded by the aspiration for the better still. Contentment, however, does not mean apathy or lack of ambition or passivity.

PATIENCE (SABR)

Patience is the willing acceptance of events without losing one's equanimity or faith in the eventual establishment of value over disvalue. It does not mean passive acquiescence in facts, without any attempt to improve them. Such passivity is not patience but a fatalistic negation of life. Ideally speaking, patience should accompany and follow the earnest striving to control the course of events.

VERACITY (SIDQ)

Veracity means commitment to truth in all affairs of life. The keeping of promises, honesty in transactions, punctuality, candidness, sincerity, the avoidance of hypocrisy or backbiting, the ready acknowledgment of one's shortcomings or mistakes, sense of responsibility for the consequences of voluntary action, etc., are all the diverse forms of the basic value of veracity. Veracity is thus one of the core values of the Islamic value system as well as of all other religions.

There is a very interesting anecdote in the life of the Prophet ﷺ that shows truth to be the foundational value of Islam. A not yet fully converted Arab told the Prophet ﷺ that he could give up only one vice for the time being. The Prophet ﷺ recommended that he give up the vice of uttering untruth. The Arab willingly promised to give up that vice, thinking that he would be free to indulge in all others. But he soon found out his error, whereupon he rushed to the Prophet ﷺ to express his total commitment to the value system of Islam.

Commitment to the value of veracity does not imply that the truth or rather the whole truth must be communicated at all times to all persons. The truthful person must also act as a responsible member of society and not lose sight of the consequences of the mechanical disclosure of the full truth quite independently of the situational context.

The consideration of the consequences of telling the truth does not imply that expediency is a higher value than truth, or that useful consequences should be preferred to the performance of one's duty. It is not as simple as this. The consideration of the consequences of an action, whether telling the truth or any other, is essentially the recognition of the organic character of the value system or, in other words, the organic character of the total well being of man. Different values cannot be served separately, as if they were all atomic foci of our commitment or, in other words, sovereign gods all claiming our unqualified surrender. Values are rather the various dimensions of the ideal state of affairs, or what ought to exist in the real world (ideal-reality). The degree of importance of any particular value depends upon the concrete total situation rather than upon the rank of the value in the abstract scale of values as such. Thus, the communication of the full truth should always be subject to the considerations of the total situation. It is not that there is any conflict between duties, but duty itself lies in resolving the conflict of values into a higher harmony or orchestration. In this symphonic approach the dissonance between two notes is overcome. It is not a compromise that keeps the conscience uneasy. It is, on the other hand, only a reminder that man is finite and limited and that he cannot achieve perfection.

WISDOM (HIKMAT)

The pursuit of wisdom and knowledge has been repeatedly stressed in the Qur'an. Wisdom has been declared to be a great gift and blessing of God. The devotion of the early Muslims to the pursuit of knowledge has few parallels in the annals of man. The avidity and keenness of the early Muslims for knowledge was partly responsible for their phenomenal success. Restrictions on the pursuit of independent reflection arose much later. The restriction on free and independent inquiry is the greatest obstacle to human progress. The belief in the infallibility of Divine revelation does not entail the finality of its interpretation.

TACT (SIYASAT)

The Qur'an prescribes tact in the day-to-day affairs of life. Tact does not imply any lack of veracity or of scruples, but only knowledge of human psychology, social causation, and the application of that knowledge for attaining ethically desirable ends. Obviously tact can also be misused. This, however, applies to almost every value that has an instrumental function such as intelligence, courage, and wealth, etc.

There is a tendency to hold that tact is not compatible with genuine morality or spirituality. Moreover, many highly ethical or spiritually developed persons are not tactful. This encourages the view that tact is the value of a worldly-wise man rather than the truly religious person. This, however, is not a balanced approach.

STRIVING (MUJAHIDA)

Striving is a prerequisite of being helped by God. The Qur'an categorically points out that God helps only those who help themselves. Striving is perfectly compatible with belief in the grace of God (*tawfiq*). Waiting for Divine help does not entail suspension of human effort. Striving must pervade every sphere of human concern. The words '*mujahida*', '*jihad*', as well as '*ijtihad*' are derived from the basic root '*jihada*', to strive. Unfortunately the word '*jihad*' has been reduced to or equated with 'holy war'. But the obligation to fight in the defense of Islam is only one form of striving for the good. A scientist striving for scientific accuracy or a wider range of generalization, a gardener striving for greater beauty and variety in the universe of flowers, a social reformer striving for a higher conception of social justice, are all striving in the way of God, to the extent that they are free from extraneous considerations such as love of money, prestige, and power, etc. Striving in the way of God is thus a matter of degree rather than of an absolute yes or no. We are all either collaborators with God or the obstructors of His will in varying degrees.

REVERENCE FOR LIFE (EHTARAM-E-NAFS)

The Qur'an clearly states that a person who saves the life of even one individual saves, as it were, entire humanity, while the person who destroys the life of even a single individual is guilty of destroying the entire human race, as it were. [91] This reverence for life implies loving care or concern for the human essence, and this in turn leads to universal kindness. The full flowering of this value generates in man a universal compassion not confined to any particular religion, race, or group. It even embraces the members of the animal and vegetable kingdoms. It suffuses man with the sense of wonder at the contemplation of the living Universe and the essential oneness of life. This feeling or attitude maybe called the cosmic feeling. This elemental experience constitutes the raw material of the mysticism of the mystic or the poet, and the monism of the philosopher.

COMPASSION (RAHM)

It is the tender and active concern for the welfare of others through providing those conditions which promote welfare and removing those which impede it. Compassion implies an imaginative sharing of the inner demands, attitudes and aspirations of the other. True compassion does not make the compassionate person feel superior to the other, but rather makes him aware of the essential vulnerability and brittleness of all finite existence. In showing compassion to others one, therefore, shows compassion to himself. The posture of superiority erodes the ontogenetic function of compassion as an intrinsic value, and brings it down to the level of a mere instrumental value for reducing suffering. The fully compassionate person identifies himself with all living beings. Since realizing the oneness of all life is the supreme wisdom, the compassionate person is also the wise person in the highest sense.

Compassion seems at times to be opposed to justice, but the conflict is only superficial. The conflict arises only when compassion (by definition, a loving concern for all life) is narrowed down to an individual or group. This leads to a conflict between justice (in the sense of penal discipline or just reward) and compassion (in the sense of forgiveness or indulgence toward the persons concerned). This conflict disappears when the enforcement of discipline or deprivation springs from a loving concern for all rather than for one or a few, and when this enforcement does not produce anger, antagonism, or arrogance in the judge or ruler.

Compassion, as a value, acquires a unique status in Islam as compassion or mercy is the Divine attribute, which is most frequently mentioned in the Qur'an. It is significant that Hindu and Buddhist ethics also stress compassion (*karuna*) and nonviolence (*ahimsa*), which flows from the former. The supreme Christian concept of love also stands for the same value.

HUMILITY (TAWAZUH)

Humility is not self-derogation or the denial of self-worth. It is the recognition that every quality or possession of the individual self has its own limitations, and that its ultimate '*ontic basis*' lies outside the control and power of the individual. For example, beauty, intelligence, strength, family prestige, musical or other talents are all given to the individual who cannot claim any individual merit for possessing them. The use he makes of them certainly goes to his credit. But here also the environment goes a long way to help or hinder him, and it is almost impossible to disentangle the extent of his individual merit from the favorable role of the environment. Consequently, self-exultation is pointless. True humility, however, is perfectly compatible with a realistic and honest self-appraisal that includes awareness of one's virtues as well as limitations.

EROS (ISHQ E MAJAZI)

Most religions tend to interpret erotic love as an obstacle in the path of spiritual development. But the Qur'anic approach is that erotic love is one of the values of the good life. The Qur'an beautifully refers to the mutual bliss of man and woman in each other's company. This bliss is not reducible to a bare physical sensation, but has a spiritual dimension. Erotic love, at its best, is rooted in the *Primal Value Elan* (PVE), which is the ontological ground of the eternal and ceaseless quest of value. It is this essential kinship between Eros and divine love, which is adumbrated in the parallelisms found in the language of love and of mysticism.

Erotic love, at its best, is far from being a pursuit of pleasure. It leads the individual from the state of loneliness and anxiety into the closest possible sense of sharing one's life with the beloved. This experience indirectly educates the individual for grasping the organic oneness of the Universe. Such spiritual development, however, takes place only if erotic love is properly regulated by higher values; divine love, truth, and justice, etc. Sexual union must be a responsible and symbolic expression of spiritual kinship. Since the sexual experience has profound repercussions on the human psychophysical organism (especially that of the woman), the casual or the purely physical approach to sex deprives the individual of the deep satisfaction of the spirit that passeth understanding.

PURITY (TAHARAT)

Purity implies both physical and psychic cleanliness. Physical cleanliness is the soil in which mental and spiritual cleanliness can grow. Cleanliness generates positive and healthy inner attitudes, while lack of cleanliness generates their opposites. Physical cleanliness consists in keeping the body free from contact with all forms of unpleasant matter. Spiritual and mental cleanliness consists in the avoidance of all forms of negative feelings or responses such as anger, fear, worry, hate, malice, and jealousy, etc., that destroy or weaken the inner serenity and bliss of man (*nafs-e-mutmainnah*). The subject of these negative feelings or spiritual poisons, as it were, suffers immensely more than does the object. Negative feelings have a role in the economy of human life, namely the removal of the sources of fear and frustration. But this vital task must be performed in a positive rather than in a negative manner.

SPIRITUAL MERIT (SAWAB)

The traditional Islamic value system attaches great importance to this value and interprets it as some spiritual gain in life after death. There is an elaborate *'calculus of sawab'*, which describes the quantum of *sawab* that accrues by reading this or that chapter of the Qur'an, or doing this action or that. *Sawab*, however, refers to the phenomenon of spiritual growth here and now through inner catharsis resulting in deeper self-understanding and a quickening of the creative conscience.

FAITH (IMAN)

Islamic faith consists of belief in God, angels, the day of judgment accepting all the prophets of God without any distinction, but Prophet Muhammad ﷺ as the last of the prophets, and finally accepting all revealed books of God without any distinction, but the Qur'an as the final and perfect revelation. Now it is indisputable that none of the above beliefs have a clear connotation or concrete content which could be claimed to be 'the' meaning of the beliefs, any deviation from which would destroy the faith. In some sense we must accept the above beliefs, but it is not clear what that sense is.

If we do not attempt to clarify our religious beliefs we do not know what we are believing in; if we clarify our beliefs there is no way of deciding which particular interpretation is 'the' true one. This inevitably leads to dogmatic interpretations, which in turn breed disputation and intolerance. The most reasonable approach, therefore, is to be content with the minimum concrete meaning of trans-empirical concepts necessary for the proper functioning of religious beliefs, namely, the integration of man as a thinking, feeling, and willing being. Indeed this is precisely the approach of the Qur'an itself, which certainly does not encourage theological hair-splitting. [92] But traditional Islamic theology and Qur'anic exegesis, even as the theologies of other religions, revel in essentially unverifiable metaphysical speculation in the garb of religious faith.

A mature faith should be content with the minimum concrete meaning of concepts such as God, revelation, creation, angels, heaven and hell, etc., rather than insist on any particular formulation or meaning as the only valid interpretation of the above concepts. Interpretative permissiveness rather than dogmatic vigor is the better part of a mature faith. This approach is amply reinforced by the Qur'anic declaration that some of its verses are categorical imperatives, while others are metaphorical statements (open to plural interpretations). But in practice religious traditions tend toward interpretative rigorism, the exclusion of dissidents from their umbrella, and to pronouncements of heresy, and renegacy, etc. However, a person who denies a particular interpretation of God or revelation does not necessarily deny the reality of God and revelation as such.

It appears to me that '*kufr*' (literally denial in the sphere of religion) is a total denial of a spiritual dimension of the Universe. But as long as a person believes either in a personal God or in an impersonal Power immanent in the Universe, he is not devoid of faith, even though he may not be a Muslim. Perhaps even a person who does not verbally affirm God or an impersonal Power, but whose actions reflect a genuine commitment to basic values such as truth, love, justice, etc., as if there were God or a Spiritual Power, should not be termed as '*kafir*'.

Who, then, is a '*kafir*'? A consistent and persistent nihilist who has lost all faith in values and is in the depth of total despair, including hatred of his own self; he is a '*kafir*'. Such a person denies all values without exception and feels like destroying his own self as well as all others. He is, therefore, the denier par excellence.

In the ultimate analysis, authentic faith, no matter what its theological complexion or content, leads to joyful surrender before the mystery of the Universe together with steadfast and ungrudging commitment to a set of values and to the duties of one's station in life. No particular conception of God or revelation should be confused with God as such, Who, in the ultimate analysis, is beyond our understanding. Hence the claim of any religion or person to possess complete and all-inclusive truth is vanity. No one religious interpretation can claim to penetrate the heart of the mystery and lay it bare and transparent to man. There is no point in the belief that only one religion or attempted solution of the cosmic mystery is valid, while all others are invalid. Hence, there is also no point in the belief of exclusive salvation for the followers of a particular chosen religion. Indeed, this is precisely the charge leveled by the Qur'an against the Jews and Christians who claimed that they alone would enter heaven. Unfortunately, the human custodians of the Qur'an fell into the same trap themselves when they started to claim the monopoly of salvation. [93] True faith can and does flourish in the soil of all religions. All people having authentic faith are spiritually akin and co-sharers in one common human destiny, no matter what its concrete nature maybe. If faith could be defined as beauty of the soul, then spiritual beauty, like physical beauty, cuts across all distinctions of creed or denomination. The belief that all men who are authentically committed to spiritual and moral values are men of faith can be combined with the belief that the Qur'an is a unique revelation and the Prophet ﷺ a unique exemplar or guide, since they bring about a quicker, richer, and more harmonious growth of the human spirit than do other guides. Muslims, however, cannot claim the privilege of a higher spiritual status or merit merely because of belonging to the Islamic community founded by the Prophet ﷺ.

PIETY (TAQWA)

Piety, in the higher sense, means something more than the mere avoidance of evil due to fear of God. It means the culture or education of the raw human impulses and drives leading to their refinement and purification. When this happens, the avoidance of evil ceases to be a matter of obeying external commands and becomes a matter of following one's own refined impulses, and hence something more or less spontaneous. The traditional Islamic value system includes this higher type of piety. [94] But traditional piety leads to a static conformity as distinguished from creative fidelity to basic values. On the *Elan* view, however, fear of God is the fear of alienation from the creative conscience or the God within man. The fear of God in this sense does not obstruct man's ceaseless creativity of values. Love of God is the eager receptivity to the Value Elan, leading to the growth of his values.

ISLAMIC BROTHERHOOD (MILLAT)

The traditional concept of the brotherhood of Muslims was and still is valid. But like reverence for life, brotherhood should be extended to mankind as such. The Islamic value system does recognize human brotherhood and, in fact, Muslims in the medieval period were far more tolerant toward non-Muslims than were Christians to Jews or Catholics to Protestants. But the idea of ideological brotherhood overshadowed that of human brotherhood. The oneness of the human family was accepted in the intra-Islamic rather than in the inter-religious sense. In other words, all Muslims, irrespective of race or region, stood equal before their Creator, their rank depending upon their piety. But the idea of the brotherhood of man (whether or not, he acknowledged the Fatherhood of God) or, in other words, the idea of humanistic love was not present, as evident from Ghazali's view that Muslims should not become friendly with non-Muslims. Mature humanistic love is perfectly non-discriminatory, even though shared values, aspirations, and memories might create a sense of group kinship among the Muslims within the wider unity of the human family. The medieval Indian *Sufi's* of the Chishti order moved toward the humanistic ideal. But in general, the idea of humanistic love was not sufficiently stressed in Muslim society to give it emotional depth and motivating power in human relations.

JUSTICE (ADL)

The word 'justice' has a wide range of application, which is only slightly less than that of the word 'good'. Greek thought placed justice as the chief among the four cardinal virtues, which included courage, temperance, and wisdom. Plato and Aristotle had defined all virtues as the just or right blending of a pair of opposites. In this sense all virtues are different species of the genus 'justice'. But justice has still other meanings, for example, impartiality, performance of duty without fear or favor, adjudication according to the established law, equity, distribution of goods or rewards on some valid principle, and, last but not least, polymorphous equality of all human beings. No one facet of justice can exhaust its total range of meanings.

Islam definitely commands right action without considering whether it benefits or harms oneself or one's nearest relations. The attitude of firmness against wrongdoing is commended. Considerations of sympathy or mercy, though laudable as such, should not deflect us from being justly firm against the wrongdoer. To waver is to be swayed by a one-sided concern for the wrongdoer at the expense of the wider social good. Where, however, the wronged person is able to forgive the wrong, the Qur'an praises such forgiveness and spirit of charity in the highest terms. But it must be conceded that justice in the sense of a polymorphous equality of consideration is not adequately present in the traditional Islamic value system. Indeed no religion whatsoever can claim polymorphous equality as a part of its value system, though Islam goes farthest in approximating to polymorphous equality, including the equality of the sexes.

Equality, in this sense, is essentially a contemporary notion of Western secular society. The traditional Islamic conception of equality is not polymorphous but limited to specific items. For example, the traditional interpretation deems all men to be equal in the sense that **(a)** all men in the mosque can stand shoulder to shoulder without any discrimination between Sultan and slave, **(b)** all free Muslim men are subject to the same laws, irrespective of their region, and language, etc., **(c)** all Muslims enjoy equal rank in the eyes of God, the only basis of higher and lower status being spiritual excellence (*taqwa*), **(d)** all individuals will be rewarded in accordance with their own merits. However, the traditional interpretation cannot be called polymorphous, since it does not include the crucial feature of equality of opportunity.

Equality of opportunity means that all individuals must be given equal opportunities for realizing their potentialities of integrated human growth and rewarded in accordance with their achievements. Obviously, equality in this sense did not exist in a society in which men were divided into rich and poor, free men and slaves, Muslims and *dhimmis*, Arabs and non-Arabs, Quraish and non-Quraish, etc. The institution of the wealth tax or the moral exhortation to give charity to the poor or needy, are obviously ameliorative remedies to mitigate the evils of social inequality rather than the positive features of an egalitarian society in the contemporary sense of the term. No society which legally permits the institution of slavery or of massive inherited wealth can ever-assure equality of opportunity in the full or strong sense as distinguished from the weak sense, which merely signifies the freedom of individuals from any legal disability or discrimination on the grounds of status, sex, religion, etc. In this 'weak' sense equality prevails today in all democratic countries. But in the 'strong' sense there is an enormous gap between the ideal and the real in capitalist as well as socialist states.

Equality of opportunity must not be confused with literal or bare equality. It is not incompatible with gradations in status, power or wealth. All that it entails is that such gradations should be earned and not inherited. Differences in power, and wealth, etc., should be the consequent reward of individual merit or work done, rather than the antecedent gift of the accident of birth. It will be seen that no religion has preached this polymorphous equality, though some religions have given greater importance to this or that dimension of equality.

CHAPTER 6

A Fresh Look at the Islamic Precept System

INTRODUCTORY REMARKS

The precept system of a religion is always deemed to be its most obvious distinguishing feature. Precepts concern the different modes of relationship of the individual with God, and are, therefore, relatively the most unaffected by and unsusceptible to developments in the cumulative knowledge and wisdom of the human family. Therefore, there is no need to reconstruct the precepts, unless of course some item may happen to prick the individual's conscience. Had, for example, Islam prescribed human sacrifice at some special occasion (which is obviously not the case) there would have been a point in altering this particular item of the precept system, assuming of course that human sacrifice was judged as utterly immoral.

PRAYER (SALAT)

One's conception of prayer is organically related to one's general world view or conception of God. The popular conception that prayer is a petition or supplication to God for specific boons such as health, wealth, or success in some specific objective is based on a more or less anthropomorphic conception of God, Who intervenes in human affairs when supplicated by His faithful devotees or even at His own Will. According to this view, where the petitionary prayer goes unheeded, the granting of the petition would have harmed the supplicant or would have involved an injustice to someone else. Further, while God radiates mercy to every creature without being supplicated, supplication is necessary for man's own spiritual growth.

The conception of petitionary prayer generates numerous intellectual difficulties, which however, do not apply to what maybe called the evocative conception of prayer. According to this conception, prayer is the evocation of the latent reserves of man through attuning the human consciousness to the promptings of the Primal Value Elan, or, in religious language, God within man. Receptivity to this Divine core of the human personality restores the equanimity that the frustrations of life ever-tend to destroy. Prayer is not a substitute for action, which alone molds the course of events in accordance with causal laws. But prayer is the spiritual attunement, which helps and encourages us to undertake the right action. The real function of prayer is cathartic and therapeutic rather than executive. Prayer is the source of inspiration rather than a means of implementation of human objectives.

The conception of prayer as the catharsis and the revivification of the soul is clearly found in *Sufism*. Even as the transfer of a fish from a bucketful of water into a flowing river gives a fullness of being to the fish, spiritual prayer transports anxious and frustrated man into the limitless ocean of spiritual bliss and serenity; the '*ananda*' of Indian philosophy, and the '*nafs-e-mutmainna*' of Islam. [95] To the immature person prayer is a substitute for magic. He is apt to believe that just as the application of scientific knowledge brings about desired results, prayer, accompanied by true faith in God, brings about desired results in accordance with mysterious spiritual laws. This conception of prayer is a hangover from the early phase of man's history when magic dominated over man's imagination. But this conception of prayer is totally incompatible with the scientific outlook.

The obligatory prayer of Islam is essentially adoratory. All the postures of prayer, such as the commencement posture, the standing posture, the bow and the full prostration, etc., heighten the feelings of total surrender to or an 'existential melting' before the Lord of the worlds. Obligatory prayers at fixed periods, however, tend to become mechanical, thus transforming the oft-repeated communion with God into a compulsory and, at times, even unwanted presence before an absent God. While it is true that the daily repetition of prayers does inevitably make them a routine affair, yet the numerous gains of regularity in prayer more than compensate this deadening effect of repetition. Moreover, when the individual maybe least expecting any spiritual ecstasy during prayer, it may suddenly descend upon him or emerge from the depths of his being, as a gift of grace from God. In the absence of regular prayer the moments of such grace are likely to be much less frequent, if not rare. Regular and disciplined prayers are thus extremely useful, if not essential for sustained spiritual growth.

A Fresh Look at the Islamic Precept System

FASTING (SAUM)

The purpose of fasting is obviously the acquisition of self-control over one's appetites and impulses. Without spiritual discipline fasting tends to become merely voluntary hunger. The spirit of fasting is not negative deprivation of food, but rather the regulation of human impulses in the service of a positive spiritual ideal. Every day can provide an opportunity to fast in this sense. For example, if one feels sleepy or lazy and is tempted to skip over some duty, the deliberate abstinence from sleep or the overcoming of laziness is a kind of fast. The obligatory fasting during Ramadan is only the minimum discipline, leaving the individual free to apply the spirit of fasting on different occasions. This does not imply any harshness or the loss of freedom and spontaneous joy of living. All that the spirit of fasting implies is that the individual must not lose his sense of direction while enjoying the good things of life. While asceticism and Puritanism exaggerate the constant awareness of this sense of purpose, Islam strikes a balance between spontaneity and discipline.

WEALTH TAX (ZAKAT)

Charity certainly provides material relief to the needy. But it has undesirable psychological repercussions upon both the giver and the receiver. The Qur'anic prescription of an obligatory tax to be paid to the state, according to a fixed percentage of one's wealth, is thus an advance upon the notion of private charity. [96] It contains the germs of the concept of the collective responsibility of the state toward the building up of a welfare society. The Qur'anic emphasis on the wealth-tax signifies the relative importance given to social justice and economic well being by Islam as compared with other religions. It must, however, be conceded that social justice in the contemporary Western sense, namely, polymorphous equality of opportunity irrespective of sex, status, and religion, etc., is a higher social ideal. It must also be conceded that tax on residual wealth needs to be supplemented by a tax on income in order to augment the total resources of the state and also to enforce austerity. Mere exhortation to spend less upon oneself and give more in charity does not suffice to solve the problem of poverty.

Again the rigid fixation of *zakat* at the rate fixed by the Prophet ﷺ or his immediate successors leads to a static approach in a field where the utmost flexibility is the prime need. The concept of *zakat* must be functionally interpreted instead of being regarded as a rigid and fixed component of the Islamic precept system. The different types of state taxes that have gradually been established such as customs and excise duties, income-tax, house tax, etc., are after all different means to the end which is also the objective of *zakat*; the welfare of the common man through the provision of different amenities. Consequently, the Muslim citizens of composite or secular states, which have their own tax systems, should not be burdened with an additional religious tax that might have serious economic repercussions on individuals belonging to the already heavily taxed group. There can be only one state and only one source of compulsory taxation. Any contribution made to religious or cultural organizations should be voluntary rather than obligatory. The functional interpretation of *zakat* would help to promote the emotional integration of the Muslim citizens of secular states with their non-Muslim fellow citizens. Moreover, under these conditions Muslims would not have the feeling of being rather second class Muslims on account of non-payment of *zakat*.

PILGRIMAGE (HAJJ)

Hajj is, perhaps, relatively more ritualistic than the other precepts. Fasting, prayer, alms-giving are not ritualistic but essentially instrumental activities. But the rites of *Hajj* are primarily ritualistic or commemorative, though they also have an instrumental function. The rites of *Hajj* are probably an exercise in blending change and continuity into an organic unity. They commemorate the episodes in the life of Abraham; the premier prophet of pre-Islamic Arabia. The inclusion of *Hajj* rites in the basic precept system of Islam must have satisfied the Arab's sense of group identity in general, and the regional pride of the Meccans in particular, and must have facilitated their authentic movement toward Islam. On the other hand, the creative genius of Islam has imbued those ancient rites with a fresh significance. Thus the circumambulation of the *Kabah*, the kissing of the black stone, the performance of animal sacrifice, the throwing of pebbles at Mina, the running to and fro between certain points, etc., all have been given a spiritual significance mainly connected with episodes in the life of Abraham.

This symbolism exercises a profound influence upon the spiritual growth of the Muslim pilgrim. At times the immediate effect is very strong but gradually wears out, while at other times it maybe more or less stable. In many cases the initial effect itself maybe negligible, while in some cases, paradoxically enough, the individual's character and conduct may even ethically deteriorate after the performance of the *Hajj* rites. [97] Much depends upon the maturity, attitudes, and expectations of the pilgrim as well as the spiritual and moral guidance available to him during the *Hajj*. If, for example, he is not sufficiently clear about the symbolism, then it should not surprise us if he fails to experience the phenomena of 'spiritual quickening'. The case is analogous to the failure of a person to be moved by a poem whose imagery is not very clear to him.

To turn to the instrumental functions of *Hajj*, they are the same as those of the weekly *Juma* congregational prayers, but on an enormously bigger scale. The growth of a sense of group identity and of emotional identification with fellow believers all over the world through joint participation in symbolic activities. The sense of Islamic brotherhood, however, can be no substitute for the brotherhood of man as such.

THE PROHIBITORY SYSTEM IN ISLAM

Every religion has a system of prohibitions, which maybe more or less elaborate. The prohibitory system of Islam is primarily based upon the Qur'an though, as is to be expected, it is supplemented by the *hadith*. In general the tone and temper of the Qur'an is permissive rather than repressive. The Qur'an does not prescribe an ascetic view of life but encourages a life-affirming ethic. There are numerous passages that draw one's attention to the sources of joy and beauty of life in this world as well as in life after death.

It is also very significant that the Qur'an discourages a casuistical approach to the system of prohibitions and injunctions. For example, the followers of Moses were discouraged from seeking unnecessary clarifications and details concerning some of the injunctions given to them. [98] The implication is that they should use their common sense and exercise their own discretion in such matters. It is again highly significant that the Qur'an only refers to a very small list of prohibited food items and expressly declares that barring these everything is permissible, according to individual likes or dislikes. This permissive approach of the Qur'an was qualified by later developments in the concrete precept system of Islam.

The prohibitory system of the Qur'an extends to the spheres of sex, food and drink, economic practices, individual and collective morality, etc. In this section, however, I shall deal with the sphere of food and drink only. The other prohibitions will be mentioned in the institutional system of Islam to which a separate chapter has been devoted.

In the sphere of food, the Qur'an prohibits only the flesh of swine, blood, carrion, and the flesh of animals offered to idols. But there is no harm in eating pork under conditions of acute hunger or distress, when no other food maybe available. [99] "This proviso suggests that the Qur'anic prohibition is not in the nature of a primitive taboo that can never be violated by a person, but that the prohibition is a restriction of some other kind. But the exact grounds of this restriction are, however, very difficult to know, if we look at things from the rational point of view.

Muslims often claim that this prohibition is based on rational grounds, since pork is injurious to the physical, mental, and spiritual health of human beings. Very often far-fetched theories or unverified explanations are put forward in support of the Qur'anic prohibition. For example, it is alleged that the sexual lewdness and propensity to dirt found in the pig corrupt the nature of those who consume its flesh. Quite apart from the consideration that this is factually incorrect, this kind of reasoning leads to obviously wrong conclusions in related fields. For example, the buffalo is a very dull and unintelligent animal, but the consumption of its milk does not have the slightest tendency to make people dull or unintelligent.

It is thus very difficult to discover a rational reason for the prohibition of pork, apart from the obvious consideration that pork may not be suitable in a hot climate which leads to ready putrefaction of fatty meat. [100] This rational justification would, however, be applicable only in hot climates and not possess a universal validity.

There are three alternatives available to us. Firstly, we may adopt the stand that our finite minds are incapable of grasping the wisdom of every single detail of the Word of God, and that we should surrender our judgment to the Divine will without questioning. This maybe called the attitude of total surrender to an external authority. The second alternative is to reject the Qur'anic prohibitions as not only invalid but also an unnecessary encroachment upon one's freedom. According to this view, food prohibitions have no ethical import and should not be given any importance even when they are found in the Qur'an. The third alternative is to acknowledge that every revelation contains traces of the conceptual and ethical framework of the space-time in which the revelation occurs. Taking this stand, a Muslim may hold that the Qur'anic prohibition may either have a rational justification, hitherto not yet grasped by us, but likely to be grasped later on, or it may represent a trace of the Judaic conceptual valuational framework. He may then accept the discipline required by the Qur'an as a symbol of his creative fidelity to the Qur'an without, however, claiming that the prohibition can be rationally justified. The spirit of this alternative is clearly distinct from that of the first alternative, even though they both agree in showing deference to the Qur'an. As regards the prohibition of blood, etc., comments are unnecessary since they are not controversial items.

The other main items in the prohibitory or rather the disapproved list are alcoholic drinks and gambling. It is significant that the language of the Qur'anic injunction to desist from the above is not as stern as in the case of the flesh of swine. If the literal sense of the Qur'anic text be followed, alcohol and gambling are to be 'avoided', while pork and blood, etc., are 'prohibited', according to the Qur'an. This distinction does not entail that alcohol is allowed by the Qur'an. But it does entail that there is a difference of degree in the demerit involved.

As regards permissible food, many orthodox Muslims think that only the flesh of such animals is permissible as have been slaughtered in the traditional Islamic or Jewish way. Consequently, they have a conscientious objection against such methods of slaughter that do not lead to the free flow of blood of the slaughtered animal. This leads to unnecessary restrictions on the consumption of the flesh of animals slaughtered by Christians, Sikhs or others, even though the animal food as such be quite permissible. A liberal approach in this matter is thus on an entirely different plane than the plea of relaxing the objection against pork, and alcohol, etc.

In the ultimate analysis, however, the true moral worth of an individual lies not in his following the rules of food and drink, but in his commitment to foundational values such as love, compassion, truth, justice, and loyalty, etc. Admittedly these words or their equivalents are common to every individual and society. But the concrete significance or use of these value words differs considerably from person to person, society-to-society, and age-to-age. Hence, an active concern for ceaseless growth in these values is a much more vital matter than the concern for implementing the food and drink rules given in the Qur'an.

In the end, a few observations are called for on the subject of music, painting, and other branches of fine art. Although there is absolutely no prohibition in the Qur'an on these activities, traditional schools of law in Islam have definitely discouraged or prohibited these activities. Undoubtedly, the fine arts have flourished in Islamic societies. But all this artistic efflorescence occurred not because of, but in spite of, the severely restrictive or puritanical approach to the aesthetic dimension of man's experience. Many fields of art had to be totally sacrificed in view of the prohibition on the visual representation of living forms. Moreover, the average Muslim suffered or tended to suffer from an uneasy conscience at the appreciation or enjoyment of dance and music. This un-Qur'anic Puritanism has been a source of profound deprivation for the average Muslim. It has conspired along with some sociological factors; to foster a somewhat unbalanced personality development in Islamic societies. The total lack of great music in the Islamic cultural *gestalt* is the most glaring instance of this unfortunate devaluation of man's aesthetic impulse. It is true that architecture tended to fill the void left by the retreat of music, and Muslim architecture tends to be as delicate and tender as a musical note. Again, the art of Qur'anic recitation was developed to a very high rank, and moved people to spiritual ecstasy. Yet, the aesthetic dimension has never attained the rank that it did in ancient Indian, medieval Christian, or Western secular culture.

To conclude, the puritanical attitude is not an internal and integral feature of the Qur'an, which contains no prohibitions against music or other fine arts. Puritanism was injected into the nascent Islamic tradition due to its birth and early growth in Arab society, which, though steeped in poetry, oratory, and martial valor, etc., was deficient in music and the softer virtues of humanity. Later on, when Islam was grafted upon Persia, and Turkistan, etc., the cultural soil or the genius of the people was much more favorable to the flowering of the fine arts, which indeed did happen in history. But the seeds of the Islamic thought-cum-value system had already been baked enough to permit of any theoretical changes in the prohibitory system. [101]

The precept system of any religion is the most obvious external sign of group membership and also the least amenable to any suggested change. Any change in the precept system is bound to be regarded as an attack on the heart of the religion and its actual displacement by a new religion or sect under the verbal garb of the old. This attitude is perfectly justified. Moreover, the Islamic precept system is quite rational and does not call for any modification in any basic sense. However, a relatively permissive approach toward the precept system instead of the traditional disciplinarian or rigorous approach is desirable in those cases where strict literal adherence to the traditional precept system leads to rather absurd consequences, very quick repetition or very long gaps between the five obligatory prayers, in areas such as Sweden, Finland, and Siberia, etc. Similarly in the above regions the literal adherence to the Qur'anic prescription concerning fasting leads to a fast, sometimes of ten minutes, and at other times, of twenty-three hour's duration. Both these situations are unhappy. The same is the case with the animal sacrifices made almost simultaneously by millions of *Hajj* pilgrims. The enormous quantity of meat, bones and skins of the animals slaughtered must be harnessed for man's betterment. Thus some new patterns to supplement these mass sacrifices are called for, if we wish to render our customs and rituals more meaningful and functionally relevant to man's contemporary needs.

CHAPTER 7

A SECULAR APPROACH TO THE ISLAMIC INSTITUTIONAL SYSTEM

INTRODUCTORY REMARKS

The Qur'an contains very few details concerning the institutional system. The details were worked out first by the Prophet ﷺ himself and later by his successors in the light of the Prophet's ﷺ example, the prevailing Semitic mores, and their own sense of equity.

It is noteworthy that *Caliph* Umar, who was second to none in his love and reverence for the Prophet ﷺ, modified the administrative policies and decisions of the Prophet ﷺ in a number of cases. Umar, for example, stopped the equal distribution of the spoils of war, as was done by the Prophet ﷺ and the first *Caliph*, Abu Bakr, and instead, distributed them according to the merits or needs of the Muslim participants in the war. Again, the Prophet ﷺ distributed the spoils without keeping any amount for the state, and Abu Bakr followed the same practice. Ali suggested the continuance of the practice, but Umar decided to institute the state treasury (*bait ul mal*), and earmark a portion of the spoils for the same. Again, most of Umar's contemporaries wanted conquered lands in the Nile valley to be distributed among the Muslim armies. But Umar refused to do so, even though some lands in Arabia had been so distributed by the Prophet ﷺ himself. [102]

Umar ordered that no Arab could be made a slave. It appears he was seriously inclined to the total abolition of slavery. But his contemporaries were not sympathetic to this move. It is interesting to note that almost two hundred years after Umar, the famous jurist, Hambal, criticized Umar's prohibition of slavery for the Arabs. Umar also ordered that a slave woman or concubine who became a mother could not be sold by her master. Umar adopted an interpretative approach to the Qur'an as distinguished from the purely literal. Thus, on many occasions he did not enforce the Qur'anic punishment of theft.

The dynamic and rationalistic approach of Umar was reflected in the thought of Abu Hanifa (d. 767), the first of the four recognized juristic leaders (*imams*) of the *Sunni's*. But with the passage of time his followers were unable to appreciate the rationale of Abu Hanifa's system, and thus Umar's dynamic approach to the institutional system of Islam gradually withered away, notably under the influence of personalities such as Shafai, Hambal, Ibn Hazm, Ibn Taymiya and others.

Muslim theologians and jurists of almost all schools of thought concede in theory the permissibility of development in the institutional system of Islam to suit changed or new conditions in accordance with the well-known principles of analogical reasoning (*qiyas*), equity (*istehsan*), and consensus of the learned (*ijma*). But the practice of Muslims, apart from notable exceptions, has been marked by a static approach, in sharp contrast to Umar. The charge of innovation (*bidat*) has ever-haunted Muslim reformers. The fear of innovation has, however, helped in preserving Islamic solidarity during and after the sociopolitical upheavals of the 13th century in the greater part of the Islamic world.

It is noteworthy that Umar did not make any changes or modifications in the precept system as formulated by the Prophet ﷺ. It is reported that Umar was initially inclined to discontinue a particular rite connected with the *Hajj*, but, on second thoughts, did not do so. [103] It seems to me this decision of Umar is highly significant. Changes in the symbolic precept system of a religion tend to erode its identity and the sense of group solidarity, which springs from performing symbolic acts.

We have seen that all religions had been functioning as complete codes of conduct until the 18th century, when Christianity in Western Europe was transformed from an institutional religion into a spiritual relationship between man and God, leaving the Christian society free to shape its political and economic institutions on democratic lines. This was the secular revolution of the 18th century, which, ever since the 19th century, has been spreading in the rest of the world, together with science, technology, democracy, and equality between the sexes. While, from the viewpoint of religious modernists this is a very happy trend, from the orthodox Islamic viewpoint, the 18th century secular revolution was the beginning of the end of religion and its degeneration into mere ritualism without any social content or message. Muslim orthodox opinion has, therefore, been relatively more opposed to secularism than orthodox sections of other religions.

A Secular Approach to the Islamic Institutional System

Liberal Muslims in Turkey, Egypt, and Iran have vigorously affirmed secularism. But their intellectuals have not bothered to give a rational and systematic justification of secularism within a carefully reconstructed Islamic thought-cum-value system. The adoption of a militant secular posture in the name of religious pragmatism (whose most glaring examples are Mustafa Kamal in Turkey and Amanullah in Afghanistan) may succeed in breaking public resistance to changes in the institutional system. This procedure, however, does not change the inner convictions and values of the people who are apt to regard secularism as a surrender of the true Islamic faith to the demand of expediency. They are unable to appreciate that secularism, implying the delinking of the institutional system from the essence of Islam, is a feature of religious modernism in general, as distinguished from religionism in the medieval sense. It is, therefore, necessary to remove the anti-religious flavor or associations of secularism. The delinking of the institutional system from the essential core of Islam or any other religion must be accepted as spiritually legitimate rather than merely politically useful. Only when this happens, will the authentic Muslim feel free to participate in the democratic shaping of the politico-economic patterns of his society (be it Muslim or plural) without any sub-conscious qualms of violating religious piety.

The above freedom must, however, remain subject to the clear Qur'anic injunctions concerning human institutions. Since, however, the Qur'an deals primarily with micro-social institutions such as marriage, divorce, and inheritance, etc., rather than the macro-social, the Qur'anic mandate will not erode secular freedom in politico-economic matters. Thus as far as the macro-social institutions are concerned, secularism will not give rise to any conflict between man-made and Qur'anic laws. Even so, a distinction will have to be made between intrinsic and instrumental prescriptions of the Qur'an. The decision whether a particular Qur'anic imperative is an intrinsic or an instrumental rule of conduct will inevitably be based on individual insight into the Qur'anic ethos and the decision will thus remain controversial. There is no harm in this provided the democratic consensus is adopted.

The political, economic, and social institutions of a group are meant to promote certain basic values with the help of some instrumental rules. Institutions thus always presuppose a set of factual beliefs concerning the most effective means for promoting the basic values of the society. Now, if the factual beliefs happen to be wrong then the resultant institutions of the society would fail in their real purpose, even if the basic values were valid. It is, therefore, vitally essential for a society to adopt the most effective means for the realization of its basic objectives, just as a sick person ought to use the most effective remedy against disease. Since man's factual knowledge has been progressively increasing, contemporary man should be more competent to prescribe better means for promoting his cherished values. Now the adoption of better means inevitably involves changes in the institutional patterns of society.

The most basic change needed in the traditional Islamic institutional system is the acceptance of **(a)** the complete legal equality of men and women, and **(b)** equality of opportunity for all human beings, as the essence of social justice. All the details of the reconstructed institutional system concerning marriage, inheritance, political, and economic matters follow from the acceptance of the equality and dignity of the human essence independently of any sex differentiation and equality of opportunity as the essence of social justice.

The reconstruction of an institutional system is not the task of any individual. In the final analysis, institutional systems grow and evolve over the centuries in response to the felt and also unconscious needs of millions of individuals. In what follows I shall, therefore, only briefly discuss some basic social and politico-economic institutions such as marriage, inheritance, democracy, and the pattern of economy, etc. The purpose of the discussion will be merely to highlight some major difficulties and the possible lines of their solution.

SOCIAL INSTITUTIONS:

MARRIAGE

Islam is the only world religion, which holds marriage to be essentially a contract, which is, in principle, terminable, as distinguished from the conception of marriage as an indissoluble sacramental union. The Islamic conception of marriage is being increasingly accepted by contemporary man in both Western and Communist societies.

A Secular Approach to the Islamic Institutional System

Islam also permits polygamy, although the Qur'anic text clearly indicates that the norm is monogamy. Polygamy was a universal institution barring Christian society. Islamic law humanized and refined this institution without abolishing it. Polygamy is certainly not self-evidently immoral, or a violation of women's freedom or dignity, as slavery was a violation of the freedom and dignity of the slave. In other words, polygamy cannot be included in the list of such manifest disvalues as murder, rape, slavery, and prostitution, etc. Polygamy and monogamy are, from the purely rational viewpoint, alternative social patterns, just as capitalism and socialism are alternative patterns of economy.

Polygamy, however, goes against the ideal of marriage as a unique union of a man and a woman. The need for a special *I-Thou* relationship without involving a third is perhaps deeply entrenched in both the sexes without any distinction, just like other common personality needs. This "*I-Thou* communion need' should not be confused with the so-called sexual possessiveness of the male. Now, polygamy enables the man to satisfy this need, but completely ignores the corresponding need of the woman. Hence, polygamy clearly discriminates against the woman. Obviously, polygamy enables her to satisfy her needs of food, sex, and motherhood. But this subtle spiritual '*I-Thou* communion need' is left permanently frustrated. The woman misses the deeper joy of a spiritual kinship or companionship with her polygamous spouse, even though she may derive material and social benefits from the marriage tie. This inevitably has deep repercussions upon the total personality structure of the woman. She turns to her children for emotional support and consolation. This dependence upon the children in turn adversely affects her own growth. The ramifications of polygamy are, thus, much greater than its defenders are likely to suspect.

Some defenders of polygamy hold that men are incorrigibly poly-erotic, and that Western or Christian monogamy is only a facade to deceive women. According to them, official polygamy not only puts an end to this deception and hypocrisy, but is ultimately more acceptable to the woman than the unofficial polygamy of the West.

It is true that men are poly-erotic. But it does not follow that the poly-erotic tendency ought not and cannot be regulated. Poly-eroticism is only the natural male attitude, which is modifiable by cultural conditioning. The love marriage stands for the fusion of the flesh and the spirit. In proportion as this conception of marriage is inwardly appropriated by the human male, his natural poly-eroticism is transformed into a deep and lifelong spiritual-cum-physical love. Man's poly-eroticism, thus, cannot constitute any valid justification of polygamy.

Defenders of polygamy make a very sweeping assumption in saying that women prefer official polygamy to the unofficial brand of the West. While no wife can remain unaffected by the marital infidelity of her husband, she deems an extra-marital affair a much lesser evil than a co-wife with equal privileges and an equal status. Polygamy would be totally unacceptable to a woman, if she could have her own way. This institution is definitely weighted in favor of the male and against the female, just as numerous medieval customs and usages were weighted in favor of the nobility and against the peasantry.

Many Islamic apologists point out that the population of women usually tends to exceed that of men, so that polygamy is natural and also inevitable. This line of argument, however, goes to prove the naturalness of polyandry in those societies, where men exceed women in number. But Islamic orthodoxy would never accept this conclusion.

Polygamy does provide a solution to the economic and sexual problems of the single dependent woman in a patriarchal society. But the economic problem is best solved by providing equality of opportunity for both sexes and the consequent economic independence of woman. The sexual problem of the single woman; however, does not admit of any solution except, either sexual permissiveness or the permission of bigamy, though not polygamy. It, therefore, seems to me that the zeal of some Islamic modernists for legally banning polygamy is misconceived. It should be left to the free will of the economically independent woman to choose between spinsterhood and the status of a co-wife, assuming she is unable, for some reason or other, to find a monogamous husband. Similarly, it should be left to the free will of the first wife to choose to live as a co-wife or obtain a divorce from her polygamous husband, and either lead a single life or seek another monogamous union. The crux of the matter is that permissiveness is the best principle, provided both men and women are economically secure and engaged in productive and self-fulfilling work. Under such social conditions, problems of cruelty, harassment, suffering of the children, and dowry system are kept at bay.

DIVORCE

The right of divorce is absolutely essential for the good life. According to the Islamic concept of marriage, as a civil contract, the right to divorce is an inherent and unconditional right of the man. The woman does not enjoy this right unconditionally, but she can stipulate this right in the terms of the original marriage contract or even afterward by mutual consent, and thus obtain divorce at her will. This was indeed a remarkable and revolutionary advance in according equal rights to the woman and has no parallel in any other religion. However, equity demands that the woman's right to divorce should be made unconditional as in the case of man.

Marriage being the most intimate form of a face-to-face association, the state or society should restrict itself to the bare minimum of regulation compatible with the stability of the family and the welfare of the children. This is precisely the Qur'anic approach, and contemporary opinion in Western and Communist societies has also come to the same conclusion.

Some divorce regulations of the traditional *Hanafi* law are, however, over-permissive, tending to make divorce too easy and casual. For instance, according to the *Hanafi* law, three consecutive pronouncements of the formula of divorce lead to irrevocable divorce, as distinct from the revocable divorce effected by a single pronouncement. Such an interpretation clearly violates the Qur'anic spirit of caution and restraint in such matters. The Qur'an clearly specifies that intending divorcees must first seek reconciliation with the help of arbitrators appointed by both the husband and the wife.[104] The *Shia* law does provide for this reconciliatory device prior to divorce.

Another *Hanafi* law, which must be examined afresh in the light of the Qur'anic texts, concerns the conditions of remarriage of a divorced wife with her former husband who had pronounced the irrevocable divorce, or whose divorce has become functionally irrevocable due to the expiry of the three/four-month reconciliation period. According to the present *Hanafi* interpretation of the Qur'anic text, such a divorced wife cannot remarry her first husband without an intervening marriage and divorce by a second husband. This rule may cause acute psychological distress to divorcees who, over the period of years, may come to realize that divorce was ill-advised and that a reunion is in the best interests of all concerned. According to the *Hanafi* law, the divorced couple cannot remarry unless the woman first marries another husband, consummates the marriage, and is divorced by him.[105] The Qur'anic text is by no means clear on this point, and some commentators have held that the Qur'anic clause, prescribing the intervening marriage and divorce, becomes operative only after two irrevocable divorces have already taken place. The rule of the intervening marriage was made with a view to checking the abuse of easy divorce and remarriage, and this basic objective is obviously sound. But four months are much too short a period for a couple to acquire full insight into their inner conflicts and personality structures. Hence, no unnecessary obstacles should be placed in their reunion, if they be so inclined, unless of course they have been twice divorced already.

POSITION OF WOMEN

Of all the major religions of the world Islam gives the highest status to the woman. It must be conceded, however, that this status falls short of the ideal of complete equality of man and woman. The concept of equality of the sexes is the unique contribution of the modern Western value system to man's cultural evolution. In other words, it is not official Christianity or other religions, but only the contemporary Western and Communist value systems that can rightfully claim to be ahead of Islam in this respect.

The equality of status of men and women has several dimensions. The most serious inadequacy in the traditional Islamic concept of equality of men and women is in respect of evidence. According to the Qur'an, the evidence of two women is equivalent to that of one man. [106] It is utterly futile to take the stand that this discrimination is based upon some inherent defect or shortcoming in women. The proper stand, probably, is to interpret the Qur'anic discrimination as a reflection of the inferior and dependent status of the average woman in Arab society. She was liable to be swayed by external pressures while giving evidence. Equality of status as a person obviously demands that the woman be at par with the man, as a voter as well as a legal witness.

Equality of status also implies eligibility to hold all positions of trust and responsibility including political offices. While the *Shariah* does not permit a woman to become the head of the state, there is no such ban in the Qur'an. [107] Women must enjoy complete equality of opportunity to pursue the career of their choice.

The third facet of equality is equal inheritance of parental property. The Qur'an fixes the share of daughters as half of the share of sons. This inequality is not as glaring as the inequality in the matter of evidence, because a reduced share in inheritance does not imply a lower legal status, but merely a lower degree of financial responsibility for maintaining the family. Nevertheless, this does violate the concept of polymorphous equality, which is an integral part of the value system of contemporary man. This concept cannot be ignored or brushed aside as a passing fashion or human aberration, since it profoundly concerns the interests as well as the dignity of women who constitute right one-half of the entire human family.

The institution of *purdah* too vitiates the concept of equality. The protagonists of *purdah* are certainly right in the sense that the primary sphere of woman's activity differs from that of man. They are also right in the sense that chastity and modesty are important values, and all those social institutions that foster them should be promoted, while those that foster their opposites should be prohibited. The institution of *purdah* certainly tends to promote the value of chastity and modesty. But it obstructs the full development of the personality of the woman. The restriction on freedom of movement, or profession and on other opportunities generates a self-image of inferior status. She may even be led to regard herself as a thing rather than as a person.

Another social psychological consequence of *purdah* is the institution of arranged marriages. The institution of *'arranged marriages'* encourages the practice of the purchase of bridegrooms by the girl's parents from the marriage market. This practice is firmly entrenched among many sections of the Hindus, and is fast spreading among the Indian Muslims. This evil can never be removed unless our women boldly repudiate the theory and practice of segregation and assert their dignity as human beings. The bridegroom should gratefully accept any gift, which parents freely give to their daughters. But self-respecting women must never tolerate the spirit of bargaining. This demands the total abolition of the *purdah* system.

The mutual association of the sexes at different social occasions is essential for the balanced development of the personalities of both men and women. Such association lends a peculiar charm and refinement to social intercourse, and helps the individual to cultivate inner restraint, as distinguished from external discipline. It is true, that if over-done, it has its own dangers, for unrestrained and too frequent mixing between the sexes tends to corrode both chastity and modesty. It is precisely here that the spirit of the Islamic ethic becomes relevant to our age. But complete segregation goes to the other extreme. As in all other areas of human activity, we have to strike an optimum balance between the extremes of unrestrained free mixing and total segregation of women.

The underlying aim of the protagonists of *purdah*; the promotion of chastity and modesty; is laudable. But the means are wrong. Maturity of character and balanced personality development are the real promoters of chastity, and these pre-requisites are not fostered but hindered by *purdah*. Not the curtailing of the freedom and equality of opportunity of one half of the human race, or treating them like perpetual minors under the guardianship or mandate of the other 'superior' half, but rather proper education and balanced training are the right means to promote chastity and modesty in both men and women.

THE LAWS OF INHERITANCE

The Qur'anic law of inheritance is a contribution to the good life and is indeed remarkable for its comprehensiveness. It prevents the concentration of wealth among the few and benefits the maximum number of relations of the deceased. But at least two provisions of the *Shariah* need to be revised, since they violate plain equity and common sense. It is significant that neither of these provisions is expressly mentioned in the Qur'an but has been inferred or developed by Muslim jurists.

The first provision relates to one's share in the property of one's grandparents, if one's parents die in the lifetime of one's grandparents. According to the present interpretation of the Qur'anic law, the grandchildren are deprived of their share for the logical reason that the chain of succession is broken, the moment their parents die in the lifetime of their grandparents. In a sense this is quite logical, but it is inequitable to deprive orphans of the wealth, which would have naturally accrued to them, if only their parents had not died prematurely. Other circumstances being the same, the orphan's need of financial security and help is greater than that of other children. [108]

The second provision concerns the share of daughters in their parent's property in the absence of any brother. The present *Hanafi* law drastically curtails the share of the daughters, if there be no male coeval heir. In such cases the residual property goes to other relatives who would not have inherited in the normal course. This is a clear case of discrimination against women. It stands to reason that at least the normal half share of daughters should not be reduced any further due to the accidental fact that they have no brother. The *Shia* law is quite rational in this respect. [109]

The Islamic law of inheritance obviously ceases to be relevant in an egalitarian socialist society where property is restricted to one's belongings, and every individual enjoys equality of opportunity. But as long as private enterprise exists, whether in a capitalist or a mixed economy, the Islamic law of inheritance will retain its relevance and promote human welfare through its judicious and balanced provisions.

PENAL CODE

Murder: The Qur'anic punishment for murder is the death sentence. But the Qur'an specifically provides for commuting the extreme penalty, provided the heirs of the deceased are willing to accept an agreed monetary compensation. This was the customary law and the Qur'an retains it.

The provision for compensation greatly helps the poor and the needy survivor and also gives a second chance to the culprit to live the good life in the future. Contemporary opinion too favors a therapeutic rather than a retributive approach to the criminal and many states have abolished the death penalty.

Theft: In the case of theft, the Qur'anic punishment is severing the hand. [110] But the Qur'anic text also clearly states that the culprit should be given a chance of seeking Divine forgiveness. If he is deprived of his hand straightway, the forgiveness clause in the Qur'an would be rendered pointless. Most commentators have, therefore, inferred, and rightly so, that severing the hand is only the extreme punishment for the third offense. However, it is not merely the number of offenses but also the total situation and the motivation of the criminal, which is crucial for determining the degree of guilt or evil involved in any offense. This stand was taken by *Caliph* Umar who is reported to have refused to sever the hand of a thief on the ground that he had been deprived of food for several days. The concept of extenuation of the degree of guilt is indeed indispensable, and is as fundamental as the concept of the degrees of good and evil. For instance, would it be rational and just to sever the hand of a person committing theft for the third or even the tenth time, when the person is a kleptomaniac? In any case, when the principle of commutation is applicable to the penalty for murder, why should it not be applied to the penalty for theft? Depriving a person of his life is a much greater evil than depriving him of his property, and if commutation applies to the greater crime, it should also apply to the lesser, that is, theft.

Adultery: The Qur'an prescribes whipping (hundred stripes) as a penalty for adultery, provided there be four witnesses to the act.[III] But the Islamic religious law (*Shariah*) prescribes the traditional Semitic practice of stoning to death as the penalty for adultery, while flogging for fornication.

The distinction between adultery and fornication is important, and a more severe penalty for the former is understandable. But what is far more important is the distinction between fornication and rape, since the former does not violate the dignity and freedom of the woman, while the latter does. It seems that the *Shariah* does not register this vital distinction.

According to the Islamic conception, the essence of marriage is a free contract between the parties to share their life, while the husband undertakes the financial responsibility for the family unit. The presence of witnesses, the formal written or oral ceremony of marriage and publicity are recommended, but do not constitute the essential part of Islamic marriage. Thus, the difference between this contractual concept of marriage and adultery or fornication is not publicity, but a recognized and enforceable obligation of the husband and wife to each other and to the children that may follow. The basic evil of adultery is thus irresponsible self-gratification. Moreover, adultery almost invariably violates the moral integrity of the parties who are pushed into the pit of secrecy and dissimulation. Adultery also causes psychological pain and economic loss to the spouse or his family. Nevertheless adultery, as an evil, can never be bracketed with such evils as murder, rape, cruelty, malice, fraud, bribery, false incrimination, and adulteration, etc. Hence there must be a more severe penalty for rape than for adultery and fornication. Now if the latter two be penalized by stoning and whipping (which amount to the death penalty as such), the manifestly greater evil of rape cannot be penalized in a correspondingly more severe manner. This would mean that a greater evil is indirectly bracketed with a lesser.

However, the Qur'anic requirement that four witnesses must testify to the deed practically averts the Qur'anic penalty of flogging and the traditional penalty of stoning to death. It appears to me that perhaps the practical erosion of a theoretically severe penalty is not an anomaly, but is meant to issue a stern warning to irrational man to keep his sex impulses in responsible check, yet to condone his unavoidable lapses and failures in a difficult task. The contemporary Western ethic of sexual permissiveness, on the other hand, merely condones without antecedently warning and exhorting the individual, and thus it becomes a rather lopsided ethic.

POLITICO-ECONOMIC INSTITUTIONS:

SECULARISM

The crucial problem of man today is what politico-economic structure best promotes human welfare. To this crucial question the answers of the traditional Muslim and the consistent secularist are basically different. Traditional Islam seeks the answer to this crucial question in the Qur'an and the *sunnah* whose directions in this regard are held to be as binding upon the Muslims as the prescriptions concerning prayer, fasting, pilgrimage, etc. The assumption underlying this answer, as already indicated, is that Islam is a complete code of life without any distinction between the religious and the secular. Indeed, this is the burden of Maududi's writings, which repeatedly emphasize the utter incompatibility between Islam and secularism.

The secular approach, on the other hand, says that the answer to political or economic issues should be sought with the help of observation and independent reflection on the cumulative experience of the human race. Thus, if actual experience were to show that socialism best promoted human welfare, one should opt for the socialist economy, whether or not it be envisaged in the Qur'an or *sunnah*. The assumption in this case is that religion is not a monolithic prescriptive system or total code of conduct, but rather a personal relationship between man and God, leaving man free to make his own independent choices in matters that are essentially social rather than transcendental.

This stand is not atheistic, nor does it imply the abolition of religion from society. But it does imply the rejection of those forms of religion, which claim supreme regulative authority in all spheres of human life. Moreover, it implies the affirmation of the spiritual autonomy of the individual and the sovereignty of society in all matters concerning the relations between man and man, as distinguished from man's personal relationship with God. Apart from such matters as belief in God, life after death, and prayer, etc., all areas of human activity, such as industry, commerce, taxation, politics, education, and administration, etc., are thus brought into the purview and jurisdiction of free collective inquiry. Now, this conception of religion is totally different from the traditional Islamic interpretation, according to which Islamic religious law (*Shariah*) should guide the Muslim in every sphere.

There is no incompatibility between secularism and religion, but the religion must be such that makes a clear distinction between the purely social (man-to-man) and the transcendental (man-to-God) spheres of life. While secularism does not reject religion, it certainly does demand a version of religion, which does not encroach upon certain matters. From the traditional perspective, such religion is a spineless pseudo-religion, which has retreated from its legitimate position of supremacy to a restricted autonomy. It is thought that such a spineless or truncated religion would gradually wither away from the stage of human life, since it would have no vital function to perform, apart from regulating rites and rituals for prayer and for occasions such as birth, marriage, death, etc. In short, there is a sharp conflict between the traditional conception of Islam and secularism.

Christianity too had to face this conflict in the 18th century, since medieval Christianity also was a complete code of life, and a good Christian had to follow the traditional institutional system in all its details. Due to the Christian Reformation, revival of Greek rationalism, the impact of science and technology upon society, and last but not the least, the growing sentiment of territorial nationalism, the medieval conception of Christianity gradually made room for the modern conception that religion ought to be a personal relationship between man and God rather than presume to regulate all the spheres of human life. The ideal of a sovereign secular democratic nation-state displaced the ideal of a multi-national Christian society subject to Divine laws promulgated by the Roman Church or the Vicar of Christ. This secular revolution of Western Europe has not yet touched the imagination of the average Muslim. [112]

It is significant that the Muslim takes special pride in claiming that his religion is a complete code of conduct. He does not realize that right up to the beginning of the modern era every world religion claimed to be a complete code of conduct. Judaism, Christianity, Hinduism, and most probably Buddhism, all offer complete guidance to their followers. Christian, Jewish, and Hindu casuistry is not any the less developed than the Islamic *Shariah*. Consequently, Islam is not unique in this respect, even though it must be conceded that the Islamic institutional system is positively superior to the traditional institutional system of the other world religions

A Secular Approach to the Islamic Institutional System

with respect to such important features as racial tolerance, social equality, religious brotherhood, status of women, laws of marriage and divorce, and equitable laws of inheritance, etc.

The difficulty of the traditional Muslim in accepting the full implications of secularism is understandable and genuine. The Islamic tradition gives primacy and pride of place to the concept of an Islamic community (*ummah*) committed to the will of the sovereign Lord of the worlds, and has no room for the concept of a sovereign nation-state whose members are autonomous and equal citizens, irrespective of their caste, color or creed. It is significant that right through the period of the Caliphate the non-Muslim citizens of the Islamic state were placed in a separate category of the protected ones (*dhimmis*). Although the *dhimmis* were treated well (in glaring contrast to the persecution of religious minorities in the Christian society of the age), the *dhimmis* did not enjoy, rather, logically, could not enjoy, equal rights in a state, which was, by definition, fused with the church of Islam. The Muslims alone ran the establishment of the Islamic Church-cum-State under the Caliph (*khalifa*). The *Caliph* was not a tribal chief but the successor to the Prophet ﷺ, who in his own turn was not the sovereign, but a messenger of the Sovereign Lord. Indeed, the thought-cum-value system of not only traditional Islam but also Christianity and Judaism was so structured that they could not include the concept of equal rights for nonbelievers. Thus the *dhimmis* regarded themselves and were regarded by the Muslims as associate members of a society in which their evidence was not admissible against a Muslim. [113] Most probably, they did not object to this discrimination, since they themselves subscribed to the medieval conception that it was the membership of a religious community which primarily determined the group-identity and legal status of the individual. Modern Western thought was the first to substitute the state as the primary unit of corporate life and of group-identity. This has gradually made religion permissive rather than obligatory and has redefined the function of religion in life. This is the essence of the secular revolution. Muslims all over the world must come to grips with this fundamental change in the medieval and modern approaches to the nature and function of religion. [114]

One simply must answer the basic question whether a religion, which abdicates the claim to regulate the totality of man's life, could still perform a vital function in the economy of life. My answer is obviously in the affirmative. In fact, the delinking of the institutional system from the core function of religion would not destroy religion, but rather strengthen it from within. Religion would then flourish and truly enrich the inner life of the genuinely religious man. It would continue to remain the source of the deepest and the most enduring joy for the individual and the means of his spiritual sustenance in the task of living.

Religion, in the final analysis, is not a matter of external discipline, but an inner and free commitment to basic ethical values, plus a mystical yearning to surrender oneself before some Power, Being, Presence, or Elan, which is judged as the source of these values. In the absence of this mystical dimension one cannot be said to be religious, though one may well be morally developed. Perhaps not all among us possess the mystical capacity in the developed sense, although we are all mystical to some degree or other, just as we are all musical to some extent. Now just as society cannot force the individual to enjoy music or poetry, similarly, society cannot force men to taste the spiritual joy of spiritual communion between man and God. However, the genuinely religious will always betake themselves to such communion, seeking inspiration for living the good life, even when religion no longer claims to legislate for every sphere of life. Thus religion would ever-inspire man to realize his spiritual possibilities in a secular society.

DEMOCRACY

Democracy implies the spiritual autonomy of the individual and the sovereignty of the state or society. Individuals are required to submit to the collective wisdom of the group in all public matters. Since, however, individuals remain free to convert others to their point of view, society ever-remains open to new ideas and insights. The traditional Islamic view of life, on the other hand, affirms the sovereignty of God and man's duty of unqualified surrender to the Word of God as interpreted by His prophets. Minor changes or modifications maybe permitted to the individual Muslim in regard to peripheral matters. But the true Muslim is not supposed to question the provisions of the sacred law in any really significant matter or issue. The supremacy of the Qur'anic injunctions signifies submission to an external authority or locus of sovereignty as distinguished from the democratic conception of the sovereignty of the people.

The sovereignty of the people or the state itself flows from spiritual autonomy, which is the ultimate basis and bedrock of democracy. The view that the prerogative to decide must rest with the majority also flows from the notion of the dignity and freedom of the individual. The logic of this convention is that agreement between free individuals enhances the probability, though not the certainty, of their being right. In the absence of certainty the minority must be given the prerogative to differ from the majority without any feelings of guilt, and the right of the minority to differ must be deemed to be as fundamental as the right of the majority to decide. Indeed, it is quite common for the majority to be in the wrong and the minority to be in the right. But then just as the majority must tolerate, nay respect, the right of the minority to differ, the minority, on its part, must respect the right of the majority to be in the wrong, and yet have the prerogative to have it all its own way.

This democratic dialogue between autonomous and theoretically equal individuals provides an inbuilt mechanism for exposing and removing the inevitable errors and evils, which the majority maybe guilty of. Like the scientific method, the democratic process is, in the long run, self-corrective. Just as the test of empirical verification acts as a check upon uncontrolled speculation, the test of democratic approval by the majority checks the chances of error or evil. Consequently, despite serious defects, democracy appears to be relatively the best form of government. [115]

Some observers think that democracy is not suitable for multi-religious or heterogeneous societies, since the different religious, ethnic, or linguistic groups are apt to function as closed and insular majorities and minorities. This difficulty is genuine but it does not invalidate democracy. After all, journeys cannot be abandoned if the road be rough. And there appears to be no better road than democracy.

In a homogeneous society the similarity of the reference group makes for more or less spontaneous cohesion and sense of participation among the individuals. On the other hand, ethnic or cultural differences; make for social psychological difficulties in the way of effective participation of the minority groups which always suffer from the fear of being dominated or discriminated against. Human nature being what it is, negative discrimination, or, at least, group partiality is very difficult to eliminate completely. But even where there is no discrimination in specific instances, psychological fears cloud the atmosphere. The minority groups maybecome defensively aggressive or extra-vocal, or more or less withdraw into a protective shell thereby becoming helpless observers cut off from the national mainstream. These difficulties, however, must be faced as thorns in the rose.

It must be noticed that homogeneity of the population is itself a matter of degree, and also that group tensions and rivalries are the inseparable shadows of all human relationships. No society, however homogeneous it may appear to be on the surface, is inwardly free from interpersonal and inter-group tensions, which develop in small cultural associations and even in families, to say nothing of the state. It is the destiny of man to feel alienated in some form at some time or other; it is the task of man to overcome this alienation as best as he can. [116]

Secular democracy, in essence and theory, does not imply or presuppose the concept of the nation-state and is quite compatible with the haunting ideal of humanism. But in the present human situation democracy in action is practically inseparable from the nation-state. Indeed, nationalism itself, if not confused with chauvinism, is not opposed to but the precondition of a viable and stable humanism. A merely sentimental ideal of human solidarity can never work in the absence of smaller and more manageable units or groupings; continental, national, or provincial. Nationalism is thus not the antithesis but rather the sub-thesis of humanism; the arc of the circle, as it were.

The same maybe said of the relationship between the different religions or churches and the ideal of the Church of man. The Church of man should not seek to destroy different churches or to assimilate them into its unitary fold, but seek a federal union or fellowship of faiths, unpolluted by the militancy of dogma or the imperialism of the spirit. The concept of conversion to the one true religion, as a pre-condition of world brotherhood in this life and of salvation in life hereafter, is a concept that does not appeal to the religious sensibility of a growing number of intelligent and sincere believers, be they Muslim, Christian, or Hindu.

At present the relations between different national and religious groups are still colored by the heritage of past antagonisms. But the economic disparities between the rich and the poor nations of the world could lead to a still more explosive antagonism in the next century. Many Western intellectuals have realized that the surging waters of uncontrolled poverty could easily engulf islands of affluence. Now more than ever, concern for the welfare of the tribe itself demands active concern for the human family. Under these conditions the traditional concern of the Muslims for the Islamic brotherhood acquires a parochial air in the global context. Muslims must realize that the brotherhood of man is a higher level of corporate existence than

A Secular Approach to the Islamic Institutional System

both the nation-state and the brotherhood of Islam. In practice, however, one never encounters mankind in the abstract but only individuals in concrete situations. And every individual must get his proper due of sympathy and help, irrespective of his caste, color, or creed.

Many traditional Muslims fear that democracy in the Western sense leads either to anarchy or to the perversion of all values due to man's essential fallibility or sinfulness. But this evaluation of democracy is not confirmed by the history of Western democratic society. Toynbee has pointed out in his monumental work how Western European society has gradually transformed traditional Christianity through integrating it into the framework of modern science and democracy, while retaining its moral impulse. This was also Matthew Arnold's interpretation of the essence of Western culture. [117] The ethical values of the Christian tradition were retained, not because of any external compulsion but because of their authentic appeal to autonomous individuals. So we can see for ourselves the outcome of democracy in Western society for the past few centuries. Despite many blunders, the record is not worse than that of the medieval age dominated by the traditional interpretation of Islam and Christianity. After all, fundamental rights, the equality of the sexes, the dignity of labor, equality of opportunity, religious tolerance, and the Parliament of man, etc., to say nothing of the purely scientific and technological achievements of the modern era, are all the contributions of men who followed where the argument led them. The debit side of the picture, however, should not be ignored. Indeed it was precisely this painful realization soon after the First World War that damped the smug enthusiasm of the 19th century European votaries of reason and progress. But is it not a sign of hope that their warnings arose when they did, and what is more, their warnings are being heeded now, and that the limitations and imbalances in patterns of Western thought and living are slowly being remedied? A new concern for the hitherto neglected spiritual dimension of life is slowly but steadily emerging in both the Western and the Communist worlds. [118]

Under these conditions the Muslims must shed their traditional 'fear of freedom' and not only intellectually accept but fully commit themselves to secular democracy. It is heartening to note that countries such as Indonesia and Bangla Desh, apart from Turkey and some Arab States, have, as a matter of principle, adopted secular constitutions, even as India, with an overwhelming Hindu majority, has freely chosen the path of secular democracy.

The Indian Muslims should not fear that a commitment to democracy would lead to their de-Islamization. To the extent that the basic moral values of the Qur'an evoke the Muslim's authentic commitment and actually shape his sensibility, his free decisions would conform with the Qur'an in the task of applying the Qur'an and the *sunnah* to the present human situation. In this process Qur'anic values will acquire new dimensions and depth and will not be ignored or rejected. To the extent of their inner power to convince and grip free minds, Qur'anic values, in the form of secular wisdom, would also permeate the institutions of secular democratic societies, whether professedly Islamic or not.

Pattern of Economy

The most crucial decisional problem of our age is to determine which pattern of economy is most desirable. Many crucial problems, which were once decisional in nature, have now become primarily problems of implementation. [119] This means there is a more or less general consensus about their theoretical solution, though difficulties of implementation still remain. The problem of capitalism versus socialism, however, still awaits a theoretical solution, and is thus the supreme decisional problem of the age. The division on this score cuts across all divisions based on race, religion, or language. Both sides are confident that they are right and will prevail. It is difficult to say that only one side is wise and the assured victor, while the other is deluded and doomed.

The solution involves making complex value judgments, and value judgments can never be clinched like scientific truths. But far more serious than this purely theoretical difficulty is the inner or existential uncertainty of honest individuals concerning the rank or grade of the different values emphasized by capitalism and socialism. For example, it is impossible to grade values such as freedom, enterprise, efficiency, security, cooperation, competition, equality, and merit, etc., in a hierarchical order claiming universal appeal. Different values serve different interests and appeal to different types of persons, or persons in different types of situations. Hence the chances of agreement become rather small. In theory it is possible to adopt the standpoint of the impartial spectator with sympathy for all and no personal axe to grind. But in practice almost all remain under the sway of their interests when they try to choose between the values in question.

A Secular Approach to the Islamic Institutional System

Even if a person renounces his economic or material interests, he cannot give up his personality needs which incline him to prefer, say, security to enterprise. Even those who turn to religion for an answer to this crucial problem remain under the sway of their interests, though they may not be aware of this.

The above difficulty, however, does not mean that the effort to be impartial and non-partisan is totally futile. It only means that we should be aware of the clash of interests and ever-try to reconcile them through an all-inclusive sympathy, without, however, claiming omniscient impartiality. In any case man ought to choose one way or the other, since the failure to choose is not less harmful than the common situation of choosing under the sway of unconscious self-interest.

Until recently I was inclined to hold that a mixed economy was the most suitable and balanced of all alternatives, since it combined the virtues of both capitalism and socialism and avoided their defects as far as humanly possible. The dovetailing of the private and the public sectors, and of centralization and decentralization in the concept of the mixed economy appeared to me as the dialectical synthesis of capitalism and socialism. But I am no longer sure of the validity of this approach.

Many observers prefer the mixed economy on the ground that selective nationalization of industries gives the state full control over the commanding heights of the economy without abolishing the private sector. From this vantage point the state can control the direction of the economy in the public interest without becoming an all-powerful monolithic producer. It is held that the coexistence of the private and the public sectors creates a proper balance between centralization and decentralization and prevents the concentration of power in either industry, finance, or the government. The thesis appears to be sound in theory, but our actual experience belies the great expectations that had been raised in several quarters by the concept of mixed economy. Let us see why this is the case.

The basic appeal of socialism, to my mind, is its ethical flavor; the promise to deliver society from man's exploitation of man and from the tyranny of social, psychological tensions and temptations to break moral or legal rules for the sake of material gains. [120] Since, however, the mixed economy does not usher in a fully cooperative society, but only brings selected industries under state control, mixed economy does not transform the basic social and moral climate of capitalist society. The aggressive and somewhat unscrupulous individualism of a competitive society continues to color human relationships. One producer remains pitted against the other, the wholesaler remains eager for a little more elbowroom from the retailer, the retailer from the consumer. Similarly, the interests of the small producer clash with those of the big producer and also the state. When the private producers and the state both need some raw material that is in short supply, the private producers are compelled to resort to sharp practices or plain unfair means just to survive in the market economy. Bureaucracy breeds several ills and producers are compelled to resort to 'therapeutic corruption', or else retire from the race. The mixed economy also generates peculiar managerial difficulties. On the one hand, state intervention and controls over the free market economy hamper productivity, while on the other, the public ever-keeps up its pressure upon the industry and the government to keep prices low. The threat of nationalization always hangs as a 'Damocles' sword in front of the private sector, which is tempted to placate and appease the government by fair means or foul.

The mixed economy thus does not lead to the moral regeneration or toning up of society expected of socialism, though it does reduce the concentration of economic power in the hands of the private producers as well as of the government.

The traditional Islamic approach to this vital matter is even less acceptable to a growing number of well-informed and intelligent observers, whether Muslim or non-Muslim. The traditional approach is that the prohibition of interest, in combination with the Islamic laws of inheritance and the wealth-tax (*zakat*) together with regular voluntary alms is quite sufficient to cure all those evils, which are sought to be removed by the extreme measures of socialism or communism.

The traditional approach is rooted in three assumptions. The first is that the moral and economic malaise of society flows from the lack of Islamic piety in the Muslims who profess Islam but (unlike the early Muslims) do not live up to its noble teachings. In other words, the fault lies in the character of the individuals and not in the character or structure of the economy as such. The traditional approach seeks to change the pattern of personal behavior, rather than the pattern of economy, or, in other words, to reform the Muslims rather than reform the Islamic polity rooted in the Qur'an and the *sunnah*.

A Secular Approach to the Islamic Institutional System

The second assumption is that the economic system obtaining at the time of the Prophet ﷺ is sacrosanct and unalterable, at least in spirit, if not the letter. Any attempt to improve it in the name of equity, reason, or progress amounts to intervention in religion (*mudakhilat fid deen*) and is not permitted by Islam.

This assumption stems from the basic fallacy of confusing instrumental with intrinsic values or confusing means with ends. Patterns of economy are obviously means to human welfare and not ends. On principle, therefore, there should be no hesitation in choosing the one or the other in accordance with their capacity to promote human welfare. The case is partly analogous to the adoption of new modes of locomotion or transportation without being troubled by the sense of disloyalty to the Prophet ﷺ. Since, however, patterns of economy have far-reaching ramifications upon human life as a whole, and some of the implications of socialism may conflict with the Qur'an and the *sunnah*, continuous reflection becomes necessary.

The third assumption is that Islam having been completed when the last Qur'anic verse was revealed to the Prophet ﷺ, the economic pattern implemented by the Prophet ﷺ is bound to be irrevocably valid for all time. [121] This assumption is rooted in a mechanistic rather than a dynamic conception of perfection. It ignores the observed fact that the concrete implementation of abstract ideals has complex results. The results almost always turn out to be poorer than the expectations of the agent due to the inevitable limitations of human functioning. But these very shortcomings stimulate creative souls to devise ways and means of remedying them, and this leads to qualitative growth of the values and ideals. On the one hand, the values shape the environment; on the other, the changing environment reshapes the values themselves in a dialectical process. In other words, new dimensions emerge in the soul and substance of old values, which are thereby not destroyed but fulfilled, just as the emergence of life does not destroy but fulfills the potentiality of matter. Likewise the concept of equality of opportunity fulfills the promise latent in the earlier concept of equality of franchise.

The concept of dialectical growth and perfection demands creative fidelity to the Qur'an. This means a concern for ceaseless growth of the Qur'anic values. This growth occurs through continued reflection upon Qur'anic values as well as full receptivity to the ever-growing human fund of concepts and values.

Islam has certainly given relatively the greatest importance to the removal of exploitation of man by man (just as Islam has given relatively the highest status and legal rights to woman). But the traditional Qur'anic measures, useful as they were, did not and will not suffice to remove socio-economic evils from their roots. The ancient and universal institution of slavery, for example, was humanized and reformed, but not abolished either by the Qur'an or by the Prophet ﷺ. A society in which slaves are treated humanely is better than a society in which they are treated brutally. But is not a society in which there is no slavery at all better still? In the same vein, is not a society in which all members enjoy equality of opportunity a still higher society than one where they are equal, merely in their right to vote?

A society that helps the needy or deprived through charity or state funds (*bait ul mal*), is certainly a better society than one in which the poor are treated with callous unconcern. But is not the ideal of *abolishing* poverty instead of merely *mitigating* it, a still higher ideal? In other words, is not an economic program, which prevents poverty better than one, which merely cures it? Rather than be content with a particular notion of social obligation at a particular stage of human history, the Muslim must enlarge and deepen the Qur'anic value of humanistic sympathy. This is the meaning of creative fidelity to the basic values of the Qur'an and the *sunnah*.

The traditional Islamic polity relies too much upon the piety of the good Muslim, and too little on legal prohibitions (such as the ban on usury) for ending the exploitation of the poor and establishing social justice. When the moral zeal and religious piety of the early Muslims (who were directly inspired by the Prophet ﷺ and the pious *caliphs*) declined, as was quite natural, and has happened with other religions also, there were not enough legal sanctions or structural safeguards in the polity to prevent the rich and powerful Muslims from indulging in pomp and luxury rather than to follow the simplicity of the Prophet ﷺ and the pious *caliphs*. Muslims, therefore, must realize the inadequacy of mere moral exhortation or religious piety to end social evils.

Mere obedience to the letter of the Qur'anic prohibition against interest is not enough. There should be perennial growth in Islamic values and institutions without any resistance to the contribution made by the human family as a whole. If, for example, today our sense of social justice demands that all sources of exploitation should be removed and equality of opportunity be maximized, we, as good Muslims, should advance from the prohibition

A Secular Approach to the Islamic Institutional System

of interest to the prohibition of unearned incomes, massive inherited wealth, unrestricted private enterprise, and a soul-killing competition that generates all kinds of immoral temptations and psychological stresses, which appear to be inseparable from the capitalist economy. Similarly, if the contemporary ideal of equality of opportunity be the more developed form of Islamic equality, in the traditional sense (*masawat*), and if our actual experience were to show that socialism is a pre-condition for establishing equality of opportunity, than, will not creative fidelity to the Qur'an and the *sunnah* demand the full socialistic transformation of society?

The establishment of a broadly egalitarian society appears to be a pre-condition of equality of opportunity. An egalitarian society probably cannot be ushered in through mere taxation measures, which reduce disparities of wealth, without restructuring society as such. Useful as they are, such measures do not bring about a substantial change in the required direction. Equality of opportunity demands restructuring the total economy and society rather than merely progressive slabs of taxation or scholarships to enable exceptionally bright children of poor parents to study in expensive schools.

Many critics of socialism maintain that the total abolition of private enterprise under full socialism leads to the concentration of both political and economic power in the executive. This tends to erode the freedom of the individual, and this is deemed to invalidate socialism. This argument has considerable weight but it is not conclusive. The fact is that in any society the freedom of the individual remains an abstract paper freedom without any concrete content, until he is economically strong enough to exercise his freedom. In other words, the potential freedom of the individual in a formal democratic society becomes kinetic only when the equality of opportunity has conferred economic strength upon the masses. Socialism is thus the economic dimension of democracy at least for the masses, though it does erode the economic power (rather than the freedom) of the select few.

Socialism is thus quite compatible with democracy. But it may, however, make it necessary to modify the concrete institutional patterns of pro-socialist democracy. The issue of restructuring the democratic *gestalt* without destroying its essence or spirit is as crucial a decisional problem as that of socialism itself. But I do not propose to discuss it here.

Many traditional Muslims as well as other shrewd observers maintain that no system can work well unless the persons running the system are good. This is no doubt true. But from this it is wrong to infer that no change is necessary in the present system, and all that is necessary is to improve the quality of our people through education, morality or religion. Both the quality of the human material and the quality of the system are important. If either one or the other is ignored the results would fail to be optimum. However, out of the two, the quality of the human material is perhaps relatively more important, since if individuals running a bad system are good, they will, in due course, get the bad system changed. But if bad men are running a good system, the good system will progressively deteriorate without much chance of self-correction. The ideal is, therefore, to have a good system run by good men.

In conclusion, I must again refer to the insuperable difficulty of arriving at the just pattern of economy, which reconciles all clashing interests and values. It is easy to decide which pattern is the most just or satisfactory, if we consciously or unconsciously identify ourselves with the interests of a particular group, say, landless or industrial labor, the small farmer, the professional classes, and big business, etc., or, if we could be definite about the relative rank of different values such as security, creativity, happiness, contentment, etc. Even if we could be clear on this latter score, we shall still not know the best way to realize these values, since experience shows that the actual consequences of our purposive acts often sharply differ from their expected or calculated consequences. This no doubt happens because the undetected variables of the complex human situation upset our plans, despite the theoretical validity of our reasoning or policymaking. For example, it is theoretically valid that competition helps keep prices low, and eliminates the inferior product from the market. But we learn from experience that this law breaks down in conditions of imperfect competition, say, unequal facilities of advertising. Thus the abstract theories or conceptual models of economics can be accepted only after their empirical confirmation. [122] Now the socialist economy is an experiment of such short duration (only about fifty years, quite unlike secular democracy which has been in action in Western Europe for about two centuries), that it becomes very difficult to be sure of the total results of the socialist economy in the long run. As for democratic socialism, it is still a vision, since no actual society as yet combines democracy and socialism in the full sense.

It appears to me that the passage of time will lead to a clearer vision and a more or less broad consensus as to the most equitable and satisfactory pattern of economy for the human family as a whole, rather than any particular section or interest group. This consensus will be greatly facilitated if the present polemical ideological approach to the problem could be substituted by an irenic sociological one. In practice this would mean two things. Firstly the formulation of an agreed list of the different dimensions of human welfare, or the different facets of the good life. Secondly, a sympathetic but critical evaluation of the main polities of the world for each separate dimension of human welfare, rather than a mere blanket evaluation.

It is true that the above procedure will not lead to complete agreement. Nevertheless, a broad consensus cannot be ruled out. Man lives by hope. It is my rational hope that just as the 19th century saw the end of slavery and the 20th is seeing the end of colonialism, the decline of racialism, and militant 'religionism', etc., the next century will see the end of polemical 'economism'. This will result in the dialectical reconciliation of the elements of value in capitalism and socialism. Recent developments in the methodology of science and philosophy sustain this hope and line of argument. [123]

SECULARISM AND THE INDIAN MUSLIM

What are the factors that hinder the inner acceptance of the secular revolution by the Indian Muslim? Secularism ruptures the traditional Islamic view that the *Shariah* embraces the totality of life, and that the organic unity of the Muslim's life should not be divided into the sphere of the sacred/spiritual and the sphere of the mundane/worldly. Now this is too radical a change for the Muslim to accept without considerable inner resistance.

The Indian Muslim has, in addition, another major difficulty, which is absent in societies where Muslims are in the majority. The Muslims of these regions are being modernized and secularized in spite of any well-thought-out rationale or reinterpretation of Islam. Important changes have already been made in these countries with regard to the laws of marriage, divorce, trade, and commerce. Islamic society in these regions is gradually becoming secular in outlook. In functional terms, this means that the area of human activities supposed to come under the purview of religious law is progressively shrinking, while the area of human activities held to be subject to man's own discretion is gradually expanding. A pragmatic secularization is going on in Egypt, Iran, and to a lesser extent in Pakistan, as distinguished from the deliberate secular revolution planted in Turkey by Mustafa Kamal.

The Indian Muslim fears that the secularization process would weaken the minority power of self-regulation or self-determination due to the proportionately much greater influence-capacity of the majority group. In the case of a homogeneous society the expanding frontiers of secularism bring about a corresponding increase in both individual and group autonomy. But in the case of minority groups this attraction is totally absent, since the minority tends to develop a fear that secularization would erode its self-determination and place it at the mercy of the majority. The minority fears that the secularization process would ultimately result in its gradual assimilation or absorption in the bigger group. The Muslim's fear of loss of group identity and importance intensifies his attraction to the traditional conception of Islam as a complete code of life. The Islamic code could be modified in accordance with the principle of reinterpretation (*ijtihad*), which is an integral part of the grand Islamic tradition. The program of secularization, on the other hand, tends to generate not only fear of loss of group identity, but also fear of the unknown destination of the ship of secularism piloted by a non-Muslim majority.

It is of crucial importance to clarify the complex issues involved in the above analysis. Unless this is done, the Indian Muslims will never be able to make a sane and balanced choice of their own free accord without the compulsion of events. The first question, which arises, is: what are the actual thought currents found in the majority? In case the basic motivating aspirations and ideals of the majority are more or less in harmony with the basic values or preferences of the Indian Muslims themselves, then there is no reason to feel afraid that their own choices or preferences would be rendered ineffectual in shaping their destiny. The reason is that the decisions arrived at through the secular democratic process would reflect the thinking of the minority no less than that of the majority. If, on the other hand, there be an essential disharmony or conflict between the basic thought and value patterns of the majority and the minority groups, then the fear of loss of self-determination would be a reasonable fear.

This is not the place to go into the actual complex details of the Indian situation. It will suffice, in the context of this work, to register my own considered judgment in regard to this crucial issue. I am convinced that in the final analysis the leitmotif of contemporary Indian society, far from conforming to traditional Hinduism in basic socio-cultural or politico-economic matters, is essentially the leitmotif of contemporary Western culture and (paradoxical as it may appear) of the Qur'anic value system itself. The distinguishing features of the Western thought-cum-value system are the scientific method and polymorphous egalitarianism. In this type of society the only group likely to lose its influence or power is the class owning unearned inherited wealth. Consequently, the vast majority of Indian Muslims, who are clearly in the category of have-nots, stand to gain rather than lose in the emerging set-up. In theory there does exist the possibility that the Indian majority, at any moment in the future, may regress or revert to its traditional mores, and by virtue of their numerical strength, the Hindus may start completely ignoring the views of the minority. This possibility, however, is not a realistic probability. World thought currents and politico-economic forces operating in Indian and human society as a whole almost certainly rule out the actual occurrence of this bare theoretical possibility, no matter what some militant Hindu revivalists may solemnly proclaim before their own charmed circle. [124]

Secularism does not necessarily lead to the total loss of group identity, which is bound to persist so long as the group maintains its distinctive style of man's *I-Thou* dialogue with God. Secularism only leads to emotional integration of the different groups. This fosters a sense of *'we-ness'*, without weakening group identity. Emotional integration on the basis of secular nationalism and the sense of belonging to the ancient Indian family, far from weakening the group, would revitalize the Indian Muslims by giving them equality of opportunity.

Like democracy, and socialism, etc., secularism too can be understood and interpreted in more than one sense. There is no reason why our brand of secularism should be the carbon copy of any particular version without regard to our own particular situational requirements. Theoretically it is possible to have a secular state with proportional representation of the different religious groups in the legislature. However, it seems to me that the adoption of rigorous secularism in the sphere of politics is in the best interests of the Indian Muslims themselves. Nevertheless, they are justified if they want to retain group autonomy in the sphere of personal laws.

It is true that interpersonal relationships such as marriage, divorce, etc., have social consequences and cannot be bracketed with the man-God relationship. But even the man-God dialogue has a social dimension, apart from its dominant transcendental function. Now, if secularism could exclude the transcendental relationship of the believer from its purview, it could also exclude some intimate personal matters, particularly in a multi-religious society. These matters could be governed by the personal laws of the group concerned, provided no gross violation of equity or natural justice were involved. Some secular states have uniform laws of marriage and divorce, while some, such as the USA, permit regional variations. Many states permit their citizens to opt either for the traditional religious law of marriage and divorce or for the civil law of the state. A strict uniformity in these matters is neither sound logic nor intelligent patriotism. Perhaps a similar option should be available to the Indian Muslims without any erosion of their religious status in their own eyes.

What is needed is not enforced uniformity but the evolution of a consensus among the Muslims after full deliberation under democratic auspices. The concrete mechanics for arriving at a consensus will have to be worked out, and though it is not an easy task, it is surely not insuperable. It seems to me that getting acquainted with the structure and working of the Roman Catholic church, the different Protestant churches as well as the relatively younger religions and reformist sects such as Sikhism, and the Arya Samaj, etc., should prove helpful in suggesting concrete mechanics for evolving the consensus of the Muslims in India and elsewhere. All problems of personal law and all other purely religious problems of the Muslims, for example, the proper method of sighting the new moon or the duration of fasts in those regions where night and day are too long or too short to make the traditional fast meaningful, should be thrashed out by a body of competent Muslims representing a cross-section of the Muslim society rather than the jurists alone.

The responsibility for taking the initiative in this matter lies with the religious as well as the intellectual leaders of the Indian Muslims. Will they do their solemn duty? I hope and trust that they would.

CHAPTER 8

CONCLUDING REFLECTIONS:

THE JUSTIFICATION PROCEDURE FOR EXISTENTIAL INTERPRETATIONS

The *Elan* conception of God and of revelation, as projected in this work, is only one interpretation of man's religious experience and there can be no finality about it. It does not imply that other interpretations are false. But the *Elan* interpretation seems to be the most adequate and valid, as it takes into full account the entire gamut of human experience and all the basic features of the cosmos, rather than a selected few. The *Elan* conception also preserves man's spiritual autonomy which is viewed as creative fidelity to God within man, and which implies the duty of ceaseless creativity of values. This conception appears to remove the various field-tensions mentioned in the work, and to restore to the traditional Islamic symbols their original power to evoke man's authentic assent. Only when religious symbols reverberate with acceptable meanings can they become the springs of action instead of remaining mere verbal professions or formal marks of a cultural tradition.

All religious thought systems are, in the ultimate analysis, rooted in existential interpretations of human experience. These interpretations serve a different purpose from scientific explanations with which they should not be confused. But no religion can be a substitute for scientific knowledge based on the empirical method. The empirical method affirms that all truthclaims concerning facts, as distinct from values, must be accepted only when they are either directly or indirectly verifiable or falsifiable in principle. In case a truthclaim is verifiable in principle but not in practice (due to technical difficulties in the actual process of verification), the truthclaim maybe accepted as a tentative working hypothesis subject to future acceptance or rejection, as the case maybe. Empiricism implies that even the factual truthclaims contained in the Qur'an be subject to the above test as a condition of their acceptance.

As is well-known, direct verifiability is possible only in the case of simple or elementary statements of the type 'the cat is on the mat', 'some birds are green', 'water is a chemical compound of hydrogen and oxygen'. But explanatory constructs or abstract conceptual models such as atom, electron, and energy, etc. cannot be directly perceived and verified. They are, however, indirectly verifiable in the sense that the predictive consequences of these concepts can be empirically confirmed. Likewise, no scientific law or generalization can ever be completely verified because of the impossibility of testing the future course of events. Nevertheless, laws are said to be verifiable in the sense that our actual experience strengthens the probability that the law is universally true and would also hold for future instances.

Now what is the difficulty in the way of claiming that, like the concept of an electron or elementary particle, which cannot be perceived, the concept of God too is a hypothesis for explaining the order and harmony of the world, though God cannot be perceived. The answer is that though the electron cannot be seen, the predictive consequences of this hypothesis can be verified. We, for instance, know what would be the case if electrons actually existed and had the structure we attribute to them. Now when actual observations, in the course of the relevant experiment, agree with the calculated consequences or states of affairs, this verifies the hypothesis in the scientific (though not in the strict logical) sense. But beliefs in God, life after death, and revelation, etc., do not have such consequences, which can be verified. We do not know, for instance, what would be the case if the hypothesis of God were true, or what would be the case, if false. When there are no antecedent predictive consequences as such the question of their verification does not arise at all. There maybe eschatological verification, provided there is life after death. But then we must first believe in life after death, and any such belief can only be a matter of faith rather than of empirical knowledge.

The empirical method, however, does not restrict the deductive or even the speculative activity of reason in the realm of pure theoretical possibilities. As is now generally accepted by philosophers, philosophical scientists, and mathematicians, the laws of logic and mathematics are not factual truth-claims, that is, they do not give any information about the actual states of affairs, but affirm the implications or what must be the case, given some initial assumptions. In other words, they tell us what must be the case, if some state of affairs is antecedently accepted as true. Whether the state of affairs is a mere possibility or an actual fact is not the concern of logic and mathematics but a matter of empirical inquiry. Now life after death, a cosmic purpose, and the eventual victory of good over evil are all logically possible, even though these beliefs do not have any verifiable predictive consequences. In other words, these beliefs are not scientific hypotheses but existential interpretations of the Universe. It is these existential interpretations that comprise the thought system of a religion. The fact that no religious thought system can be conclusively established as true does not imply there is nothing to choose between different religions, one being as good or bad as the other. Some criteria, such as simplicity or interpretative economy, internal consistency, range of unification, harmony with authentic values, and the maximum reinforcement of man's quest for value, could be used as non-coercive norms of preference in the field of religion. Let us now explain the nature of the above criteria.

INTERPRETATIVE ECONOMY

This means that the interpretative element in the thought system should be the minimum required for sustaining man's quest for value. Unquestioning faith in putative factual beliefs concerning matters outside the range of human experience, e.g., detailed accounts of life after death, the tortures of hell or the rewards of heaven, the creation of the earth, the birth of Adam as the first man, the dialogues between God and the angels and prophets, etc., are no longer easy for the scientific temper and outlook of contemporary man, who is taught that in the absence of factual evidence, suspension of belief is more respectable than either acceptance or rejection. Contemporary man can only commit himself to a sense of mystery while contemplating the Universe and his own inner being, rather than accept a religious ontology, cosmology and eschatology. The smaller the number of factual and existential interpretative beliefs demanded by a religion, the less will be its element of unverifiable faith, and thus the greater will be the probability of universal agreement.

INTERNAL CONSISTENCY

Every existential interpretation of the Universe leads to a conceptualization of our experience together with a corresponding set of attitudes toward the Universe. For example, the interpretation that God is the loving Creator and Sustainer of the Universe suggests that self-preservation should be possible without destroying other creatures of God. But the fact that nature is red in tooth and claw prima facie belies this possibility.

RANGE OF UNIFICATION

Like a scientific theory an existential interpretation may apply to a wider or a restricted range of human experience. Theism, for instance, accounts very well for the cosmic order and harmony but does not account equally well for the different forms of cosmic disharmony; the struggle between good and evil, or between life and death.

HARMONY WITH VALUES

If some ethical values of a religion do not harmonize with the authentic values of the individual, a conflict is born. If authentic harmony is not achieved, the individual remains a divided self or an inauthentic being, giving lip loyalty to the religion. In some cases the person may not be fully aware of his own authentic values and the conflict may remain more or less obscure to him. The full power to evoke man's authentic commitment to its value system is thus a major test of the validity of a religion.

MAXIMUM REINFORCEMENT OF MAN'S QUEST FOR VALUE

The quest for value is the basic *elan* of which all-specific instincts or drives are the concrete forms. Man cannot help the pursuit of value, nor can he escape failure and frustration in his quest. This frustration generates self-destructive attitudes and responses such as rage, hate, bitterness, despair—the logical culmination of which—is suicide. But man's will to live and to overcome his negative impulses lead him to find ways and means of reinforcing his quest for value, just as his concern for his bodily health and vigor prompts him to seek cures for the diseases which afflict him. Indeed the urge to reinforce the quest for value is as universal as the primary quest for value itself. The search for motivational reinforcements to fight back negative and self-destructive attitudes is perhaps yet another form of the basic quest for value. This search is not unreasonable or irrational, even as the desire to live or the will to power cannot be called irrational. However, a particular means of motivational reinforcement maybe rational or irrational. Some methods of reinforcing the quest for value may work in the short but not in the long run. Alcohol, drugs, hypnosis, music, prayer, and phantasies, etc., come in this category.

The most effective form of reinforcement comes through religious or philosophical faith; that the Universe is not the accidental product of blind chance, but the expression of a rational purpose, which may transcend our limited minds, but is nevertheless operative in the cosmos. A conceptual reinforcement like the above has many advantages over the biological or emotive reinforcements of different types. Drugs, for instance, may not be available when needed, while man's authentic beliefs become the deepest part of his being. Again, music does not have the same appeal to all, while sex also loses its attractions in old age. But authentic faith consoles and fortifies the human ego in every situation, provided it does not raise any intellectual difficulties for the believer.

In the final analysis, no one religion or conception of God can claim to satisfy alike all humans, just as no music, architecture, or style of life can have a strictly uniform appeal. The conception of God or any philosophical interpretation, for that matter, depends upon extra-logical factors. A permissive approach is thus the only wise and valid approach in such matters. The exact conception of God to which an individual subscribes should not be given greater importance than the basic values by which he lives and which are reflected in his actual conduct. Pursuing good in one's life is more important than pursuing the only true definition or conception of God. Again, having the religious attitude is more important than commitment to a particular religion.

THE RELIGIOUS ATTITUDE

The religious attitude, as I understand it, is the individual's sense of oneness or emotional integration with the cosmos (rather than merely with his family, nation, species, etc.) and his sense of responsibility and fidelity to the promptings of the *Primal Value Elan* embedded in the heart of all things. Emotional integration with the cosmos implies that the individual feels no bitterness, frustration or resentment. This, however, does not imply the absence of the spark of Divine discontent, or the tension between the 'is' and the 'ought', which is most poignantly felt by the religious person. He yearns to contribute his best toward the overcoming of this tension as far as lies in his power. Indeed, it is only a very superficially religious or naive person who feels that since God is in heaven above, everything is well with the world below. This kind of faith is unaware of and, therefore, untroubled by the tragedy, brutality, sordidness, and absurdity of life. His faith is a shelter and shield that protects him from a full confrontation with the realities of life. But the mature individual is fully aware of the complexities, polarities, and contradictions of reality. He, however, finds a deep satisfaction and a sense of joy through the fulfillment of his duties and obligations even in the face of the tragic dimension of life. The highest level of cosmic integration is reached when the individual establishes an *I-Thou* relationship with the Primal Value Elan. This *I-Thou* relationship increases his receptivity to the pulsations and promptings of the Elan.

The religious attitude, as I understand it, is inseparable from authenticity or self-awareness, which is as difficult as sighting a pinhead lying in the bottom of a deep dark well. Self-awareness requires the courage of self-acceptance and is, therefore, rare. Man is ever-haunted by the temptation to brighten his self-image or boost his ego, and to conceal his blemishes. Authenticity is man's capacity to hear the cry of his innermost being in the stillness of solitude. This solitude is not identical with physical loneliness. Even a physically lonely man maybe very far from lasting solitude, if he be oppressed by his own thoughts, memories, or fancies shadowing him all the time. Even in the midst of physical loneliness such a man finds himself suffocated by the clamor of desires and impulses that are other than his own authentic being.

The concept of authenticity, as I understand it, implies that no dogma or belief that fails to evoke an unqualified assent from the depths of one's being should be accepted, no matter how central or important the belief in question maybe in the religious tradition. Even if the individual maybe mistaken in his views, the very authenticity of his quest is its own reward.

Authenticity wells forth from the depths of man's consciousness just like true love. However, solitude, communion with nature, silence, fasting, meditation, evocative prayer all help promote authenticity. A total surrender to the *Value Elan* or God within sometimes leads to an existential 'melting', as it were, of man's puny agitated self into an ocean of peace and serenity that passeth understanding. In such brief moments man may weep. But the tears he sheds are fit for purifying the angels.

The religious attitude, as defined here, is the universal need of man, and will nourish rather than destroy different religious traditions of the human family. What such an attitude will dissolve and destroy is the crust of ethnocentricity, intolerance, and a spiritual myopia that fails to reveal basic similarities behind the diversity of religions.

The nearest analogue of the above approach is found in *Sufism*. In the *Sufi* idiom, '*Shariah*' refers to the outward practice or conformity with the law without any reference to inner spiritual growth, while '*tariqat*' and '*haqiqat*' refer to stages of the inner purification and evolution of the soul. The ultimate *Sufi* ideal is the obliteration of the seeds of evil in the finite individual through the death (*fana*) of his individual ego or will (*nafs*) and a total joyful surrender to God's will (*razi ba raza*). What thus remains in this purified state (*baqa*) is free from all traces of evil. This state has been viewed as the absorption of the ego into God.

THE UNITY AND VARIETY OF RELIGION

An impartial study of different religions makes it quite clear that all religions manifest the principle of unity in variety and variety in unity. The unity is due to the oneness of the basic faith that all religions express, according to their own genius; the variety is due to the diverse concrete conditions in which the different religions arise and develop. Thus, for example, it is inconceivable that the ritual of a daily bath or the custom of seasonal mass bathing in rivers could have been found in Islam, which arose in a desert region. Similarly, it is inconceivable to expect the ethic of complete non-violence and its corollary of vegetarianism in the Arctic regions of the world, which are perennially covered with snow and where not a blade of grass can grow.

Apart from the above-mentioned differences, which are rather easily correlated with the environment, the comparative study of the developed religions reveals that many differences in the basic beliefs of different religions are either superficial or verbal. In the case of genuine differences, the different beliefs are only different versions or species of a more basic generic belief. For example, the beliefs of Divine incarnation and of prophecy, though certainly different from each other, are, in the final analysis, two different versions or species of the more fundamental conviction that God intervenes in history to guide man on the right path. The theory of incarnation holds that God incarnates Himself but the incarnation is never literally equated with the infinite God. The incarnation is rather viewed as a finite and temporal manifestation of the infinite and eternal God. The theory of prophecy, on the other hand, holds that the mode of Divine intervention in history is through the revelation of the Divine will or word to a human being, rather than through descent or revelation in a human being. A little honest reflection would show that, in the final analysis, neither of the two conceptions can claim to be fully intelligible or transparent to the human mind, and that both conceptions are essentially full of mystery.

The same remarks apply to the belief in life after death and the belief in re-birth. Both these beliefs are different versions or species of the more basic conviction of man; that the Universe is subject to a moral law, and as a man soweth so shall he reap. Both these beliefs affirm the continuity of life. But one belief posits linear continuity, while the other the cyclical form of continuity. The net functional results of both these beliefs is to encourage man to lead the good life for the sake of his own good, if not from the higher motive of doing one's duty without hope of reward or fear of punishment.

Further analysis will confirm that all the other beliefs of different religions such as the belief in angels, devils, demons, miracles, efficacy of prayer, and boons, etc., also exhibit a basic unity in variety.

The traditional Muslim approach that all non-Muslims are *kafirs*, with the exception of Jews and Christians, who are the *'people of the book'*, is incompatible with numerous Qur'anic verses that God's messengers and prophets have been sent in all ages and to all peoples. The Qur'an further points out that of the large number of God's messengers the names of only a few have been mentioned in the Qur'an. [125] This clearly implies that there must have been Indian, Chinese, or African prophets to guide their peoples. Consequently, there is no reason why the people of India or China should be excluded from the category of the *'people of the book'*. The fact that the Qur'an does not mention any Indian or Chinese prophet by name cannot be used as an argument against the clear statement found in the Qur'an itself that God has sent His prophets to all peoples of the world.

Concluding Reflections

Some traditionalist interpreters hold that since only some and not all prophets are given a revealed book and since prophets occupy different ranks, even if Rama, Krishna, and Buddha were prophets of God, there is no justification for holding the Hindus or Buddhists to be the *'people of the book'*. This approach overlooks the fact that the *Vedas* are viewed as revealed (*sruti*) in the ancient Indian tradition and are contrasted with the secondary sources (*smriti*) of religious truth. Moreover, there are striking parallels and similarities of ideas and expressions between the Qur'an and the Upanishads no less than between the Qur'an and the Bible. Indeed many of the attributes of God, mentioned in the Qur'an and the Upanishads, are identical. [125a] In view of such facts the exclusion of Hindus or Buddhists from the category of the *'people of the book'* appears to be inconsistent with Qur'anic teaching. Thus, Muslims are spiritually akin not merely to the Jews and the Christians, but all religious groups are spiritually akin to each other. There should be no discrimination between Semitic religious groups and the non-Semitic ones simply on the ground that only the Semitic prophets are mentioned by name in the Qur'an, while Muslims are left guessing about the identity of the pre-Islamic Aryan, Dravidian, Chinese, or American prophets. A discriminatory approach leads to a parochial preference for a particular race or region.

Again, most Muslims have a highly confused notion of the exact meaning of polytheism (*shirk*). They hold, for example, that the Christian concept of Trinity is essentially incompatible with monotheism or Divine Unity, and hence all Christians are guilty of polytheism, the most unpardonable of sins. However, this extreme indictment of the Christian is mollified by the admission that Jesus was God's messenger whose authentic doctrine was as unitarian as the Islamic doctrine itself, but unfortunately got corrupted by later Christians. The traditional attitude of Muslims to the Christians is thus essentially ambivalent. This approach is the product of a superficial understanding of the Christian concept of trinity. Even if a Christian affirms that Jesus was not an ordinary mortal, but was the Son of God, he does not imply that there are two separate Divinities; God, the Father, and God, the Son. The Father and the Son, and also the Holy Ghost are ultimately three aspects of one Supreme Being, the All-Powerful, Self-Existent, and Eternal God, exactly as is the God of Judaism or Islam. The Christian conception of Divine incarnation *in* man, though opposed to the Islamic conception of Divine revelation *to* man, does not turn Christians into polytheists. All it implies is that there are some basic differences in the Christian and Islamic conceptions of Divine Self-revelation in history. The fact is that mutual misunderstandings and ignorance have resulted in a distorted perspective of each other's religion all through the centuries.

The same remarks apply to the popular Muslim view that the Hindus are polytheists, since they are idol worshippers. The truth of the matter is that according to the Hindu conception, the idols are concrete images or symbols of a finite god (*devta*) interpreted as a differentiated finite aspect or manifestation of the Brahman; the absolute and undifferentiated Cosmic Ground or the eternal Self-Existent Essence (*sat*) of all finite existents. In other words, neither the idols are interpreted as intrinsically Divine beings, nor are the finite gods, symbolized by the idols, regarded as plural Gods possessing supreme power. The finite gods are regarded as finite manifestations of the infinite Brahman, just as the physical idol is regarded as the symbol of the god. The function of the symbol is to facilitate one-pointedness in the devotee rather than to mediate between the worshipper and his chosen deity or aspect of the one Supreme God. Consequently, Hindus, as a religious group, cannot be regarded as polytheists, even though, obviously, their version of Divine unity does not exactly correspond with Islamic monotheism.

Functionally speaking, belief in one God means having only one focus of surrender or submission, while belief in more than one God means divided loyalties. Thus a person who verbalizes belief in one God maybe in the grip of, say, moneymaking, lust for power, revenge, jealousy, sex, or some other dominant passion. Functionally speaking, such a person surrenders himself to plural authorities, and thus worships more than one God. [126]

Shirk, in the ultimate analysis, is infidelity to the authentic promptings of one's creative conscience or God within man. This creative conscience is the spark of Divinity or the *Primal Value Elan* embedded in the heart of all things, but fully revealed only in the depths of man's consciousness. In the words of Bishop Butler, it is this conscience, which has full authority, but unfortunately, not full power over man. [127] Faith in one God ultimately means restoring complete power to the authority of the creative conscience, while '*shirk*' means the dispersal of the power of conscience among rival authorities. *Shirk* in this sense is the loss of the integrity of the individual.

There is another kind of shirk which is very often committed by the traditional Muslim without his least suspicion. This maybe called 'conceptual idolatry'. In this type of shirk some human conception of God is identified with the intrinsic nature of God. Such a rigid fixation upon a particular conception of God virtually amounts to the worshipping of a conceptual or mental idol. This conceptual fanaticism is a very subtle form of idolatry that escapes detection within the traditional Islamic conceptual framework. Yet this, rather than idolatry, in the popular sense, is more prevalent in the modern age. The well-known story of *Moses and the Shepherd* in Rumi's great *Masnavi* clearly refers to conceptual idolatry. [128]

What are the implications of the above analysis? The first implication is that in the field of religion the cardinal virtue is not fanaticism but rather tolerance. It should be obvious to any intelligent and enlightened person that a knockdown proof of the exclusive truth or validity of his own religion is absolutely out of the question. Equally obviously, forceful conversion of others is also out of the question. Even the ideal of peaceful persuasion is not a realistic ideal in view of the fact that the individual is culturally conditioned by his milieu. Let us examine this last point more fully.

The child is born in a family and acquires the ideas and norms of his milieu as naturally as it assimilates its mother's milk. Thus it becomes a Catholic if the family be Catholic, and a Buddhist if the family be Buddhist. The religious symbols and practices associated with its childhood leave a profound and permanent impact upon the child's sensibility for the rest of its life. The wider environment and experience of the child no doubt foster its unique individuality, but they cannot altogether break the spell of its early cultural conditioning. Consequently, conversion to a new religion, implying the shaking of the early foundations, becomes extremely difficult. Even when it does take place, the individual projects his previous depth images and associations upon the new canvas of ideas and values. To shift the imagery, the pull of cultural gravitation is so great that only a few individuals can manage to transcend the natural ethnocentricity of the individual. No doubt, mass conversions to Islam or Christianity have taken place in the past, and conversion to Islam is still on at a considerable pace in some African societies. But these facts do not falsify the thesis that conversion is extremely difficult from one developed religion to another, though not from a primitive cult to a developed religion, particularly when the new religion promotes group interests. [129]

The inhibition against conversion does not rule out social change. What happens is that the inevitable changes in society and the influence of other groups stimulate one's own group leaders and cultural innovators to reform and revitalize their ancient heritage and thus make it relevant to contemporary needs, rather than embrace the religion or philosophy of the alien successful group. Now, is it wisdom to oppose these movements of inner reform in different religions in the name of converting others to one's own true religion? Is it wisdom to expect that other religious groups will merge their separate identity with our own, just because we are convinced that our own religion is true? In the light of the concepts of cultural conditioning and self-interpretation, is it wisdom to expect mass conversions of the followers of the different developed religions, and (when they refuse to get converted) to blame them for their ignorance, pride, and prejudice, etc.?

Another reason, which rules out complete religious uniformity, is that every religion has plural versions, which, at times, considerably differ from each other. These plural versions emerge in response to diverse needs or situations. Different versions appeal to different individuals having different personality needs and intellectual capacities. Now, if an intellectual type of Muslim is not satisfied with the version of Islam current in his own milieu, he can easily accept some more adequate version free from these intellectual difficulties. He need not embrace a new religion when he can replace an unsatisfying version by a superior version of the same religion. Exactly the same remarks apply to a Hindu or a Christian.

The actual course of events in Asian and African countries that have come under the impact of Western culture and modern Christianity confirm the above theoretical analysis. The sincere and untiring efforts of the Christian missionaries have not resulted in any mass conversions to Christianity, barring, of course, the more positive response of the relatively primitive or simpler societies. The impact of Western culture and religion has rather acted as a challenge to the inner growth and development of the non-Christian religions. [130]

The conclusion of the above analysis as well as historical facts is that the approach of religious monolithism must give way to the approach of religious pluralism. Every intelligent and enlightened believer in Islam, Christianity or Hinduism must prepare himself to accept a multi-religious and multicultural world society as distinguished from a mono-religious human family. This approach implies the acceptance of tolerance and inter-

Concluding Reflections

religious fraternalization and cooperation. It also implies the clear acceptance of plural versions of the same religion and the awareness that no religion as such is superior or inferior to any other religion. It is only a particular version of a religion that can claim to be superior to the corresponding version of another religion. For example, it could rightfully be claimed that Azad's version of Islam, with its accent on democracy, universal brotherhood, and social justice, is superior to the version of Hinduism, accepted by a dogmatic and rigidly conservative pundit of Varanasi, who refuses to teach Sanskrit to non-Brahmans or to approve of inter-caste marriages or friendships. Similarly, the version of Hinduism accepted by Vivekananda, with its accent on the essential oneness of all life and the ethic of cosmic compassion and humanism, is definitely superior to the version of Christianity, as accepted by a rather parochial Christian missionary, belaboring under the idea of the white man's burden and believing in the exclusive salvation of the Christians. Thus, while qualitative differences do exist between different versions of a religion or between different versions of different religions, no religion as such can properly be said to be a higher or a lower religion, as far as the major developed religions of the world are concerned. Indeed, if the highest version of the different religions are taken into account, they would be found to be remarkably similar to each other. Indeed, the higher versions of the different religions would be found to be nearer each other than the higher and lower versions of the same religion. For example, the *Sufi* version of Islam is functionally closer to the Vedantic version of Hinduism or the mystical version of Christianity than it is to the orthodox legalistic version of Islam itself, at least in the functional sense.

The above vital truth is not generally and sufficiently realized because the followers of a religion are generally inclined to identify themselves with the higher version of their religion and to compare it with the lower version of other religions, thereby feeling happy at the superiority of their own religion. In other words, the followers of different religions unconsciously try to boost their own self-image at the expense of other religious groups. They think that granting of equal status to different religions would deprive their own religious tradition of its unique importance and role in the world. The failure to see the essential unity and variety of all religions is at bottom the failure to transcend or outgrow an immature group-pride or ethnocentricity.

Every world religion maybe said to be a spiritual seed that has grown and blossomed in a particular soil. The unity of the different religions is due to the essential similarity in the seeds of different religions, while diversity is due to differences in the soil. All world religions are, in the final analysis, human responses to the cosmic situation under Divine guidance, since man's quest for truth is ultimately rooted in the *Primal Value Elan* or God within man. The origin and development of the different religions is thus a complex process in which the natural environmental and social factors interact with the spiritual dimension of man's experience. Religions are thus the fruit of Divine guidance given to man at a concrete time and place, which constitute the temporal pole of the complex bipolar process of revelation. This temporal pole leaves situational traces in the content and application of the Divine revelation. This is how differences between religions arise even though the source of man's guidance is rooted in the same *Primal Value Elan*.

All religions are thus different languages of the human spirit seeking to express man's experience of wonder and mystery, when he contemplates himself and the Universe. Just as every language has its own grammar and vocabulary, so does every religion have its own characteristic and recurring metaphors and modes of interpreting the basic mystery of the microcosm and the macrocosm. The concrete interpretations may differ not only in details, but sometimes even in a more basic sense. Yet, as pointed out above, even these basic differences are rooted in a still more fundamental similarity or unity of interpretation and function. Hence as long as a religious interpretation reinforces or deepens man's quest for value, the label of the religion is unimportant. To give an analogy, if lovers feel deeply fulfilled through Sanskrit poetry, there is no point in prescribing German or French for this purpose. If, however, a particular religion does not provide complete inner satisfaction but generates doubt in the individual and if the doubt persists in spite of all possible efforts to resolve it, then the basic function of religion is not served. In such a case the individual should no longer try to cling to the interpretation in question. The criterion of religious truth is existential and not merely logical. Religion must inspire man for the joyful acceptance of the burden of life. It is better to be an authentic and sincere Hindu, Jain, or Sikh believer with an integrated personality and possessing the deep inner peace that passeth understanding than a Christian or a Muslim who is unable to commit himself to the beliefs, which he merely verbalizes. When, however, a religion starts to bear on social concerns or relationships it cannot be maintained that one religion is as satisfactory as the other. If, for example, a particular religion prescribes child sacrifice as a means of promoting the fertility of the tribe or the soil, the principle of religious permissiveness *ipso facto* ceases to be applicable.

Concluding Reflections

Islam, as projected in this work, is a universal religion. Since, however, the higher philosophical versions of other religions are also capable of functioning as universal religions, the really important thing is not to make claims on behalf of a particular religion, or even to strive for its formal propagation, but rather to work for the concrete establishment of the basic values of the religion, such as universal compassion, social justice, world brotherhood, inner freedom, dignity of man, and equality of opportunity for all. All those who sincerely work for the establishment of the above ideals, no matter under what religious or even secular labels, such as democracy, socialism, or communism, should be encouraged to persist in promoting the above values under the umbrella of their own respective religious or secular value systems.

Those who strive to propagate the above-mentioned values are propagating the basic values of Islam, whether or not the word 'Islam' occurs in their vocabulary or thinking. If the same remarks are also true of Christianity or Hinduism, then there should be all the more reason to rejoice that they are all different versions of one basic truth. Even Communism which, in some respects, is the arch enemy of religion has a dimension of faith, which makes it a religion in the functional though not in the formal sense. [131] It is, therefore, not surprising that the Communist way of life inspires in its true followers a loyalty and self-effacing dedication which one associates with religious martyrs or saints. Likewise, Communism has its own lip believers who use Communist labels or slogans for promoting their own personal interests rather than the values of Communism.

At present there is no doubt a political confrontation between the atheistic humanism of Communist society and the liberal humanism of the West. There is also talk of an inter-religious united front of the theistic brotherhood against atheistic Communism. But it would be as futile to think in terms of a united inter-religious fraternity confronting atheistic Communism, as it is futile to think in terms of warring religions.

It seems to me that classical religions are ways of life whose center is either God, as an external Creator, or God within man, while Communism is a way of life whose center is man himself. In this sense, therefore, there is a prima facie conflict between theism and atheistic humanism. But perhaps this conflict is a passing phase of human history, for, if man is rooted in God or Spirit, humanism must eventually flower into theism with the passage of time. It would, however, be a mature theism that would affirm the Divine dimension in the unfinished and free depths of the human ego, rather than a theism that would smother the divinity, authenticity and autonomy of the human spirit in the arms of an authoritarian external Creator.

It seems to me that, despite its limitations, Communism has played and will continue to play in the future a constructive role on the human scene. Communist thought has been the largest single factor in highlighting the concepts of social causation and of ideology, and the Communist movement in highlighting the ethic of egalitarianism. [132] Whether or not we accept the Communist ethic of revolution, the limitations of democratic persuasion for speedily establishing social justice and equality of opportunity are becoming clearer to the common man all the world over. The vested interests seem to have a will and a way to defend their interests, against which the ordinary man finds himself almost helpless, despite the political power of the vote in a democratic society. In this predicament Communism becomes relevant, as it claims to show a way out and to deliver the goods to the common man. It is, therefore, essential for all Muslims and other religious persons to come to terms with the sociological insights and ethical values of Communism, and to reconstruct democratic socialism, so as to make it an effective and viable instrument of speedy social justice and a cooperative world order.

The Russo-Chinese split in the Communist faith has created a new situation, pregnant with tremendous possibilities for the welfare of the human family as a whole. Both the Communist wings would be induced to consolidate their own power and isolate the 'traitor to the true faith' without caring for the ideological purity of their political allies. Western society, for its part, would be tempted to play one Communist wing against the other to contain the 'Communist menace' to the free world. But out of the tortuous round of this gigantic power-game there might emerge mutual understanding and insight into the elements of value in the two competing ways of life. This was precisely the outcome of the medieval confrontation between Islam and Christianity, as also between the much earlier confrontation between the Indo-Aryan and the original Indic culture. The dialectical reconciliation between Capitalism and Communism (in some form too difficult for me to envisage right now) rather than the unipolar liquidation of one or the other appears to be the destination of man. The spirit of Islam, as understood and projected in this work, and the spirit of Indian culture, from the Upanishads to Tagore and Aurobindo, under the

Concluding Reflections

auspices of democratic socialism, could play a significant role in the task of reconciliation and the ceaseless growth of the human spirit.

A SELF-INTERPRETATION OF THE PRESENT WORK

This work is an attempt to integrate the Islamic thought system with the well-established concepts of contemporary thought and also to develop traditional Islamic values and institutions in the light of my own quest for truth. My quest is not an exercise in Islamic apologetics, but a reinterpretation of the basic Islamic vision in the light of a critical methodology of philosophy and the natural and social sciences, without rationalizing or distorting Islamic beliefs to suit any pre-conceived theory. It is an independent work, which, however, does take into account the views of some recent Islamic thinkers in the Indo-Pakistan subcontinent.

The principal methodological concepts which have guided the detailed reinterpretation are as follows: field tension and field integration, empiricism, existential interpretation, personification, interpretative economy and tolerance, social causation, emergent evolution of concepts and values.

The principal assumptions of this work are:

1) All factual truth claims must be settled empirically in accordance with the scientific method.

2) Philosophy cannot give us any knowledge of facts, but is an activity of clarification of the concepts of ordinary language, science, religion, etc., so that the classical conception of metaphysics or theology, as a super-science, breaks down.

3) Scientific explanation is only one type of interpretation of the given and does not exhaust the total spectrum of man's response to his experience. An existential response to the Universe is *sui generis*, though it has points of contact with the ethical, aesthetic and scientific responses. Though not capable of proof, existential interpretations have their own logic of validity.

4) Language has plural uses or functions which, when confused with each other, generate unnecessary pseudo-problems. The language of the Qur'an must, therefore, be analyzed from the functional point of view prior

to its interpretation.

The work challenges the traditional assumption that religion must guide the total conduct of life, and squarely affirms secularism in its place. The delinking of the politico-economic institutions from the purview of religion enables Muslims in both Islamic and mixed societies to shape their polity in a secular democratic manner without being emotionally or conceptually '*fixated*' upon the past. As is well-known, many Islamic modernists in Turkey, Iran, and Arab countries take this stand, but they do not seek to give a theoretical reinterpretation of basic Islamic concepts and values. Consequently, their secularism does not fuse with their spirituality, and the two do not blend into one organic and integrated worldview or vision of the good life. Their secularism remains useful, but it fails to inspire authentic Muslims.

The work tries to put forward an existential interpretation of the human situation in terms which should appeal, not only to Muslims, but theists in general, perplexed agnostics, and perhaps even to some so-called atheists. This becomes possible because their denial of God does not imply the denial of the *de facto* cosmic law and order and of values in the Universe. The work takes the stand that affirming an immanent cosmic purpose makes the *de facto* presence of values more intelligible, while the existential personification of the cosmic purpose intensifies man's quest for value and enriches the quality of his inner life, even as music and poetry do so at different levels. Personification of the cosmic purpose or the establishing of an *I-Thou* relationship with the supreme Source of values is, however, viewed as permissive rather than obligatory, and is deemed to perform an ontogenetic rather than an onto-*Noetic* function. The usual polarity between *Theism and Atheism*, and *Idealism and Materialism* is thus transcended. But this irenic approach must not be confused with a pragmatic approach rooted in situational compulsions. The work also puts forward a sociological interpretation of history, which is compatible with religious faith, with social facts of life and with the ideals of democracy and socialism.

The work does not claim to give 'the' true definition of Islam. All definitions of any living cultural tradition can only be connotative recommendations made by persons who maybe insiders or outsiders. In the final analysis, the answer to the question whether or not one is an insider can only come from the person himself. If his answer is a '*yes*', rooted in his authentic existence, he should not bother about the verdict of others.

Concluding Reflections

"And do thou (O Reader!)
Bring thy Lord to remembrance in your very soul,
With humility and in reverence,
Without loudness in words,
In the morning and evenings;
And be not thou of those who are unheedful."

-- *Qur'an 7:205*

"... seek refuge, then, in Allah. It is He, Who hears and sees (all Things)."
-- *Qur'an: 40:56*

"... forgive me my faults on the Day of Judgement."
-- *Qur'an 26:82*

"... peace to all who follow guidance!"
-- *Qur'an 20:47*

"Ameen!"

Afterword

Quest for Islam was first published some thirty-five years ago. At the time several close friends and colleagues who broadly shared my basic approach to the study of religions, including Islam, expressed their fear that neither the Muslim religious establishment nor the common believer would ever-appreciate my work because of its radical departure from traditional Islamic thinking. They did, however, laud my boldness in expressing my authentic views without any fear of being dubbed by the community as an apostate, or atheist, or as a political opportunist. They also felt that the common man, ever-burdened by hunger, sickness and insecurity, looked to religion for getting solace, consolation and emotional support, without caring for such ideals as logical consistency, spiritual autonomy or self-realization and the rest. I, however, was not discouraged by their honest response and went on traveling on a road, which at that time only a few awakened fellow Muslims dared to travel. I dare say, now I don't feel myself so lonely on this road.

What has brought about this significant change in the outlook of a large number (though not yet in the majority) of Muslim believers? It is well-known that information and factual knowledge grow much faster than change in mental habits and attitudes. Changes in the sphere of religious beliefs and social attitudes are the slowest. What, however, is not sufficiently understood is that religious symbols and creeds are not clear and demonstrable, but rather highly complex truthclaims that are understood in different ways by different persons with varying backgrounds. As a result, quick and easy agreement between people of very varied backgrounds is indeed extremely difficult. However, human creativity, continually increasing knowledge and the lessons of experience lead to profound changes in how believers learn to deconstruct their cultural (including religious) heritage and to redefine their cherished concepts and values in the light of expanded knowledge and experience. I have already explained in the foregoing pages how and why the great Islamic intellectual and cultural tradition began to stagnate after peaking first in Syria and Iraq and later in Iran, central Asia and Spain as well as India under Mughal rule.

The words, symbols and images of a sacred or cherished belief/value system remain the same but some creative individual or individuals (who deeply cherish the tradition but outgrow some of its perceived limitations) discover or project a new meaning or significance into it. Thus, a new paradigm of the old religion emerges in society. The older custodians and guardians of the tradition are naturally reluctant to accept the new paradigm. To them, their paradigm of the faith or religious tradition is not a paradigm, but rather the true faith or religion itself. From their point of view those who suggest or accept a new paradigm forfeit their right to identify themselves with the symbols, images and sacred history of the religion as such. Conflict and controversy thus remain entrenched in society and act as a drag on the peaceful flowering of the new paradigm among the body of believers.

However, I remain optimistic that Muslims in general all over the world will gradually gravitate to the paradigm I have presented in Quest for Islam and elaborated in my different works. The human spirit cries out for inner peace and harmony in society. The literal meaning of the Arabic word Islam is peace through submission to one Supreme Creator. Conflict arises only when hubris propels some individual or individuals to claim they have grasped the one and only true conception of the nature and will of the Creator. Such people begin to lose their sense of mystery, inadequacy, humility and respect for other members of the human family who may entertain different ideas or conceptions of the Supreme, as it is itself rather than as others imagine or conceive it to be.

The other major source of conflict is the human passion for power and domination. My study of the Qur'an has given me the deep assurance that the Islamic revelation is not a rigid and closed code or set of rules and prescriptions that admit of no flexibility or possibilities of further

Afterword

orthogenetic growth. It is a plain fact of the sacred history of Islam that the vision of the Prophet as well as the polity that he instituted or approved of evolved before the very eyes of the Prophet's Arab audience. Moreover, the Qur'an itself repeatedly invites men of understanding to reflect on nature, society and the very core of the human self as such. The miracle of the Qur'an was and is its inherent capacity to inspire faith, joy, hope, and fructify humanity's latent spirituality and reflective conscience. In simple words, the Qur'an definitely exhorts people of understanding to reflect, to wonder, to probe the self, to strive and to act as the most excellent of God's creation. Is this not rather different from the supposed obligation of a good Muslim to follow the *Shariah* rigidly in letter and spirit without raising any 'ifs and buts'?

This approach to the Qur'an implies that the good Muslim should reflect on both the text and the context of the Qur'anic revelations and the peculiar situation or situations of the Prophet before determining the right course of action. Moreover this decision must take into account the distinction between intrinsic values and instrumental rules. This approach to the good life removes the rather self-imposed insularity of Muslims from non-Muslims in general and fosters the idea of a larger brotherhood or fraternity of good souls, collectively trying to preserve and promote shared basic spiritual and ethical values despite some secondary disagreements. This approach will enable Muslims to become equal partners with all fellow citizens of multi-ethnic secular democratic states all over the world.

Muslims must not confuse secular democracy with atheism or immoral or unscrupulous politics. Muslims should also ponder over the new wave concept of gender justice that implies that men and women should have equal status and opportunities of polymorphous growth. Even if Muslims feel reluctant to accept gender equality in the literal sense because of some Qur'anic personal laws other communities will move ahead and Muslim women will feel the pinch of discrimination and of gender inequality. To my mind, giving the status of complete equality to the female half of the human family is not any violation of Qur'anic injunctions. Rather it amounts to the full fruition or development of the ideal of gender justice found in the Qur'an. To give a parallel example, the Qur'an did not prohibit the institution of slavery, though it did prescribe humane treatment of slaves, both male and female. But does the legal prohibition of slavery violate any Qur'anic injunction? To the contrary, such legislation actually promotes the idea of human dignity and compassion, which are the basic values of the Qur'an as of all humanist ethics in general.

Coming to the situation of the Indian Muslims living in a secular democratic state, I am very optimistic that India has a bright future in the days ahead. The constitution of India is a landmark in world history, though there are several friction points in our machinery of governance. Once the teething troubles of our nascent democracy are over, we shall realize the inherent shortcomings and limitations of our outlook and political vices. At present we are weathering a savage storm raging at different levels of our society and state—rising expectations, the lust for easy and quick money, the clamor for rights without awareness of duties, the vicious effects of caste and tribal exploitation for ages past, the social psychological wounds inflicted on the Muslim minority in India and the Hindu-Sikh minorities in Pakistan due to the partition of 1947.

The rectification of these and still other wrongs is going on slowly and imperceptibly, despite all the ravages of totally unscrupulous politics and violence in present day India. We must, therefore, persevere in the right course and not allow the rigors of fighting the storm to defeat or deflect us.

In any case the dark clouds have several silver linings. The deprived and downtrodden (no matter what their religion or region) for ages are looking up to the sky, while the wings of the erstwhile lords of the earth (no matter what their origin) are having their wings clipped. The women of India are on the march and no power, theological or male chauvinistic will be able to block their path to full empowerment and equality of opportunity in the course of time. It is my honest faith and hope women (as the bearers of the Divine gift of maternal love) will exercise power more ethically and compassionately than men have done in the past.

Afterword

The course of history is seldom straight or clear to the traveler. However, as we move on the vision improves and we begin to see more clearly the direction and the distance to the goal, provided we keep open our eyes and ears, remain intellectually honest and consistent and continue to act according to our lights.

Let me end this afterword with a prayer found in the first chapter of the Holy Qur'an,

> *Thee do we worship, and Thine aid we seek.*
> *Show us the straight way,*
> *The way of those on whom Thou hast bestowed Thy Grace, those whose (portion) is not wrath and who go not astray.*
> (surah 1, verses 5-7)

Notes and References

'Q' stands for Qur'an. The first number after 'Q' stands for the *surah*, while the number/numbers after the colon for the verse/verses in the chapter. Since the numbering of the verses (though not the text or the numbering of the *surahs*) slightly differs in the different standard Qur'anic recensions, the reader should be prepared for slight deviations from the numbering given here. I have throughout followed the numbering in Pickthall's English translation of the Qur'an.

✻✻✻

1) Q 16:40

2) An interpretation which makes the Universe a chance product of the blind dance of atoms will tend to promote the attitudes of egocentricity, irresponsibility and a carefree pursuit of pleasure without any thought for the morrow or for others. On the other hand, the interpretation that the Universe is the creation of God, or that it is the teleological expression of an immanent impersonal *Elan* will tend to promote the ethic of responsibility and social concern. Whether or not the tendency realizes itself in concrete behavior patterns would, however, depend upon many other factors; both internal and external.

3) Consult Whitehead's classic *Science and the Modern World*.

4) Western thinkers have outgrown, or are doing so, the extreme and rigid anti-metaphysical positivist stance of the period between the two world wars when Logical Positivists dubbed metaphysics as either poetry or nonsense. Contemporary linguistic analysts, far from rejecting metaphysics,

recognize metaphysical statements or the metaphysical use of language as an important area of human discourse, which must be charted or explored for removing the mistakes likely to result from confusions and ambiguities of different types. However, due to the impact of the positivist critique of metaphysics, the traditional meta-theory of metaphysics as a super science has been changed to metaphysics as a language game. It seems to me this change is all for the good. Consult Waismann, *How I see Philosophy* and also *The Principles of Linguistic Philosophy*.

5) All men have some capacity for this existential response to the Universe. But some exceptionally sensitive souls have the capacity for mystical response, which is *sui generis*. This response which is a 'state of mind-body' is a unique organic whole having points of contact with the perceptual, moral and aesthetic dimensions of experience, but not reducible to any one particular dimension. Mystical experience maybe accompanied by peculiar bodily changes such as palpitation, sweating, and shivering, etc. Its satisfactory interpretation, however, leads to catharsis and an inner integration of the individual on whom descends a peace that passeth understanding.

The interpretation is made in terms of concepts, which refer to the 'Other', but these concepts are not themselves experienced or directly perceived. Thus God, Spirit, Incarnation, revelation, and life after death, etc., are never directly encountered by the person, but these concepts convince or grip him as the truth about the 'Other' on the basis of his mystical experience without the props of reasoning. Most religious persons do not distinguish between mystical experience and its conceptual interpretation, and suppose that the questioning of their interpretation amounts to a questioning or denial of their experience itself. They do not realize the essential relativity and the organic connection of the interpretation with the conceptual framework inherited by the individual from his milieu. See James classic, *The Varieties of Religious Experience*.

6) The traditional Islamic six-fold classification of conduct into **(a)** obligatory (*farz*), **(b)** highly recommendatory (*wajib*), **(c)** recommendatory (*masnun*), **(d)** permissible but not commended (*makruh*), **(e)** disapproved (*mamnti*), and **(f)** prohibited (*haram*) is partly similar to the distinction between intrinsic and instrumental values.

7) Stoning is prescribed by the Islamic religious law (*Shariah*), though this is virtually a paper penalty only.

Notes and References

8) See Whitehead, *Religion in the Making* and Tillich, *Dynamics of Faith*. For Russell's views, consult *Sceptical Essays* and *Why I am not a Christian*. Freud's critique of religion is developed in his *The Future of an Illusion*.

9) Freud holds the total human psyche or self to consist of three layers or levels; the *'id'*, the *'ego'*, and the *'super-ego'*. The *'id'* is the deep un-conscious reservoir of man's irrational drives, the *'ego'* is the normal conscious self, which knows, feels, and wills, while the *'super-ego'* is the conscience or the 'internalized censor', performing the role of an invisible but ever-present policeman and judge.

10) This explains why the pragmatic or utilitarian approach to religion ever-fails to convince most men, even though some philosophers and also men of the world may think they have hit upon the real justification for or the true theory of religion

11) See Erich Fromm's influential work *The Fear of Freedom*.

12) The Christian concept of original sin is a recognition of the fact that man's nature is tainted. But this concept takes us to an extreme position. On the other hand, Rousseau's and later Marx' concept of the essential goodness of human nature are romantic glorifications of man who has the germs of both good and evil in his essential nature.

13) The American philosopher, William James, divides persons into tender-minded and tough-minded, the former but not the latter, having an inner personality need for a loving personal God.

14) The German philosopher Paulsen's work *Introduction to Philosophy* was widely read at the turn of the century, while the British philosopher, Lloyd Morgan became well-known for his theory of *Emergent Evolution*.

15) The Qur'an is full of references to the absolute power of God, the Creator, Sustainer, and Ruler of the heavens and the earth and all that lies between them. The sovereignty and majesty of God suggest the utter helplessness of man in the face of Divine power and will. On the other hand, a few Qur'anic verses state or imply that man has been given the power to choose between good and evil. Obviously it is futile to try to prove either the theory of pure libertarianism or of pure pre-destinarianism with the help of the Qur'an, which merely draws man's attention to the supreme power of God as well as man's responsibility and duty as a created being to make a free surrender to God. In the final analysis no putative proof, whether philosophical or Qur'anic, can be conclusive. Reflective thought or philosophical analysis can only remove confusions or reveal hidden contradictions in our beliefs, thereby preparing us for an existential interpretation of man in the Universe. The interpretation that man is a free or potentially free agent would promote conscious value-oriented striving; the interpretation that man is merely a complicated machine would promote the pursuit of pleasure; the interpretation that man is a prisoner of a Divinely ordained fate would promote the negative surrender to his fate. The Qur'anic verses cited in favor of the theory of predestinarianism are: Q15:21; Q 25:2; Q2:284; and Q 74:56. Versus cited in support of the theory freedom of will are: Q13:11 and Q18:30.

16) Q 85 :21–22.

17) See Ghazali *Ihya id Ulum (Bulaq 1872) vol. II* p. 157, as quoted in Grunebaum, *Islam*, p. 225.

18) For a lucid and authentic account of the main doctrines and practices of the *Sufi's*, see Nicholson's classic English translation of Al- Hujwiri's *Kashf Al Mahjub*. Al-Hujwiri, popularly known in Indo-Pakistan as Data Sahab, died about 1075 in Lahore, where his grave was especially visited by the venerable Chishti saint, Khwaja Moinuddin of Ajmer (d. 1235/36).

19) See Aziz Ahmad, *Studies in Islamic Culture in the Indian Environment*. See also Mujeeb, *The Indian Muslims*.

20) Afghani was highly critical, nay hostile, to Syed Ahmad and his approach to Islam. For his angry criticism see Baljon, *The Reforms and Religious Ideas of Sir Sayyid Ahmed Khan*, pp. 98-100.

21) The term 'communitarianism' as used in this work does not carry any technical meaning as a sociological concept. It merely highlights the view that the religious community (*ummah*) is the primary macro-social group instead of the nation, race, caste, or class etc.

Notes and References

22) Q 3:47.

23) It seems to me that the valid meaning of *taqdir* is merely this, that every individual has an inherited psychophysical constitution, which delimits or pre-inclines the individual in a particular conative direction. There is, however, no pre-determination of the individual's future in any mechanistic sense. The future of the individual is open within the framework of his pre-determined potentialities. Potentiality does not imply a sealed fate but only a particular direction and range of the individual's capacities, and of his possible growth. Individual initiative or effort can and does make a difference to the concrete unfolding of the individual's potentialities or inherited psychophysical endowments. In this sense every man is born with a *taqdir*.

24) *I died as a mineral and became a plant,*
I died as plant and rose to animal,
I died as animal and I was man.
Why should I fear? When was I less by dying?
Yet once more I shall die as man, to soar,
With angels blest; but even from angelhood
I must pass on; all except God doth perish.
When I have sacrificed my angel-soul.
I shall become what no mind ever-conceived.
Oh, let me not exist! For Non-existence
Proclaims in organ tones: "To Him we shall return".

See Nicholson (ed.), *Rumi, Poet and Mystic (Selections)* p. 103.

25) In their earliest phase both Christianity and Islam faced persecution from hostile rulers of the period. The persecution of Muslims came to an end after the Prophet's ﷺ migration from Mecca to Medina in 622 and the consequent establishment of an Islamic state after the expulsion of the Jews from Medina. But Christianity did not become a state religion for more than 300 years after Christ, until the conversion of the Roman Emperor Constantine (d. 337). See Kellet, *A Short History of Religions*.

26) For further details consult Bronowski and Mazlish, *The Western Intellectual Tradition*.

27) Contemporary philosophers of science in the West now fully acknowledge the limitations of the scientific method no less than its undeniable value and achievements. See Cohen and Nagel, *Introduction to Logic and Scientific Method*.

The balanced positivistic temper of Kant's Critical Philosophy has reasserted itself in the main Western tradition after a brief ascendancy of either a rigid empiricism or a rigid rationalism, both of which ignored the different dimensions of man's complex experience. Now eminent Western philosophers and scientists concede that our factual knowledge is extremely limited and selective, immense areas and levels of experience still remaining entirely outside the concepts and categories of natural science. As and when the frontiers of our awareness expand, the present conceptual framework of science will have to be revised to accommodate what are now termed by some as '*paranormal facts*', but which are liable to be rejected by others as delusions, precisely because they do not fit into the present conceptual framework.

The distinguished British philosopher C.D. Broad has cogently dealt with this issue in his critical studies in the field of paranormal facts. Now even Russian thinkers have started taking interest in this matter. See Broad, *Religion, Philosophy and Psychical Research*.

28) Iqbal expressed his views on this matter in a number of his poems. He also criticizes the Turkish reformer Ziya Gokalp for championing the cause of the equality of the sexes in the Western sense. See his *Reconstruction of Religious Thought*, pp. 169-70.

29) *Al-Hilal* was the famous Urdu Journal published by Abul Kalam Azad from Calcutta before the First World War. Azad could not complete the commentary, but the first volume is by itself a lasting contribution to philosophical theism.

30) See the beautiful passage:
'*let him look at the food he places before himself. What is it-a grain of wheat? Well! Let him place that grain into the hollow of his hand, and let him think over what stages it had got to pass through before it could emerge into its present form. Was it possible for this insignificant grain to come into existence had not the entire framework of life participated actively in its growth, and*

that, in a particular manner? And when such a system of organized cooperation is at work, could it be said that it has no organizer to direct its operation?'

(Azad) *Tarjuman Al Qur'an, Vol. I*, p. 38.

31) Q 16:68–69.

32) Parvez's approach to *hadith* seems to me to be substantially the same as that of Syed Ahmad or Iqbal. Since, however, Parvez spells out in great detail what Iqbal only hints at or implies, the views of Parvez on *hadith* have attracted a lot of opposition from orthodox circles. This together with his radical socialist interpretation of Qur'anic verses, rather than his conception of God, revelation, angels, and *Jinn* etc., has led one thousand Pakistani divines to pronounce Parvez as an apostate from Islam.

33) For further details consult Aziz Ahmad, *Islamic Modernism in India and Pakistan*.

34) Even these contain some repetitions, so that in the final analysis, only four or five verses maybe said to deal specifically with politico-economic issues in the structural or institutional sense. The first verse deals with the prohibition of usury (Q 2:275), the second with the procedure of contracts (Q 2:282), the third with the rules of distribution of spoils of war (Q 8:41), and the fourth with political ethics in the face of treachery by others (Q 8:58). Apart from these the Qur'an contains numerous exhortations for decent public or economic behavior as well as specific rules from which other rules can be deduced. Indeed this was done by the Prophet ﷺ, his immediate successors and later jurists. But the point is that all these rules and their derivatives are of the nature of moral commands for the pious Muslim and not institutional or structural guidelines for the framing of a polity, which is left unspecified.

Piety is always individual, while polity is always social, and the two should not be confused. It is this confusion (which exists even among Muslim intellectuals), which tends to blur the urgent need for devising the most suitable polity for human society in general rather than preaching or even sincerely practicing the traditional Islamic piety.

35) See Fyzee, *A Modem Approach to Islam* and Fazlur Rahman, *Islam*. The hue and cry raised against the latter in Pakistan several years ago was most unfortunate and violated man's fundamental right and duty to seek truth without fear.

36) A number of books have recently come out. Their able authors sincerely lament over the Muslim's inner resistance to secularism and modernism, but shirk follow-up work on the writings of Syed Ahmad, Iqbal, and Azad. See Abid Husain, *The Destiny of the Indian Muslim*; Musheerul Haq, *Muslim Politics in Modern India*; Moin Shakir, *Khilafat to Partition*; M. Mujeeb, *Islamic Influence on Indian Society*; Imam (ed.), *Muslims in India*; Baig, *The Muslim Dilemma in India*. The last work is a candid but impatient, rather alienated plea for the 'instant modernization' of the Indian Muslim. The same writer's earlier autobiographical work, *In Different Saddles*, is however a most absorbing and rewarding study.

37) Rumi's *Masnavi* is the crowning glory of the liberal and rationalistic approach of Umar and the mystical approach of Ali. What Ghazali achieved through philosophical analysis; Rumi achieved through poetic insight, expressed in anecdotes and fables. Many of the anecdotes or stories of the *Masnavi* refer to historical persons. But scholars say Rumi did not bother about the factual truth of the reported instances. This, however, does not detract from the validity of Rumi's approach. The anecdote about *Moses and the Shepherd* is briefly as follows:

The prophet Moses once came across a shepherd who was deeply engrossed in expressing his love and devotion to God as if God had physical attributes. Annoyed by the ignorant impudence of the lad, Moses admonished him to desist from such blasphemy. On learning of his unwitting sin the shepherd uttered a cry of remorse and fled into the hills and jungles, leaving behind his flock. Immediately afterward God revealed to Moses that he was wrong in chiding the shepherd who was engaged in an act of true communion with God. God then warned Moses that his own conception of the Divine Being might not be adequate to the glory of God. The implication is that one should never equate one's conception of God with God Himself. This poses the danger of worshipping one's subjective conception of God rather than God, without suspecting in the least that this was a very subtle form of idolatry.

See Arberry, *Tales from the Masnavi*.

38) Shah Waliullah also applies this concept when he holds that the distinction between monism (*wahdatul wajud*) and theistic creationism (*wahdatul shahud*) is merely verbal, both formulations having the same significance.

39) Gibb's *Mohammedanism* is excellent and so is Fazlur Rahman's *Islam*. Maududi's *Towards Understanding Islam* is also highly commendable. Among larger works Muhammad Ali's *The Religion of Islam* is excellent.

40) According to the orthodox view, the exact position of the verses in the different *surahs* and their sequence were also revealed to the Prophet ﷺ.

41) The traditional thought system has been quite hospitable to supernatural stories or anecdotes even though the Qur'an categorically affirms that the Prophet ﷺ could perform no miracles in support of his claim to be an inspired messenger of God. Numerous stories concerning the Prophet ﷺ, Ali and later saints have become an integral part of the tradition. In the *Nahj al Balagha*, which is a collection of the speeches and writings of Ali several supernatural stories or miracles are attributed to the Prophet ﷺ, and even more significantly, claimed by Ali himself. A lot of material in the work appears to be interpolated. *hadith* literature also attributes miracles to the Prophet ﷺ. Here is one example of such stories or anecdotes:

The angel Gabriel awakened the Prophet ﷺ from his sleep and took him to a celestial winged horse (*Al Buraq*). When the Prophet ﷺ mounted the animal he shied away. But when Gabriel told him who the rider was, the *Buraq* took off steadily and alighted in Jerusalem. Here in the Aqsa mosque Abraham, Moses, and Jesus among other prophets welcomed the Prophet ﷺ who led them in a congregational prayer. Later Gabriel procured a very fine ladder, which was used by the Prophet ﷺ for climbing to the heavens. When the Prophet ﷺ reached the first heaven the angel guarding the gate stopped him. On being told by Gabriel that the Prophet ﷺ had permission to enter, the angel allowed entry to him. The Prophet ﷺ saw such and such things in the first heaven. He then proceeded to the second heaven where again his entry was checked in the same manner. The procedure was repeated at each gate of all the seven heavens, where he met different prophets, including Abraham ﷺ, who was stationed in the highest heaven. After his coming into the presence of God the Prophet ﷺ returned to Mecca. On the way back the Prophet ﷺ was accosted by Moses ﷺ who was eager to know what had transpired. The Prophet ﷺ told him his community had been commanded to pray fifty times a day. Moses ﷺ thought this was too great a burden upon the community and advised the Prophet ﷺ to plead with God to lighten it. The Prophet ﷺ returned to God and pleaded for a reduction. God then reduced the obligatory prayers to twenty-five. Moses met the Prophet ﷺ again on his way back and told him that even this was too great a burden. The Prophet ﷺ thereupon went back to God Who reduced the prayers still further. This procedure was repeated a number of times until the obligatory prayers were reduced to five. Moses was not satisfied with this result, but the Prophet ﷺ refused to plead with God for any further concessions. For details see Guiilaume (ed.), *Ibn Ishaq's The Life of Muhammad* pp. 182-187. A more or less similar version is also found in Bukhari's famous collection of the sayings of the Prophet ﷺ.

42) Q 4:34; Q 2:228.

43) See Augustine, *City of God*.

44) See Jame's classic essay '*The Will to Believe*' in his book with the same title.

45) According to biologists, the path of evolution is far from being a straight route, which one would normally associate with a rationally guided process under the complete control of an all-powerful God. Many lines of evolution come to a dead end as if an experiment were being abandoned when it proved fruitless. This is what is meant by 'blind alley' in Zoology, and this involves enormous waste.

Mutations are sudden substantial changes as distinguished from variations, which are slow and minute changes. Mutations also maybe beneficial or harmful to the species. The concept of mutations put forward by De Fries after Darwin cannot be smoothly reconciled with Darwin's theory that like produces like, but not just like. For a very comprehensive and balanced discussion of the issue see Simpson's standard work, *The Meaning of Evolution (abridged edition)*. See also Bergson's classic *Creative Evolution*.

46) See the classic article by Flew in his *New Essays in Philosophical Theology*. See also Blackstone, *The Problem of Religious Knowledge*.

Notes and References

47) This permissive approach to a personal God is similar to the Hindu view that '*nirguna and saguna Brahman*' are both equally valid, depending upon the intellectual level or emotional needs of the person.

48) I have occasionally used PVE as an abbreviation for *Primal Value Elan*.

49) For a lucid and detailed treatment of the subject, see Azad, *Tarjuman al-Qur'an, Vol. I*.

50) For the description of the five stages, see Faruqi, *The Muj'addid's Conception of Tawhid*.

51) '*To realize one's inability to comprehend Him is the true comprehension; Holy is He Who has not kept any road to Himself open to His creatures except by way of realizing their incapacity to know Him*', (Abu Bakr), as quoted in *Faruqi*, ibid., p. 139.

52) For further details see Watt, *Muhammad at Mecca*, which gives references from original sources.

53) For details see Tyrell's excellent *Personality of Man*.

54) Consult James, *The Varieties of Religious Experience*.

55) See Cragg, *The Event of the Qur'an*.

56) In the case of 'inspired' cultural works a couplet, poem, or theory may come to an individual in a flash, but he maybe unable to understand them fully without mental labor. Again, such an 'inspired' poet or scientist may prefer another's interpretation to his own original understanding.

57) The term 'numinous' derived from 'numen' was first used by the German religious thinker, Rudolph Otto, in his well-known *The Idea of the Holy*. It is not translatable into English. It implies the quality or the power of evoking mute wonder and the sense of benign power and holiness, prompting the person to surrender himself completely before the 'numinous' Being.

58) This does not imply the view that the meaning is revealed, while the words are not.

59) See James, *The Will to Believe*.

60) Q 44:43–54.

61) Refer to the Introduction, p.42.

62) For further details consult Pitcher, *The Philosophy of Wittgenstein*, and also Ramsey, *Religious Language*.

63) The mythical types of Qur'anic statements deal with themes whose interpretation is highly problematical but not impossible like that of the *muqatta'at*; the letters of the Arabic alphabet placed before a few Qur'anic *surahs*. Their interpretations are all highly speculative and arbitrary, hence futile.

64) Q 68:17–27

65) Q 2:6,7; Q 50:38; Q 24:35

66) Even out of the 250, many verses naturally repeat the same theme, so that the number of independent injunctions is much less.

67) Q 13:2; Q 90:18–19

68) For a clear and cogent treatment of the issues involved, see Latif, *The Mind Al-Qur'an Builds* and the introduction in Muhammad Ali's English translation (without the Arabic text) of the *Qur'an*. Sec also the stimulating and fresh treatment of the subject in Schuon, *The Dimensions of Islam*.

69) Q 24:35; Q 57:3

70) See Comte, *The Positive Philosophy*.

71) The famous Swiss psychoanalyst, C.J. Jung and also Cassirer have made notable contributions in this field. See Langer, *Philosophy in A New Key*.

72) Q 15:26–40; Q 7:11–18

73) The Qur'an has only two or three myths in the sense in which there are Hindu, Greek, Roman, or German myths. In the Qur'an the parable and metaphor displace the myth, which is the primitive type of discourse. The most striking feature of the language of the Qur'an is the creative use of parables and metaphors and its very simple but extremely elegant rhymed prose. While there are about forty parables in the Qur'an, the only candidates for the label 'myth' (apart from Adam's creation) seem to be a dialogue between God and the angels (Q 2:30–33) and God's offering of the trust to the earth and the mountains and their refusal (Q 33:72). However, there are several verses whose meaning remains obscure and problematic. Unverifiable speculative explanations of such verses are futile. It is difficult to classify such passages as either mythical, parabolic, or metaphorical—for example, references to *Zul Qarnayn, Gog and Magog* (Q 18:84–98; Q 21:95–97); some remarks about Solomon (Q 38:31–41); references to *Harut* and *Marut* (Q 2:102), the story of the *sleepers in the cave* (Q 18:9–20)

74) Q 17:90–93; Q 29:50,51; Q 18:111

75) Q 7:203

76) Some orthodox theologians hold that the Qur'an itself attributes two miracles to the Prophet ﷺ, namely, the splitting of the moon (Q 54:1–3) and *'miraj'* or the ascension of the Prophet ﷺ (Q 17:1,60). As regards the first issue, the verses of the Qur'an are clearly too ambiguous and vague to warrant the traditional interpretation that the moon split asunder at the raising of the Prophet's ﷺ finger. As regards the second matter, the Qur'anic text does not make the meaning clear as to whether the ascension was a bodily journey or a spiritual one. It is significant that even the companions of the Prophet ﷺ were divided on this issue. The spiritual interpretation, being simpler of the two, is more acceptable to the critical mind.

77) Q 3:45–49; Q 20:17–22

78) I owe this point to late Prof. Hamieduddin Khan of Aligarh.

79) It is significant that Bukhari's famous collection of authentic reports (*Sahih*) has been divided into 30 parts (following the division of the Qur'an) and the book is or used to be read as a ritual in some quarters.

80) This does not mean that no importance was given to *hadith* in the early period. Indeed the entire Islamic precept system is the product of the sayings and doings of the Prophet ﷺ, who alone was competent to spell out the abstract injunctions of the Qur'an. Moreover, in view of the Prophet's ﷺ acknowledged status in the eyes of his companions and their successors it is inconceivable to hold that they did not attach the utmost significance to his sayings, until two hundred years or so after his death. Indeed the work of Bukhari became necessary precisely because too much interest had already been taken in the past with too little caution to sift the genuine reports from the spurious. The change that took place in the age of Bukhari, more than 200 years after the death of the Prophet ﷺ, was thus not so much a new founded concern for *hadith* as its systematic and critical study. The reasons for this change were both the desire to sift the true from the spurious reports (which admittedly were in abundant circulation due to one reason or another), and also the need for using authentic sayings of the Prophet ﷺ for settling juristic differences in different regions of the Islamic commonwealth. Nevertheless the fact remains that Abu Bakr and Umar (and later on Uthman and others who were second to none in their love and regard for the Prophet ﷺ, did not reduce *hadith* to writing, in contrast with the supreme caution and expedition with which the Qur'an was put into writing in the order in which it had been memorized during the lifetime of the Prophet ﷺ himself. This clearly reflects the degrees of significance given to the Qur'an and the *hadith* in the very early period. It has been suggested by some authorities that perhaps Abu Bakr and Umar feared that the recording of the Prophet's ﷺ sayings involved the risk of their getting mixed up with the Qur'an. For a detailed and balanced discussion of the issue, see Muhammad Ali's comprehensive work, *The Religion of Islam*.

81) For further details see Shibli's classic *Al-Faruq*.

82) The actual number of separate non-repetitive reports in the main Bukhari corpus is the same, that is, 2,180. This goes up to over 7,000 in the above corpus, wherein Bukhari counts the same report twice, thrice, or even more, whenever there is even a slight difference in the chain of transmission of a report. Zubaidi's collection, therefore, is a complete and unabridged edition (in the functional sense) of the Bukhari corpus. **83)** See Baljon, op. cit., p.79.

84) These and similar themes are included in *hadith* literature.

85) Q 3:31; Q 4:64, 65, 69.

86) See Tillich, *Dynamics of Faith*.

87) Many sociologists as well as theologians tend to hold that the evolutionary approach to the idea of God is incompatible with prophetic or revealed religion, that is, the view that inspired prophets have proclaimed the existence and unity of God from the very beginning of man's history. However, no contradiction arises if we realize that the concrete interpretation of the Divine message is inevitably made by human beings in terms of the concepts and categories of their milieu. In this context the Qur'anic reference to Abraham's search for God is illuminating. Though Abraham was a prophet, yet, according to the Qur'an itself, he apprehended the truth only gradually, or, in other words, as a result of a spiritual evolution. (Q 6:76–80.) The Qur'anic reference to the degrees of excellence of the different prophets is also significant in this context (though the Qur'an affirms that no prophet should be rejected). It seems to me that the degrees of excellence refer to the stages in the conceptual, moral, and spiritual evolution of man. (Q 2:253; Q 3:84)

88) In this respect there is a basic similarity between Marx and several post-Darwinian thinkers such as Bergson, Driesch, Lloyd Morgan, and Alexander, among others, who put forward the concept of levels of Being; mechanistic, vital, conative, mental, spiritual, each superimposed upon and fused with the previous level, and each having its own autonomous laws. According to the above thinkers, these levels emerge in the course of evolution due to an inner impulse inherent in primal reality toward growth and development, though these thinkers do not view this impulse as 'numinous' in the sense in which Otto has used this word. Marx's view that matter is not inert and passive like billiard balls which need an external push for their motion, but that matter is inherently dynamic, as also Marx's view that the philosophical concept of matter was an abstraction from the concrete reality of 'matter-in-motion' comes very close indeed to the concept of *Elan* as described above. However, Marx did not reflect upon the nature and significance of the subjective *Elan* apart from the empirical study of the objective expressions of the *Elan*.

89) Marx glorified the scientific method and rejected all idealistic speculation as either a game of abstract or empty words or as an unconscious ideological legitimization of the vested interests of rulers and priests who gave primacy to ideas over things and avoided physical labor without which things cannot exist. Marx's Sociological Positivism was a strand of the post-Hegelian positivistic revolt against metaphysics, represented by Comte, Dilthey, and Avenarius, etc., and (in a different way) by Kierkegaard. Marx's meta-theory of metaphysics as an ideological legitimization of one's interests is quite different from Wittgenstein's meta-theory of metaphysics as a language game. Nevertheless, both agree in drawing our attention to the function or use of words as distinct from their prima facie grammatical form. Again both the meta-theories ignore, in varying degrees, the existential use or function of language. For a comprehensive and masterly treatment of the meta-theory of philosophy advanced students of philosophy may consult Vol. III of Jasper's monumental work *Philosophy*. See also Mannheim, *Ideology and Utopia*, and Cornforth's, *Dialectical Materialism*.

90) An anecdote reports that the lady saint was once seen walking with a bowl of water in one hand and a plate of burning coals in the other. When asked for an explanation of her strange behavior she replied she was going to quench the fires of hell with the bowl of water and put fire to paradise with the burning coals. See Margaret Smith, *Readings from the Mystics of Islam*.

91) Q 5:32.

92) Q 2:68–71; Q 5:101,102.

93) Q 2:111–113; Q 23:52,53; Q 3:84,85.

94) Some non-theistic moralists hold that religious morality is inferior to purely humanist morality, because the former is essentially rooted in the fear of hell or the hope of heaven, while the latter springs from pure respect for the moral law or the welfare of society without any expectation of reward in the hereafter. This objection is valid in the case of religious morality motivated by fear (*taqwa*) in the lower sense, but not *taqwa* in the higher *Sufi* sense of love of God. See the anecdote mentioned above.

95) This was how the famous Indian mystic of Bengal, Ramakrishna (d. 1886) described his mystical experiences.

96) The Qur'an does not mention the exact rate of *zakat*, but the traditional annual rate is a fortieth part of one's total wealth after deducting one's reasonable expenditure.

97) There is a popular belief among Muslims in the sub-continent that contact with the sacred 'Black Stone' of the *Kabah* brings out the real inner traits of the person. Consequently, those who manage to put on a facade of goodness are exposed after performing the *Hajj*.

98) Moses ordered his people to sacrifice a cow. Instead of carrying out the order they started putting questions about the age, color, and breed of the animal. They did carry out the order in the end but the purpose was defeated, according to the Qur'an (Q 2:67–71).

99) Q 2:173.

100) According to food chemists, all land animals including the pig have an identical protein structure. Birds and water animals each have their own protein structure, but the fat content varies in different species within the three main types of land, air, and water organisms. A high fat content increases the time and blood supply needed for digesting food, thereby reducing the available fund of energy for other desirable physical and mental activities.

101) Even *Sufism*, with all its liberalism, does not acknowledge the true worth or value of music, even though *Sufi's* of the Chishtia order do listen to religious songs accompanied by musical instruments. But they do not appreciate pure instrumental music as an art form. Other *Sufi* orders, especially the *Nakshbandi*, firmly prohibit even religious songs.

102) See Shibli's *Al Faruq*.

103) The rite of *Ramal* was walking with stamping of the feet in the precincts of *Kabah* to create an impression of collective strength, when the Muslims were numerically few and were continually harassed by the Meccan nonbelievers. The rite had been initiated by the Prophet ﷺ. Umar's initial reasoning was that after the establishment of Islam in the whole of Arabia no social psychological justification was left for continuing the practice. See Shibli, ibid.

104) Q 4:35.

105) Q 2:229, 230, 232.

106) Q 2:282.

107) It maybe recalled that when in the 1966 Presidential election in Pakistan, late Fatima Jinnah (sister of the founder of Pakistan), was a candidate against Ayub Khan, the latter (reportedly) got issued a religious ruling (*fatwa*) from the *ulema* to the effect that the *Shariah* prohibited a woman from being head of the state. Ayub Khan was a religious liberal and had introduced many reforms during his regime, while Maududi, who had been opposed to the liberal approach of Ayub Khan, veered round to the support of a woman candidate. Such is the ethics of political struggle!

108) Parvez and also many others in India and Pakistan have been pressing for this change, and public opinion appears to be gaining ground in its favor.

109) According to *Shia* law, if there be no male issue, the entire property will be inherited by the daughter/daughters, there being no residuary heirs. According to *Hanafi* law, if there be no male issue, but one daughter, she will inherit one half of the property, the remaining half going to the residuary heirs. If there be no male issue, but two or more daughters, they will inherit two-thirds of the property, the remaining one-third going to the residuary heirs. See Amir Ali, *Muhammadan Law*.

110) Q 5:38, 39.

111) Q 24:2–6.

112) Refer to Introduction pp. 47 – 49.

113) See Hitti, *History of the Arabs,* pp. 353 – 354.

114) The pull of the old cultural tradition makes some Indian Muslims disapprove of the ideal of complete equality between the citizens of a secular state. Some persons claim that they would prefer to remain associate citizens with limited political rights but with full freedom to manage their own educational affairs and personal laws. A little reflection reveals that the logic of such ideas is a hangover from religio-political institutions of the medieval period. These ideas are also the result of the frustration of Indian Muslims and their disillusionment with the consequences of Pakistan, as far as their own interests in India are concerned.

115) For a clear and balanced discussion of the merits and demerits of democracy, see Joad, *Guide to the Philosophy of Morals and Politics*. Concrete democratic processes and structures must, however, be continually restructured to maintain and enhance their utility in the ever-changing human situation.

116) For a superb analytical and sociological treatment of the problem of alienation, consult Schacht, *Alienation*.

117) See Toynbee, *An Historian's Approach to Religion*, and Matthew Arnold, *Culture and Anarchy*.

118) See the well-known works of Toynbee and Russell. Also see Julian Huxley, *Religion Without Revelation*, and Carr, *What is History?*

119) Issues pertaining to casteism, racialism, linguism, federalism, religious tolerance, and equality of opportunity, etc., were decisional problems until the mid-19th century. But today they are problems only in the sense that numerous obstacles exist in the implementation of their more or less agreed theoretical solutions.

120) See Tawney's classic *The Acquisitive Society*. See also MacIver and Page, *Society: A Textbook of Sociology*.

121) Q 5:3.

122) See the candid report on the American economic scene in the works of Vance Packard, notably, *The Waste-Makers*.

123) The studies being conducted in American centers of research and the growing cultural cooperation between the capitalist and socialist blocs is bound to bear fruit in the coming years. Some impartial comparative studies of the concrete patterns of decision-making, role of pressure groups in politics, the merits and demerits of the different economic systems, etc., have already appeared, and will be followed by many more. See Brezenski and Huntington, *Political Power, USA/USSR*. See also Galbraith, *The Affluent Society*, and Schumpeter, *Capitalism, Socialism and Democracy*.

124) The internal differences in the Jana Sangh and a measure of liberalization in their approach to religious minorities and backward sections of Indian society reflect the power of the situational logic of history or the objective working of social reality. This, however, must not be misconstrued as sociological or historical determinism. See Popper, *The Poverty of Historicism*.

125) Q 40:78.

125A) See Bhagwan Das, *The Essential Unity of All Religions*.

126) See the profound Qur'anic verse, 45:23.

127) The English Bishop Bulter (d. 1752) wrote the well-known, *Analogy of Religion*.

128) Refer to Note 37.

129) The continuing conversion of British Protestants to the Roman Catholic Church does not contradict the above thesis, since these conversions are really within the wider unity of the great Christian tradition.

130) All 19th century reform movements in Hinduism and Islam in India were responses to the Christian and European challenges, just as the medieval reform movements in Hinduism, viz., *Bhakti* and Sikkhism, were responses to the Islamic challenge to a much older culture.

131) In the functional sense commitment to the scientific method and democracy is the religious faith of Western Europe, as pointed out by Toynbee. See his *An Historian's Approach to Religion*.

132) It seems to me that Communists tend to overestimate the role of Marxian ideas at the expense of the liberal humanist-socialist tradition of the West, while the non-Communists tend to do the opposite.

Supplemental Essay

Modernism and Traditionalism in Islam

'Modernism' and 'Traditionalism' in the sense of basic life attitudes are universal concepts. Every religion in every age has its modernists and traditionalists. In this essay, however, I propose;

(a) To elucidate the contemporary Western meaning of modernity and traditionalism in the sphere of religion and then show how far this conception of religious modernity applies to Islamic modernism and traditionalism;

(b) In the place of the two-dimensional modernist-traditionalist framework suggest a multidimensional framework for accommodating the different religious approaches found in contemporary Islam;

(c) Elucidate the relationship between traditionalism and modernism in general with special reference to Islam.

The word 'modernism' was first used to describe certain tendencies in late 19th Century Protestant Christianity. Ever since then considerable progress has been made in the philosophy, sociology and semantics of religion. Thus modernity in religion now signifies something more than modernism in the original Christian sense, namely,

(a) Emphasis on rationalism and the scientific method,
(b) Abjuration of dogma and supernaturalism,
(c) Higher criticism of the Bible. Religious modernity in the contemporary sense is a development of the above line of thinking.

THE ESSENTIAL FEATURES OF RELIGIOUS MODERNITY

The following points constitute its essential features:

(1) Stress on the fully integrated human personality as distinguished from a fragmented or compartmentalized one. This integration takes into account all the dimensions of human experience like reason, feeling, and morality, etc., without suppressing any basic existential or personality need.
(2) Distinction between religious experience and its conceptual interpretation.
(3) Distinction between the essential core and the concrete *gestalt* of a religion.
(4) Distinction between salvation in the sense of continuous spiritual growth and in the sense of the 'saving' of souls in life after death.
(5) Distinction between intrinsic and instrumental values.
(6) Stress on the cultivation of basic spirituality rather than any one of its diverse forms as represented by particular religions.
(7) Emphasis on spiritual autonomy and the reconciliation of any possible conflict with religious authority.
(8) Emphasis on ceaseless creativity of values and extra dimensional progress, as distinguished from the conservation of values and intra-dimensional progress. In other words, the stress is on creative fidelity rather than mechanical conformity to the past.

The above-mentioned eight points sum up the essential features of religious modernity in the West and are more or less self-explanatory. I shall however, comment on the first three points which are foundational:

The concept of the dimensional integration of personality is a much more inclusive and richer concept than of rationalism. Full integration includes the cultivation of reason but is not reducible to it. The hallmark of 19th century religious modernity in the West was rationalism, which was a legacy of the previous age of reason and enlightenment in Europe. But this mono-dimensional approach has given way to a multidimensional approach.

The second basic feature of religious modernity is the distinction between religious experience and its conceptual interpretation. This distinction applies to all forms of human experience and not merely the religious. Religious modernity emphasizes the significance and role of both experience and interpretation in the religious sphere. But, it insists that the two should not be confused, as is actually the case with most popular conceptions of different religions. Religious experience is sui-generis and cannot be reduced without remainder to other forms of experience like the aesthetic, the moral and the logical etc. Hence, religious modernity is not synonymous with pure ethicism or humanism, which are attempts to reduce religion to the purely ethical dimensions of human experience. Religious modernity does not accept humanism or ethical religion as fully adequate, because of their reductionist approach to the purely religious dimension of human experience. Man's growth remains incomplete without the flowering of his potential spirituality or spiritual sense as distinguished from his moral potentiality or moral sense. The distinction between the spiritual and the moral sense is analogous to the distinction between the moral and the aesthetic sense. The quest for the existential interpretation of man's experience is a deeply ingrained human personality need. Like religious experience, this quest is also sui-generis and different from the quest of scientific explanation. Mere descriptive knowledge and scientific explanation do not fully satisfy man's yearning for an existential interpretation or significance of the human situation within the total cosmic context. This interpretation, however, is a distinct activity from the original and primary religious experience of man as such. Most religious persons do not make any distinction between religious experience and its interpretation. Consequently, they suppose that the denial of their particular interpretation amounts to a denial of the experience as such. Moreover, they are not aware of the essential relativity of all interpretation to socio-cultural space-time. In other words the popular traditionalist believers of different religions remain unaware of **(a)** the distinction between experience and interpretation, **(b)** the organic connection of the interpretation with the socio-cultural conditions and the inherited conceptual framework of the society in which a particular religion grows.

The systematic conceptual interpretation of religious experience is essential and indispensable. The supposed selfsufficiency of mere morality or even religious experience is a romantic illusion born of difficulties or rather man's despair at arriving at a final and universally acceptable conceptual interpretation of the human situation.

Sober religious modernists in the West like Whitehead, Bergson, Hocking, Tillich, Niebuhr, Marcel and Buber etc., thus do not reject a metaphysical or philosophical theology, as superfluous, but attempt to reconstruct the basic religious concepts of the Christian or Jewish tradition. Their aim is to remove the conceptual difficulties that flow from the traditional meaning given to such concepts as God, Son of God, creation, revelation, prophecy, providence, and grace, etc. Such reconstruction has always been attempted by all creative interpreters of the different religious traditions. But the distinguishing feature of modern and contemporary religious reconstruction is that it must be done under the umbrella of science and the scientific method.

The third foundational feature of religious modernity concerns the distinction between the essential core and the concrete *gestalt* of a religion. This distinction has been suggested and developed as a result of the growth of sociology of religion on the one hand, and the phenomenology of religion on the other. The sociology of religion shows that all religious traditions have socioeconomic determinants as well as dimensions. The phenomenology, of religion, on the other hand, draws our attention to the nature of the essential core of the total religious *gestalt*. This core consists of a thought-cum-value system in organic interaction with the general conceptual framework prevalent in the parent society in which the religion originates. This thought system is the same as the conceptual interpretation mentioned above.

The value system underlies concrete rules, regulations and precepts of a particular religion and should not be equated with these concrete rules etc. The thought system and the value system jointly entail the precept system of a particular religion and give meaning to its symbolic life. The concrete *gestalt* of a religion, on the other hand, is influenced by the concrete conceptual and social soil in which the religion grows. The concrete personality or *gestalt* of different religions, however, includes a system of institutions over and above the thought-cum-value system, even as a living organism has secondary qualities distinct from its essential attributes.

The practical significance of this apparently academic distinction is crucial. Once this distinction is conceptually registered, we are at once liberated, as it were, from an emotional fixation upon a particular cultural *gestalt* whether Islamic, Christian or Hindu. The confusion between the pure essence and the accidents of its concrete exemplification in social space-time is removed. The 'Idea of Islam' in the Platonic sense generates both conceptual space and an inner freedom of movement without thereby repudiating Islam. The possibility of conflict between loyalty to the past and aspirations for the future is reconciled. As a member of the kingdom of ceaseless growth, man is liberated from enslavement to the past as distinguished from a creative fidelity to his religious tradition.

The foregoing analysis of Western religious modernity should also throw into relief the profile of its contrary, that is, religious traditionalism. But the difference between the two is a matter of degrees, rather than of kind, at least as far as Protestant Christianity is concerned. Consequently, the concepts of religious modernity are not totally absent from the traditionalist frame of reference, but are only much less emphasized.

SOME FEATURES OF ISLAMIC MODERNISM

Let us see to what extent the foregoing account of religious modernity applies to Islam. For obvious reasons I shall concentrate on the Indian scene.

All Islamic modernists accept in varying degrees the first three foundational points of Western religious modernity. But in general they are much more cautious and conservative than their Western counterparts, whatever the reason maybe.

All Islamic modernists have put a question mark against the traditional or popular Islamic thought system. Sir Syed's Qur'anic exegesis and commentary represents his attempted reconstruction in the religious thought of Islam, under the impact of Western science and rationalism. Iqbal and Azad also reconstruct the thought-cum-value system in the light of modern conditions.

The approaches of Sir Syed, Iqbal and Azad in this matter show significant differences. Sir Syed assumes, on the one hand that the Qur'an as the word of God, could not contain any error and, on the other, he also holds the scientific propositions of his time as indisputable. Consequently, he tried to reconcile any apparent conflict between the two as best as he could. Iqbal and Azad on the other hand, were never bothered by any such problem, since they held the Qur'an to be primarily an inspirational document rather than a textbook of physics or geography. The portions of the Qur'an dealing with facts of nature deliberately presupposed the scientific frame of reference prevalent in the age of revelation. Any deviation from that framework would have baffled and mystified the people concerned, instead of helping, them in their religious quest. The spheres of revelation and of scientific knowledge being different, no clash arises between the two. The Qur'an is the infallible source of value judgments and the fount of wisdom, while the scientific method is the source of all factual judgments and the laws of nature. The later modernists like Sindhi and others accept Azad's standpoint.

Valuable and ambitious as these reconstructions are, they nevertheless fall short of the depth and range of the reconstructive essays of a Whitehead or a Tillich etc. Perhaps one of the reasons for this general shortcoming of Islamic modernism is the lack of pure and professional practitioners among the Islamic modernists. Sir Syed, Afghani, Abduh, Iqbal, and Azad, all were public figures, engaged in extensive political work. Perhaps no Islamic modernist with the exception of Sindhi would accept all the implications or rather the philosophical foundations of the Western concepts of democracy, spiritual autonomy and sovereignty of the people. In the full Western sense of these terms, they cannot be reconciled with the traditional Islamic concept of revelation. The modernist reconstruction of this concept at the hands of Sir Syed, Azad and even Iqbal fails to overcome the conflict or incompatibility between the claims of revelation and man's spiritual autonomy, which are the basis of democracy and the sovereignty of the people. However, the thought system of classical Muslim philosophers like Ibn Sina, and Ibn Rushd etc., embraced this delicate theme of revelation. The concepts of *Nous, Agent Intellect,* and *First Intellect* etc., and the grades of emanation and illumination etc., were nothing but their bold and honest attempts to construct a critical theory of revelation and its relationship with reason.

The main tasks that Islamic modernists have set for themselves are concerned more with a critique of the status of *hadith* on the one hand, and on the other, with the implications of the distinction between the core and *gestalt* of Islam. Here their approach and achievements are creditable. Let us consider these two points separately.

All modernists concede that while *hadith* is very important for living the good life, it is not binding in the sense in which the Qur'an is. All Islamic modernists would perhaps vacillate in their attitude, should any part of the Qur'an may contradict plain common sense, clear observation, or one's conscience. But they would not hesitate to reject any *hadith* that may come in this category even if it satisfied all the canons of authenticity prescribed by the science of *hadith*.

Supplemental Essay: Modernism & Traditionalism in Islam

Theoretically, the status of the word of the prophet has always been lower than that of the word of God. It is significant that for the first almost two hundred years no attention was paid to the collection and arrangement of *hadith*. During this period Islamic jurisprudence (*fiqh*) was the only discipline that supplemented the Qur'an. It is also significant that the school of the greatest Muslim jurist Imam Abu Hanifa (d. 767) was known as the school of reasoned opinion (*ahlur-ray*). But later on when the other schools of jurisprudence emerged and differences of opinion arose, the attention of scholars and theologians was naturally drawn to the possibility of using *hadith* as a criterion of validity. It was in the period after Bukhari (d. 870) that the concept of revelation or *wahy* was fully developed. This led to the distinction between the 'open' and 'implicit' revelation (*wahy-i-khafi and wahy-i-jali*). The interpretation of *hadith* as an implicit revelation certainly raises the status of the word of the Prophet ﷺ, making it barely distinguishable from the word of God. If the Qur'an was openly revealed, while the *hadith* was implicitly revealed, then for all practical purposes, the Qur'an and the *sunnah* become the joint final authority. In other words, Qur'an and *hadith* become the ultimate court of appeal and the infallible criterion of validity.

Bukhari and other traditionalists certainly held that in the case of an irresolvable conflict between the word of the Prophet ﷺ and the word of God, the latter was to prevail. But since the Qur'an confines itself to general principles, broad precepts and value judgments, numerous concrete details of *hadith* could not possibly be judged according to the above criterion. Consequently, they tended to acquire practically the same status as the word of God. It was at this time that the doors of re-interpretation or *ijtihad* were closed. One of the essential features of Islamic modernism is, therefore, a vigorous protest against this closure, as well as against the practical nullification of the distinction between the word of God and the word of the Prophet. Different modernists may differ in their assessment of the status of *hadith*; but they certainly agree that it cannot be accepted as infallible in the sense in which the Qur'an is infallible.

Let us now turn to the distinction between the essence and total *gestalt* of Islam. All Islamic modernists have attempted the task of the distillation of the pure essence of Islam.

The medieval version of Islam had a considerably strong puritanical flavor, resulting in either the prohibition or the discouragement of music, dancing, sculpture, and most forms of painting etc. Islamic modernists protest against this Puritanism, and opt for aesthetic liberalism. They stand for the harmonious growth of the human personality without suppressing the aesthetic impulse in man. It is significant that this approach of aesthetic liberalism is not something foreign to the Qur'an. Rather the contrary approach was foreign to the spirit of the Qur'an.

Sir Syed was quite clear that dress, food and living habits, and marriage customs, etc., of the Prophet ﷺ were the accidents of time and place. Certainly, Sir Syed would not have gone to the extent of questioning the validity of social laws expressly found in the Qur'an. But he insisted that contemporary conditions be taken into account while applying Qur'anic laws. Sir Syed, thus, would have distinguished between eternal Islam and temporal *Mohammadanism*. Following this distinction, one could say that the followers of Abraham or Jesus were Muslims without being *Mohammadans*. For all his liberalism, however, Sir Syed was acutely class conscious and biased in favor of the upper and middle classes.

Similarly, Iqbal criticized democracy based on the counting rather than the weighing of heads. In spite of his intellectual attainments, Iqbal's approach to social problems, particularly the position and status of women was out of tune with his dynamic approach in other spheres of life. He shrank back from the full reconstruction of the value system and institutional system of Islam. There was some inexplicable resistance in his mind on this score.

Azad on the other hand, had a more liberal outlook on social matters. Perhaps this was due in large measure to his political affiliations after the First World War. But since he did not write much about such matters during the last twenty-five years of his life, it is difficult to assess the exact degree of his religious modernity.

The names of Ubaydullah Sindhi, Niyaz Fatehpuri (d. 1965) Akbarabadi, K.G. Saiyidain, Ajmal Khan, A.A.A. Fyzee, Caliph Hakim (d. 1959) and Ghulam Ahmad Parvez of Pakistan, must be mentioned in this context. All the above have a modernist approach.

THE LIMITATIONS OF ISLAMIC TRADITIONALISM

In view of what has already been said about Islamic Modernism, only some brief comments will be made on Islamic Traditionalism.

Supplemental Essay: Modernism & Traditionalism in Islam

Contemporary Islamic traditionalists like Abul Hasan Ali Nadwi, Maulana Tayyib, Maududi and others are certainly aware of some of the distinctions and concepts that constitute the core of religious modernity. But they do not concern themselves with the implications of these concepts. The traditionalists often chide Muslims for verbally professing beliefs without understanding their implications or acting in accordance with them. It appears to me that the traditionalists are guilty of the same charge, though the concepts or beliefs may differ in the two instances. Maududi, for example, does make a distinction between intrinsic and instrumental values, and also between essence and *gestalt*, even though his conception of essence maybe rather crude. Yet he totally fails to deduce their implications, or to apply them to the human situation. This is due to his views about *hadith* and *sunna*. He may allow a few superficial changes or modifications here and there, but he is essentially fixated upon the concrete *gestalt* of medieval Islam. Hence the revivalist strand in his thought, as distinguished from the traces of conservatism, found in certain aspects of Sir Syed's or Iqbal's outlook. It is a pity that in the estimation of his followers and admirers, Maududi, stands for a dynamic Islam. Unfortunately the word dynamic is a prize or prestige word like democracy, justice, humanism, and equality, etc., and hence used very loosely.

The basic limitation of all Muslim traditionalists is their rather uncritical and crude conceptual framework for dealing with religious experience, and relating it with other dimensions of human experience. Their phenomenology and sociology of religion and their conceptions of God, revelation, and creation, etc., fail to remove the intellectual difficulties or dissonances that flow from these concepts. To begin with, the traditionalists are not even aware of all the difficulties. But even when they do register these difficulties, and attempt to overcome them through the reconstruction of these concepts, their attempts lead to patch work structures and halfway houses. Due to their lack of consistency and organic unity, they fail in evoking an integrated conceptual response to the mystery of man in the Universe. The traditionalists are too involved with the conceptual models of the past to be able to look at them with a measure of critical detachment. Moreover, they presuppose that the slightest change in those models must inevitably destroy or weaken the value structure of Islam. Consequently, in spite of making the distinction between the core and the *gestalt* of Islam, they fail to see that the core itself is not static or inert as Democritus and Dalton imagined the atom to be.

The core is rather like the Rutherford's atomic nucleus consisting of a charge of electricity. The implication is that no conceptual model employed by man for the interpretation of his experience can be accepted as final. Even our modernists, barring one or two are not sufficiently aware of the depth and range of modifications necessary in the tradition, in order to effect a real breakthrough in Muslim society. Even the basic values of Islam, like brotherhood, and equality, etc., as understood in the ancient and medieval period of Islam require a thorough revision to become alive again for contemporary man exposed to the thought of Marx, Freud and Einstein. Unless this is done, many new sociopolitical and economic patterns are liable to be rejected straightaway by Islamic societies, even though they maybe for more effective promoters of the basic intrinsic values of Islam, than the traditional patterns hallowed by time. It is, therefore, quite misleading to declare that traditional Islam is perfect, and only Muslim's need to be reformed.

PATTERNS OF RELIGIOUS RESPONSE IN ISLAM

The two-dimensional modernist-traditionalist framework though valid in its own way, fails to draw our attention to the different responses or approaches to Islam or any other religion. I have suggested an eight dimensional framework for this purpose. This scheme can be applied to different religions at every stage of their history. But it applies primarily to the later stage of a religion, when sufficient growth has already taken place. In a sense, there is a tension between modernity and traditionalism at every stage of human history. But the early period of every religion is taken up by the articulation and crystallization of the different facets and strands of the tradition, rather than by the tension between modernity and traditionalism. The reason is that traditionalism presupposes an antecedent tradition, which takes time to grow. The tension between modernity and traditionalism does not result in a simple uni-linear movement either toward or away from a given tradition. There are separate cycles or spirals of modernity-traditionalism, each cycle consisting of the following stages:

- Felt disvalues of given tradition.
- Articulation of protest.

Supplemental Essay: Modernism & Traditionalism in Islam

- Growth of momentum of protest.
- Crystallization of new values.
- Inception of a new tradition.
- Growth of the new tradition.
- Felt disvalues of given tradition.

In one sense, the process of crystallization or the formative period of Islam ended in 632 A.D. In another sense, it ended with al-Ghazali's magnum opus, *Ihya ul-Ulum* (near 1100 AD) that attempted to combine the three major strands or impulses in Islam, after their prolonged crystallization over a period of about 400 years. These are the impulses of rationalism, mysticism and legalism. Each of these impulses took about 150 years for its full unfolding. In yet another sense the formative period of Islam will, or at least, should last forever. There is a very striking analogy between the above three senses of development on the one hand, and the three or four stages of human development on the other. In one sense man is complete at the moment of birth, in another sense he is complete only after the attainment of puberty, while in another and the most important sense, man is never complete, but always continues to grow.

It is thus about 1100 A.D. that the process of articulation of the Islamic genius was completed. At this stage the eight point scheme becomes fully applicable. The situation remains the same ever since then with the exception of one major or rather crucial development, namely the scientific revolution of the West. The impact of science on Islam is, however, beyond the scope of this paper.

The following are the patterns of religious response in Islam:

- Selective Reduction.
- Pietistic Conservation.
- Activist Conservation.
- Piecemeal Adjustment.
- Transformation.
- Substitution.
- Agnosticism-Nihilism.
- Cultural Emergence.

I will make extremely brief explanatory comments on the above types of religious attitudes.

Selective reductionism: The individual reduces the tradition to a few selected features of the tradition without creating or adding any new features. In other words, he prunes the tradition. An example is Abdul-Wahhab in the 17th century.

Pietistic conservatism: The individual tries to conserve the tradition as it exists in his age and believes in simple piety and the sincere practice of faith without much ado about sociopolitical improvements in the environment. Examples are the members of the Tablighi Jamat in present day India.

Activist Conservatism: The individual believes in not only conservation of the tradition and simple piety etc., but maintains that an active participation in sociopolitical movements calculated to reform society is a part of their religious duty. Examples are the members of the Jamat-i-Islami.

Piecemeal adjustment: The individual is dissatisfied with some feature or features of the tradition, but hesitates to undertake any systematic and sustained thinking with a view to come to a definite conclusion. Under-pressure of circumstances, however, he just makes piecemeal adjustments to remove his difficulties, for example, the average Indian Muslim today.

Transformationism: The individual is not only highly dissatisfied with the tradition but is also skilful and gifted enough to think independently. In the process, he completely transforms the tradition. Examples are the members of the Bahai faith.

Substitutionism: The individual is so much attracted by another tradition that he substitutes it, in place of his original tradition. Examples are those Muslims who are converted to some other secular or religious faith, such as, Christianity, or Communism, etc.

Agnosticism-Nihilism: The individual is utterly perplexed. Nihilism is only the ultimate stage of despair. The individual has no faith left in any system of values. Examples are the Muslim Beatniks, etc.

Emergentism: The individual appreciates the elements of value in the tradition but is dissatisfied with the elements of disvalue. But instead of merely pruning the tradition, he also believes in its creative growth.

Supplemental Essay: Modernism & Traditionalism in Islam

Cultural emergents combine continuity with change and thus represent the fusion of conservation and creativity. Examples are Sir Syed, Iqbal, and Ubaydullah Sindhi, etc.

THE RELATIONSHIP BETWEEN MODERNITY AND TRADITIONALISM

The creation of new values and the conservation of the old that have stood the test of time are both equally necessary. In fact they depend upon each other. The creation of new values pre-supposes a valuational base or support. Similarly, the effective maintenance of this base demands awareness of the subtle changes in the nuances and rhythms of human experience. Eternal and intelligent vigilance is the price of keeping old values alive in the condition of dynamic interaction with the environment rather than as showpieces in the museum of man's heritage.

Creativity ever-spurs man to go ahead in the realm of values and to yearn for the better rather than be content with the good. The function of tradition on the other hand, is to strike a note of caution, lest the pace of change increase to the point of giving diminishing returns. The function of tradition is not the stoppage of growth but only the regulation of the speed of growth. The conservative approach thus, has its own function in the economy of human progress, provided it does not over-reach itself.

Creativity and conservation should, therefore, dovetail into and supplement each other. Without creativity conservation leads to fossilization, while without conservation, creativity leads to irresponsible experimentation. While such adventures in the realm of art and literature may not be injurious, they could prove catastrophic in the realm of moral and social relationships. The new sex morality of Western Europe and America, according to which the game of sex maybe played between any two willing parties without any mutual obligation arising therefrom, has played havoc with the spiritual growth of the contemporary Western man. It appears to me that the West is gradually realizing its fallacy and that a more balanced interpretation of sex is in the process of crystallization. Similarly the limitations of different movements like nationalism, capitalism, socialism, and scientism, etc. are being acknowledged. Humanity would have been spared countless tears, had human judgment been more balanced and well-informed. But man is neither a mathematician nor a fly in the fly bottle, or a rat in a maze. He is an honest evaluator who commits errors of evaluation. He blunders and pays the penalty in the course of time and gradually forges ahead.

It is precisely man's constant blundering that grips the imagination of the champions of the traditional interpretation of Divine Revelation. They constantly reiterate man's incapacity to regulate his own affairs and point out that the only way open to man is the complete submission to the word of God and the example of His Prophet ﷺ. These persons are, however, not aware of the different meanings of submission to God. They accept only one conceptual model or meaning, namely the model of the dutiful son or subject submitting himself completely to the will of the authoritarian father or king who acts through his agent.

Similarly the traditionalists do not realize that their concept of revelation is based on the conceptual model of human communication through the spoken language. This model generates its own conceptual difficulties, which the traditionalists tend to ignore in the interest of preserving the integrity of their faith. This evasion of conceptual difficulties has, however, very harmful consequences, though apparently it may serve to keep the faith alive. This type of conceptual pain killing, as it were, leaves man with no intellectual motivation to explore other possible conceptual models for the interpretation of the Prophet's ﷺ religious or mystical experience of which the Qur'an is the concrete product. Thus the traditionalist Islamic approach remains unconvincing to the mind alive to the complexities of the human situation. Those individuals whose conceptual framework has kept pace with the continual developments in the natural and social sciences of the modern west have outgrown the conceptual clothes or models, which appealed to medieval man whether Muslim, Hindu or Christian. These are the people who yearn for a new language and idiom for the articulation of their own authentic religious experience. It appears to me, however, that the Islamic tradition is not a monolithic mausoleum but a garden where a hundred flowers have bloomed, and may still bloom. While getting depressed at the arid deserts of extreme orthodoxy and conservatism that we have to cross in the 1400 year old journey of Islam, we must not lose sight of the magnificent mountains and deep rivers that also greet and cheer the traveler. I refer to such liberal intellectuals as al-Farabi, Ibn Sina, al-Ghazali, Ibn-Rushd, Ibn Khaldun, Rumi, Ibnul-Arabi, Khayyam, and al-Beruni, and others. Those who reject the Islamic tradition outright, unnecessarily deprive themselves of the resources that ought to have been judiciously harnessed for cultural growth, instead of being indiscriminately spurned.

Supplemental Essay: Modernism & Traditionalism in Islam

Every age must look afresh and reinterpret its heritage of concepts and values. The task of revaluation and reconstruction of the Islamic thought-cum-value system will ever remain incomplete as long as man continues to grow and exercise the privilege and the duty of the ceaseless creativity of values.

In the context of Islam such a fresh look by Indian Muslim intellectuals is absolutely essential for giving enlightenment and guidance to the common Muslim who stands totally baffled and perplexed by the antagonistic pulls of theocracy and democracy, clericalism, and secularism, traditionalism and modernity. The average Muslim is more or less a split personality and must be helped to integrate himself. There can be no doubt that the integration needs to be oriented toward modernity. Like, it or not, the human family, as a whole is steadily moving in this direction. The angularities and imbalances that are inevitably generated in different societies are also in the process of being corrected, although this process is bound to take a fairly long time to be completed. Different religions are at different stages of modernization, and within the same religion, different groups are likewise at different stages. Even within these groups individual differences obviously exist. But the push of science and the pull of theology are definitely working to the advantage of modernization.

The need of the age is an authentic dialogue between Islamic modernists and traditionalists. The spirit of polemics only generates mutual resistance in both the quarters helping neither the cause of modernity nor the cause of traditionalism. Unfortunately, many Muslim modernists and traditionalists have a genius for giving offense to each other through various devices. The traditionalist is prone to lament over the opportunism and disloyalty on the part of the modernist. The modernist, on the other hand, is irritated at the fixation or rather fossilization of the conservative or traditionalist mind. The way out of this unfortunate predicament lies in greater tolerance and an authentic dialogue between modernity and traditionalism. The outcome of such a dialogue, to my mind, should be the reconciliation between the two through the liberating concept of 'cultural emergents' that combine continuity with change. The effective promotion of this approach is much more difficult than the downright denunciation of modernism or traditionalism, just as, in a very important sense, living the good life is much more difficult than rejecting life through suicide.

The study of the history of other religions is very useful for a deeper insight into our own religion. It is always easier to detect the psychological defense mechanisms and motives of self-interest, etc. in the case of others than in one's own. The same applies to groups. The limitations of other religions are much more easily grasped than those of one's own. Consequently a critical sociological survey of other religions helps us in a better understanding of the stages and laws of growth of our own culture or religion, its strength and its limitations. This comparative sociology of religions tends to dissolve our natural ethnocentricity and group self-conceit. Self-conceit prompts us to treat our own religion as a class by itself, and hence exempt from sociological laws that apply only to religions other than our own. Having outgrown this natural ethnocentricity and 'group snobbery', if I may call it, we are in a much better position to appreciate the points of excellence of our own religion and its unique contribution to the economy of the human family at large. Moreover, the realization of the variegated changes wrought by time in the fabric of the religious tradition, sets our creative imagination at work. Fresh visions are stirred that make us forward-looking, and growth-oriented as distinguished from backward looking and tradition-oriented.

Creative growth, however, implies the conservation of the values of the past. Cultural borrowing from others is one of the means of such growth. Early Islam was conspicuous for its spirit of assimilation of Greek, Iranian and Indian cultures. The cross-fertilization of intercultural concepts and values is an ever-recurring world process, though it usually operates at the unconscious level. Its conscious practice, however, does not render it any the least objectionable.

Cultural assimilation need not be confused with imitation or a patchwork synthesis. At its best, cultural assimilation is neither imitative nor synthetic but creative. It pre-supposes a critical evaluation of the culture of others no less than one's own. It is precisely this creative fusion that leads to 'cultural emergents'.

The basic ingredients of the different world religions are essentially the same, namely a thought-cum-value system, a precept system and an institutional system that is an organic part of the total cultural *gestalt* but not included in the religious core. Provided the genius of a particular religion has been grasped, its basic nuclear content can be preserved and cherished in the midst of a conscious assimilation of other concepts and values without impairing the basic integrity and personality of that religion.

The concepts and values, which to my mind, need to be consciously integrated into a dynamic Islam are the basic concepts and values of

Western modernity, and one or two concepts or values of Indian culture. I have described the concepts and values of Western modernity in a paper: *What is Modernity?* I shall, therefore, not repeat them here. But the value of 'authenticity' as it has emerged in Western Europe under the stimulus of existentialist thought, was-not included in that paper. Hence, a brief elucidation of this value would not be out of place here.

The contemporary age is the age of spiritual crisis and nihilism. A simple faith, whether in religious or secular values, has become more or less impossible for the sensitive and informed person, unless he first goes through a period of intense self-searching. One is, therefore, sorely tempted to cut short this arduous and long journey in the dark night of the soul in order to reach quickly the haven of faith and certitude. Man is eager to end the painfulness, nay the torture and agony involved in the loss of faith and a naked exposure to a total nihilism. The stress on authenticity is an appeal to man not to fall a prey to intellectual dishonesty, self-alienation, and the compartmentalization of his personality, in order to escape doubts or the awareness of conflict between his different attitudes and beliefs.

CONCLUSION

There is no unbridgeable chasm between modernism and traditionalism. The ideal is to be a growth-oriented person rather than be a traditionalist or modernist in the chronological sense. The growth-oriented approach implies that no one vision, whether of a Ghazali, a Wali Ullah, or Sir Syed or an Iqbal, or for that matter, Gandhi, Tagore, Russell, Marx or Mao, can be accepted as final. Ghazali's great synthesis in the 11th century between the strands of rationalism, mysticism and legalism was an achievement even as the *Summa* of St. Thomas was in later Christendom. Similarly, Ibn Sina, Ibn Rushd, Ibn Taymiya, Ibn Khaldun and Wali Ullah, each in his own way has left us with a synoptic vision. But no vision or interpretation can be allowed to become static.

The conceptual interpretation of the totality of human experience is a collective and progressive enterprise that should transcend the barriers of region and time, language and religion. The task of interpretation can never be completed. Human experience grows, yielding fresh factual data. This, in its turn, reacts or should react upon the conceptual interpretation in the lap of which the data first confronted man. This dialogue between experience and interpretation (leading at times to the discovery of fresh facts and at others to the formulation of fresh interpretations) is a part of the unending human adventure or man's quest of value. To give only one example of this dialogue, the conquest of poverty and disease and the control of human population are profoundly modifying, in the Christian framework of ideas, the conception of a Personal God, and, by implication, of revelation. On the other hand, it was the concept of a Supreme and Just Creator that had centuries earlier helped in the emergence of the concepts of cosmos and science. The important thing to note is the organic character of the interpretative framework, which attracts data from every dimension of human experience. This interaction between science and religion is rather marginal in Islam, since the impact of science and technology has just begun. The moment it gains momentum, similar changes are most likely to follow in Islam.

The reconstruction in the meaning of traditional symbols and images takes time. There may said to be a 'conceptual lag', just as there is a cultural lag. The concept of conceptual lag makes us tolerant toward the tradition-oriented person. In this respect, the methodological approach of some Western philosophers is also relevant. These philosophers avoid philosophical disputes, holding that different philosophical theories are merely varying formulations of the same set of facts. They differ because they select different facts for emphasis: Hence the important thing is not the verbal formulation but rather the full awareness of the complexity of the situation concerned. Provided this complexity is grasped, any formulation maybe retained. This principle may aptly be called the 'principle of formulational tolerance'. This principle together with the concept of conceptual lag should help our modernists in carrying out an authentic and fruitful dialogue with the traditionalists, as recommended above.

The principle of formulational tolerance is not an innovation in the cultural tradition of either Islam or Hinduism. The well-known story of *Moses and the Shepherd*, in the *Masnavi* of Maulana Rumi (d. 1273), is perhaps the most striking and pregnant recommendation for the acceptance of this principle. Indeed, Rumi goes on to say that the violation of this principle leads one to 'conceptual idolatry', that is, the worship of one's conception of God, rather than God Himself. Similarly, Waliyullah's concept of *Tatbiq* is very fruitful.

Earlier still, both Ghazali and Ibn Rushd had posited the principle of 'formulational dualism'. According to this principle, truth must be communicated to suit the mental level of the hearer. This dualism must

Supplemental Essay: Modernism & Traditionalism in Islam

lead us to what I call 'formulational pluralism'. This concept releases us from the monopolistic grip of traditional formulations on the one hand, and the formulations or jargon of our own pet interpretative systems, whether Marxism, Positivism, Idealism, Theism, Vedantism, or whatnot, on the other.

Every interpretative or value system no matter who the individual or which the historical tradition has limitations which must be acknowledged and overcome. These limitations are due to the spatio-temporal traces, which cling to the very individual in spite of this creative dynamism. This applies to every historical individual and epoch including the Prophet ﷺ and the *Khilafat-i-Rashida*.

The quest of growth must not, however, blind us to the power of the symbols and images of a tradition. These symbols must be retained and at the same time they must be reconstructed. If the symbols are discarded, the new ideas and values have no legs to stand upon, or no vessels to be poured into. If on the other hand, the symbols are retained, it becomes very difficult to make them first absorb or assimilate and then convey the new ideas and values in question. The symbols cast their shadows and tend to obscure and distort the fresh stirring of the human soul. Moreover, even if this difficulty be overcome, there is another dilemma. If the symbols are retained in their traditional sense, the reformer is heard and understood by the group, but the group does not move forward or toward the vision of the leader. If the symbols are nominally or formally retained but their meaning or significance radically altered, he is liable to be charged with hypocrisy by those members of the group who rightly or wrongly have no reason to feel dissatisfied with the tradition. Every creative individual, therefore, has to solve this predicament. Provided he feels an emotional involvement with the tradition and genuinely finds many elements of value in the historical personalities and events of that tradition, he should go ahead to reconstruct the tradition in question. The charge of hypocrisy cannot after all be treated as more demoralizing than the charge of *kufr* or apostasy that was the order of the day in medieval times nay, right up to our own.

The charge of hypocrisy will be valid only if the individual distorts his authentic meanings in order to get an audience. But, if the recommended changes in the meanings of the traditional symbols are not concealed but fully and frankly acknowledged, then their employment for facilitating the genuine and creative growth of the community can never be regarded as hypocrisy. Indeed this is the only way to further the cause of Cultural Emergentism. Socrates, Buddha, Jesus, Muhammad and Gandhi, and in an important sense, even Marx, followed the same principle.

APPENDIX 1:
INTRODUCING JAMAL KHWAJA & HIS WORKS

Jamal Khwaja has written seven major books, numerous articles and scholarly essays. Anyone interested in the intersection of Islam and Modernity will find Khwaja to be a reliable guide. Readers of his work will be informed, inspired, and intellectually liberated. Muslim readers will feel emotionally aligned with the Qur'an and find themselves empowered to live as authentic Muslims in the heart of the multicultural global village.

Khwaja's work is the definitive contemporary discussion regarding Islam and Modernity. Explore it. You will be profoundly rewarded.

Some illuminating excerpts from his works are presented below. They will enable readers to see for themselves the clarity, range and depth of his writings.

❖ ❖ ❖

Jamal Khwaja was born in Delhi in 1928*. His ancestors had been closely connected with the Islamic reform movement, inaugurated by Sir Syed Ahmed Khan, the founder of the famous M.A.O. College, Aligarh in the second half of the 19th century, and the Indian freedom movement under Gandhi's leadership in the first half of the 20th century. After doing

---

* Jamal Khwaja was born in Delhi on August 12, 1926. However, most official records show 1928 as the year of birth.

Appendix 1: About the Author

his M.A. in Philosophy from the Aligarh Muslim University, India, he obtained an Honors degree from Christ's College Cambridge, UK. Later he spent a year studying the German language and European existentialism at Munster University, Germany. At Cambridge he was deeply influenced by the work of C.D. Broad, Wittgenstein and John Wisdom, apart from his college tutor, I.T. Ramsey who later became Professor of Christian Religion at Oxford. It was the latter's influence, which, taught Khwaja to appreciate the inner beauty and power of pure spirituality. Khwaja was thus led to appreciate the value of linguistic analysis as a tool of philosophical inquiry and to combine the quest for clarity with the insights and depth of the existentialist approach to religion and spirituality.

Khwaja was appointed Lecturer in Philosophy at the *Aligarh Muslim University* in 1953. Before he could begin serious academic work in his chosen field, his family tradition of public work pulled him into a brief spell of active politics under the charismatic Jawahar Lal Nehru; the first Prime Minister of India. Nehru was keen to rejuvenate his team of colleagues through inducting fresh blood into the *Indian National Congress*. He included young Khwaja, then freshly returned from Cambridge, along with four or five other young persons. Khwaja thus became one of the youngest entrants into the Indian Parliament as a member of the *Lok Sabha* (Lower House) from 1957 to 1962. While in the corridors of power, he learned to distinguish between ideals and illusions, and finally chose to pursue the path of knowledge, rather than the path of acquiring authority or power. Returning to his *alma mater* in 1962, he resumed teaching and research in the philosophy of religion. Ever since then Khwaja has lived a quiet life in Aligarh. He was Dean of the *Faculty of Arts* and was a member of important committees of the University Grants Commission and the *Indian Council for Philosophical Research* before retiring as Professor and Chairman of the *Department of Philosophy* in 1988. He was a frequent and active participant in national seminars held at the *Indian Institute of Advanced Study* in Shimla.

He was invited to deliver the *Khuda Bakhsh Memorial Lecture* in Patna. He was one of the official Indian delegates at the *World Philosophical Congress, Brighton*, UK, in 1988, also at the *International Islamic Conference Kuala Lumpur*, Malaysia, in 1967, and the *Pakistan International Philosophy Congress, Peshawar*, Pakistan, in 1964. He has visited the USA and several countries in Western Europe. He performed the *Hajj* in 2005.

Appendix 1: About the Author

Khwaja's written works include,

1. Five Approaches To Philosophy: A discerning philosopher philosophizes about the philosophy of philosophy with wisdom and clarity, 1965.

2. Quest For Islam: A philosophers approach to religion in the age of science and cultural pluralism, 1977.

3. Authenticity And Islamic Liberalism: A mature vision of Islamic Liberalism grounded in the Qur'an, 1986.

4. Essays On Cultural Pluralism: A philosophical framework for authentic interfaith dialogue, 2015.

5. The Call Of Modernity And Islam: A Muslim's journey into the 21st century, 2015.

6. Living The Qur'an In Our Times: A vision of how Muslims can revitalize their faith, while being faithful to God and His messenger, 2012.

7. The Vision Of An Unknown Indian Muslim: My journey to interfaith spirituality, 2015.

Please visit
www.JamalKhwaja.com
for more information

Appendix 1: About the Author

1. Five Approaches to Philosophy
A Discerning Philosopher Philosophizes About The Philosophy Of Philosophy With Wisdom and Clarity

This monograph attempts to describe the different, approaches to philosophy, their situational and conceptual fields, their interrelations and limitations. The possibility of combining them into a multidimensional approach is also discussed.

The key notion underlying this essay is that the actual doing of philosophy must be rooted in a critical and comparative meta-philosophy. Most philosophers are so busy in establishing truths, or analyzing words and sentences, as the case maybe, that they tend to neglect meta-philosophy. This leads to methodological isolationism and a polemical instead of an irenic approach to philosophical problems.

Excerpts

The present human situation is characterized by scientific uniformity and progress in the midst of philosophical controversy and religious and cultural diversity. This is perhaps the most significant feature of the contemporary situation. This generates the basic conceptual field for the critically oriented contemporary philosopher. It maybe called the meta-philosophical field. Methodological, questions like the nature of philosophical, metaphysical, ethical and logical statements, the theories of meaning and truth, and the nature and dynamics of philosophical or ethical controversy, etc., arise within this field. Controversy and disagreement in the midst of progressively expanding scientific and technological standardization appear as anachronisms to the contemporary mind. It is impelled to find the causes and the cure of this incongruity. This leads to an unprecedented interest in meta-problems of almost all the branches of knowledge. The value judgment underlying this quest is that avoidable controversy or conflict is bad and must be overcome. The contemporary analytical and meta-philosophical approaches are the new instruments to serve this basic value, even as previous metaphysical systems were the instruments of serving and defending some value system or other, embedded in past cultural traditions. In other words, harmony or agreement is the motif of contemporary meta-philosophy. It maybe said that this is the motif of all philosophy and religion as such. This is probably true. But the range of harmony sought by contemporary philosophers is immensely wider than the range previously sought. Moreover, there is a distinction between a democratic harmony among autonomous individuals freely committing themselves to values, and the harmony that ensues as a result of the commitment to an external *Authority*. No doubt the philosophical theologian claims that since his acceptance of the *Authority* is based upon universally valid reasons, the harmony that accrues is rooted in reason rather than a dogmatic or arbitrary surrender to an *Authority*.

If philosophical theories and systems are conceptual patterns, then how and in what sense can they be true or false? A landscape or a musical composition maybe good or bad. But there is no sense in judging them to be true or false. If, however, philosophy claims to be a conceptual picture of the Universe, as a portrait is of an individual, say, Napoleon, then the terms true or false are applicable to philosophy. But in the case of a portrait, we have the original subject as well as the painting, and the two can be compared. Now where is the original subject in the case of the Universe? Surely, the observed features of the Universe are there. But a philosophical theory is not descriptive. Consider the case of a number of architects, each pressing his design for acceptance by the town planners. There is no standard or Platonic design, with reference to which the claims of the architects could be tested and settled. Even if there were such design, but was in principle inaccessible, there would be no point in claiming truth for a particular design. All that legitimately could be claimed by an architect was that his particular design had such and such advantages under specified conditions, apart from aesthetic value.

Appendix 1: About the Author

The choice of a valid conceptual field on the basis of the criteria suggested is ultimately a function of reflection and not of an investigation of the facts. Thus the possibility of eventual disagreement among philosophers cannot be eliminated, even though the choice is not arbitrary. Two persons may agree to the rules and yet differ in their application. Philosophical disagreement is thus unavoidable. No approach can eliminate disagreement without any remainder. But the type of disagreement that remains on the multidimensional approach would be the unavoidable minimum like the unavoidable minimum friction of a well-constructed and well-oiled machine or moving body. It would be a fraction of the disagreement that results from a non meta-philosophical or a mono-dimensional approach. The disputes about the nature and tasks of philosophy are a function of a one sided fixation upon selective Paradigms of philosophical questions and answers. The monopolistic grip of selective instances of a general concept is a fairly widespread phenomenon. Marx's theory of the determinants of social change, Freud's theory of the determinants of neuroses, and the different theories of truth or of knowledge, the different theories of the nature of ethical judgments, etc., are all reminders of how the fondness for particular instances or paradigms leads to a general theory concerning the subject matter. Rather than accept or reject any particular theory of philosophy, we must try to see how far it is illuminating, and how far misleading.

2. QUEST FOR ISLAM
A PHILOSOPHER'S APPROACH TO RELIGION IN THE AGE OF SCIENCE AND CULTURAL PLURALISM

Quest for Islam is a systematic exposition of Islam in the light of contemporary knowledge by a practicing Muslim. A seminal work, it successfully resolves intellectual difficulties created in traditional interpretations by new knowledge. Among other things, it organically integrates core Islamic values with the requirements of plural societies and secular democracies. It thus adds a fresh dimension of value to the Islamic thought-cum-value system. It will appeal greatly to Muslim intellectuals perplexed by the assault of modernity on traditional values and institutions.

EXCERPTS

The Universe has some basic features which maybe said to be its warp and woof, and which remain the same throughout history, e.g., the features of law and order, harmony and beauty of nature, man's moral sense, as distinct from concrete moral codes, the struggle for survival of the species and of individuals, pain and suffering, hope and joy, birth, growth, decay, and death. Natural science does not concern itself with the significance or meaning of these features of the Universe, that is, whether they are just accidental features and could, therefore, disappear from the cosmic scene, as accidentally as they appeared; or whether they stand rooted in the constitution of the Universe and thus have an *ontic* status or permanent reality. Now the way in which one interprets these features simultaneously influences the personality orientation of the individual, and is in turn, influenced by the original bent of the personality itself.

In other words, there is a dialectical relationship between the existential interpretation and the personality orientation. The interpretation becomes important, since it influences man's inner responses to the Universe in a most subtle manner, though the interpretation has no *prima facie* bearing upon

Appendix 1: About the Author

man's empirical, ethical, or aesthetic response. But the fact is that different existential interpretations constitute different ways of treating the Universe or relating oneself to it, and this inevitably influences the individual's lifestyle and also raises the question as to which particular style is right, and why so. To give an analogy, the practicing scientist does not concern himself with the question whether or why nature behaves uniformly, but takes it for granted, as if it were self-evident or necessarily true, or because it works. But the denial of causal uniformity does not involve any logical contradiction; nor can it be logically proved.

We accept it for two reasons: first, our actual experience suggests as if it were true; and, second, if it were not true, no point would be left in our scientific inquiries, which we deem as valuable and worth pursuing. Likewise, there would be no point left or, to be more accurate, the urge to pursue values would be far less intense, if values were chance and ephemeral products of the blind dance of atoms, without the conservation and growth of values being ontologically guaranteed, despite all seeming obstacles. The concept of God is precisely one particular form of this faith. Belief in God implies that values like truth, goodness, and beauty are neither chance products, nor ultimate and un-derived features of the Universe, but have their source in the ultimate and Supreme Being with whom man could establish an '*I-Thou*' dialogue. The existential interpretation is neither a hypothesis, nor a partly justifiable postulate; it is a motivational re-enforcer that integrates the individual's thoughts and feelings into a stable inner way of life or mode of treating the Universe, as distinct from ad hoc and ever-variable responses or attitudes.

If, and when, the interpretation does not harmonize with the scientific conceptual scheme, a revision of its concrete sense may remove the prima facie discord. We may say, for instance, that God's love for His creation is not the same as a mother's love for her child, or that what appears as evil works as an instrumental good in a larger context. This task involves redefining, analyzing, explaining, making distinctions or comparisons either in the spirit of a free exploration of the given data or in the spirit of a defensive reconciliation between theology and science. In the former case, the role of reason is primary, while in the latter, it is secondary. The theologian explores

Appendix 1: About the Author

new meanings of traditional concepts in a spirit of defensive reverence to the tradition, while the philosopher freely reflects upon the validity of the religious interpretation. He checks whether the actual data of human experience harmonize with the religious interpretation. This activity, however, does not involve deductive or inductive reasoning but existential elucidation, that is, the illumination of one's hidden depth attitudes, choices, interpretative responses, or images. An existential interpretation, which is chosen by the philosopher, is thus functionally similar to, but genetically or methodologically different from, religious faith. An existential interpretation of some kind or another is unavoidable.

We can only opt for this or that interpretation, but we cannot opt to do away with all interpretation as such. We may claim to avoid all contact with metaphysics or religion, which we may view as the hallmarks of a pre-scientific mentality. Yet the fact is that we cannot live as integrated human beings without some kind of worldview or total perspective on the cosmos. This total perspective, be it religious or philosophical, is at bottom always an existential interpretation of the basic features of human experience cosmic law and order, the mysteries of birth, growth and death, the beauty as well as the fury of nature, good and evil, joy and tragedy. Religious faith is the pre-logical acceptance of an interpretation because of its existential grip over the believer.

3. Authenticity and Islamic Liberalism
A Mature Vision Of Islamic Liberalism Grounded In The Qur'an

"Authenticity and Islamic Liberalism" is a collection of four original and highly stimulating papers on the liberal existentialist approach to religion with special reference to Islam in India. Each paper deals with an independent theme; yet, a consistent analytical existentialist approach makes them a well-orchestrated and balanced exposition of what may best be called "Islamic Liberalism."

Excerpts

Every religion has a nuclear core of basic beliefs and values embedded in a wide cultural matrix comprising myths, ancient collective memories, folklore, customs, and stereotyped images, etc. All these elements are enmeshed and the ordinary believer hardly cares to separate the nuclear core from the total cultural matrix of faith and practice. The total cultural tradition is the spiritual atmosphere in which he lives, moves and has his being. The German religious thinker of the 20th century, Bultmann, called the gradual process of distilling the nuclear core of Christian thought and value system from the cultural matrix of the Christian tradition, the 'demythologization of Christianity. This concept, however, has universal and timeless relevance to all religious traditions. Several creative thinkers and savants of Islam; Al-Beruni (d. app. 1040), Ibn Sina (d. 1037), Ibn Rushd (d. 1198), Al-Ghazali (d. 1111), Ibn Arabi (d. 1240), Jalaluddin Rumi (d. 1273), Fariduddin Attar (d. 1229), Ibn Khaldun (d. 1406), Shah Waliullah (d. 1763), and others attempted to grasp the essence of Islam.

Sir Syed attempted to distill the nuclear essence of Islam in the framework of modern thought, as he understood it. He was not a professionally trained philosopher, social scientist or historian. But his extraordinarily sharp intellect, intuitive insight and common sense, and above all, his intellectual honesty and moral courage enabled him to distill the nuclear core of Islam from its concrete historical forms in space and time. It is instructive to recall that in his earlier pre-critical phase, Sir Syed had adhered to the conventional ideas of his milieu, though even then he had come under the influence of the, relatively, liberal philosophical theology of Shah Waliullah, of Delhi. However, soon after the failure of the great Indian rebellion of 1857 against British imperial rule, when Syed Ahmed was roughly forty-five, he outgrew his honestly held ideas and values and became clearly aware of their limitations, without, however, ever-rejecting the nuclear core of his Islamic faith. Those who were unable to appreciate the spiritual pilgrimage of the great man and the organic growth of his ideas charged him with having abandoned Islam or distorting the faith for ulterior motives. Half a century later Abul Kalam Azad passed through a similar experience.

Azad's principled separation of politics and religion, in the Indian context, is right. His writings and public utterances do not make it sufficiently clear what course he proposed for predominantly Muslim societies. It needs pointing out that secularism is right not only in the case of mixed societies but also in the case of predominantly Muslim societies. The rationale behind this approach is that the social customs and the polity (which Muslims inherited from its original Jewish and Arab environment) must be de-linked from the core of the Islamic faith and value system. The primary scope of the *Shariah* ought to be restricted to pure spirituality as the essence of religion (*deen*). Polity, in the modern age, ought to be guided by democratic decision making based on autonomous and informed inquiry, as is being done in the case of natural sciences. The first to affirm the principled separation of religion from politics were the founding fathers of the American constitution, although they themselves were deeply committed to the Christian faith and to value based politics. Their reason was that the union of religion and politics, inevitably, makes the established religion intolerant of other religions. This was the precise and precious lesson America had learned from the experience of the European peoples.

The principled separation of church and state, however, does not mean or imply that politics has no need to be regulated by moral and spiritual values. I strongly feel that many who strongly oppose secular politics and insist that the lasting strength and beauty of true Islam lies, precisely, in preserving and promoting the 'organic unity of religion and state', consciously or subconsciously equate secular politics with immoral or unethical politics. They do so because of their still deeper conviction that morality and spirituality are not possible without belief in a personal God or without following religious laws or prescriptions in every walk of life. I submit that this belief is a half-truth. This is not the place to debate this complex issue. I have fully discussed this issue in my other published works.

Appendix 1: About the Author

4. ESSAYS ON CULTURAL PLURALISM
A PHILOSOPHICAL FRAMEWORK FOR AUTHENTIC INTERFAITH DIALOGUE

Ours are times when religion is systematically being used; unconsciously by some and deliberately by others, in the service of politics and personal gain, rather than spirituality. However, perceptive and honest minds among all religious communities view different religions as diverse "languages of the spirit," each valid and nourishing in its own way.

An impartial study of different religions shows the underlying unity in the diversity of religions. All religions are attempts to satisfy the human sense of wonder and awe at the inscrutable mystery of the Universe. This common function produces the unity while the diverse conditions in which different religions arise and grow produce the diversity.

EXCERPTS

Now, though Mahavira and Buddha denied *Brahman* and the sanctity and infallibility of the Vedas, they both accepted basic moral and spiritual values and the principle of *karma*. It is, therefore, reasonable to hold that the followers of Mahavira and Buddha, or for that matter, the followers of any other religious tradition (provided they eschew the moral evils or vices mentioned above) do not come under the purview of the above verses of the Gita. In other words, the approach of the Gita is so catholic that notwithstanding its own commitment to *Vaishnavite Anthrotheism* (faith in the divinity of Sri Krishna), it seems to permit the conceptual elimination of even God/Brahman from one's value system for agnostics and others. Possibly, this is the explanation of how and why both Jainism and Buddhism, after an extended period of conflict with Brahmanical orthodoxy, and even a measure of persecution by the custodians of the Vedic tradition, eventually came to be regarded as unorthodox schools or sects of Hinduism in the larger sense.

Appendix 1: About the Author

Blessed are the good and simple and authentic believers in a caring Personal God. Blessed are they who can plumb the depths of their being and can hear *'the music of the spheres'* and see *'the light of a thousand suns blaze forth all at once'*, and act dutifully without attachment to the fruits. Blessed too are they whose journey in inner space brings them to *'Brahman without attributes'*, and fortifies the *'Atman'*. But what about those whose honest and sustained quest for truth meets with a bewildered inner silence and the darkness of an unending night of the soul, and yet they remain sensitive to truth, goodness and beauty, and go on responding to the call of duty for its own sake? This is the crucial question facing and dividing humanity today.

An impartial study of different religions shows the underlying unity in the diversity of religions. All religions are attempts to satisfy the human sense of wonder and awe at the inscrutable mystery of the Universe. This common function produces the unity while the diverse conditions in which different religions arise and grow produce the diversity. However, the differences in belief, on a deeper analysis, turn out to be merely different ways of performing the same function in the basic economy of human life. In other words, different beliefs turn out to be different versions or species of a more basic generic belief. For instance, the belief that God reveals His will to a human messenger or prophet and the belief that God incarnates Himself in human form are two different versions or species of the more fundamental conviction that God intervenes in history to guide man on the right path. Neither of the two beliefs is fully intelligible or transparent to the human mind and both are full of mystery. Likewise, the basic Aryan belief in repeated rebirths in this world and the basic Semitic belief in one single eschatological rebirth are twin species of the more fundamental conviction that as a man soweth, so shall he reap in one form or the other. Both beliefs posit the continuity of life, either in the 'linear' or the 'cyclical' sense, and both motivate man to the same end.

Appendix 1: About the Author

If one looks at history from the humanist perspective the political or religious conflicts of the human family in the past turn into humanity's march (in circuitous and halting stages) toward a global federal unity. The victory of an Alexander and the defeat of a Porus in India, the almost total destruction of Baghdad by a Hulagu and the devastations in north India by a Nadir Shah, the compassion of an Ashoka, the statesmanship of an Akbar, the aberrations of a Hitler, all become the achievements or failures of the human family. With charity for all and malice toward none, the historian passes judgment on the deed, rather than the doer. His standards remain consistent, but he takes into account that human ideas and ideals are subject to the law of evolutionary growth. In short, his range of sympathy gradually becomes universal instead of remaining congealed at a particular parochial level determined by his birth or early conditioning.

It is significant that the data of history are not given to the truth seeker, as are the data of nature to the scientific investigator through sense perception or experiments under controlled conditions of observation. The data of history are themselves, in part, constructs out of surviving remains of past things or events. Moreover, no two historians select exactly the same set of data out of the total range available. Historians select their own unique 'effective' data for a systematic narrative and analysis of the past. The historian fits these data in his favored framework of ideas and values out of several alternatives available. No such framework, as such, can be proved as conclusively true, or valid. Yet, one must have some basic frame of orientation (as pointed out by Erich Fromm) in order to understand or existentially respond to the human situation in totality.

Religions and philosophies, in different ways, perform this function. They hold their effective data together and enable one to arrive at a total perspective on the human situation as such. Thus, a historian having a *Hindutva* frame of orientation would tend to view Sultan Mahmud's destruction of the Somnath temple, Gujarat, in the 10th century as an Islamic attack on Hindu India. A historian with a humanist sociological orientation would view the same episode as a medieval Sultan's lust for booty. This admission, however, does not amount to unrelieved relativity of historical interpretation as such.

Appendix 1: About the Author

Let me explain this point further. A reliable contemporary Persian record of Mahmud's time states that after returning to his capital, covered with glory and laden with booty, the Sultan sent some valuable gifts to a venerated divine of Ghazna; Qazi Abul Hasan Baulami. The Qazi returned the royal gifts and severely chastised the Sultan for violating the *Shariah*, which prohibited the desecration of any place of worship. Obviously, the honest and bold response of the Qazi had no effect upon the Sultan and the general course of events in medieval time. However, the above authentic story makes it quite clear that the primary '*leitmotif*' of the medieval Sultans was personal aggrandizement and expansion of power, not the promotion of Islam or forcible conversion. In this sense and to this extent, therefore, the humanist interpretation of history becomes more valid than the *Hindutva* interpretation that rejoices in Muslim baiting and distortion of the past. By the same token those Muslims who glorify Sultan Mahmud as an Islamic hero, misinterpret or distort Islam and also harm Muslims and all of humanity.

Appendix 1: About the Author

5. THE CALL OF MODERNITY AND ISLAM
A MUSLIM'S JOURNEY INTO THE 21ST CENTURY

The Call Of Modernity And Islam is a timely and welcome anthology of ten scholarly essays that focus creatively on the urgent need to re-energize Islamic culture and institutions. The essays span an enormous disciplinary range. Professor Khwaja moves back and forth with consummate ease between religion, science, philosophy, history, and the social sciences to paint a fully integrated, big picture of the encounter between Islam and modernity.

EXCERPTS

The predicament of Muslims in the modern age is that their religious tradition stands for the unity of religion and state while the modern mind stands for the separation of religion and state. The Islamic tradition is that Islam is not merely a spiritual discipline, but a complete way of life, including a polity (*Shariah*). Though not inspired like the Qur'an, the *Shariah* is deemed as all embracing and sacrosanct. Only the *ulema* are empowered to modify it according to a definite procedure. But it would be absurd to claim or expect that the *Shariah* should be binding on the Parliament of a sovereign secular state. Muslims in general hold that a sovereign secular democratic state is bound to fall headlong into 'Satanic' politics and the amoral pursuit of power. In other words, they equate the separation of religion from politics with immoral politics. They honestly tend to hold that the secular approach to politics destroys or erodes true Islam, which is a seamless and complete map of conduct according to Divine guidance.

This is the spiritual predicament of traditional Muslims all over the world including the followers of Maududi's school of Islamic thought that is, relatively, liberal, but falls short of the fully integrated and spiritualized religious sensibility of the modern mind. Western educated Muslims in general, and, particularly, those belonging to plural societies are, increasingly, becoming aware of this predicament. But they lack the moral courage and credentials to question the validity of the time honored traditional approach and the exclusive authority of the *ulema* in such matters. Another reason why the educated Muslim laity is reluctant to assert itself is the lack of proper grounding in religious learning and the Arabic language. These perplexed believers silently wait for the day when the *ulema*, on their own, will take the initiative to revise or redefine the proper scope of the *Shariah*. The *ulema*, hardly aware of the complex issues of modernity (understandably) suffer and, unconsciously, go on the defensive when confronted with the immense gap between medieval learning and the much more developed natural and social sciences in the modern age.

I submit, in all humility, they, in the best interests of all concerned, should ponder on the full implications of four basic truths: (a) granted that all Muslim believers must accept the Qur'anic text as infallible, no human interpretation of the text can claim to be infallibly true; (b) interpretation, in some form or other, necessarily, enters into all efforts at understanding the Qur'anic text; c) the proper understanding of any communication involves a frame of reference within which the 'addressee' interprets the words or expressions used in the original communication; (d) the frame of reference as well as the concrete meanings or usages of words, necessarily change in the course of time. These truths apply to all communications or languages including the 'Word of God'. It follows that whosoever interprets the Qur'an, whether one be an Arabic-speaking lay person or scholar, necessarily, interprets the Scripture relative to one's own set of Arabic usage and understanding of the context of the communication.

Appendix 1: About the Author

6. LIVING THE QUR'AN IN OUR TIMES

A VISION OF HOW MUSLIMS CAN REVITALIZE THEIR FAITH, WHILE BEING FAITHFUL TO GOD AND HIS MESSENGER

In the past, authentic Muslims, including the closest Companions of the Prophet, often differed sharply in their political and social beliefs. In our times, the challenges posed by modernity have made such differences especially toxic. In this work, the Author clarifies the core teachings of perennial Islam and their continuing relevance to our daily lives.

EXCERPTS

Perennial Islam, as joyful submission to one Supreme Creator and acceptance of the Qur'an as the '*Word of God*', revealed to Prophet Muhammad, is one thing; the surrender to a static *Shariah* conceived as a perfect and total guide for the believer in every walk of life, is quite another. To remain rooted in the perennial spiritual values of the Qur'an, as exemplified in the life and character of the historical Muhammad ﷺ, the '*Seal of the Prophets*' is one thing; to hold that this implies that believers should actively strive to become 'carbon copies' of the Prophet's ﷺ actions and lifestyle is quite another. Rootedness in the basic Qur'anic values does not imply a mechanical and un-reflective adherence to Qur'anic injunctions without making a distinction between 'intrinsic' values and 'instrumental' rules. Likewise, genuine reverence and love for the Prophet ﷺ does not imply the uncritical acceptance of the many miracles or myths found in the popular versions of the Islamic faith, especially the dramatic detailed events and dialogues mentioned in the stories of the Prophet's journey (*Miraj*) to God's Throne. To deny such myths or miracles in no way diminishes his sublime spiritual status and his authentic mystical experiences, or his amazing achievements

Appendix 1: About the Author

as a historical figure. Muslims generally believe that Prophet Muhammad ﷺ must have possessed supernatural powers on the ground that earlier prophets performed miracles. Prophet Muhammad ﷺ being the greatest, God must have endowed him with similar, if not greater, powers, so it is held to be the case. Muslims commonly cite the Qur'anic verse (54:1) as evidence that Prophet Muhammad ﷺ performed the miracle of splitting the moon *(shaqq ul Qamar)*. Numerous saints and mystics of Islam are also credited with possessing extra-ordinary powers through Divine grace. *Sufi* tombs attract numerous devotees (both Muslim and others) who seek the intervention of the saints in securing various material benefits for themselves. However, the Qur'an gives no warrant at all for accepting this traditional image of Prophet Muhammad ﷺ. Indeed, the Qur'an categorically denies that Prophet Muhammad ﷺ possessed supernatural powers with the sole exception of the gift of Divine revelation *(wahy)*. In other words, the Qur'an is the only miracle, which Prophet Muhammad ﷺ claimed to possess.

Millions and millions of Muslim believers will surely and rightly continue to venerate Prophet Muhammad ﷺ as the perfect exemplar for humanity. An ever-swelling number of non-Muslims of eminence now also acknowledge the administrative, moral and spiritual genius of Prophet Muhammad ﷺ as one of the super-architects and shapers of human destiny on the world scale. The crucial question is what should be the concrete form, in the modern age, of a true Muslim's veneration for Prophet Muhammad ﷺ. In answer to the above crucial question, I submit that true reverence and fidelity to Prophet Muhammad ﷺ consists in trying to make his basic values and objectives, rather than the details of the Prophet's ﷺ conduct, the pivot of our own lives and activities.

The promotion of Prophet Muhammad's ﷺ basic values (even if this task today requires modifying his instructions given in particular situations) is the real meaning of following his example *(sunnah)* in an ever-changing world. This is, precisely, what Caliph Umar had done. The following considerations should help perplexed Muslim believers to realize this liberating truth. First, development or growth takes place in different fields of human activity despite interruptions, retrogressions and reverses. This applies not only to factual knowledge but also to human ideals, values and institutions. Thus, have arisen fresh interpretations of the good life. Universal human rights, rule by consent, peaceful transfer of power, tolerance of dissent,

Appendix 1: About the Author

gender equality, and equality of opportunity, are some of the ideals that are the fresh characteristics of the modern age.

Static norms of perfection cannot but arrest the natural movement of ideas and ideals. No particular stage of development can be said to be perfect. It maybe thought that for the committed Muslim, at least, the Qur'an is beyond the shadow of imperfection. The crucial point is that the Qur'an has to be understood by human beings whose conceptual framework is bound to change with the passage of time. This framework will always remain subject to various imperfections or limitations. Thus, even if we concede the Qur'an, as the Word of God, to be perfect, its human understanding will always remain a matter of perfection aspired to rather than perfection achieved. Ceaseless growth toward perfection rather than perfection as such is all that man can hope for. Second, a clear distinction should be made between basic values and instrumental rules. The Muslim segment of the human family will not advance forward, but move in ruts alone, if Muslims do not sift the instrumental prescriptions of the Prophet from his basic goals and objectives. The making of this distinction between basic objectives and the means for realizing them should not be confused with the rather facile view that the end justifies the means.

Third, a clear distinction will also have to be made between matters of personal taste and matters of morality and spirituality. Real and honest commitment to the values of the Prophet ﷺ does not mean that the individual give up his inclinations and preferences in matters of taste.

Fourth, the reported sayings and doings of the Prophet Muhammad ﷺ are not sufficiently authentic despite the arduous efforts by dedicated and gifted Muslim researchers to separate the chaff from the grain. Though it is true that several Qur'anic texts are inexplicable or will remain vague unless read in the light of the reported sayings or doings of the Prophet ﷺ there is no justification for bracketing the Qur'an and the *hadith* as equally authentic, or binding. Respect for the latter does not mean unquestioning acceptance. Keeping the above four considerations in mind should help us to realize that the real meaning of fidelity to Prophet Muhammad ﷺ is not the literal imitation of his conduct but the honest and intelligent endeavor to translate the basic values of the Qur'an and hence of the Prophet ﷺ into practice in an ever-changing human situation.

Appendix 1: About the Author

Mere conformity to the instrumental rules without intelligently searching for what exactly right action means in the ever-changing human situation society will yield only marginal benefits. The principled acceptance of the semantic distinction between prescriptive Qur'anic verses referring to basic values and those referring to instrumental rules prepares the ground for the believer's own free commitment to basic values without any loss of spiritual autonomy. This transforms obedience to the 'Word of God' into the enjoyment of inner freedom. The Prophet's character beautifully exemplifies these basic values that can never be exhausted by the instrumental rules of the *Shariah*. The character of the historical Muhammad , however, is a perennial source of inspiration to humankind in its ceaseless (but ever-incomplete) aspiration for attaining perfection and truth. The authentic and prayerful reflection on the Qur'an touches the deepest chord of the authentic human conscience, which is itself the Divine spark in humanity after the individual learns to deconstruct his or her natural ethnocentricity. This is, indeed, the miracle of the Qur'an.

❖ ❖ ❖

Reading or reciting my favorite Qur'anic *surahs* or verses, in the original Arabic, profoundly moves me and millions of Muslims, and also many others. However, other scriptures can, and do inspire others, in the same way. I accept this fact with a sense of wonder and humility at the power of different 'sources of inspiration and inner light'. Individuals do get inner light and inspiration from a variety of historical sources, but the ultimate or apex Source is one. The crucial question is not where the light comes from; the crucial question is whether there is light in the inner world of the individual. Any deeply committed believer (no matter what his religion) who acts righteously (according to his authentic values), and concedes that his own faith or conceptualization of the Supreme Mystery of Being is not the only window to the inscrutable mystery, is, to my mind, a fellow pilgrim on the journey of the spirit. To give an analogy from the realm of human love, if one truly loves, no matter whom he loves, he/she attains to the highest level of bliss and blessedness. Obviously, in the realm of love every lover has his or her own beloved and this love brings one into the portals of the Divine.

Appendix 1: About the Author

The fruit of spirituality blossoms on different theological creeds. The essence of spirituality or religious faith, at its best, is the realization of the truth of the unity of all existence and the striving to translate this idea into concrete action. I would, therefore, submit that in the modern age the bare minimum connotation or core of the Islamic faith is as follows: all that exists is the creation of one supreme, self-existing being, and the Qur'an is the revealed 'Word of God' to Prophet Muhammad ﷺ—as the final exemplar and guide for the Muslims in the never ending and ever-evolving quest for the good life. This approach, however, does not imply that no other human exemplars and guides perform the same function for other believers. The ideal of spiritual pluralism is embedded in the Qur'an itself when we read it without the gloss of its various interpretations in the course of history, especially when one tries to discover the underlying spirit and thrust of the Qur'an and the authentic life of Prophet Muhammad ﷺ, without importing myth or miracle, or resorting to the personality cult.

Creeds and dogmas of any historical religion may appeal to one but leave the other indifferent, may fascinate one but amuse the other. However, the divine flame of spiritual wonder, the wordless but prayerful surrender to the cosmic mystery and retreat into inner silence of the spirit (*shoonya*) is, to my mind, the only '*jewel that shines by its own light*'. Once we accept this we begin to see that different creeds, dogmas or thought patterns are, in essence, different languages or alternate linguistic systems for conceptualizing the mystery of the cosmos beyond human comprehension. Keeping alive the sense of wonder and awe while contemplating the totality (viewed as the Supreme Mystery) is, functionally the same as ever-living in the presence of the Supreme Creator and ever-engaged in 'righteous action'. This approach to Islam and all other religions promotes the good life far more effectively than believing that any one particular creed or dogma is a precondition of salvation.

7. THE VISION OF AN UNKNOWN INDIAN MUSLIM
MY JOURNEY TO INTERFAITH SPIRITUALITY

"In this book I have recounted important facets of the story of my inner intellectual and spiritual growth. It is the story of how, a relatively, dogmatic model of Islam developed into the paradigm that I now accept.

In one sentence, my journey has taken me from an honest acceptance that Muslims alone will win salvation to an equally honest acceptance of the beauty and validity of interfaith spirituality."

EXCERPTS:

What is not generally known or fully appreciated today is the heroic resistance of some Congressmen (especially Muslim Congressmen) to avert partition. When the All India Congress Committee met to ratify the earlier decision of the Working Committee, jointly taken by Sardar Patel, Nehru, and others who had consented to partition, Maulana Hifzur Rahman, one of the most clearheaded intellectuals among the *ulema*, voted against the resolution. The case of Badshah Khan is the most tragic of all those who strongly and honestly resisted the idea of partition, but failed to avert the day when there was *'darkness at noon'* on August fifteenth, 1947. The division of the Indian family must have been an inner torture for all Indian nationalists, but there were some silver linings of subjective satisfaction that their long struggle, appreciated by their own people, had borne some fruit. Gandhi became (very rightly) the father of independent India, Nehru its Prime Minister, Sardar the architect of its consolidation, Rajendra Babu the President of the Union, Azad the conscience keeper of the Party, Rajagopalachari, the wise old pilot of the *'rath'* of modern India, and so on. However, Badshah Khan, the brave tragic hero, became a villain and a traitor to his own countrymen and was put into prison in his own land by those he had liberated from foreign yoke. A tragedy of this sheer poignant intensity is,

Appendix 1: About the Author

perhaps, without parallel in world history.

Little did the architects of a sovereign homeland for Indian Muslims realize that slightly less than half of the total Muslim population of India would be excluded from the proposed 'homeland'. In other words, that almost half the Indian Muslims, even after the creation of the homeland, would still remain at 'the mercy of the Hindus' in independent India. Little did the ardent champions of Pakistan in Uttar Pradesh, Bihar and other areas of Hindu dominance realize that the logic of Pakistan, as a Muslim homeland, would precipitate the parallel idea that India was or ought to be a Hindu homeland. Little did the ardent dreamers of Pakistan belonging to and living in India realize that those who did not go or could not go would have to live under the shadow of a continuing suspicion of divided loyalties. Little did the young hearts and minds of the dreamers understand the logic of politics and human passions.

The root limitation of the RSS (*Rashtriya Swayamsevak Sangh*) philosophical vision and interpretation of Indian history is its 'ahistorical' and totally abstract notion of the *'Rashtra'*. From the RSS angle of vision, the *'Rashtra'* is some eternal and pure Aryan collective entity that is the special creation or manifestation of the *Absolute Brahman*, and is thus, something apart from the common rung of humanity. The RSS intellectuals and ideologues hold that the *'Rashtra'* is the pure historical microcosm of the *Brahmanical* macrocosm and *Bharat* is the territorial locus of this historical process. This stand implies that the language, thought, culture, customs, and institutions of the Aryans of *Bharat* during the golden period of its sacred history (before the scourge of foreign invasions and conquests) were all perfect. Muslims and Christians corrupted them and attempted to destroy the soul of *Bharat*. The Muslims and the British eventually conspired to vivisect the body of 'Mother India' before being compelled to vacate the unholy aggression against India down the centuries. The RSS vision goes on to claim that the soul of India is immortal and destined to conquer all opposition. It is for *Bharat* to teach and for all others to learn the infallible wisdom and truth eternally enshrined in the Vedas. The wisdom of the Vedas is complete and needs no further growth through exposure to and dialogue with other thought systems, cultures and religions. In fact, all these are cultural or conceptual aberrations to be swept aside by Vedic

Appendix 1: About the Author

wisdom of a resurrected *Bharat*, freshly emancipated from centuries of accursed foreign rule.

The above philosophical and historical vision and interpretation of Indian history is a species of a closed 'ahistorical' pattern of understanding the concrete growth of the Indian people in history. This type of conceptualization of history completely ignores the concrete processes of the growth of nations and the evolution of human ideas and ideals through continual interaction and dialogue. This approach totally brushes aside the mutual give and take between different wings of the human family in both peace and war. It also ignores the fact that the invader or a foreigner of yesterday becomes the son of the soil tomorrow, provided he settles down, works, dies and mingles with the air and dust of his chosen land, just like those who may have arrived earlier on the common soil.

I foresee that the leaderless Indian Muslims (presently confused, demoralized, in the grip of a besieged mentality) after two or three general elections will join the mainstream of secular Indian politics instead of functioning as vote banks for political managers, be they secular or religious. The bewildered Indian Muslims (including the erstwhile champions of a separate homeland for Muslims) are now realizing the tremendous folly they committed in 1947. They are fast coming round to the view that they should vote for the man who is honest and has the right agenda in view (irrespective of his religion or caste). I am pretty confident that well-educated Muslims having a broad humanist outlook and vision will soon emerge on the Indian scene. The same applies to *Dalits* and OBC's (Other Backward Classes). Nitish Kumar of Bihar has already captured the imagination of the people of India, while Narendra Modi of Gujrat is more likely to take on the image of a boss who gets things done rather than of a statesman and democratic leader. It is my faith in the genius of India that the common man is soon going to see through the dirty tricks as well as honest deceptions of our establishment. Young India is developing the clarity, courage and conviction to embrace the politics of integrity without importing religion, region or caste into the game of power.

The persons who win the free and fair vote of the people must honestly view themselves as servant leaders of the great Indian family, rather than

Appendix 1: About the Author

the leader of any particular group. The servant leader will be fully alive to the fact that the Indian family, in its own turn, is an arc (a very large one indeed) of the still larger circle of humanity. Accordingly, he will fully understand the limitations of the dictum, *'my country, right or wrong'* and will take the lead in applying the Gandhian-Nehruvian ethical approach to national and international politics. Today several Christians, upper caste Hindus and Muslims who are compassionate humanists stand rather marginalized in the corridors of caste centered Indian politics. This must go and the 'Obama moment' should arrive. Reinhold Niebuhr and Gandhi inspired Martin Luther King. Likewise, Gandhi inspired Nelson Mandela. When will Gandhi inspire another Indian after Jawaharlal? When will it be? Who will it be? Where in India will it be? All I know is that it will be. Much earlier, Rabindra Nath Tagore had described the land of his dreams in his prayer in the *Gitanjali* in these immortal lines:

Where the mind is without fear and the head is held high;
Where knowledge is free;
Where the world is not broken up into fragments by narrow domestic walls;
Where words come out from the depth of truth;
Where tireless living stretches its arms towards perfection;
Where the clear stream of reason has not lost its way into the dreary desert sand of dead habit;
Where the mind is led forward by thee into ever-widening thought and action:
Into that heaven of freedom, let my country awake.

And I, as an Indian Muslim, dream of the day when every Indian Muslim heart will resonate with Tagore's prayer and will cease to bother whether the poet was a Muslim or a Hindu.

APPENDIX 2: SELECT BIBLIOGRAPHY

The books mentioned in the following list have been selected from writings, which have influenced the Author's thinking and approach to the subject of the present work. Only those books have been listed which are of a high standard but not too technical for the general reader. The list is confined to English works only either in the original or in translation. For Urdu or Persian writings of the authors discussed by me I refer the reader to the titles listed in the works of Aziz Ahmad.

A

Al-Hujwiri, *The Kashf-Al-Mahjub,* London, 1936.

Allport, G. W., *The Individual and His Religion,* N.Y., 1960.

Ameer Ali, *The Spirit of Islam,* Calcutta, 1902; *Mohammedan Law,* 2 Vols., Calcutta, 1912.

Arberry, A. J., *Tales from the Masnavi,* London, 1961.

Aron, R., *The Opium of the Intellectuals,* London, 1957.

Arnold, M., *Culture and Anarchy,* Cambridge, 1932.

Augustine, *City of God,* N.Y., 1950.

Aurobindo, *On Yoga,* Pondicherry, 1957.

Ayer, A. J., *Language, Truth and Logic,* London, 1950.

Azad, A. K., *Tarjuman-al-Qur'an (Vol. I),* Bombay, 1962.

Aziz Ahmad, *Intellectual History of Islam in India,* Edinburgh, 1969.

Aziz Ahmad, *Islamic Modernism in India & Pakistan,* Bombay, 1967.

Aziz Ahmad, *Studies in Islamic Culture in the Indian Environment,* London, 1964.

B

Baig, M. R. A., *In Different Saddles,* Bombay, 1967.

Baig, M. R. A., *The Muslim Dilemma in India,* Delhi, 1974.

Baljon, J. M. S., *The Reforms and Religious Ideas of Sir Syed Ahmad Khan,* Lahore, 1958.

Basham, A. L., *The Wonder That was India,* Calcutta, 1967.

Bergson, H., *Creative Evolution,* London, 1922.

Bergson, H., *Two Sources of Morality and Religion,* London, 1935.

Blackham, H. J. (Ed.), *Objections to Humanism,* Pelican, 1965.

Blackstone, W. T., *The Problem of Religions Knowledge,* Englewood Cliffs, 1963.

Bhagavan Das, *The Essential Unity of All Religions,* Benares, 1939.

Broad, C. D., *Religion, Philosophy and Psychical Research,* London, 1953.

Bronowski, J. & Mazlish, B., *The Western Intellectual Tradition,* Pelican, 1963.

Brzezinski, Z. & Huntington, S. P., *Political Power,* U.S.A./U.S.S.R./N.Y., 1963.

C

Campbell, C. A., *Selfhood and Godhood,* London, 1957.

Carr, E. H., *What is History,* Pelican, 1967.

Carrel, A., *Man the Unknown,* Bombay, 1959.

Cassirer, E., *An Essay on Man,* New Haven, 1944.

Cohen, M. R. & Nagel, E., *Introduction to Logic and Scientific Method,* London, 1951.

Cole, G. D. H., *The Meaning of Marxism,* London, 1948.

Comte, A., *The Positive Philosophy,* N.Y., 1969.

Cornforth, M., *Dialectical Materialism, (3 Vols.),* Calcutta, 1955.

Cragg, K., *The Event of the Qur'an,* London, 1971.

D

De-Boer, T. J., *History of Philosophy in Islam,* London, 1933.

Dewey, J., *The Common Faith,* Yale, 1936.

F

Farooqi, B. A., *The Mujaddid's Conception of Tawhid,* Lahore,

Fazlur Rahaman, *Prophecy in Islam,* London, 1958.

Fazlur Rahaman, *Islam,* London, 1966.

Flew, A.G.N. & McIntyre, A., *New Essays on Philosophical Theology,* London, 1955.

Freud, S., *The Future of an Illusion,* London, 1934.

Fromm, E., *The Fear of Freedom,* London, 1960.

Fromm, E., *Man for Himself,* London, 1950.

Fromm, E., *The Sane Society,* N.Y., 1955.

Fyzee, A. A. A., *A Modern Approach to Islam,* Bombay, 1963.

G

Galbraith, J. K., *The Affluent Society,* London, 1961.

Gandhi, M. K., *Hindu Dharma,* Ahmedabad, 1950.

Gibb, H. A. R., *Muhammadenism,* London, 1949.

Gibb, H. A. R., *Modern Trends in Islam,* Chicago, 1947.

Gopal, R., *Indian Muslims: A Political History,* Bombay, 1959.

Grunebaum, G. E. Von., *Medieval Islam,* Chicago, 1954.

Grunebaum, G. E. Von., *Islam : Essays in the Nature and Growth of a Cultural Tradition,* London, 1955.

Guillaume, A., (Ed.) *Ibn Ishaq's Life of Muhammad,* London, 1955.

H

Hakim, K. A., *The Islamic Ideology,* Lahore, 1961.

Haq, M. U., *Muslim Politics in Modern India,* Meerut, 1970.

Haq, M. U., *Islam in Secular India,* Simla, 1972.

Hayakawa, S. I., *Language in Thought and Action,* London, 1965.

Heinemann, F. H., *Existentialism and the Modern Predicament,* London, 1953.

Hick, John, *Faith and Knowledge,* N.Y., 1957.

Hitti, P. K., *History of the Arabs,* London, 1956.

Holt, P. M. et. al. (Ed), *Cambridge History of Islam, (2 Vols.),* Cambridge, 1970.

Hooron, E. A., *Up From the Ape,* N.Y., 1946.

Horney, K., *Neurosis and Human Growth,* London, 1953.

Hume, D., *Dialogues Concerning Natural Religion,* Edinburgh, 1947.

Husain, S. A., *The Destiny of Indian Muslims,* London, 1965.

Huxley, A., *Ends and Means,* London, 1957.

Huxley, J., *Religion Without Revelation,* London, 1957.

Huxley, J. (Ed.), *The Humanist Frame,* London, 1961.

I

Imam, Z. (Ed.), *Muslims in India,* New Delhi, 1975.

Iqbal, M., *The Reconstruction of Religious Thought in Islam,* Lahore, 1962.

Isherwood, M., *Faith Without Dogma,* London, 1964.

J

James, W., *The Varieties of Religious Experience,* N.Y., 1902.

James, W., *The Will to Believe,* London, 1927.

Jaspers, K., *Way to Wisdom,* New Haven, 1954.

Jaspers, K., *Philosophy, (Vol. III),* Chicago, 1970.

Joad, C.E.M., *Guide to the Philosophy of Morals and Politics,* London, 1938.

Jung, C.G., *Modern Man in Search of a Soul,* London, 1961.

K

Kabir, H. (Ed.), *Maulana Abul Kalam Azad: A Memorial Volume,* London, 1959.

Kierkegaard, *Concluding Unscientific Postscript,* Princeton, 1968.

Kellet, E. E., *Short History of Religions,* London, 1948.

L

Lamont, C, *Humanism as a Philosophy,* London, 1952.

Langer, S. K., *Philosophy in a New Key,* N.Y., 1951.

Latif, S. A., *The Mind Al-Qur'an Builds,* Hyderabad, 1952.

Liebmann, J. L., *Peace of Mind,* N.Y., 1955.

M

MacIver, R. M. & Page, *Society,* London, 1957.

MacIver, R. M., *Social Causation,* N.Y., 1964.

Macquarrie, J., *Existentialist Theology,* London, 1955.

Mannheim, K., *Ideology and Utopia,* London, 1949.

Maududi, A. A., *Towards Understanding Islam,* Delhi, 1940.

Menninger, K., *Man Against Himself,* Harvard, 1971.

Mehta, V., *The New Theologian,* Pelican, 1965.

Mead, M., *Sex and Temperament,* N.Y., 1950.

Mead, M., *Male and Female*, N.Y., 1955.

Mill, J. S., *On Liberty*, London, 1912.

Miller, J.D. B., *The Nature of Politics*, Pelican, 1962.

Mohammad Ali, *The Religion of Islam*, Lahore, 1936.

Morgan, C. L., *Emergent Evolution*, London, 1923.

Moreland, W. H. S. & Chatterjee, A. C, *Short History of India*, London, 1944.

Mujeeb, M., *The Indian Muslims*, London, 1967.

Mujeeb, M., *Islamic Influence on Indian Society*, Meerut, 1972.

N

Nasr, S. H., *Ideals and Realities of Islam*, London, 1966.

Nehru, J., *Glimpses Into World History*, London, 1949.

Nehru, J., *The Discovery of India*, Calcutta, 1946.

Nicholson, R. A., *Rumi, Poet and Mystic*, London, 1950.

Niebuhßr, R., *Moral Man and Immoral Society*, N.Y., 1955.

O

Ogburn, W. F. & Nimkoff, M. F., *A Handbook of Sociology*, London, 1956.

Otto, R., *The Idea of the Holy,* Pelican, 1959.

P

Packard, V., *The Waste-Makers,* Pelican, 1960.

Paulsen, F., *Introduction to Philosophy,* N.Y., 1928.

Pitcher, G., *The Philosophy of Wittgenstein,* N.Y., 1964.

R

Radhakrishnan, *Eastern Religions and Western Thought,* Oxford, 1940.

Radhakrishnan, *The Principal Upanishads,* London, 1953.

Radhakrishnan, *Recovery of Faith,* London, 1963.

Ramsey, I. T., *Miracles,* Oxford, 1952.

Ramsey, I. T., *Religious Language,* London, 1973.

Reid, L. A., *Ways of Knowledge and Experience,* London, 1961.

Rhine, J. B., *New Frontiers of the Mind,* Pelican, 1950.

Robinson, J., *Honest to God, London,* 1963.

Robinson, M., *Islam and Capitalism,* London, 1974.

Russell, B., *Sceptical Essays,* London, 1956.

Russell, B., *Why I am not a Christian,* London, 1961.

S

Sartre, J. P., *Existentialism and Humanism,* London, 1952.

Schacht, R., *Alienation,* N.Y., 1970.

Schumpeter, J. A., *Capitalism, Socialism and Democracy,* London, 1961.

Schuon, F., *Dimensions of Islam,* London, 1970.

Shakir, M., *Khilafat to Partition : A Survey of Major Political Trends among Indian Muslims during 1919-1947,* New Delhi, 1970.

Shibli, Al-Farooq: *Omar the Great,* Lahore, 1962.

Simpson, G. G., *The Meaning of Evolution,* N. Y., 1954.

Smith, M., *Readings from the Mystics of Islam,* London, 1950.

Smith, W. C, Modern Islam in India, Lahore, 1943.

Smith, W. C, *Islam in Modern History,* Princeton, 1957.

Snow, C. P., *The Two Cultures,* N.Y., 1964.

Sundarlal, *Gita and the Qur'an,* Hyderabad, 1957.

T

Tarachand, *Influence of Islam on Indian Culture,* Allahabad, 1963.

Tagore, R., *Religion of Man,* London, 1931.

Tawney, R. H., *The Acquisitive Society,* London, 1961.

Tawney, R. H., *Equality,* London, 1964.

Tennant, J., *Philosophical Theology,* Cambridge, 1969.

Thouless, R. H., *Psychology of Religion,* Cambridge, 1950.

Tillich, P., *Dynamics of Faith,* London, 1957.

Toynbee, A. J., *A Historians Approach to Religion,* London, 1965.

Tyrell, G. N. M., *The Personality of Man,* Pelican, 1948.

U

Umaruddin, M., *Ethical Philosophy of Al-Ghazali,* Aligarh, 1962.

V

Vidler, A. R. (Ed.), *Objections to Christian Belief,* Pelican, 1965.

Voltaire, *Candide,* Middlesex, 1947.

W

Waismann, F., *How I see Philosophy,* London, 1968.

Waismann, F., *The Principles of Linguistic Philosophy,* London, 1968.

Wach, J., *Sociology of Religion,* 1957.

Watt, M., *Faith and Practice of Ghazali,* 1953.

Watt, M., *Islam and the Integration of Society,* London, 1961.

Watt, M., *Mohammad at Mecca and Madina,* Oxford, 1953.

Watt, M., *Truth in the Religions,* Edinburgh, 1963.

Webb, S. and Webb, B., *Soviet Communism,* London, 1947.

Weber, M., *From Max Weber: Essays in Sociology,* London, 1948.

Whitehead, A. N., *Science and the Modern World,* N.Y., 1954.

Wisdom, J., *Philosophy and Psycho-Analysis,* Oxford, 1953.

Z

Zafarullah, *Islam: Its Meaning for Modern Man,* London, 1962.

INDEX

A

Abduh, Muhammad, *34, 35, 278*
Abraham, *120, 141, 158, 188, 259, 265, 280*
Abu Bakr, Caliph, *79, 84, 112, 119, 152, 195, 261, 264*
Abu Daud, *154*
Abu Hanifa, *153, 196, 279*
Adam, *36, 41, 71, 79-80, 84, 94, 145-147, 227, 263*
Adultery, *11, 82, 123, 206*
Afghani, Jamaluddin, *34-35, 49, 254, 278*
Ahmad, Sarhindi, *32*
Ahmad, Sir Syed, *34-41, 50, 53, 62, 66, 149-150, 254, 257-258, 277-281, 285, 289, 293*
Al-Bistami, *128*
Akbar, Emperor, *32-33, 307*
Al-Beruni, *63, 286*
Ali, Caliph, *25, 29*
Alienation, *110, 117, 182, 212, 269, 289*
Aligarh Movement, *35, 39*
American Jew, *47*
American Revolution, *33*
Amir Ali, *22, 39, 268*
Apologetics, *241*
Apostasy, *68, 291*
Aquinas, *66*
Arabic, *2, 27, 36, 38, 56, 86-87, 121*
Arberry, A.J., *64, 258*
Aristotle, *27-30, 42, 86, 160, 183*
Arnold, Matthew, *49, 63, 213, 269, 321*
Asceticism, *86, 187*
Asharites, *26, 27*
Atheism, *242, 247*
Atheist, *45, 77, 123, 242, 245*
Atheistic, *22, 45, 207, 239*
Attar, Fariduddin, *33, 302*
Augustine, Saint, *91, 127*
Aurobindo, Sri, *64, 240*
Authentic, *11, 13, 24, 30, 93, 52-53, 63, 68, 74, 84, 97, 99-100, 108-109, 112, 115, 117-118, 121, 124-125, 132, 135-136, 146-147, 150-158, 168-170, 173, 181, 188, 197, 213-214, 225, 227-234, 238, 242, 245, 254, 264, 286-291*
Authority, internal & external, *14, 190, 210*
Ayesha, *119*
Azad, Abul Kalam, *39, 50-54, 56, 60, 113, 237, 256-258, 261, 277-280, 303*

B

Basri, Hasan, *25, 173*
Beauty, *1, 4-8, 50, 54, 99-100, 104, 110, 114, 134, 141, 148, 150, 170, 177-178, 182, 189, 294, 304*
Bentham, Jeremy, *13*
Bergson, Henri, *20, 37, 42, 108, 260, 265, 275*
Bible, *12, 84, 149, 233, 273*
Biological strife, *7, 98-99*
Blunt, Wilfrid Scawen, *49*
Buddha, Guatam, *84, 120, 148, 233, 292*

Bukhari, Imam, *154-155, 158, 260, 264-265, 279*
Bultmann, Rudolf, *64, 302*

C
Caesar, *42, 43*
Calvin, John, *43*
Chiragh Ali, *39*
Christian monotheism, *233*
Christianity, *20, 33, 42-44, 62, 73, 85-87, 103, 137, 196, 202, 208-209, 213, 235-240, 255, 273, 277*
Communism, *55, 61, 216, 239-240, 284*
Communitarianism, *35, 43, 47, 53, 55, 58, 254*
Compassion, *112, 164-165, 177-178, 191, 237, 239, 248, 307*
Conceptual idolatory, *235, 290*
Conceptual lag, *66, 290*
conditioned, creative Conscience, *11, 14, 52, 54, 100, 106-108, 151, 180, 234, 278*
Consensus, *43, 55, 57, 76, 83, 88, 128, 196-197, 214, 220-221, 224*
Contentment, *80, 174, 220*
Continuity and change, *60, 65, 287*
Conversion, religious, *212, 235*
Copernicus, *23, 44*
Creation, *2, 6-7, 12-13, 17, 19, 20-21, 26-28, 36, 40-41, 57, 74, 84, 89, 98-99, 101, 107,-108, 115, 137, 142-146, 227, 247, 251, 263, 276*
Creativity, *42-43, 46, 50,65, 89, 158-159, 163, 182, 220, 225, 274, 285*
Cultural conditioning, *2, 107, 151-152, 199, 235-236*

D
Darwin, Charles, *3, 20, 23, 34, 41, 97, 105, 161-162, 260*
Death, *4-5, 8, 16, 23-24, 61, 69, 71, 74, 75-76, 79-80, 84-85, 90-91, 97, 134-135, 141, 158, 161, 168, 207*
Defense mechanism, *20, 24, 63, 288*
De-Islamization, *214*
Democracy, *35, 45, 49, 55, 60-61, 82, 167, 196, 198, 210-214, 219-220, 223, 237, 239, 242, 247-248, 269, 278*
Democratic socialism, *220, 240*
Descartes, *37, 44, 160-161*
Dhimmis, *85, 184, 209*
Divine,
- attributes, *26, 41, 50-51, 79, 111*
- guidance, *51-52, 72, 238*
- incarnation, *37, 232, 233*
- providence, *22, 56*
- regulation of history, *144, 159, 170*
Divorce, *34, 191, 200-202, 209, 221-224*
Dravidian prophets, *149, 233*
Dysteleology, *20*

E
Economy,
- mixed, *205, 215-216*
- pattern of, *198, 214-216, 220*
- traditional Islamic approach, *21, 216*
Ego, *40-44, 79, 114-115, 134-135, 229-231, 240, 253*
Ego fortification, *99*
Ego hood, *29, 42, 135*
Empirical method, *225-226*
Equality of opportunity, *55, 172, 184, 187, 198, 200, 202, 204-205, 213,*

217-219, 223, 239-240, 248, 269, 313
Eros, 6, 171, 179
Ethical factors, 165, 167
Ethnocentricity, 27, 63, 231, 235, 237, 288, 314
Eve, 79, 84, 145
Evil, 7-8, 13, 20, 22-23, 34, 46, 49, 53-54, 60, 63, 71-72, 77-78, 81-83, 90-96, 99, 115-116, 133-134, 147-148, 158, 165, 168-169, 172, 174, 182, 184, 203, 205-206, 211, 216, 218, 227-228, 231, 253-254
Evolution, 3, 7, 11-12, 17, 20-21, 34, 42, 45, 53, 66, 68, 93, 97-98, 105-106, 108-110, 135, 160-162, 202, 208, 224, 231, 241, 260
Existential interpretation, 3-8, 13, 18, 39, 46, 96-97, 99-100, 109-110, 114, 133, 141-142, 161-162, 168, 173, 225, 227-228, 241-242, 254, 275
Existentialist approach, 13, 37, 43, 50, 112, 139

F

Factual knowledge, 7, 9, 17, 19, 40, 67, 99, 171, 198, 245, 256
Faith, 1-2, 5, 7, 8, 12, 14-15, 17, 19, 22, 24, 30-31, 32, 36-37, 39, 44, 47, 52-53, 59, 62, 70, 73, 76-81, 89, 91-92, 110-116, 122, 125, 133-137, 146-147, 150, 158-159, 169, 172-174, 180-182, 186, 197, 226-234, 239-242, 246-248, 253, 284, 286, 289
Farabi, 27-30, 37, 112, 128, 286
Fasting, 2, 75, 78, 153, 155, 187-188, 193, 207, 230

Field,
- integration, 10-13, 15, 17, 25-29, 31, 34-35, 39, 61, 64, 67, 241
- isolation, 12, 17, 113
- rationalization, 12
- repression, 12
- tension, 10-11, 17, 25-30, 67, 225, 241
Finalistic fallacy, 158
Flogging, 123, 206
Freedom, 15, 20, 55, 58, 77, 93-95, 132, 163, 190, 213
Freedom,
- fear of, 15, 213, 253
- of the will, 26, 93
French Revolution, 33
Freud, Sigmund, 11, 23-24, 107, 253, 282, 298
Fromm, Eric, 15, 159, 307, 253
Fyzee, A.A.A., 60, 257, 280

G

Gabriel, 28, 41, 73, 118-121, 257, 259
Galileo, 44
Ghazali, Imam, 30-31, 66-67, 128, 171, 183, 254, 258, 283, 286
Gibb, H.A.R., 64, 259
God, 2-10, 13-32, 34-42, 46, 50-55, 59-60, 69-87, 89-128, 132-155, 158-162, 168-177, 180-186, 190, 196, 207-212, 223-235, 238-239, 242, 252-261, 265-266, 277-281, 286, 290
God,
- and mystery, 112
- difficulties raised by evolution, 97
- difficulties raised by pain and evil, 90
- difficulties raised by semantic considerations, 100
- Elan conception, 105-108, 113, 115,

125, 162, 225
- *ontogenetic function of, 110-112*
Gokalp, Ziya, *59, 256*

H
Hadith,
- *prescriptive specificity, 155*
- *sociology of, 152*
- *status of, 155*
Hajj, *2, 188-189, 193, 196, 267, 294*
Hambal, Imam, *153, 195*
Heaven and Hell, *36, 41, 85, 137, 173, 180*
Hedonism, *16, 19*
Hifzur Rahman, *56, 316*
Hinduism, *2, 62, 75, 78, 84, 86, 91, 153, 155, 158, 172, 188, 193, 207, 208, 222, 230, 237, 270*
Humanism, *16, 32-33, 48, 53, 59-60, 212, 237, 239, 275, 281*
Hume, David, *44, 325*
Humility, *41, 147, 171, 178, 246*
Husayn, Imam, *61*
Husayn, Taha, *58, 61*

I
Ibn Arabi, *30-33, 112-113, 128*
Ibn Hazm, *111, 196*
Ibn Rushd, *27-28, 67, 137, 278, 286, 289-290*
Ibn Taimiya, *289*
Ideologies, *82, 164*
Immortality, *28, 134-137, 168-169*
Infallibility, *131-132, 176*
Inheritance, *56, 82, 155, 171, 197-198, 202, 204-205, 209, 216*

Institutional system, *3, 35-36, 42, 55, 69, 81, 153, 155, 159, 190, 195-198, 208-209, 280, 288*
Interest, *63, 82-83, 218, 264*
Internationalism, *48, 55*
Interpretation, *2-19, 22, 29, 31, 33, 35-41, 46, 50, 53-57, 63, 66-69, 74-75, 89-100, 110-118, 126-127, 130-146, 149-162, 172, 180-188, 201, 204, 208, 225-229, 241-243, 252*
Interpretation of surah Fatiha, *113*
Iqbal, Muhammad, *35, 39-50, 53, 56, 58, 66, 108, 257, 280*
irenic approach, *30, 33, 221, 242*
Islamic brotherhood, *48, 172, 182, 189*
Islamic Communitarianism, *35, 43, 53, 55*
Islamic modernism, *35, 257, 273, 277*
I-Thou Communion, *109, 199*

J
Jahiz, Muslim scholar, *27*
James, W., *20, 37, 96, 129, 134, 252-253, 261-262, 326*
Jami, Persian poet, *33*
Jaspers, Karl, *40, 326*
Jesus, *14, 36, 84, 120, 139, 150, 233, 259, 280*
Jews, *121-122, 149, 181, 232-233, 255*
Justice, *1, 8-9, 12, 44, 48, 77, 81-82, 90, 133, 144, 164, 170, 178-181, 183, 191, 224, 281*

K
Kabah, *123, 188, 267*
Kamal, Mustafa, *197, 221*

Index

Kant, Immanuel, *40, 44, 66, 256*
Karma, *91, 137, 144*
Kepler, Johannes, *44*
Khadijah, *118*
Kierkegaard, *37, 266, 327*
Kindi, *27, 37*
Kleptomania, *123, 205*
Krishna, Shri, *84, 233*
Kufr, *181, 291*

L

Language game, *102, 112, 252, 266*
Language of religion, *28, 90, 106, 114*
Language of the Qur'an, *121, 139, 191, 241, 263*
League of Nations, *46*
Leibniz, *37, 99*
Life affirmation, *21, 100*
Life after death, *2, 8, 18, 28, 37, 69, 76, 80, 99, 133-137, 173, 180, 207, 227, 232, 252*
Locke, John, *37, 44*
Luther, Martin, *43, 319*

M

Malik, Imam, *153*
Marriage, *9, 85-86, 167, 171, 197-203, 206, 208-209, 221, 224, 280*
Marriage,
- *arranged, 203*
- *inter-religious, 54, 122, 237*

Marx, Karl, *21-23, 161-164, 253, 265-266, 271, 282, 289-292*
Mary, *38*
Mathematics, *18, 30, 37, 160, 226, 227*
Maududi, Maulana, *54-60, 207, 259,* *268, 281*
Metaphor, *5-6, 26-28, 38, 50, 103-104, 111, 122, 140-143, 174, 181, 238, 260*
Metaphysics, *8, 15, 18, 30, 241, 251-252, 266*
Methodology, *16, 31, 36, 221, 241*
Mill, John Stuart, *23, 49, 328*
Miracles, *17, 30, 36, 38-40, 144, 148-157, 232, 259, 263*
Modernity, *33, 60, 273-277, 280-283, 285, 287, 289*
Morality, *11, 15-16, 26, 29, 32, 43, 46, 52, 60, 66, 75, 109, 112, 134-136, 156, 176, 220, 266, 274-275, 285, 322*
Moses, Prophet, *66, 120, 149-150, 189, 258-260, 267, 290*
Mueller, Max, *49, 63*
Muhammad, Prophet, *1-2, 38, 53, 74, 77, 84, 118-120, 132, 148-150, 180, 260-261, 292*
Music, *192, 210, 229, 242, 267, 279*
Mutation, *19, 98, 161, 260*
Mutazilites, *26, 27*
Mystery, *41, 50, 70, 73, 97, 105, 108, 111, 112, 135, 143, 169, 181, 232, 238*
Mystical,
- *experience, 29, 31, 33, 79, 111-112, 118, 127, 130, 252, 267, 286*
- *silence, 111, 112*
Myths, *30, 84, 144-146, 263*

N

Nadvi, A.H.A., *23*
Nationalism, *16, 35, 43, 46-48, 55, 66, 208, 212, 223, 285*
Naturalistic fallacy, *112*

Index

Newton, Isaac, *20, 44*
Niebuhr, Reinhold, *64, 275*
Nihilism, *16-17, 46, 283-284, 289*
Non-being, *102*

O

Omnipotence, *13, 26, 71, 77, 94, 98, 108, 120*
Ontogenetic, *110-112, 178, 242*
Ontological Commitment, *17, 173*
Optimism, *110, 162, 169*
Otto, R., *37, 261, 265, 329*

P

Pain and evil,
- problem of, *54, 96, 99, 115*
- sources of, *20, 90-96*
Painting, *11, 192, 280*
Pakistan, *45, 57-60, 166-167, 221, 248, 254, 257, 268-269, 280*
Pan-Islamism, *49, 50*
Parable, *123, 141, 145, 263*
Para-normal fact, *125-128*
Parvez, Ghulam Ahmed, *56-58, 257, 268, 280*
Penal code, *82, 205*
Permissiveness, *180, 200, 207, 238*
Persian mystical tradition, *33*
Personal law, *142, 223-224, 247, 269*
Piety, *34, 49, 52, 85, 113, 166, 172, 182-183, 197, 216, 218, 257, 284*
Pilgrimage, *2, 63, 155, 188, 207, 303*
Plato, *28, 30, 86, 183*
Plural society, *32, 33, 45, 58*
Polygamy, *55, 199-200*
Polytheism, *233*
Poverty, *16, 21-22, 60, 80, 93-94, 158,* *187, 212, 218, 270, 290*
Precept system, *3, 153, 155, 159, 185, 188, 190-193, 196, 264, 276, 288*
Prince, Morton, *128, 129*
Principle of formulational tolerance, *66, 290*
Private enterprise, *205, 219*
Prohibited foods and drinks, *191*
Prophecy, *2, 29, 37, 40-41, 52, 69, 72, 77, 232, 276, 324*
Psychical research, *128, 256, 322*
Psychoanalysis, *19, 23, 25, 107*
Purdah, *166-167, 203, 204*
Puritanical attitude, *192*
Purpose, *7, 44, 50, 55, 57, 69-71, 81, 89, 98, 105, 107, 140-145, 160-163, 187, 198, 225, 227, 229, 238, 242, 267, 282*

Q

Quest for Islam, assumptions, *241*
Qur'an, *11-14, 23, 27-42, 50-61, 70-77, 81-89, 111-113, 117-125, 127-133, 136, 139-159, 173, 176-182, 187-199, 201-207, 210, 214-219, 223, 225, 232-233, 243, 246-248, 251-254*
Qur'an,
- *as a miracle,* *38, 148-151, 247*
- *Numinous quality of,* *150-151*

R

Rahman, Fazlur, *60, 257, 259*
Ramsey, Ian Thomas, *64, 262, 294, 329*
Rationalistic fallacy, *37*
Raziq, Ali Abdel, *58-59*
Religion,
- plural versions of, *236-237*

Index

- unity and variety of, *231*
Religionism, *16, 45-48, 197, 221*
Religious attitude, *229-231, 283*
Renaissance, *33-34*
Revelation, *2, 17, 28, 36-41, 51-52, 56, 59, 72-77, 80, 117-137, 148-151, 154, 159, 176, 180-182, 191, 225-226, 232=234, 238, 245-247, 252, 257, 269, 276-279, 281, 286, 290*
Revelatory content, *125-127, 131-132*
Reverence for life, *177, 182*
Righteous action, *52, 173, 315*
Rousseau, *44, 253*
Roy, Rammohun, *64*
Rumi, Jalaluddin, *33, 42, 66, 108, 235, 255, 258, 286, 290*
Russell, Bertrand, *11, 253, 269, 289, 329*

S

Sadiq, Jaffar, *25, 29*
Salvation, *52, 72, 77, 86, 181, 212, 237, 274*
Sanskrit, *62, 103, 237-238*
Satan, *36, 72, 79, 80, 97, 145-147*
Schleiermacher, Friedrich, *37*
Schweitzer, Albert, *64*
Science and religion, *15, 17-18, 21, 34, 290*
Science, *3-4, 6-7, 10-18, 21, 30, 34-41, 44, 59, 64, 87, 105, 109, 111, 114, 147, 155, 160, 196, 208, 213, 221, 241, 251-252, 256, 276-277, 283, 286-287, 290, 332*
Scientist, *5, 20, 52, 86, 128, 143, 147, 177, 226, 256, 261*
Secular revolution, *44, 56, 196, 208-209, 221*

Secularism, *43-46, 49, 54-61, 88, 196-197, 207-209, 221-223, 242, 258, 287*
Self-interpretation, *63, 83, 236, 241*
Semantics, *20, 140, 273*
Sex morality, *66, 285*
Shafai, *153, 196*
Shaw, George Bernard, *108*
Shibli, Nomani, *39, 153, 264, 267, 330*
Sindhi, Ubaidullah, *56, 278*
Slavery, *83, 155, 157, 184, 195, 199, 218, 221, 248*
Socialism, *45, 49, 54-57, 61, 66, 82, 199, 207, 214-223, 239-242, 270, 285, 330*
Sociology, *19, 21, 57, 63, 152, 161, 269, 276*
Sociology of religion, *63, 276, 281, 288, 332*
Socrates, *61, 67, 75, 120, 292*
Spiritual merit, *53, 78, 85, 180*
Striving, *42, 99-100, 136, 163, 168-169, 174, 176-177, 254*
Struggle for power, *163-165*
Suffering, *4, 7, 24, 54, 77, 90-96, 100, 108, 110, 119, 158, 168, 178, 200*
Sufism, *28-31, 112, 186, 231, 267*
Suicide, *92, 163, 228, 287*
Symbols, *66-68, 126, 158, 225, 234, 245-246, 290-291*

T

Tagore, *64, 240, 289, 319, 331*
Technology, *16, 18, 22, 24, 64, 103, 196, 204, 208, 290*
Theocracy, *60-61, 88, 287*
Theologian, *7, 20, 26-33, 36-37, 55, 75, 92, 96-97, 111, 121-122, 128, 133, 154, 157, 173, 196, 263-265, 279, 327*

Theology, *3, 7, 11, 18, 25-27, 29, 90-91, 98, 180, 241, 260, 275, 324, 327, 331*
Theory and practice, *60, 120, 203*
Tillich, Paul, *11, 64, 158, 253, 275, 278, 331*
Time, *3, 10-11, 19, 25-37, 40-44, 63-68, 72, 74-76, 84, 94, 103, 114, 119-123, 130-133, 137, 139, 144, 149-150, 155, 159, 173, 175, 191, 196, 217, 238, 245*
Tolerance, *23, 32, 36, 53, 66, 88, 94, 209, 213, 235-236, 241, 269, 287, 290*
Tolstoy, *49, 64*
Toynbee, *213, 269-270, 331*
Tradition, *7, 10-23, 29, 31-36, 41, 44, 48, 50, 52-56, 59-73, 78-81, 88-105, 108, 114-133, 137, 145, 148, 150, 152, 154, 158-159, 164, 167-168, 171, 180-184, 191-193, 198, 201-202, 206-213, 216-225, 230-237, 241-242, 245-246, 252, 256-259, 269, 273*
Traditionalism, *60, 159, 273-277, 280-282, 285-289*
Trust in God, *80, 167, 174*
Turkey, *45, 197, 213, 221, 242*

U
Umar, *58, 88, 124, 152-154, 195-196, 205, 258, 264, 267, 312*
Unconscious motivation, *23*
Universal religion, *85, 239*
Upanishads, *233, 240*

V
Value Elan, *105-116, 130-132, 146, 151, 162, 168, 179, 182, 186, 229-230, 234, 238*
Value, instrumental and intrinsic, *8-9, 115, 141, 156, 178, 217, 247, 274, 252, 281, 311, 313*
Value judgment, *18, 99, 103, 152, 214, 278, 296*
Value,
- quest for, *46, 63, 111, 114, 134, 143, 162-163, 170, 227-229, 238, 242*
- conservation of, *110, 274*
Vedas, *84, 233, 305, 317*
Veracity, *112, 125-126, 133, 175-176*
Verification, *13, 109, 140, 143-144, 160, 211, 225-226*
Vested interests, *56, 57, 240, 266*
Vivekananda, Swami, *64, 237*
Voltaire, *44*

W
Waliullah, Shah, *33, 35, 41, 122, 259, 302*
Waraqa, *118-119*
Wealth tax, *2, 82, 86, 141, 155, 184, 187*
Whitehead, Alfred North, *6, 11, 251, 253, 275, 278, 332*
Will to live, *41, 134, 163, 169, 228*
Wisdom, *11, 41, 50, 59, 71-72, 75, 82, 87, 90, 96, 98, 114, 125, 145-146, 171, 176, 178, 183, 185, 190, 210, 213, 236, 278*
Wittgenstein, Ludwig, *40, 103, 262, 266, 294*
Women, position of, *9, 202*

Z
Zahbi, Imam, *153*
Zubaidi, *154, 264*

More information about the Author
and his various works can be found at the Author's website

www.JamalKhwaja.com
Get FREE Downloads of Essays & Articles by the Author

Or, visit
www.AlhamdPublishers.com